FEATURE WRITING
FOR NEWSPAPERS
AND MAGAZINES

SIXTH EDITION

FEATURE WRITING FOR NEWSPAPERS AND MAGAZINES

The Pursuit of Excellence

EDWARD JAY FRIEDLANDER

University of South Florida

JOHN LEE

Professor Emeritus, The University of Memphis

Boston   New York   San Francisco
Mexico City   Montreal   Toronto   London   Madrid   Munich   Paris
Hong Kong   Singapore   Tokyo   Cape Town   Sydney

Editor-in-Chief: *Karon Bowers*
Series Editor: *Jeanne Zalesky*
Project Manager: *Lisa Sussman*
Senior Marketing Manager: *Suzan Czajkowski*
Production Supervisor: *Beth Houston*
Editorial Production Service: *Westwords/PMG*
Composition Buyer: *Linda Cox*
Manufacturing Buyer: *JoAnne Sweeney*
Electronic Composition: *Westwords/PMG*
Cover Administrator: *Joel Gendron*

For related titles and support materials, visit our online catalog at www.ablongman.com.

Between the time Web site information is gathered and then published, it is not unusual for some sites to have closed. Also, the transcription of URLs can result in typographical errors. The publishers would appreciate notification where these errors occur so that they may be corrected in subsequent editions.

ISBN-13: 978-0-205-48466-9   ISBN-10: 0-205-48466-2

Library of Congress Cataloging-in-Publication Data

Friedlander, Edward Jay.
   Feature writing for newspapers and magazines : the pursuit of excellence / Edward Jay Friedlander, John Lee.—6th ed.
      p. cm.
   ISBN 0-205-48466-2
1. Feature writing.   I. Lee, John, 1931- II. Title.
PN4784.F37F75 2007
070.4'4—dc22
                                                                    2007020885

Printed in the United States of America

10   9   8   7   6   5   4   3   2   1   11   10   09   08   07

Credits appear on page 321, which constitutes an extension of the copyright page.

CONTENTS

CHAPTER TEN

Legal and Ethical Considerations for Writers 307

PREFACE

READERS SERVED AND TEXT OBJECTIVES

Welcome to the sixth edition of *Feature Writing for Newspapers and Magazines,* a book that has served in college and university classrooms for more than two decades. This staying power, buttressed by trend-setting writing examples, periodic updates and timely tips from some of America's best feature writers, has made it the premier text in its field and the ideal guide for two types of writers.

One kind of writer will find work as a reporter with a weekly or daily newspaper. Such a person will be hired primarily to cover the news: fires, club meetings, murders, bake sales. At some point, it's likely that some icy editor who doesn't even know the reporter's first name will assign something called a "feature story." The feature story may at first appear to be on a hopeless topic—perhaps the story of a wealthy civic leader who opens a boutique specializing in silk flowers—or it may be extraordinary, such as the story of Edward Zepp by Madeleine Blais found in Chapter 2 of this book.

The other kind of writer to whom the book speaks is the aspiring magazine staffer or budding freelance magazine writer. The magazine staffer will walk much the same editorial road as the newspaper writer, though the twists and turns may not look and feel the same. For the freelance writer, the path may be more tortuous. Freelance is another word for self-employed. (And, in many cases, "self-employed" is a synonym for unemployed.) Self-employed writers are in many ways like newspaper feature writers and magazine staffers but are additionally burdened with the awesome tasks of finding and selling their stories.

For either set of writers, this book's purpose is to explain. With luck, the book will explain well, and will show them—through suggestions and work from some of the best newspaper feature and magazine article writers in the United States—how they, too, can achieve excellence in writing.

WHAT'S NEW TO THIS EDITION?

One of the true pleasures of guiding a textbook through six editions is the ability to refine the editorial content to achieve maximum effectiveness. The changes in this sixth edition are significant. The book itself has been redesigned for easier reading. Several new examples of writing excellence have been added to aid the student writer. All 10 chapters have been revised and updated to match the steady growth of journalistic techniques and technology. Among the new materials you will find:

- Biographies of three new Pulitzer winners for feature writing—Sonia Nazario of *The Los Angeles Times* (2003), Julia Keller of the *Chicago Tribune* (2005), and Jim Sheeler of Denver's *Rocky Mountain News* (2006)—now appear in Chapter 1.

- A thoroughly revised examination of Internet-assisted research has been provided in Chapter 4 to keep pace with one of the fastest growing aspects of American journalism.
- Chapter 4 also contains an expanded examination of a burgeoning new market for freelance writers—electronic magazines.
- Invaluable case-history comments and writing aids from several new Pulitzer winners—Nazario and Sheeler—are scattered through Chapters 5 and 6.
- Chapter 6 also includes excerpts from new Pulitzer Prize–winning feature articles. As with all writing examples in this book, the excerpts are accompanied by a careful analysis of the authors' writing techniques.
- Chapter 7 includes a discussion about the multimedia journalism potential for the three Pulitzer Prize–winning stories featured there, as well as the actual multimedia used to present the 2006 Pulitzer Prize–winning feature story.
- Chapter 8 contains a new National Magazine Award-Winner, and introduces a previously undiscussed writing form—the essay.

DEFINING EXCELLENCE

Of course, excellence is difficult to define, which is why the authors have relied on newspaper journalism's best known award, the Pulitzer Prize, as one convenient gauge, and major magazine honors, such as the National Magazine Awards, as another. As a result, you will now find more than 25 years of Pulitzer feature material included in the book, and you'll read tips and comments from many of the award-winning journalists and magazine writers.

The range of stories is far reaching. You'll read riveting medical features ("Mrs. Kelly's Monster," by Jon Franklin); sordid crimes ("Death of a Playmate," by Teresa Carpenter); truly inspirational profiles ("Like Something the Lord Made," by Katie McCabe); celebrity interviews ("Cybill Shepherd," by Ed Weathers); sad stories ("Ashes to Dust," by Linda Wilson); massively researched backgrounders ("The Bureaucracy: How Did It Get So Big?" by Saul Pett); even a couple of macho pieces from men's adventure magazines.

But no matter what the topic, the country's best newspaper feature and magazine article writers all offer about the same basic advice, guidance proffered long ago by iconoclast and journalist H. L. Mencken of the Baltimore *Sun*. Said Mencken: "There are no dull subjects. There are only dull writers."

So read on. Then write hard. And write well.

ACKNOWLEDGMENTS

The authors wish to thank the following individuals for their contributions to the first edition of this book: Robert Byler of Bowling Green State University, Jane Clarke of the University of Missouri at Columbia, G. Robert Holsinger of Ohio State University, W. Wat Hopkins of Virginia Polytechnic Institute and State University, Bud Kliment of the office of the administrator of the Pulitzer Prize Board at Columbia University, Clint Miller of the office of the Attorney General of Arkansas, and Roy Paul Nelson of the University of Oregon at Eugene.

The following reviewers of the second, third, fourth, fifth and sixth editions are also gratefully acknowledged: Mark Arnold of California Polytechnic State University, Linda Bowen of California State University-Northridge, Steve Byers of the University of Wisconsin-Madison, Steven E. Chappell of Truman State University, James P. Corcoran of Simmons College, John Erickson of the University of Iowa, Jon C. Hughes of the University of Cincinnati, F. Mitchell Land of Stephen F. Austin State University, Carolyn Lepre of University of Tennessee, Thom Lieb of Towson State University, John Lowery of Miami University, Wanda Mouton of Stephen F. Austin State University, Gene Murray of Grambling State University, Cornelia Lynne Nash of Shippensburg University of Pennsylvania, Alan Neckowitz of James Madison University, David Okeowo of Alabama State University, Chip Scanlan of the Poynter Institute for Media Studies, Kenneth Sexton of Morehead State University and Larry C. Timbs, Jr. of Winthrop University. The authors also wish to thank Bruce Plopper of the University of Arkansas at Little Rock for a thoughtful review of libel and invasion of privacy law in Chapter 10.

Edward Jay Friedlander
John Lee

CHAPTER ONE

THE NEWSPAPER FEATURE STORY

THE FEATURE: HELEN'S STORY

"Garcia," says the editor. "I've got an assignment for you."

The city editor of the *Chronicle* hands Helen Garcia a sticky yellow note bearing only a name and telephone number.

"It's a feature story," the editor says. "The chief mechanic at the biggest cab company in the city says he can get 300,000 miles out of an ordinary automobile engine before it has to be rebuilt, and he's willing to tell us about it. Most of our readers would love to discover some way to get that kind of use out of their cars.

"This could be a very well read story."

Garcia, less than ecstatic, takes the note. She is hoping for a major, hard-news story. Instead she gets a feature. Garcia, two months out of college and just transferred to the *Chronicle*'s city desk after a probationary period rewriting news releases from public relations sources, barely remembers how to write a feature. Walking to her desk, she strains to recall the features she wrote in college.

The concept, she remembers, is to write something like a nonfiction short story: quotation-filled, descriptive, entertaining, informative.

As Garcia taps out the mechanic's telephone number, she hopes writing this feature will be like swimming after years of little or no practice; she hopes the technique will return to her naturally, and quickly, before she sinks to the bottom of the pool or, in this case, finds herself banished back to rewriting news releases.

The mechanic agrees to an interview. But first Garcia needs to do some research. She checks the newspaper's electronic library for previous stories about the cab mechanic, then calls the service managers of the city's three largest automobile dealerships to determine whether coaxing 300,000 miles from an auto engine is as unusual as it sounds. The service managers confirm the oddity. Garcia knows the story will be even stronger if she contacts a nationally recognized source, so—on a tip from one of the service managers—she calls the National Institute for Automotive Service Excellence (NIASE), which tests and certifies many automobile mechanics. Eventually, she reaches an expert, who—like the service managers—confirms the novelty of the mechanic's claim. Using several key words garnered from the interview with the NIASE expert, she conducts multiple Internet searches to locate examples of high-mileage automobile engines and the service techniques used to achieve long engine life. She also makes a note to talk to some of the cab company's employees after she finishes interviewing the mechanic.

Then Garcia hurries out to her first professional feature interview.

Just over an hour later, she returns to the newspaper with her assorted pages of interview notes. Three hours after that, the mechanic's story is told to the *Chronicle*'s readers on page one of the newspaper's local news section. And with that, Garcia has successfully passed one more test of her journalistic ability.

Garcia's experience with the *Chronicle* is not at all unusual. Most of America's daily newspapers have a circulation of less than 25,000. Assuming that you're lucky enough to find a job with a daily newspaper, you'll likely begin your career at a small one such as the *Chronicle*. Beginning reporters working for small-circulation dailies are expected to be able to write both news and feature stories. Often a reporter's first months on the job may consist of even more feature writing than weighty news writing, until a "beat" is assigned or the reporter otherwise gains the confidence of the editor.

Feature writing, then, is a crucial weapon in the arsenal of writing talents required of the professional print journalist, particularly in the twenty-first century, when various new media forms are focusing more and more on such popular stories.

An Overview

As Garcia correctly remembered, a feature story is a journalistic article that is typically both original and descriptive. Some feature stories are geared toward entertainment with little information. Other features inform, but entertain little. The best combine both aspects.

Let's take another look at that definition, step by step.

A feature story is *original* in two ways. First, it is original in respect to the way it is written. Simple news stories are commonly written in what is called the inverted pyramid style. This rigid form, which began to evolve at about the time of the American Civil War, demands that a story begin with a one-paragraph lead of one or perhaps two sentences summing up the essence of the story. The lead is short, typically less than 35 words. The rest of the story is written in a declining order of importance, with information proceeding from the most important to the least important.

The inverted pyramid made sense during the Civil War because stories often were filed using telegraph lines, which could be disrupted at any time. In that situation, it obviously was a good idea first to send a summary—or what journalists today call the lead of the story—and then to transmit the rest of the story with information in a declining order of importance. The inverted pyramid style of news writing makes even more sense today, for two reasons. First, readers can quickly scan the story by reading the lead and perhaps a few additional paragraphs. Second, busy editors can cut news stories simply by removing less important material from the bottom of the story.

Unlike the news story's inverted pyramid style, the feature story's form is more fluid. Feature stories probably date to the beginning of world journalism, but they began to assume their modern form in the United States in the "penny press" of the 1830s. They most strongly resemble short stories in structure. For example, they have distinct beginnings, middles and ends. Feature stories, unlike news stories, aren't intended for the scanning reader. They must be read completely in order to make sense. They also must be edited carefully by removing various sections from throughout the text, rather than just from the end.

Features are also *original* because they can be about virtually any subject that falls within the realm of "human interest," unlike news stories, which presumably are written only because they cover newsworthy events.

Human interest obviously means what "interests people," and a good rule of thumb is that anything that interests the feature writer and the editor is also likely to interest a substantial number of readers. Human interest stories can be about both "people" and "things," but journalists know that "people" stories typically are more interesting and are more often read than are stories about "things." For that matter, stories about unusual events are more interesting than stories about usual events, but you'll read more about that later.

In summary, if you've found a story about a person, and something about that individual is unusual, you probably have a good feature story idea.

In that sense, Garcia's cab mechanic article is an example of an acceptable feature story. What the cab mechanic accomplished by getting 300,000 miles of service from an automobile engine isn't breaking news by anyone's definition. Most readers, for instance, probably have a friend of a friend who has nursed a family sedan almost that far. But the story has a human quality because it is about the mechanic and his ideas rather than about an automobile engine. The story also carries an element of oddity because obtaining that much mileage from an engine is, in fact, unusual.

Actually, feature stories need not even have the element of oddity for them to contain human interest. Some feature writers maintain they can write a good feature story about absolutely anyone and have, in fact, proved it by opening the city telephone directory at random, pointing to a name, and then doing a feature story on the person they've selected.

How? Let's look at an example. Pretend you have opened your city telephone directory and randomly selected page 72. You stab your finger at a name halfway down the first column.

The name you have picked is Roger Grub. Grub lives in a middle-class suburb of the city. On the surface, you have nothing that would suggest a feature story. Your next step is the city directory (found in almost every newspaper office or online), which lists name, address and occupation. From the directory you learn that Grub is the manager of the produce section of a large supermarket.

This fact suggests that you might be able to interview him for expert tips about how shoppers can select the choicest samples of produce. You call him, ascertain he is still the produce manager, explain your story idea and set up an interview.

During the interview, you discover that Grub is a third-generation produce manager and that, indeed, he does have strong ideas on how shoppers can best select fruits and vegetables.

As the interview progresses, you discover there are other, even better feature possibilities with Grub. For instance, you learn that he is an amateur historian who has a large collection of turn-of-the-century postcards of your city. His collection, in fact, is the largest in the state. Later, you find out that he is also an amateur gardener in the process of developing a new strain of bug-resistant tomatoes.

Any one of these angles has individual feature possibilities.

Feature stories tend to be *descriptive,* another element of the definition. News stories are supposed to be objective, which often precludes description. For example, the news writer would rarely describe the subject of a news story by height, weight, hair color, and kind and type of clothing, unless that description were vital to the story. Yet the feature writer routinely uses this type of description.

For instance, here's a partial description of Garcia's cab mechanic:

> Jones patted the greasy cab motor, then stroked a three-day stubble with his oily, callused hand, and said, "This one ain't gonna make 300,000 miles."

That kind of description, evoking imagery, is encouraged in a feature story. But it would likely be edited out of any news story.

A feature story must remain, above all, *journalistic,* in addition to being original and often descriptive. By that, the feature writer is expected to subscribe to the same standards of journalistic accuracy as the news writer. He or she must verify the information, quote accurately and be fair and precise with description.

And the feature writer follows journalistic "style." Style is nothing more than a uniform approach to punctuation, capitalization, abbreviation, titles and, in some cases, spelling. Most American newspapers today have a fairly uniform journalistic style that is also quite similar to the style of the major American wire service—the Associated Press. At one time, however, newspaper reporters would have had to master a local style every time they moved to a new newspaper. For example, one newspaper in Denver might publish a local story about a man and refer to him as *Mr.* throughout the article, but a competing local newspaper might call him *Mr.* on first reference, then use only his last name throughout the rest of the story. If a wire service were later to use the same story, it probably would use a third style. By the early 1960s, American wire services were using a similar style and many newspapers across the country began to adopt it. Now a reporter who thoroughly learns wire service style will have to relearn only minor style differences when moving from newspaper to newspaper.

In summary, a feature is subject to the same accuracy and style requirements as any other story in the publication.

Finally, a feature story traffics in *entertainment* or *information* or both. Garcia's cab mechanic story obviously is laden with information regarding automobile engine maintenance. It should also have entertaining moments, perhaps through examples or "anecdotes" told by the mechanic. However, there is nothing wrong with a feature that's very entertaining, with little valuable information. "Entertainment" in this context can mean an interesting, amusing—or moving—feature story. For example, if Garcia were assigned to do a personality profile about a man in a local nursing home celebrating his 100th birthday, a successful story might paint only an emotionally charged word portrait of the elderly gentleman, without offering much useful information about how he had lived so long.

A feature story, then, is significantly different from a news story. The feature has a beginning, a middle and an end, and is intended to be read completely and edited with care. The feature can be written about almost anything, but commonly is written about an unusual person, place or activity. It is accurate, usually filled with description and may be sheer entertainment, information-oriented or a combination of both.

NEWSPAPER FEATURE STORY TYPES: NEWS AND TIMELESS FEATURES

Unlike flavors of ice cream, there are only two basic kinds of newspaper features.

One type is the *news* feature, which usually is tied to a breaking news event, is placed in the same general location as the breaking story, and is often written under deadline pressure. This type of news feature is called a "sidebar," in that it is a "side" article that accompanies the main news story. A variation is a news feature that appears after the publication of the hard news story. Such a follow-up story is often called a "second-day" feature.

The other basic kind of feature is the *timeless* story, which does not have to be used immediately in the newspaper and can sometimes be written leisurely over a period of two or three days or even weeks or months.

The news feature is perhaps a little less common than the timeless feature in most American newspapers. This may be because the news feature often results in at least two stories on a given event: the news, or "cover," story and its news feature. Two stories, of course, mean the editor will have to find twice as much space and commit twice the staff time to coverage of a single event. At many newspapers where space and personnel are at a premium, editors are often reluctant to make that decision. In addition, feature stories, because of their use of description and detail, are often very difficult to write under deadline pressure. Thus, because of space, staffing, and time problems, many editors are prone to ignore feature angles on breaking local stories.

For example, assume you are the editor of a small-town afternoon newspaper. Your deadline is about noon. A school bus filled with children on a field trip crashes at about 9 A.M. you learn about the accident shortly before 10 A.M. You could easily assign a reporter to the story, who could gather the facts by telephone and have the news story written by noon. However, if you want a sidebar feature about the crash—perhaps a personality profile of the heroic bus driver who pulled injured children from the wreck—the story would be far more difficult to write by the noon deadline because it would probably require an interview with the driver, who might not be immediately available by telephone. In addition, the thorough feature writer would want to see the crash site firsthand and interview witnesses as well as surviving children. That means more time. All of this would be difficult for one reporter to accomplish by the noon deadline and probably would require assigning a second reporter to write the feature.

A good editor would assign the second reporter to do the feature if a reporter were, in fact, available. If the editor lacked personnel, the available reporter could write the news story for deadline and the feature for publication on the following, or second, day of the coverage.

It is also possible, of course, to write a news feature about a continuing news event and to publish that feature on a day when there is nothing about the main event in the paper. For example, if gasoline prices have been skyrocketing for the past few weeks, it might be appropriate to research and write a feature about the expense of getting a gallon of gasoline from the well to the neighborhood service station. Here's another example.

A child is bitten by a rabid skunk. A feature writer is assigned to do a story on the medical treatment required for humans who have been exposed to rabies. This story might follow the original news story by four, five or even more days. Both of these examples, however, are generally known as second-day stories.

The other basic type of feature, the *timeless* feature, is described by just what the words imply—a story frozen in time. Like frozen food, the timeless feature will keep for a long time without spoiling. A timeless feature might be written in early March and held until April or even May before it is published. The careful feature writer, of course, will check back with the subjects of the story before it is published to ascertain that no facts have changed since the interview. In most instances, nothing will have happened. In other cases, ages or addresses will have to be updated. In rare instances, feature writers will find that major changes will have occurred, perhaps even including the death of the featured subject or of others in the story.

An example of a timeless story would be the one on which Garcia worked. The cab company mechanic's tips on vehicle maintenance are as true in March as they will be in April, May or even June. But the cab mechanic might have retired, quit his job, been fired or dropped dead since Garcia's interview with him. Thus, updating the timeless story is necessary.

The news feature and the timeless feature have a number of characteristics in common. They are original, both in form and in subject matter. They both use description to give them life. They are held to tight journalistic standards of accuracy. They inform or entertain, and sometimes they do both. In short, they both fall within the definition of what a feature story is supposed to be.

In addition, news and timeless features share at least one other characteristic: They are popular with readers. Many studies have shown that readers of general-circulation newspapers tremendously enjoy well-written features. And a feature story with a photograph is an almost unbeatable recipe for high readership because studies have shown that pictures also have extremely high readership value.

And in that sense, feature stories are a lot like ice cream. Few ice cream lovers are neutral about a hot fudge sundae smothered with rich, foamy whipped cream and capped with a blushing cherry. And few newspaper readers are neutral about a well-written, anecdotally rich, professionally illustrated news or timeless feature.

Categories and Appeals

Feature stories, while journalistic, are first and foremost *stories,* with beginnings, middles and ends. These stories—albeit with different characters in different circumstances—tend to recur so frequently that they can be divided into familiar *categories* built around topics of universal *appeal.*

Let's look at the categories first.

There are at least 15 widely recognized types of newspaper features, and many more when individual variations within categories are considered. All can be either news or timeless features, with the exception of the "commemorative" feature, which is almost always tied to a breaking news event.

Remember that while some categories are about things, people are more interesting. The effective feature writer will try to transform the "thing" feature into a "people" feature.

Here are the categories, with examples:

The Business Story.　The problem with the business story is that it is easy to write a lackluster little feature about what a business sells (such as live lobsters), makes (such as cardboard caskets) or provides (such as removal and replacement of aircraft warning lights for television and radio towers). Such stories, however, are boring (except to the owner of the business), and interesting stories are usually very hard to come by because business owners are fearful of tarnishing their images and (unlike government agencies) are not required to provide you with any information unless shares in the business are traded on the stock exchange.

Here's how you can handle the business feature. In most cases, you should focus on an employee or the owner of the business. If the business has competition, you should look for a timely or unusual angle—a reason for writing the story about that particular business at that particular time—and then try to concentrate on an individual. You should also mention the competition to avoid the appearance of giving the business free advertising space. On the other hand, if it is a business with no competition, you could zero in on why the owner started the business and what impediments he or she faced on the road to success. Success is a universal appeal often used by storytellers.

Examples: If fees for personalized automobile license plates in your state are increasing, you write a feature story about the metal-fabricating company that manufactures the tags, focusing on the employee who makes the personalized plates. A veterinarian who specializes in treating exotic animals opens an office in your town. You write a feature about her after following her through a day's medical rounds at the city zoo, where she is a volunteer.

Above all, be aware that you are not writing a free advertisement for the business. If your article reads like copy you would expect to see from the business's advertising agency, press the "delete" button on your computer and start over.

The Commemorative Story.　Commemorative stories are news features pegged to the anniversary of an earlier news event. The commemorative story is usually written initially at the first anniversary, with other stories following at five-year intervals. Depending on the event, you can interview people who originally were involved in the story, or, if the individuals are dead or otherwise unavailable, you can write an article capturing the mood of the anniversary.

Examples: On the anniversary of the Japanese attack at Pearl Harbor, you interview a local resident who was aboard the battleship *Arizona.* On the anniversary of the assassination of President John F. Kennedy, you interview a local resident who was the Dallas police officer who arrested assassin Lee Harvey Oswald. On the anniversary of the September 11, 2001, terrorist attacks on New York City and Washington, D.C., you interview survivors. Or you write an article capturing the sights and sounds of the last day of operation of a 100-year-old downtown hotel.

The Explanatory Story.　You can show the reader how electricity or natural gas reaches consumers' homes, how a check written at a store in a distant city reaches the local bank, how a television newscast is assembled or how a radio commercial is created. Again, you should focus on a person in the process. Be forewarned: This type of story requires saturation research; you have to know almost as much about the process as does the expert in your story.

The First-Person Story.   In the typical first-person story, something dramatic happens to the writer that is so personal that nothing less than the first person singular ("I") is appropriate. For example, read the first 45 words from an award-winning *New York Times* feature about toxic shock syndrome.

> I went dancing the night before in a black velvet Paris gown, on one of those evenings that was the glamour of New York epitomized. I was blissfully asleep at 3 A.M.
>   Twenty-four hours later, I lay dying, my fingers and legs darkening with gangrene.

You have the flavor now.

If you are involved in an airplane crash, a nearly fatal automobile accident with a drunk driver or perhaps a sky-diving experience, the first-person story may be appropriate. Otherwise, consider writing it in the second person, "you." For example, if you get an exclusive interview with a movie star, you might want to write the story this way.

> You've always wanted to meet a movie star. Tuesday you got your chance. Tom Cruise was in town.

The Historical Story.   The historical feature is usually loosely pegged to a breaking news event, which gives the feature writer an excuse to do some research in the library and to show readers how their community or world has changed.

Examples: Crews installing new water lines encounter long-buried streetcar tracks, which provide you with a "news hook" to explain how the city was once served by a sophisticated trolley system. Or, construction of a new building is delayed while a pioneer cemetery is moved; you focus on the families buried in the cemetery and explain how they contributed to the development of the community.

The Hobbyist Story.   Everyone collects something, ranging from stuffed aardvarks to matchbook covers. Some hobbyists have extraordinary collections. As a feature writer, your job is to make certain that you are writing about the right collector—the one with the biggest, best or most unusual collection in your area. Check this out by talking to other collectors who can identify dealers, who in turn can lead you to national publications that provide a clearinghouse for collectors across the country. If you're about to interview a collector with 10,000 rubber ducks, and the editor of the national publication serving rubber-duck collectors says that's a big collection, you're in business.

The How-To Story.   The interview with one or more experts who advise the reader how to accomplish a tricky task is a meat-and-potatoes newspaper feature story. Because experts make a living charging customers for such information, they are often reluctant to give much free advice in an interview. Consequently, you may find yourself calling a number of professionals before you are able to piece together a coherent, helpful account. These stories are usually timeless articles but can be news features if they are pegged to a season (such as how to save money by chopping down your own Christmas tree) or a news event such as a flood (for instance, how to dry a wet carpet).

Example: Like Helen Garcia, you write a story about a mechanic who offers tips for nudging 300,000 miles from an automobile engine.

The Invention Story. You have probably heard about an inventor who is developing a lightbulb that never burns out or perhaps toothpaste that stains teeth red when they are inadequately brushed. Inventors are good feature material. But there's a hitch to this kind of story: Inventors usually will not give interviews until they have formally applied for a patent to protect their ideas, and conservative inventors will not discuss their ideas until a patent has actually been granted, a process that often takes years. Timing is the key.

The Medical Story. People get sick. And people die, some well before their time. There are strong feature stories in illness and death, albeit tough ones to write.

Let's look at stories of illness first. Serious illnesses require huge amounts of money. Some people don't have adequate medical insurance. Thus, relatives of a sick person—often of a sick child—frequently seek out feature writers to chronicle the family's financial plight in hopes that the story may trigger donations. If the medical insurance is adequate but the disease is unusual, the medical story often is focused on the struggle to find the appropriate treatment. If the ill person has recovered from the disease, a story can be written tracing the struggle to overcome the illness.

A variation on the illness story is the medical breakthrough story, which often focuses on a doctor who has succeeded in isolating the cause of a disease.

Stories about impending death are extremely difficult to write because of the emotional toll on both the interviewee and the feature writer. Nonetheless, such stories are occasionally written. A person who learns of terminal illness undergoes certain attitude changes. Eventually, many people approaching death find comfort in leaving a message for the living—perhaps a warning to live life fully or to avoid the habits that have brought on the disease. The feature story carries that message.

The Number Story. This kind of feature uses interviews with experts and a familiar number, such as "10," to put a problem—and sometimes a solution—in perspective.

Examples: You interview police officers and traffic engineers for a story dealing with the city's five deadliest intersections. You interview physicians and nurses to write a story about 10 ways to prepare a child for a visit to the hospital. Or you survey gourmet fast-food eaters to find the town's 10 best hamburgers.

The Odd-Occupation Story. Who washes the outside windows of the city's tallest building? What's a workday like for a modern grave digger? Who heads the city police bomb squad, and what does that work involve? And who changes the little lightbulbs on top of the local television station transmitting tower?

Every community has scores of individuals with unusual jobs—occupations that are dangerous, unappealing or simply strange. Such stories should prove interesting to your readers. A cautionary note: In the past, some fairly ordinary occupations became "odd" when a woman selected a traditionally male job—such as automobile mechanic—or a man opted for a traditionally female-filled position, but less feature value exists today in sex-role stories. A male "nanny" might be interviewed in a wider feature about child-care experts, but not merely because he is a man looking after a child.

The usual story approach requires you to find a person who has held an odd occupation for some time and who enjoys it, and to interview that person about how the job is performed, why he or she chose the field, or both.

The Overview Story.   Some kinds of features—for example, stories dealing with missing children or with arson—can be supported with voluminous statistics from various official sources. These statistics can be used to provide the reader with an informational overview of the problem, in addition to the emotional, humanistic qualities you will want to inject into the story.

Example: You gather statistics from police and fire departments, insurance companies and the FBI to paint a portrait of a "typical" business arson. You begin the story with a description of a well-known arson in your town, introduce the reader to the information you have gathered from official sources, then move to interviews with two arson investigators who take the reader through the steps used to solve the fire you described at the beginning of the story.

The Participatory Story.   Participatory stories go back to the days of Nellie Bly of Joseph Pulitzer's *New York World.* Bly, whose real name was Elizabeth Cochrane, had herself committed to a New York State insane asylum in order to write about conditions there. Frank Sutherland, a reporter for *The Tennessean* in Nashville and later president of the Society of Professional Journalists, did the same thing in Tennessee about 75 years later. And the participatory story was the trademark of writer George Plimpton, who, among other things, joined a football team and acted in a movie to obtain stories.

Hunter S. Thompson, who used to write for *Rolling Stone* magazine, called this blatant injection of the writer into the story "Gonzo journalism." Gonzo or not, there is nothing intrinsically wrong with living a role in order to write about it, unless you misrepresent yourself to write about the intimate details of other people. And even that may not be wrong in the case of investigative reporters such as Bly and Sutherland, who had no other means to investigate serious social problems. However, most feature writers using this approach will, like Plimpton, make arrangements beforehand and will "live" the story with the permission of the participants.

Examples: You want to write about the life of a sanitation worker, so you make arrangements with the city to work as a garbage collector for two days. Or you want to know the fear of being a convenience store clerk on the night shift in a high-crime area, so you talk the store's manager into hiring you for five nights.

The Profile Story.   You can profile practically anyone or anything. Of course, profiles are usually written about people, with their cooperation. You usually pick someone of interest, ask the subject for an interview, research and then interview the individual and finally talk to other people who know the subject. If the subject is uncooperative—as was Sam Walton, the richest man in America until Microsoft's Bill Gates took his place—you can do what one *Washington Post* writer did. The *Post* writer talked to scores of people who knew the shy Wal-Mart founder in his little hometown of Bentonville, Arkansas, and then wrote a story based on their views of the man.

The profile—with or without cooperation—should paint a word portrait of the subject. The reader should come away from the profile with an understanding of how the person looks, sounds and thinks.

Groups, institutions, events and things can be profiled, too. In fact, in the early 1980s writer Tracy Kidder even profiled the birth of a computer in his award-winning book, *The Soul of a New Machine.*

The Unfamiliar Visitor Story.   A visitor often offers a unique perspective on a local problem, culture or event. If the visitor is available for an interview, his or her perspective can often help readers understand their world better.

Examples: Your community suffers from 10 percent unemployment, and you interview a visiting Chinese political scientist about how unemployment is handled in the People's Republic of China. Or a Middle Eastern terrorist group sets off a bomb in a European airport, killing a local resident; you interview Arab students attending a nearby university to obtain their perspective on terrorism.

Some of these features tend to be further categorized because they are published in specific newspaper "sections" such as business, entertainment, fashion, food, health, home, lifestyle, religion, sports and travel. For example, profile stories often appear in business, entertainment, health, lifestyle, religion and travel sections. On the other hand, first-person and participatory stories often wind up in newspaper Sunday "magazines." And commemorative, historical and unfamiliar visitor stories frequently find their way into a newspaper's primary news section.

Now let's look at the other tool to help you find a good story—a topic with a universal appeal or attraction.

Flip through any thorough book explaining how short stories, novels, plays and dramatic scripts are written and you will find that most successful fictional stories are constructed around topics of universal appeal. Love is a common subject, for example. Variations of each appeal abound. Love's variations include love conquers all, love given but not returned, and sacrifice for love, among many others. Stories about adventure, animals, children, crime, death, disaster, failure, greed, health, humor, mystery, politics, religion, self-improvement, sex, success, treasure and vengeance also have a broad appeal.

Not every feature has a readily apparent universal appeal, but the best ones do seem to clearly make a statement to and about all of us. Later in this chapter, you'll read more about how appeals are integrated with story categories.

NEWSPAPER FEATURE WRITERS: THE RIGHT STUFF

Writer Tom Wolfe wrote a book in 1979 titled *The Right Stuff,* which dealt with America's first astronauts. The book's title referred to the character, courage and other personality traits of those early space travelers.

Newspaper feature writers also have to have the "right stuff" to be successful.

In the case of feature writers, the right stuff includes the ability to enjoy all kinds of people, curiosity, a keen sense of observation, a good knowledge of the language, an appreciation for the power of the printed word and the ability to organize material and to write relatively quickly. (Knowing how to use a good thesaurus and dictionary doesn't hurt either.)

Let's take the ability *to get along with various kinds of people* first.

At the beginning of this chapter, you met Helen Garcia, a new reporter for the *Chronicle*. Garcia, as you recall, was sent to interview a mechanic who worked for the local cab company. The mechanic had a formula for squeezing 300,000 miles from each cab engine, and Garcia was assigned to write a feature on the man and his ideas.

If Garcia had been reared in a typical middle-class home and educated at a state university, she could be expected to have certain fairly predictable societal values. Predicting anyone's attitude is treading on dangerous ground, because it is difficult to generalize about people in our pluralistic society. Surveys have shown, however, that newspaper reporters do share some common characteristics. They are, for example, often political moderates who view themselves as Democrats or Independents. As a group, they are somewhat less religious than most Americans. They are also middle class and college-educated, on the whole.

All of that suggests that Garcia might not be able to communicate easily with a devoutly religious neo-Nazi who has only completed the sixth grade. But as a feature writer, she must understand her subject if she is to write about him accurately.

This dilemma is common to the newspaper feature writer, the magazine writer and the book-length nonfiction writer as well. Did Truman Capote, in researching his book *In Cold Blood,* understand the two cold-blooded murderers who had slaughtered a Kansas farm family? Did Norman Mailer, who wrote about Utah murderer Gary Gilmore in *The Executioner's Song,* come to know Gilmore?

Capote didn't particularly like his Kansas murderers. Nonetheless, he wrote a compelling book. Mailer found Gary Gilmore vicious, but he, too, still produced a stunning work. And if Garcia finds her cab mechanic to be an unpleasant person who nonetheless really does know how to coax 300,000 miles from an automobile engine, the story should still be done, and done well.

How? The answer is that every person in our society is unique, and the chances are pretty good that you will encounter many people whose values do not exactly coincide with yours. You are not a police officer or a minister or a social worker. Your job description includes neither judging nor saving the people you write about. You are a reporter, a writer. Your job is to observe and to write about these people.

In short, your right stuff inventory should include the ability to get along with all kinds of people, even if you personally find them to be disgusting or immoral. In that sense, a feature writer deals with feature-story subjects in much the same way as a good lawyer deals with clients. The lawyer tries not to let personal feelings get in the way of the primary consideration, which is assisting the client.

Curiosity is another characteristic the strong feature writer must have or cultivate.

If you are the type who will never run to the top of the hill to see what is on the other side, you probably will never see the visual clues all around you that can lead to the unforgettable feature story.

For example, that strange little restaurant you drive by every day may be owned by an Albanian refugee who used to be that country's deputy minister of defense. But you will never know and will consequently never write a feature about him because you lack the curiosity to stop at the restaurant.

Of course, someone might one day tell your city editor about the restaurant and its owner, and the editor might then assign you to do a feature. Editors, however, are not wildly enthusiastic about feature writers who only wait for assignments.

The solution is to learn to look at life with an insatiable curiosity. Why do sidewalks have cracks in them? Why is peanut butter sticky? What do zoo animals eat?

A third characteristic the successful feature writer needs is an ability to *observe* surroundings keenly.

If Garcia is to do an acceptable feature on her cab mechanic, she must describe the mechanic and his surroundings so as to put the reader "in" the garage. The reader should "see" the mechanic, his workplace, his tools and his engines. The reader should have a feeling for the way the mechanic walks, talks and smells.

How? It's accomplished by being alert to your environment. You can practice this by walking into an unfamiliar room and making a mental note of all the significant features of that room. For example, the next time you are sitting in a restaurant, waiting for service, note the color and texture of the walls, the floor and the table surface. Look at the windows and see if they are clean. See whether the salt and pepper shakers on the table are full, and read the advertising you find on the table. Then, look around the restaurant and start cataloguing the customers. Are they predominantly men or women, young or old, well dressed or casual, fat or thin? Are they in groups or alone? If they are in groups, are they talking or staring into space?

When you have mastered the restaurant exercise, try other environments. If you commute to school or work, cast a new eye on the route that you travel, noting details about land features and various buildings, including any Albanian restaurants.

Eventually you should be able to walk into a strange setting, such as a cab company garage, and soak up the surroundings in a few minutes of looking and note taking. After a lot of practice, you should be able to do the same thing with people's appearances.

Describing people, of course, is a chancy business. If Garcia is 5 feet, 2 inches tall and the cab mechanic is 5 feet, 8 inches tall, she might be tempted to describe the mechanic as being "tall." The mechanic is actually a little on the short side when compared with the average height of American men. Garcia, of course, is very short. Thus, description should be written carefully. Feature writers generally describe only what is clearly observable, only what is obvious.

Sometimes, if a story requires a more risky description, such as describing a scientist as having a mind like a steel trap, the feature writer will check his or her observations with a second source, such as a friend of the subject or the actual subject. "Have your friends ever described you as having a mind like a steel trap?" the feature writer might ask. "No. They sometimes say I have a mind like a finely tooled machine," the subject answers, giving the writer an equally acceptable, more accurate description.

The feature writer also needs to have a solid *knowledge of the language* and a fine appreciation of the power of the printed word and of the varied meanings of words that may seem similar but have subtle differences. For example, Garcia describes the cab mechanic as having an oily rather than a dirty hand. "Oil" and "dirt" mean approximately the same thing to many people, but there is a difference, especially when you are describing someone who makes his living around automobile engines. A writer who has a strong appreciation of this kind of difference, of the subtlety of words, is often called a wordsmith.

A wordsmith cares about each word and knows the value of compositional techniques such as the simile and the metaphor, alliteration and personification. A wordsmith labors over each word, frequently turns to a thesaurus, and chooses a word the way a shopper selects a golden onion at the supermarket.

The last bit of right stuff the feature writer should have is the ability to organize and to write *quickly,* which seems to fly in the face of the studied precision of the wordsmith. While some features may have a deadline that gives the writer only a few hours in which to gather, organize and write the feature material, many features are written somewhat more leisurely. But "leisure" is a relative term at newspapers. It may mean only two or three hours for the interview and two or three hours (perhaps spread over several days) to write the feature.

The wordsmith, then, must write speedily, probably mentally organizing the story while returning from the interview. When the time comes to write the story—and that may be the same day or several days later—the writer does one draft of the story on the computer terminal, then polishes that in a few minutes, quickly completing the story. The writing process for the typical feature, wordsmithing and all, often takes the same time as some people might take to write a letter to a friend.

In sum, the right stuff for the newspaper feature writer means the ability to handle people of all kinds; curiosity; the knack to capture people, places and things on paper; and the seemingly contradictory abilities to write effectively and relatively quickly.

For the most part, these qualities are not inherited. They are learned; they are cultivated. These qualities, say some of America's Pulitzer Prize–winning feature writers, are gleaned largely from trial and error. But they are present in all truly outstanding feature writers.

A PROFILE OF THE PULITZER WINNERS

The Pulitzer Prize is perhaps newspaper journalism's greatest honor. Created with money left by *St. Louis Post-Dispatch* and *New York World* publisher Joseph Pulitzer, it was first awarded in 1917. Prizes are given for fiction, nonfiction, drama, U.S. history, biography or autobiography, poetry, music and journalism. Journalists compete in numerous categories, ranging from reporting to photojournalism to feature writing.

The Pulitzer Prize, like a product with a fine word-of-mouth reputation, doesn't lack "customers." The Pulitzer Board doesn't even solicit submissions because it has more business than it can handle. Instead, America's newspaper editors eagerly but quietly select and send examples of their organizations' best work each February to the Pulitzer offices at Columbia University in New York City. Then, each spring, bleary-eyed journalism juries sift through the entries in various categories, looking for the best of the best. Winners get a cash prize—now $10,000—and the recognition that their peers have judged their work to be superlative.

Most of America's best newspaper feature writers haven't won a Pulitzer Prize. There are too many writers for too few Pulitzers. Some of those unrecognized writers will never win a Pulitzer or any other major award because they're not interested in competing. Others don't enter contests because they believe they can't win. Although the Pulitzer Prize for feature writing singles out only one outstanding feature writer among many each year, the writers and their winning entries should be studied because they set a standard for features of national quality.

A Pulitzer was first given for feature writing in 1979, to Jon Franklin, then a feature and science writer for *The Evening Sun* in Baltimore.

Franklin, a high school dropout, served eight years in the Navy, then enrolled in the journalism program at the University of Maryland and graduated with honors three years later. He joined the Baltimore *Evening Sun* in 1970, serving on the newspaper's rewrite staff until 1973, when he became a feature writer. As a feature writer, he specialized in science generally and medicine specifically.

Franklin, long interested in how the human brain functioned, wrote about a woman named Edna Kelly who had brain surgery to try to stem the development of a tumor she called "the monster." The story is a blend of the *medical* and *explanatory* feature categories. Franklin's story, "Mrs. Kelly's Monster," is memorable because it deals simply with a human being and her problem. And the Pulitzer jury found the story compelling enough to call it the best in the country. Franklin, by the way, won the Pulitzer again in 1985, this time for explanatory writing about brain research.

PULITZER PRIZES OF THE 1980s.
You'll find that most of America's best newspaper feature stories—the Pulitzer Prize winners—have been about ordinary people involved in extraordinary situations.

For example, Madeleine Blais, then a writer for *The Miami Herald's Tropic* magazine, won the Prize in 1980 for a package of five stories. One, an essay on friendship, is atypical. The other four are simple stories of people with problems. One is a *profile* of writer Tennessee Williams. Two deal with families with unusual afflictions. The fifth is a *profile* of Edward Zepp, an 83-year-old man who felt he had been unfairly given a dishonorable discharge from the Army in World War I. Zepp took a train from his home in Florida to the Pentagon in Washington to plead his case. In "Zepp's Last Stand," Blais wrote about the crusade, a crusade that Zepp won.

Blais, with a bachelor's degree in English and Latin from the College of New Rochelle and a master's in journalism from Columbia University, worked for *The Boston Globe* and *The Trenton Times* before writing for *The Miami Herald*. Interestingly, all of Blais's Pulitzer stories—except the Zepp article—were sold, or "freelanced," to the *Herald*. Her work impressed the editors, and she was hired and then wrote the Zepp article that completed the prize-winning package.

Teresa Carpenter, then a writer with *The Village Voice,* won the award in 1981 for three freelanced features about the senseless killings of a suburban New

(continued)

A PROFILE OF THE PULITZER WINNERS   CONTINUED

York housewife, a popular political activist and a *Playboy* model. The *profile* about the model, "Death of a Playmate," is the basis for the Bob Fosse movie *Star 80*.

Carpenter had reported from Hawaii for a Japanese business magazine and a New Jersey monthly before beginning her freelancing career. The freelancing encompassed *The Village Voice,* and eventually she became a *Voice* staffer. Her educational background includes an English degree from Graceland College in Iowa and a master's degree in journalism from the University of Missouri.

The winner for 1982, Saul Pett of the Associated Press, broke the Pulitzer feature pattern in several ways. First, Pett, in his sixties when he won the award, was older than previous feature Pulitzer winners. In addition, he won the Prize after a long news career that began with a degree in journalism from the University of Missouri, followed by a job as a copy boy for the New York *Daily News,* a six-year reporting stint for the now defunct International News Service, and more than four decades with the AP. Unlike Franklin, Blais and Carpenter—who researched and wrote their stories under deadlines ranging from a few weeks to a few months—Pett took nearly half a year to research and write his winning entry. Pett's entry required that kind of time-consuming research: It is a thoughtful, long—almost 10,000 words—story of the U.S. government, called "The Bureaucracy: How Did It Get So Big?" The article is really an *overview* story about a government that the story notes "is owned by everybody and run by nobody."

Nan Robertson, then a *New York Times* reporter who found herself suffering from toxic shock syndrome, won the 1983 Prize with a gripping 6,500-word *first-person* story about her struggle against death, a struggle that cost her the end joints of eight of her fingers. Robertson, who received the assignment for "Toxic Shock" when she was in a hospital intensive-care ward, also gives readers a definitive account of the nature of toxic shock. The article drew 2,000 letters and eventually was reprinted in about 400 newspapers.

Robertson was the first woman reporter to win the Pulitzer at the *Times,* which has had more than 100 winners since 1917. A native Chicagoan and a Northwestern University journalism graduate, Robertson worked for five daily newspapers before

joining the *Times* in 1955. She was a bureau reporter in Washington and Paris before becoming a writer for the *Times* cultural section.

The next Prize was won by Peter Rinearson, then an aerospace reporter for *The Seattle Times*. His entry, an *explanatory* collection of 12 stories, is titled "Making It Fly" and is about the multiyear struggle of the Boeing company to design and sell the 757 jetliner. Rinearson's concept is simple; the stories, however, have vast scope and include sources from three continents.

Rinearson, a University of Washington journalism and political science major, began his career at *The Seattle Times* with an internship, and two years later he was hired full-time. He covered the legislature, city hall and special projects until he was assigned the aerospace beat. He was 28 years old when "Making It Fly" was published, and he won the Pulitzer Prize for feature writing when he was 29.

Alice Steinbach, then a Baltimore *Sun* writer who in 1985 won a Pulitzer for her profile called "A Boy of Unusual Vision," demonstrates once again that a simple human story can be compelling. The story is about a blind Baltimore boy named Calvin Stanley, who, she writes, "rides a bike, watches TV, plays video games and does just about everything other 10-year-old boys do." But Steinbach's story is really about how love can overcome the most formidable obstacles.

Steinbach, like Blais and Carpenter, freelanced for newspapers and magazines before joining a newspaper staff. She was hired by the *Sun* in 1981 as a feature writer. A Baltimorean, she had studied at the University of London.

The 1986 prize was won by John Camp, then a reporter for the *St. Paul Pioneer Press*. Camp's *profile* of a rural Minnesota family, "Life on the Land: An American Farm Family," was published in five parts. The seasons give structure to the first four parts. The final part of the series is a 12-page special section summarizing the year and the family in words and pictures. Covering the family required 10 trips—more than 4,000 miles of travel.

Camp began his newspaper career as editor of an Army paper in Korea. After his discharge from the Army, he worked as a general assignment reporter in Missouri and, after earning a graduate degree, moved to Miami where he spent eight years as a reporter and editor for *The Miami Herald.* He joined the *St. Paul Pioneer Press* in 1978. Camp has a bachelor's degree in American studies and a master's in journalism, both from the University of Iowa.

Steve Twomey, then a reporter for *The Philadelphia Inquirer,* won the 1987 feature-writing Pulitzer for an *overview* of the value of aircraft carriers. Twomey's story—"How Super Are Our Super-carriers?"—also explores life aboard the giant warships. Twomey joined the *Inquirer* in 1973 as a general assignment reporter and subsequently covered politics, education and labor for the newspaper. Later he was the paper's Paris correspondent. Twomey has a bachelor's degree in journalism from Northwestern University.

The 1988 Pulitzer Prize was awarded to Jacqui Banaszynski, then of the *St. Paul Pioneer Press,* for a three-part feature about a Minnesota farmer and political activist who became ill with acquired immune deficiency syndrome. "AIDS in the Heartland" is both a *profile* and a *medical* feature because it paints a compelling word portrait of the activist while conveying to the readers the dying man's message.

Banaszynski has a bachelor's degree in journalism with honors from Marquette University. After graduation, Banaszynski worked for newspapers in Indiana, Wisconsin, Oregon and Minnesota, covering a wide range of general assignment stories and specialized beats, including women and minorities, energy and environment and politics and government. She joined the *St. Paul Pioneer Press* in 1984 and was assigned to special projects and features a year later.

Like Rinearson, Camp and Banaszynski, David Zucchino, then of *The Philadelphia Inquirer,* won his Pulitzer for a series of features about one topic: discrimination in South Africa during the 1980s. Zucchino's 1989 Prize-winning series of *profiles,* "Being Black in South Africa," explains how nine South African blacks—a grieving father, a housemaid, a war veteran, a politician, a mother, a nightclub owner, a manager, a factory worker and a field-worker for the South African Council of Churches—cope with that country's racial segregation laws.

Zucchino joined the *Inquirer* in 1980 after seven years as a reporter for the Raleigh, North Carolina, *The News & Observer* and the *Detroit Free Press.* He became a foreign correspondent for the *Inquirer* when he was only 30 years old, covering the Middle East and, later, Africa. He has a degree in journalism from the University of North Carolina at Chapel Hill.

PULITZER PRIZES OF THE 1990s.

Dave Curtin was a police reporter with the *Colorado Springs Gazette Telegraph* in 1989 when he learned about a devastating gas explosion in a house 16 miles east of town. He rushed to Colorado Spring's Penrose Hospital in time to see Adam, 6, Megan, 4, and their father, Steve Walter, arrive by army helicopter and ambulance. "When I saw them," Curtin recalls, "I thought that I would be reporting on a triple fatality." Instead, Curtin spent six months following the children and their father through a remarkable recovery from serious burns. The *profile* and *medical* story, "Adam & Megan: A Story of One Family's Courage," written to help the Walter children reintegrate into the community despite painful disfigurement, won the 1990 Pulitzer Prize for feature writing.

Curtin, a journalism graduate from the University of Colorado, covered sports, police and general assignment stories for three Colorado dailies before joining the *Gazette Telegraph* in 1988 as a police reporter.

In the late 1980s, residents of Florida's Tampa Bay area were confronted with numerous accounts of abandoned babies. Some of these newborns were found dead in trash cans. Others were found alive, such as a baby boy that nurses at Tampa General Hospital dubbed Jack-in-the-box because he was found in a videocassette recorder carton. When Jack-in-the-box's mother was arrested, Sheryl James, then a *St. Petersburg Times* staff writer, decided to explore the issue of child abandonment by focusing on the woman. After six months of patient effort, James persuaded the baby's mother to talk about her crime. The result is a four-part *profile* series, entitled "A Gift Abandoned," that won the 1991 Pulitzer Prize for feature writing. James, by the way, was a Pulitzer finalist in 1992, for a series she wrote about organ transplants.

James has a bachelor's degree in English from Eastern Michigan University as well as a teaching certificate. After graduation, she wrote for a Michigan city magazine and then a North Carolina daily newspaper before joining the St. Petersburg paper in 1986.

The 1992 and 1993 Pulitzer Prize–winning feature stories have several similarities. Both stories are lengthy, emotional, personal accounts of events that altered the lives of their authors. The 1992 Prize was won by Howell Raines, then of *The New York Times,* for "Grady's Gift," a *Times* magazine Sunday cover story that is a blend of the *first-person* and *profile* feature categories. Raines's story is a tribute to

(continued)

A PROFILE OF THE PULITZER WINNERS   CONTINUED

Gradystein Hutchinson, who was a maid in his home in Birmingham, Alabama, when he was a child and who had a profound influence on his views about civil rights and race relations. George Lardner Jr., then of *The Washington Post*, won the 1993 feature Pulitzer for "The Stalking of Kristin," which is a mixture of the *first-person, profile* and *explanatory* feature story categories. Lardner's feature reveals flaws in the criminal justice system that permitted the murder of his 21-year-old daughter, Kristin, by a former boyfriend, who later killed himself.

Raines and Lardner, like Pett and Robertson before them, were veteran journalists when they won Pulitzers. Raines, who has a bachelor's degree from Birmingham-Southern College and a master's degree from the University of Alabama in Tuscaloosa, had worked for newspapers and television stations in Alabama, Georgia and Florida before joining the *Times*. When he won his Pulitzer, he had written two books and was the Washington editor of the *Times*. When Lardner won his Prize, he had more than 35 years of journalism experience, including newspaper jobs in Massachusetts and Florida and three decades with *The Washington Post*. He has bachelor's and master's degrees in journalism from Marquette University.

By contrast, the winner of the 1994 Pulitzer for feature writing was a relative newcomer to journalism. Isabel Wilkerson, then of the Chicago bureau of *The New York Times*, had about 10 years of journalism experience when she won her Pulitzer for three stories: a 2,800-word *profile* of a fourth-grader from Chicago's South Side and two shorter stories about floods that ravaged the Midwestern United States during the summer of 1993. Wilkerson was the first African American woman to win a Pulitzer Prize in journalism and the first black American to win for individual reporting.

Wilkerson, with a bachelor's degree in journalism from Howard University, was a reporting intern for newspapers in California, the District of Columbia, Florida and Georgia before joining the *Times* in 1984.

Ron Suskind, then a senior national affairs reporter for *The Wall Street Journal*, won the 1995 feature Pulitzer for a *profile* that explores some of the same issues that Wilkerson wrote about the year before. In a two-part story published in the spring and the fall of 1994, Suskind paints a compelling word portrait of an inner-city Washington, D.C., high school student who aspires to attend the highly competitive Massachusetts Institute of Technology. Suskind's story of the struggle of Cedric Jennings to attend MIT also became a book in 1998, titled *A Hope in the Unseen*.

Suskind received a bachelor's degree in government and foreign affairs from the University of Virginia and also completed a master's degree in journalism from Columbia University. He had more than a decade of experience in journalism when he won the Pulitzer, having started his career as an interim reporter for *The New York Times*. After working for the *Times*, he moved to the *St. Petersburg Times* as a writer covering crime and general interest stories, then relocated to a Boston business magazine, and then became a reporter for *The Wall Street Journal*.

Rick Bragg's 1996 Pulitzer Prize was the fourth for feature writing to be won by a *New York Times'* writer. Bragg's award also catapulted the *Times* into first place among newspapers that have won the feature Pulitzer.

Bragg's Pulitzer Prize was awarded for five "elegantly written stories about contemporary America," according to the citation given to the then Atlanta-based *New York Times'* correspondent. Bragg's short features, all of which were written on a tight deadline and most of which were published on the front page of the *Times*, include the following: an *odd-occupation* story about how low-income blacks in New Orleans participate in the Mardi Gras celebration; a sidebar *profile* about the reaction of Oklahoma City police, firefighters and medical technicians to the April 19, 1995, terrorist blast that destroyed the Murrah Federal Building; a blend of a *profile* and an *explanatory* story about a South Carolina sheriff who extracted a confession from a mother who drowned her two sons; a *profile* of a childless laundress who gave her life savings of $150,000 to the University of Southern Mississippi for scholarships; and an *overview* article about the United States' aging prison inmates as exemplified by five infirm Alabama prisoners.

Bragg grew up near Jacksonville, Alabama, attended Jacksonville State University briefly, and then spent a decade as a reporter for Alabama newspapers, including the weekly *Jacksonville News, The Daily Home* in Talladega, *The Anniston Star* and *The Birmingham News,* before joining Florida's *St. Petersburg Times* in 1989. At the *St. Petersburg Times,* Bragg worked as a reporter at suburban bureaus before becoming Miami bureau chief. After brief duty at *The Los Angeles Times,* he joined *The New York Times* as a reporter in 1994 and won the Pulitzer two years later. His writing prowess and his wittiness also are displayed in *All Over But the Shoutin',* his 1997 tribute to his mother, and *Ava's Man,* a 2001 book about his grandfather. A collection of Bragg's journalistic stories can be found in *Somebody Told Me: The Newspaper Stories of Rick Bragg.*

Lisa Pollak won the feature-writing Pulitzer in 1997 with her story, "The Umpire's Sons," and in the process earned the third such accolade for the Baltimore *Sun.* Pollak's long article is a combination of *profile* and a *medical* feature about an American League baseball umpire whose son died of a genetic disease and whose remaining children are afflicted with the same malady. Pollak, with a bachelor's degree in American culture from the University of Michigan and a master's degree in journalism from Northwestern University, worked for *The News & Observer* in Raleigh, North Carolina, and *The Charlotte Observer* before joining *The Sun* in 1996. She became a broadcast journalist in 2004.

Thomas French of the *St. Petersburg Times* earned the 1998 feature-writing Pulitzer Prize—the 20th such award—for a book-length *profile* about crime and punishment.

Although French's approach to feature writing is unlike that of most of the other journalists who won the Pulitzer for feature writing, his route into the profession was rather typical: French, who grew up in Indiana, graduated from Indiana University in 1980 with a major in journalism. He joined the *St. Petersburg Times* a year after graduation and covered police, courts and general assignment news before he became a feature writer. However, over time he began to specialize in meticulously researched and extremely long, detailed stories published over many days. "Angels and Demons," which won the 1998 Pulitzer over about 150 other entries, is such a story. The seven-part story recounts the horrific 1989 murders of an Ohio mother and her two teenage daughters while on vacation in Florida and the three-year investigation and 1994 life-and-death trial that followed. Reporting and writing took more than a year and included an examination of more than 4,000 pages of police and court documents.

Angelo B. Henderson, then of *The Wall Street Journal*'s Detroit bureau, won the 1999 feature-writing Pulitzer Prize for a chilling *profile* of a Detroit druggist who confronted and killed an armed robber. Henderson paints a word portrait first of the pharmacist and then of the robber. After describing the main characters, Henderson takes readers to the drugstore on the day of the 1997 robbery and the single deadly gunshot, which was later ruled justifiable homicide. Henderson ends the feature with an examination of the aftermath of the shooting for both the white druggist and the black armed robber's family.

Henderson, the first African American man to win a feature-writing Pulitzer, earned his bachelor's degree in journalism from the University of Kentucky. After four internships while at the university, Henderson began full-time work as a reporter for the *St. Petersburg Times.* He left about a year later for the Louisville *Courier-Journal,* where he was a business writer. He then joined the *Detroit News* as a reporter and later became a business writer and columnist there. Although he won the Pulitzer at *The Wall Street Journal,* he eventually returned to the *Detroit News.*

J. R. Moehringer, then *The Los Angeles Times* Atlanta bureau chief, won the twentieth century's final Pulitzer Prize for feature writing with "Crossing Over," a 10-part, 9,600-word poetic *profile* of Mary Lee Bendolph and her Alabama hometown of Gee's Bend. Moehringer visited Gee's Bend for periods ranging from one week to two weeks over a full year. Through Bendolph's eyes, Moehringer described the potential effects of a proposed ferry for Bendolph's isolated 180-year-old river community and its population, many of whom are descendants of slaves. In a story stylistically reminiscent of Steinbach's "Boy of Unusual Vision," Moehringer effectively reduces the long struggle for equal rights in the United States to the relationship between the people of a rural African American community and the residents of the neighboring, predominately white community of Camden, Alabama.

Moehringer, who received a bachelor's degree in history from Yale, began his newspaper career as a news assistant at *The New York Times.* In 1990 he

(continued)

A PROFILE OF THE PULITZER WINNERS   CONTINUED

became a reporter for the *Rocky Mountain News* in Denver, then moved to the Orange County edition of *The Los Angeles Times* in 1994. Three years later he became Atlanta bureau chief for the *Times,* a job he held until 2000, when he went to Harvard on a Nieman Fellowship. He is now based in Denver, covering the West for *The Los Angeles Times.*

PULITZER PRIZES OF THE 2000s.

Tom Hallman Jr. of *The Oregonian* in Portland won the 2001 Pulitzer Prize for feature writing for "The Boy Behind the Mask." Although it was the first Pulitzer Prize–winning feature in a new century, Hallman's four-part story, a blend of a *profile* and a *medical* feature about a severely disfigured 14-year-old boy who seeks dangerous surgery to improve his appearance, has many of the same characteristics of the work of Banaszynski in 1988, Curtain in 1990 and Pollak in 1997. To report and write about Sam Lightner's long struggle to look like other children, Hallman spent "hundreds of hours, over more than 10 months, poring over medical records, reading Lightner family journals, hanging out at the Lightner house, attending school with Sam, interviewing Sam's friends, and twice traveling across the country with the family," notes Jack Hart, managing editor of *The Oregonian.* Hallman, by the way, was one of two finalists for the feature-writing Pulitzer in 1999.

Hallman, a native of Portland, has a bachelor's degree in journalism from Drake University in Iowa. After graduation, he worked as a magazine copy editor in New York City and for small daily newspapers in Oregon and Washington before becoming a police reporter for *The Oregonian* in 1980. Hallman was a senior writer when he wrote his award-winning feature.

The 2002 Pulitzer Prize was awarded to Barry Siegel, then a *Los Angeles Times* correspondent and senior writer. Siegel won for "A Father's Pain, a Judge's Duty, and a Justice Beyond Their Reach," a *profile* of a Utah judge, the distraught father whom the judge sentenced to jail for negligence in the exposure-related wilderness death of his little boy, and the young father's ultimate suicide. Siegel, like 2000 winner and colleague Moehringer, wrote a powerful story about people struggling with challenges.

A 1971 Pomona College honors English graduate who earned a master's degree in journalism from Columbia University in 1972, Siegel began his journalism career as a summer intern at *The Oregonian.* Siegel found his way to *The Los Angeles Times* in the mid–1970s after intermediate stops as a staff writer at *LA* and as the West Coast news editor for *Woman's Wear Daily.* He is the author of numerous nonfiction books and novels.

Siegel's *Los Angeles Times* colleague, Sonia Nazario, won the 2003 Pulitzer Prize for a *profile* about a 17-year-old Honduran boy's eight attempts to cross the United States border to find his mother in North Carolina. Nazario, in classic *participatory* story style that also included components of *explanatory* and *overview* story types, spent nine months reporting, including riding on the top of railroad freight cars on the "Train of Death," evading bandits (who stole her photojournalist's cameras) and hitchhiking in 18-wheelers through Mexico. She then spent seven weeks transcribing 110 reporter's notebooks and about one year writing and editing 12 drafts that ultimately yielded a story published in six parts over two weeks in four versions: English and Spanish in different print and Internet versions. The final English print version was the second longest Pulitzer feature—French's was longer—at more than 30,000 words, with the Internet version expanded to 34,000 words.

Nazario, who grew up in both Argentina and the United States, began her journalism career as an unpaid freelance reporter for *El Pais* in Madrid, Spain, in 1980 while she was a college student. Between her junior and senior years, she was a summer intern for the *Washington Post.* After earning her bachelor's degree in 1982 in history from Williams College, she became a full-time journalist for *The Wall Street Journal,* reporting from New York, Atlanta and Miami between 1982 and 1986. In 1988, she completed a master's degree in Latin American studies from the University of California at Berkeley and also began covering social issues for the *Journal* from Los Angeles. She became a urban affairs writer for *The Los Angeles Times* in 1993 and one year later, became a projects and urban affairs reporter for the *Times.* Nazario, who won numerous national journalism awards before winning the Pulitzer, also alcohol or drugs. In 2006, "Enrique's Journey" was updated and expanded to book-length. The book also was published in Spanish as *La Travesía de Enrique: La Arriesgada Odisea de un Niño en Busca de su Madre.*

No feature-writing Pulitzer Prize was awarded in 2004 for the first time in the history of the feature Pulitzers. In 2005, however, Julia Keller, a *Chicago Tribune* cultural affairs reporter, won the award for a three-part, 14,000-word series about a 10-second Fujita-level 3 tornado that leveled a 117-year-old Utica, Illinois, tavern called the Milestone Tap and killed eight people, while sparing nine others in the building. The *Tribune* covered the immediate effects of the Utica tornado, but editors asked Keller to cover the story as a feature. She resisted because she believed the killer storm had been well reported, but nonetheless she spent seven months piecing together what happened on that evening in April 2004. Keller's story— "Utica, Illinois"—a mixture of an *explanatory* and *overview* story, ultimately took seven months to report and became a three-part series that the Pulitzer board called "gripping" and "meticulously reconstructed."

Keller earned a bachelor's and a master's degree in English from Marshall University in Huntington, West Virginia, a small Ohio River city where she grew up. She earned a doctorate in English at Ohio State University in 1995. She began her journalism career as an intern for columnist Jack Anderson and later worked for the Ashland, Kentucky, *Daily Independent* and the *Columbus Dispatch* in Ohio. She studied at Harvard University as a Nieman Fellow prior to joining the *Tribune* in 1998.

To mark Veterans Day on November 11, 2005—nearly three years after the United States invaded Iraq—the *Rocky Mountain News* in Denver published a 24-page, full-color 12,000 word *profile* about a team of Colorado-based Marines who were assigned to help families bury Marine Corps relatives who were killed in the Iraq War. Reporter Jim Sheeler and photographer Todd Heisler each won a Pulitzer on 2006 for the series titled "Final Salute."

Prior to reporting and writing "Final Salute," Sheeler specialized in covering the impact of the war in Colorado. In fact, he covered the funeral of the state's first casualty in March 2003. Sheeler's Pulitzer Prize–winning story required more than 10 months to report and write and required travel to three addi-

tional states: Nevada, South Dakota and Wyoming. The publication drew more than 1,000 e-mails and letters from all over the world.

Before joining the *News* in 2002, Sheeler worked as a freelance writer, primarily for *The Denver Post,* where he started a Sunday feature obituary column called "A Colorado Life." He previously worked for the Boulder *Daily Camera* and the weekly *Boulder Planet.* Born in Houston, Texas, he graduated with a bachelor's degree in journalism from Colorado State University in 1990. He co-authored *Life on the Death Beat: A Handbook for Obituary Writers.* A collection of his obituaries is titled *After Words: Obituaries of Ordinary People Who Led Extraordinary Lives.*

The winners of the Pulitzer for feature writing, for the most part, received journalism training in college and won their Prizes while in their thirties or forties. They wrote about topics of universal appeal: Franklin about an unsuccessful medical battle; Blais about the persistence of the human spirit and a legal success; Carpenter about crime; Pett about politics; Robertson about health; Rinearson about business success; Steinbach about motherly love; Camp about love of the land; Twomey about adventure at sea; Banaszynski about love and death; Zucchino about economic, political and social success and failure; Curtin about children; James about a child who was at first unloved; Raines about love for a friend; Lardner about crime and a lost loved one; Wilkerson and Suskind about a child and persistence of the human spirit; Bragg about people and how they confront life, death, disaster and crime; Pollak about love and death; French about love and loss and crime and punishment; Henderson about crime and its consequences; Moehringer, Hallman and Nazario—like Blais, Wilkerson and Suskind before them—about the persistence of the human spirit and love; Siegel—like Carpenter, Lardner and French before him—about crime and punishment; Keller about nature and chance; and Sheeler about duty, honor and love.

And, with the exception of Pett's story about the bureaucracy, Rinearson's about the construction of the Boeing 757 and Twomey's about warships, the Pulitzer Prize–winning features have been simple stories about common people in uncommon circumstances. They have been the kind of stories you could write.

THE ANATOMY OF A NEWSPAPER FEATURE STORY

Baltimore *Evening Sun* feature and science writer Jon Franklin covered a Johns Hopkins medical school press conference in 1973, at which researchers announced they could identify chemical sensors in the brain. The announcement stimulated Franklin's interest in brain research. Franklin explains:

> It got me interested in this. It was the first time that I had heard of any way that you could directly link something that happened in the brain with something that happened in the mind. I was fascinated by the idea. People had been arguing about whether there was a distinction between brain and mind for . . . many thousands of years [and] it struck me that this was a real turning point in the way that we look at ourselves. It seems to me that there haven't been all that many discoveries in the history of science that have really fundamentally changed the way we look at ourselves. And I thought that this was one of them.

Five years later, Franklin wrote a series on the human mind, and "Mrs. Kelly's Monster" was the opening story. The article, published in two parts, was designed to humanize a complex subject, Franklin says. The timeless "people" article won the Pulitzer Prize for feature writing the following year.

Franklin started work on "Mrs. Kelly's Monster" by asking the University of Maryland's medical school public relations director for help. She put him in touch with a surgeon, who then put him in touch with Edna Kelly.

So, are you ready? Here's the first story to win the feature-writing Pulitzer Prize, a story about the human mind and medicine written by two-time Pulitzer Prize–winning feature and science writer Jon Franklin. Notice the quantity and quality of description in the story and how scenes come to life when Franklin uses the sound of the heart ("pop . . . pop . . . pop, pop, pop . . . pop . . . pop-pop-pop") to intensify the suspense. Note how strategically described events foreshadow the suspenseful climax. Look for a problem that is resolved.

PULITZER PRIZE WINNER

JON FRANKLIN

MRS. KELLY'S MONSTER

Introduction　In the cold hours of a winter morning, Dr. Thomas Barbee Ducker, University Hospital's senior brain surgeon, rises before dawn. His wife serves him waffles but no coffee. Coffee makes his hands shake.

Downtown, on the 12th floor of the hospital, Edna Kelly's husband tells her good-bye.

For 57 years Mrs. Kelly shared her skull with the monster. No more. Today she is frightened but determined.

It is 6:30 A.M.

"I'm not afraid to die," she said as this day approached. "I've lost part of my eyesight. I've gone through all the hemorrhages. A couple of years ago I lost my sense of smell, my taste, I started having seizures. I smell a strange odor and then I start strangling. It started affecting my legs, and I'm partially paralyzed.

"Three years ago a doctor told me all I had to look forward to was blindness, paralysis and a remote chance of death. Now I have aneurisms; this monster is causing that. I'm scared to death . . . but there isn't a day that goes by that I'm not in pain and I'm tired of it. I can't bear the pain. I wouldn't want to live like this much longer."

As Dr. Ducker leaves for work, Mrs. Ducker hands him a paper bag containing a peanut butter sandwich, a banana and two fig newtons.

Downtown, in Mrs. Kelly's brain, a sedative takes effect. Mrs. Kelly was born with a tangled knot of abnormal blood vessels in the back of her brain. The malformation began small, but in time the vessels ballooned inside the confines of the skull, crowding the healthy brain tissue.

Finally, in 1942, the malformation announced its presence when one of the abnormal arteries, stretched beyond capacity, burst. Mrs. Kelly grabbed her head and collapsed.

After that, the agony never stopped.

Mrs. Kelly, at the time of her first intracranial bleed, was carrying her second child. Despite the pain, she raised her children and cared for her husband. The malformation continued to grow.

Rising action　She began calling it "the monster."

Now, at 7:15 A.M. in Operating Room 11, a technician checks the brain surgery microscope and the circulating nurse lays out bandages and instruments. Mrs. Kelly lies still on a stainless steel table.

A small sensor has been threaded through her veins and now hangs in the antechamber of her heart. Dr. Jane Matjasko, the anesthesiologist, connects the sensor to a 7-foot-high bank of electronic instruments. Waveforms begin to move rhythmically across a cathode ray tube.

With each heartbeat a loudspeaker produces an audible popping sound. The steady pop, pop, pop, pop isn't loud, but it dominates the operating room.

Dr. Ducker enters the operating room and pauses before the X-ray films that hang on a lighted panel. He carried those brain images to Europe, Canada and Florida in search of advice,

(continued)

PULITZER PRIZE WINNER   CONTINUED

and he knows them by heart. Still, he studies them again, eyes focused on the two fragile aneurisms that swell above major arteries. Either may burst on contact.

The one directly behind Mrs. Kelly's eyes is the most dangerous, but also the easiest to reach. That's first.

The surgeon-in-training who will assist Dr. Ducker places Mrs. Kelly's head in a clamp and shaves her hair. Dr. Ducker checks his work. "We can't have a millimeter slip," he says, assuring himself that the three pins of the vice are locked firmly against the skull.

Mrs. Kelly, except for a 6-inch crescent of scalp, is draped with green sheets. A rubber-gloved palm goes out, and Doris Schwabland, the scrub nurse, lays a scalpel into it. Hemostats snap over the arteries of the scalp. Blood splatters onto Dr. Ducker's sterile paper booties.

The heartbeat goes pop, pop, pop, 70 pops a minute, steady.

It is 8:25 A.M.

Today Dr. Ducker intends to remove the two aneurisms, which comprise the most immediate threat to Mrs. Kelly's life. Later, he will move directly on the monster.

It is a risky operation, destined to take him to the hazardous frontiers of neurosurgery. Several experts told him he shouldn't do it at all, that he should let Mrs. Kelly die. But the consensus was he had no choice. The choice was Mrs. Kelly's.

"There's one chance out of three that we'll end up with a hell of a mess or a dead patient," Dr. Ducker says.

"I reviewed it in my own heart and with other people, and I thought about the patient. You weigh what happens if you do it against what happens if you don't do it. I convinced myself it should be done."

And Mrs. Kelly said yes.

Now, the decision made, Dr. Ducker pulls back Mrs. Kelly's scalp to reveal the dull ivory of living bone.

The chatter of the half-inch drill fills the room, drowning the rhythmic pop-pop-pop of the heart monitor. It is 9 o'clock when Dr. Ducker hands the 2-by-4-inch triangle of skull to the scrub nurse.

The tough, rubbery covering of the brain is cut free, revealing the soft gray convolutions of the forebrain.

"There it is," says the circulating nurse in a hushed voice. "That's what keeps you working."

It is 9:20.

Eventually, Dr. Ducker steps back, holding his gloved hands high to avoid contamination. While others move the microscope into place over the glistening brain, the neurosurgeon communes once more with the X-ray films.

The heart beats strong, 70 beats a minute, 70 beats a minute, 70 beats a minute.

"We're gonna have a hard time today," the surgeon says, to the X-rays.

Dr. Ducker presses his face against the microscope. His hand goes out for an electrified, tweezerlike instrument. The assistant moves in close, taking his position above the secondary eyepieces.

Dr. Ducker's view is shared by a video camera. Across the room, a color television crackles, displaying a highly magnified landscape of the brain. The polished tips of the tweezers move into view.

It is Dr. Ducker's intention to place tiny, spring-loaded alligator clips across the base of each aneurism. But first he must navigate a tortured path from his incision, above Mrs. Kelly's right eye, to the deeply buried Circle of Willis.

The journey will be immense. Under magnification, the landscape of the mind expands to the size of a room. Dr. Ducker's tiny, blunt-tipped instrument travels in millimeter leaps.

His strategy is to push between the forebrain, where conscious thought occurs, and the thumb-like forward projection of the brain, called the temporal lobe, that extends beneath the temples.

Carefully, Dr. Ducker pulls these two structures apart to form a deep channel. The journey begins at the bottom of this crevasse.

The time is 9:36 A.M.

The gray convolutions of the brain, wet with secretions, sparkle beneath the powerful operating theater spotlights. The microscopic landscape heaves and subsides in rhythm to the pop, pop, pop of the heart monitor.

Gently, gently, the blunt probe teases apart the tiny convolutions of gray matter, spreading a tiny tunnel, millimeter by gentle millimeter, into the glistening gray.

Dr. Ducker's progress is impeded by scar tissue. Each time Mrs. Kelly's monster flooded her brain with blood, scars formed, welding the structures together. To make his tunnel, Dr. Ducker must tease them apart again.

As the neurosurgeon works, he refers to Mrs. Kelly's monster as "the AVM," or arterial-venous malformation.

Normally, he says, arteries force high-pressure blood into muscle or organ tissue. After the living cells suck out the oxygen and nourishment, the blood drains into low-pressure veins, which carry it back to the heart and lungs.

But in the back of Mrs. Kelly's brain, one set of arteries pumps directly into veins, bypass-ing the tissue. Over the years the unnatural junction, not designed for such a rapid flow of blood, has swollen and leaked. Hence the scar tissue.

Some scar welds are too tight, and the damaged tissue too weak, to endure the touch of metal. A tiny feeder artery breaks under the pressure of the steel probe. The television screen turns red.

Quickly, Dr. Ducker catches the ragged end of the bleeder between the pincers and there is a crackling bzzzzzzzt as the electricity burns it shut. Suction clears the field of blood and again the scene is gray. The tweezers push on.

"We're having trouble just getting in," Dr. Ducker tells the operating room team.

Again a crimson flood wells up. Again Dr. Ducker burns the severed bleeder closed and suctions out the red. Far down the tiny tunnel, the white trunk of the optic nerve can be seen.

It is 9:54.

Slowly, using the optic nerve as a guidepost, Dr. Ducker probes deeper and deeper into the gray.

The heart monitor continues to pop, pop, pop with reassuring regularity, 70 beats a minute, 70 beats a minute. The neurosurgeon guides the tweezers directly to the pulsing carotid artery, one of the three main blood channels into the brain. The carotid twists and dances to the elec-tronic pop, pop, popping of the monitor.

Gently, ever gently, nudging aside the scarred brain tissue, Dr. Ducker moves along the carotid toward the Circle of Willis, near the floor of the skull.

This loop of vessels is the staging area from which blood is distributed throughout the brain. Three major arteries feed it from below, one in the rear and the two carotids in the front.

The first aneurism lies ahead, still buried in gray matter, where the carotid meets the circle. The second aneurism is deeper yet in the brain, where the hindmost artery rises along the spine and joins the circle.

Eyes pressed against the microscope, Dr. Ducker makes his tedious way along the carotid.

"She's so scarred I can't identify anything," he complains through the mask.

It is 10:01 A.M. The heart monitor pop, pop, pops with reassuring regularity.

The probing tweezers are gentle, firm, deliberate, probing, probing, probing, slower than the hands of the clock. Repeatedly, vessels bleed and Dr. Ducker cauterizes them. The blood loss is mounting, and now the anesthesiologist hangs a transfusion bag above Mrs. Kelly's shrouded form.

(continued)

PULITZER PRIZE WINNER   CONTINUED

Ten minutes pass. Twenty. Blood flows, the tweezers buzz, the suction hose hisses. The tunnel is small, almost filled by the shank of the instrument.

The aneurism finally appears at the end of the tunnel, throbbing, visibly thin, a lumpy, overstretched bag, the color of rich cream, swelling out from the once-strong arterial wall, a tire about to blow out, a balloon ready to burst, a time-bomb the size of a pea.

The aneurism isn't the monster itself, only the work of the monster which, growing malevolently, has disrupted the pressures and weakened arterial walls throughout the brain. But the monster itself, the X-rays say, lies far away.

The probe nudges the aneurism, hesitantly, gently.

"Sometimes you touch one," a nurse says. "And blooey, the wolf's at the door."

Patiently, Dr. Ducker separates the aneurism from the surrounding brain tissue. The tension is electric.

No surgeon would dare go after the monster itself until this swelling time-bomb is defused. Now.

A nurse hands Dr. Ducker a long, delicate pair of pliers. A tiny, stainless steel clip, its jaws open wide, is positioned on the pliers' end. Presently the magnified clip moves into the field of view, light glinting from its polished surface.

It is 10:40.

For 11 minutes Dr. Ducker repeatedly attempts to work the clip over the neck of the balloon, but the device is too small. He calls for one with longer jaws.

That clip moves into the microscopic tunnel. With infinite slowness, Dr. Ducker maneuvers it over the neck of the aneurism.

Then, in an instant, the jaws close and the balloon collapses.

"That's clipped," Dr. Ducker calls out. Smile wrinkles appear above his mask. The heart monitor goes pop, pop, pop, steady.

It is 10:58.

Dr. Ducker now begins following the Circle of Willis back into the brain, toward the second, and more difficult, aneurism that swells at the very rear of the circle, tight against the most sensitive and primitive structure in the head. The brainstem. The brainstem controls vital processes, including breathing and heartbeat.

The going becomes steadily more difficult and bloody. Millimeter, millimeter, treacherous millimeter the tweezers burrow a tunnel through Mrs. Kelly's mind. Blood flows, the tweezers buzz, the suction slurps. Push and probe. Cauterize. Suction. Push and probe. More blood. Then the tweezers lay quiet.

"I don't recognize anything," the surgeon says. He pushes further and finds a landmark.

Then, exhausted, Dr. Ducker disengages himself, backs away, sits down on a stool and stares straight ahead for a long moment. The brainstem is close, close.

"This is a frightening place to be," whispers the doctor.

In the background the heart monitor goes pop, pop, pop, pop, 70 beats a minute, steady. The smell of ozone and burnt flesh hangs thick in the air.

It is 11:05 A.M.

TOMORROW: THE MONSTER

The following is the second part of "Mrs. Kelly's Monster," published the next day. Note that the first six paragraphs review the previous day's story for readers who may have missed it.

It is 11:05 A.M., the Day of the Monster.

Dr. Thomas Barbee Ducker peers into the neurosurgery microscope, navigating the tunnels of Mrs. Edna Kelly's mind.

A bank of electronic equipment stands above the still patient. Monitor lights flash, oscilloscope waveforms build and break, dials jump and a loudspeaker announces each heartbeat, pop, pop, pop, 70 pops a minute, steady.

The sound, though subdued, dominates the room.

Since 8:25 A.M., when an incision was opened in the patient's scalp above the right eye, University Hospital's chief neurosurgeon has managed to find and clip off one of two deadly aneurisms.

Now as he searches for the second aneurism he momentarily loses his way in the glistening gray tissue. For 57 years the monster has dwelled in Mrs. Kelly's skull, periodically releasing drops of blood and torrents of agony, and in the process it altered the landscape of the brain.

Dr. Ducker stops and ponders, makes a decision and pushes ahead, carefully, carefully, millimeter by treacherous millimeter.

The operating room door opens and Dr. Michael Salcman, the assistant chief neurosurgeon, enters. He confers briefly with Dr. Ducker and then stands in front of the television monitor.

Thoughtfully, he watches the small tweezer instrument, made huge by the microscope, probe along a throbbing, cream-colored blood vessel.

An aneurism on an artery is like the bump on a tire that is about to blow out, Dr. Salcman says. The weakened wall of the artery balloons outward under the relentless pressure of the heartbeat and, eventually, it bursts. That's death.

He says the aneurisms appeared because of the monster, a large malformation of arteries and veins in the back of the brain. Eventually Dr. Ducker hopes to remove or block off that malformation, but today the objectives are limited to clipping the two aneurisms.

Then, those hair-trigger killers out of the picture, he can plan a frontal assault on the monster itself.

But that will be another day. This day the objectives are the aneurisms, one in front and one in back. The front one is finished. One down, one to go.

The second, however, is the toughest. It pulses dangerously deep, hard against the brain's most sensitive element, the brainstem. That ancient nub of circuitry, the reptilian brain, controls basic functions like breathing and heartbeat.

"I call it the 'pilot light,'" says Dr. Salcman, "because if it goes out . . . that's it."

Dr. Ducker has a different phrase. It is "a frightening place to be."

Now, as the tweezer probe opens new tunnels toward the second aneurism, the screen of the television monitor fills with blood.

Dr. Ducker responds quickly, snatching the broken end of the tiny artery with the tweezers. There is an electrical bzzzzzzt as he burns the bleeder closed. Progress stops while the red liquid is suctioned out.

"It's nothing to worry about," he says. "It's not much, but when you're looking at one square centimeter, two ounces is a damn lake."

The lake drained, Dr. Ducker presses on, following the artery toward the brainstem. Gently, gently, gently, gently he pushes aside the gray coils. For a moment the optic nerve appears in the background, then vanishes.

The going is even slower now. Dr. Ducker is reaching all the way into the center of the brain and his instruments are the length of chopsticks. The danger mounts because, here, many of the vessels feed the pilot light.

The heartbeat goes pop, pop, pop, 70 beats a minute.

Dr. Ducker is lost again in the maze of scars that have obscured the landmarks and welded the structures together.

Dr. Salcman joins his boss at the microscope, peering through the assistant's eyepieces. They debate the options in low tones and technical terms. A decision is made and again the polished tweezers probe along the vessel.

(continued)

PULITZER PRIZE WINNER   CONTINUED

The scar tissues that impede the surgeon's progress offer testimony to the many times over Mrs. Kelly's lifespan that the monster has leaked blood into the brain, a reminder of the constant migraines that have tortured her constantly since 1942, of the pain she'd now rather die from than further endure.

Back on course, Dr. Ducker pushes his tunnel ever deeper, gentle, gentle, gentle as the touch of sterile cotton. Finally the gray matter parts.

The neurosurgeon freezes.

Dead ahead the field is crossed by many huge, distended, ropelike veins.

The neurosurgeon stares intently at the veins, surprised, chagrined, betrayed by the X-rays.

Climax   The monster.

The monster, by microscopic standards, lies far away, above and back, in the rear of the head. Dr. Ducker was to face the monster itself on another day, not now. Not here.

But clearly these tangled veins, absent on the X-ray films but very real in Mrs. Kelly's brain, are tentacles of the monster.

Gingerly, the tweezers attempt to push around them.

Pop, pop, pop . . pop . . . pop . . . . pop . . . . pop . . .

"It's slowing," warns the anesthesiologist, alarmed.

The tweezers pull away like fingers touching fire.

. . . . pop . . . pop . . pop . pop, pop, pop.

"It's coming back," says the anesthesiologist.

The vessels control blood flow to the brainstem, the pilot light.

Dr. Ducker tries to go around them a different way.

Pop, pop, pop . pop . . pop . . . pop . . .

And withdraws.

Dr. Salcman stands before the television monitor, arms crossed, frowning. "She can't take much of that," the anesthesiologist says. "The heart will go into arrhythmia and that'll lead to a . . . call it a heart attack."

Dr. Ducker tries a still different route, probing clear of the area and returning at a different angle. Eventually, at the end of a long, throbbing tunnel of brain tissue, the sought-after aneurism appears.

Pop, pop, pop . pop . . pop . . . pop . . .

The instruments retract.

"Damn," says the chief neurosurgeon. "I can only work here for a few minutes without the bottom falling out."

The clock says 12:29.

Already, the tissue swells visibly from the repeated attempts to burrow past the tentacles.

Again the tweezers move forward in a different approach and the aneurism reappears. Dr. Ducker tries to reach it by inserting the aneurism clip through a long, narrow tunnel. But the pliers that hold the clip obscure the view.

Pop, pop . pop . . . pop . . . . pop . . . . .

The pliers retract.

"We're on it and we know where we are," complains the neurosurgeon, frustration adding a metallic edge to his voice. "But we're going to have an awful time getting a clip in there. We're so close, but . . ."

A resident who has been assisting Dr. Ducker collapses on a stool. He stares straight ahead, eyes unfocused, glazed.

"Michael, scrub," Dr. Ducker says to Dr. Salcman. "See what you can do. I'm too cramped."

While the circulating nurse massages Dr. Ducker's shoulder, Dr. Salcman attempts to reach the aneurism with the clip.

Pop, pop, pop . pop . . pop . . . pop . . .

The clip withdraws.

"That should be the aneurism right there," says Dr. Ducker, taking his place at the microscope again. "Why the hell can't we get to it? We've tried, 10 times."

At 12:53, another approach.

Pop, pop, pop . pop . . pop . . . pop . . .

Again.

It is 1:06.

And again, and again, and again.

Pop . . . pop . . . pop, pop, pop . . . pop . . . pop-pop-pop . . .

The anesthesiologist looks up sharply at the dials. A nurse catches her breath and holds it.

"Damn, damn, damn."

Falling action

Dr. Ducker backs away from the microscope, his gloved hands held before him. For a full minute, he's silent.

"There's an old dictum in medicine," he finally says. "If you can't help, don't do any harm. Let nature take its course. We may have already hurt her. We've slowed down her heart. Too many times." The words carry defeat, exhaustion, anger.

Dr. Ducker stands again before the X-rays. His eyes focus on the rear aneurism, the second one, the one that thwarted him. He examines the film for signs, unseen before, of the monster's descending tentacles. He finds no such indications.

Pop, pop, pop, goes the monitor, steady now, 70 beats a minute.

"Mother nature," a resident surgeon growls, "is a mother."

The retreat begins. Under Dr. Salcman's command, the team prepares to wire the chunk of skull back into place and close the incision.

It ends quickly, without ceremony. Dr. Ducker's gloves snap sharply as a nurse pulls them off.

It is 1:30.

Dr. Ducker walks, alone, down the hall, brown paper bag in his hand. In the lounge he sits on the edge of a hard orange couch and unwraps the peanut butter sandwich. His eyes focus on the opposite wall.

Back in the operating room the anesthesiologist shines a light into each of Mrs. Kelly's eyes. The right pupil, the one under the incision, is dilated and does not respond to the probing beam. It is a grim omen.

If Mrs. Kelly recovers, says Dr. Ducker, he'll go ahead and try to deal with the monster itself. He'll try to block the arteries to it, maybe even take it out. That would be a tough operation, he says, without enthusiasm.

"And it's providing that she's in good shape after this."

If she survives. If. If.

"I'm not afraid to die," Mrs. Kelly had said. "I'm scared to death . . . but . . . I can't bear the pain. I wouldn't want to live like this much longer."

Her brain was too scarred. The operation, tolerable in a younger person, was too much. Already, where the monster's tentacles hang before the brainstem, the tissue swells, pinching off the source of oxygen.

Catastrophe

Mrs. Kelly is dying.

The clock in the lounge, near where Dr. Ducker sits, says 1:40.

(continued)

PULITZER PRIZE WINNER   CONTINUED

"It's hard even to tell what to do. We've been thinking about it for six weeks. But, you know, there are certain things . . . that's just as far as you can go. I just don't know. . . ."

He lays the sandwich, the banana and the fig newtons on the table before him, neatly, the way the scrub nurse laid out instruments.

"It was triple jeopardy," he says, finally, staring at his peanut butter sandwich the same way he stared at the X-rays. "It was triple jeopardy."

It is 1:43, and it's over.

Dr. Ducker bites, grimly, into the sandwich.

The monster won.

Source:© 1978. The Baltimore *Evening Sun.* Reprinted by permission.

Structurally, "Mrs. Kelly's Monster" chronologically seeks a solution to a problem. You'll read more about this kind of structure in Chapter 6.

The story as a whole also uses classic five-part dramatic unity. Traditionally, the drama has an *introduction,* which describes the situation, the setting and the characters. The second part is the *rising action* that introduces complication. The third part of the structure is the *climax,* or turning point, in the story. The fourth part, the *falling action,* shows opposing forces overwhelming the hero or heroine until *catastrophe,* resolution or explanation occurs.

Put another way, a problem such as Mrs. Kelly's disease is introduced and suspense is maintained while the reader learns whether the problem can be successfully resolved. The problem may overwhelm the subject—as in Mrs. Kelly's case—or the subject may struggle and win.

Let's look at this another way. In the typical inverted pyramid structure used in a simple news story, the information at the top of the pyramid—the lead—is the most important and is represented by wide lines in the diagram. As the reader gets deeper into the story, the value of the information decreases, represented by narrower lines.

News Story Structure

Lead

In "Mrs. Kelly's Monster" and many other feature stories with dramatic unity, the action is relatively unimportant in the introduction phase but gets more important—and thus wider—toward the climax, narrows some with falling action, then widens a little at the end.

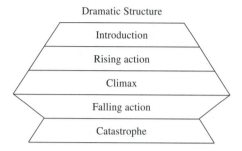

Dramatic Structure

Let's analyze "Mrs. Kelly's Monster." The first paragraphs *introduce* the reader to Dr. Ducker, Mrs. Kelly and the monster. These paragraphs also provide a sense of time and place using a parallel construction, involving the doctor and the patient, that you will recognize from motion picture and television productions.

In the next 100 paragraphs, the reader feels *rising action* and dread, with the use of suspense and foreshadowing devices such as Dr. Ducker's comments: "We're having trouble just getting in," and "This is a frightening place to be."

Then the reader moves into the *climax,* face to face with the monster.

A few dozen paragraphs later, the reader begins to see *falling action:* "'There's an old dictum in medicine,' he finally says. 'If you can't help, don't do any harm. Let nature take its course. We may have already hurt her. We've slowed down her heart. Too many times.' The words carry defeat, exhaustion, anger."

Catastrophe, although well foreshadowed, does not begin until the final paragraphs of the story: "Mrs. Kelly is dying."

While many successful features introduce the reader to some kind of problem or conflict that is later resolved, not every feature lends itself to this kind of structure.

For example, Steinbach, who won the 1985 feature Pulitzer, wrote about a person with an unresolved problem—blindness. Steinbach says that she didn't worry about conflict in that story.

> I don't have any rules about there's-got-to-be-a-conflict. I think there's got to be a story that says something beneath the story. There has to be a moment that clicks in the reader's mind, and they think, "I know why I'm reading this story. I know what this story is about." I know that when I see it, but I don't know that I could ever teach anybody that. You read a story and when you're finished, you feel that a little piece has been added to your knowledge about the world. From the letters I got about Calvin's story, I like to think that a lot of people found some tiny little chip had been added to their knowledge about the way the world works, and how some people function in it.

Camp, who won the 1986 Pulitzer with the story of a rural family, notes that the problem in his story—the farm crisis—also was unresolved. And Camp says that what conflict there was in the story was subtle: "There's obviously a conflict going on beneath the surface of this story and that's the disaster of the farm culture, but there's not any conflict within the family. They are like instruments expressing the frustration of the people but they like their culture. They are not struggling against it, they are struggling for it," he explains.

"Mrs. Kelly's Monster" uses a type of ending often called the *circle technique* or the *tie-back*. The idea is that the ending repeats a word, phrase, description or theme used at the beginning of the story. Here's the story's second sentence, followed by the next-to-the-last sentence:

> His wife serves him waffles but no coffee.
> Dr. Ducker bites, grimly, into the sandwich.

Food, which Franklin notes symbolizes life, completes the circle. You'll read more about feature endings in Chapter 6.

In addition, there's superb description of atmosphere in "Mrs. Kelly's Monster." One of the special attributes of all quality feature writing is that the writer shows rather than tells the reader. For example:

> The tough, rubbery covering of the brain is cut free, revealing the soft gray convolutions of the forebrain.

The story also uses the present tense. Dr. Ducker "rises" in the morning. If the story had been written in past tense, "rose" would have been used. Editors disagree about whether newspaper features should be written in the present tense. Here's some guidance. Unless you place a subject in time and space (such as *The editor, sitting in his office last Tuesday, said, "Good feature."*), present tense may be used. If you use the present tense, know why you are using it. Franklin uses it to give readers a sense of immediacy. And whatever tense you choose, use it consistently.

A final note. Not every feature lends itself to the techniques Franklin used, such as chronological as well as problem and solution structure, dramatic unity with suspense, atmosphere, and present-tense immediacy. But when you've got a good story to tell, you should be prepared—like Franklin—to use all of the storyteller's tricks to tell your tale.

THE FUTURE: TRENDS IN NEWSPAPER FEATURE WRITING

American newspapers have long been engaged in an economic struggle with competitive media such as magazines and radio and particularly television. Newspapers now are also increasingly competing for readers against both the old media and the new media in forms as diverse as Internet-based citizen journalist bloggers, multimedia journalists and podcasters from competitors, and even social network communicators. All of this competition is taking its toll. Newspaper circulation is declining in total numbers in most parts of the

United States and particularly when measured against population growth, and many remaining core readers are slowly defecting to these new interactive new media forms.

Why? Internet-based journalism has immediacy. Printed newspapers are a day late. Internet news, with its color and sound, can have significant emotional impact. Printed newspapers lack the impact of the Internet's images. Most Internet news is free. Most newspapers are not. Internet news can be tailored to a reader's interest. Customizing printed newspapers is difficult and expensive at the level of a single postal code and not yet economically possible at the level of a single home address. And if newspapers can probe more deeply than television, Internet stories can drill down past newspaper stories into bedrock.

This media war has produced numerous dead and walking wounded. The most obvious battle casualties are afternoon, or "PM," metropolitan newspapers. For example, each year increasing numbers of afternoon newspapers shut their doors, or convert to morning or "all day" publication, with home delivery in the mornings but only newsstand sales later in the day. And in the last years of the twentieth century and the early years of the twenty-first, even morning and all-day newspaper circulation began to stagnate or decline.

Almost all newspapers have mobilized to meet the challenge of the electronic competition in general and the Internet in particular by launching their own Web sites with frequent updates, still and video image enhancements, sound snippets, staff and citizen-journalist blogs, and numerous links to other information sources. In essence, newspapers are becoming news centers that publish on the most appropriate news platform first with all of the multimedia tools in their toolkit.

In summary, newspapers are capitalizing on their strengths. Newspapers have large news-gathering and editing staffs backed by accessible and deep electronic libraries that allow them to quickly produce thoroughly reported and well edited coverage with all of the power of the permanent written word. And with their Internet sites, newspapers also can provide immediacy, impact, low price, customization and depth as needed. It's likely that both newspapers and their Internet sites will survive and thrive, although they'll increasingly likely serve different types of news consumers.

Even the Pulitzer Prize Board has recognized the new media forms. In 2007 the Pulitzer Board agreed to allow newspapers to submit online material to support stories in most Pulitzer categories, including Internet material as varied as databases, graphics, and still and video photojournalism.

Which brings us to features. The big local news stories of the day may be covered—albeit superficially—by every radio and television station and blogger and podcaster in town, but that detailed, powerful feature about the 100-year-old man in the nursing home probably won't be broadcast because it isn't "visual" enough to warrant 60 seconds of valuable time in a local newscast nor will it be reported by independent bloggers or podcasters because of a lack of news-gathering resources.

Increasingly, some media experts are betting that the printed feature and its repackaged Web-based cousin may, in fact, be the newspaper's ultimate secret weapon—especially the exhaustively researched, brilliantly written and well-illustrated feature, such as those written by journalists like Franklin, Blais, Carpenter, Pett, Robertson, Rinearson, Steinbach, Camp, Twomey, Banaszynski, Zucchino, Curtin, James, Raines, Lardner, Wilkerson, Suskind, Bragg, Pollak, French, Henderson, Moehringer, Hallman, Siegel, Nazario, Keller, Sheeler and others.

Feature writers such as Franklin and his colleagues often have generous deadlines and extraordinary topic, style and space freedom, commodities available to few newspaper feature writers years ago and still unavailable to most feature writers on small-circulation dailies. However, media experts expect this trend toward unshackling the newspaper feature writer to spread from the well-heeled metropolitan newspapers—which can afford the luxury of creative freedom—to the small-town dailies increasingly confronted with new media competitors. As a result, the average space allocation for feature stories in a small-circulation daily is quickly becoming at least a portion of the front page of one section and additional space inside that section. This space is typically increased in proportion to advertising on Wednesdays, Thursdays and Sundays and decreased at other times. The newspaper's Internet version can offer even more room for features. Web enhancements for features published on the Internet can include significantly expanded written and photojournalistic coverage and audio interviews, graphs and illustrations, Internet links to original and supplemental sources, live interviews with the journalists, multiple video segments, interactive public opinion polls and other intriguing packages.

In addition to providing more space for traditional news and timeless feature stories, many newspapers of all circulation sizes are experimenting with hybrid forms of storytelling that blend breaking news story techniques with compelling feature story characteristics.

Pulitzer-winner Pett applauded the changing feature story.

> Features have more of a base now, more depth to them. The good ones are more comprehensive. All of this, of course, requires more time to do, more space to write it in. I think it's a far more adult business now than it was years ago. If your editor (then) said, "Do a profile" on a well-known person, you would dash down to the morgue or library and read what clips the library had on him, then you'd hop in a cab and go interview the subject for 20 minutes, come back and sit down and write it. And that was supposed to be a penetrating profile. That's a lot of baloney. It never was. And the public rightfully either yawned or turned away from things like that. I as a reader would have, too. They wanted something more.

Some observers also have suggested—with all of this color and intriguing design coupled with thorough news stories and long, sparkling features—that printed and Internet newspapers are beginning to look like magazines. Whether newspapers are becoming "newszines" is debatable; what is not debatable is that newspapers are engaged in a fierce struggle with many media forms, and one of the most powerful weapons in the arsenal is the well-crafted feature story. And clearly, newspaper publishers and editors are recognizing the value of feature writers and are permitting them the freedom they need to produce the kinds of stories that will hold readers' attention in an electronic century.

CHAPTER TWO

THE NEWSPAPER FEATURE STORY IDEA

WHAT NEWSPAPER READERS WANT TO READ

Newspapers in the United States traditionally try to perform five roles. There are formal names for these roles—the *commercial, information, opinion, public forum* and *entertainment functions.* But readers call the various parts of the newspaper package "advertising," "news," "editorials," "letters to the editor" and "the comics."

The names the readers use are self-explanatory, with the exception of "the comics." What readers really mean when they talk about comic strips is the newspaper's ability to entertain and emotionally and intellectually intrigue with material ranging from an advice column to the crossword puzzle to the funny feature story about the local lady with a parakeet she thinks can recite Edgar Allan Poe verse.

[handwritten: NO, Not really]

Comics, columns, crosswords and features are extremely important to readers, surveys show. Much of this entertainment material is provided by national syndication services. Therefore, what local entertainment material is available—even a talking-parakeet feature—becomes especially valuable.

The basic secret to writing features that readers will like is to recall that although features come in both news and timeless varieties (and a talking-parakeet feature would be, for example, timeless), they are, more importantly, also thing- or people-oriented. A feature about how tombstones are manufactured would be a "thing" story, of course, but an article about the woman and her wondrous bird would be essentially a "people" story.

Which would *you* rather read?

You probably selected the bird story because strong features—including the parakeet article—are almost always people stories. In addition, the parakeet story has some traditional news characteristics that add to reader appeal.

You remember news characteristics: qualities such as conflict, human interest, importance, prominence, proximity, timeliness and unusualness. Let's look at each quality and see how these characteristics can add punch to a feature story.

Most of us live our lives with little major daily *conflict,* which may explain why professional football and boxing are so exciting to some people. Thus, real-life conflict is unusual and interesting for most of us—televised games or a midnight mugging notwithstanding. Consequently, an explanatory feature examining why a 12-year-old Florida boy killed his mother and little brother fascinated readers of *The Miami Herald.* And a profile tracing a mother's year-long successful search for her missing 15-year-old daughter had equal appeal for readers of the *Arkansas Democrat-Gazette* in Little Rock. Conflict comes down to this: Would you rather read a story about a dramatic, emotional cross-country search for a missing child or a business story about a wealthy local woman who opened a boutique specializing in Scottish woolens?

Human interest is hard to define. Most editors say stories about children, animals or sex have automatic human interest value. So do stories about health, if supermarket tabloids such as the *National Enquirer* and the Sunday newspaper supplements such as *Parade* are any measure. Consequently, a story about a little girl and her father combing the city for her missing puppy has guaranteed reader appeal. So does a medical feature about a young woman struggling to cope with acquired immune deficiency syndrome or one about a doctor at the state research hospital trying to find a cure for cancer.

Importance refers to universality. The more people affected by the subject of a feature, the more readers the story will attract. For example, a how-to story advising readers of a clever way to cut home electricity bills by 50 percent has more importance—and probably more readers—than a how-to feature about constructing an ant farm. Why? Paring down the electric bill has more appeal to most people than does accumulating ants.

The governor of your state has *prominence.* Most probably, your best friend does not. A hobbyist story about the governor's model train collection has more reader appeal than a story about your friend's similar train collection. Names make news, the saying goes. Names also make features.

Proximity simply means closeness to your readers. A story about someone who lives 1,000 miles from the newspaper's readers has less appeal than a similar story about someone in the newspaper's home circulation area. So, an odd-occupation feature about a local university professor who junks his teaching career to open an auto salvage yard has more reader appeal than does a story about a lawyer in another state who decides to become a crop duster.

Timeliness means little to feature writers, unless they are writing a news feature. However, *unusualness* is extremely important to the feature writer. A university teacher who turns junkman is, in fact, unusual. A junkyard owner who earns his doctor of philosophy degree and becomes a university teacher is equally unusual. On the other hand, a male registered nurse is less unusual, and probably is not worth a story. Verification is the key to deciding if a story is truly unusual. When *Chronicle* reporter Helen Garcia was assigned the cab mechanic feature, she checked out the mechanic's claim.

Consequently, if you want to write a profile about a man who traps animals for a living, you probably have a sufficiently unusual story for broad reader appeal. Nonetheless, you should find out how many full-time trappers there are in the country and, if possible, in your circulation area. How? Census information may help, but your best information will probably come from the companies that buy pelts. In addition, there may be an association of trappers you can check, or your state game and fish department may have records of trapping licenses. As you pursue the number of trappers to qualify your subject for unusualness, you also should be asking questions to determine whether your chosen trapper is, indeed, the best choice. Is your trapper the most experienced or the most well known? Is he the most successful, or is he at least typical? Is he respected by other trappers?

As you can see, the talking-parakeet story also has unusualness—assuming the little fellow really can muster up verbs and nouns—as well as human interest and proximity.

Of course, you can write a feature without conflict, human interest, importance, prominence, proximity or unusualness, but if your feature has none of these qualities, it is probably not going to be very interesting. And dull features don't appeal to anyone except perhaps the subject of the article.

HOW TO GET IDEAS

If you become a reporter who occasionally receives a feature assignment, such as Garcia, you will rarely have to worry about unearthing feature story ideas. The ideas will come from your editor, and your most serious problem probably will be transforming the editor's occasional sows' ears into silk purses.

On the other hand, if you are a full-time newspaper feature writer—especially one assigned to a Sunday magazine or a features section—you will be expected to formulate many of your own assignments. Pulitzer Prize winner Madeleine Blais of *The Miami Herald* explains why: "At a magazine (published by) a newspaper, usually the editors will allow a writer to pick stories because they don't want writers spending months on material they don't like."

Feature writers get ideas from a variety of sources. They read newspapers and magazines both for national articles that can be localized and for area news stories that can be turned into features. That process is called "writing off the news." For example, Teresa Carpenter's Pulitzer Prize–winning *Village Voice* features about three killings were stimulated by news stories. So was Dave Curtin's Prize-winning *Colorado Springs Gazette Telegraph* feature about two children who were severely burned in an explosion. And so were Sheryl James's stories in the *St. Petersburg Times* about a mother who abandoned her baby. Pulitzer winner James explains: "In 1989 and 1990, authorities found a rash of abandoned babies in South Florida. After several of these had been written about in typical metro-daily news stories, my editor, Sandra Thompson, asked me to look into one of these cases. The story was already on my story idea list. But in all fairness, feature writers often have long, neglected story lists, and I am not at all certain I would have gotten around to the story had it not been assigned. Most of my stories are self-assigned, but I always appreciate a good suggestion."

Thomas French, the *St. Petersburg Times* writer who won the 1998 Pulitzer for a long series about the 1989 murders of an Ohio woman and her two daughters, also derived his story from a news event, but only after a significant conceptual detour. French originally wanted to write a definitive series about life in St. Petersburg, Florida, as it approached the year 2000. One segment focused on police and the courts, and French's broad series was eventually realigned as a story about faith, called "Angels and Demons."

And *The Los Angeles Times* writers who won the 2000 and the 2002 Pulitzer Prize for feature writing both got story ideas from previously reported incidents. J. R. Moehringer, who won in 2000 for a long, poetic profile of Mary Lee Bendolph and her Alabama hometown of Gee's Bend, says the story was suggested by a *Times* researcher:

Edith Stanley, the formidable researcher in Atlanta, first brought Gee's Bend to my attention in 1998, just after I became bureau chief. In a small Alabama newspaper Edith spotted a squib about a proposed ferry on the Alabama River, and we both thought there was far more than a ferry at stake. I'd always been drawn to stories about places, stories that explore where we are and how that translates into who we are. But I'd never run across a place quite like Gee's Bend. Later, when I drove into Gee's Bend for the first time, I was even more fascinated. The sense of ghosts and spirits lurking everywhere, behind every tree and tropical vine, was over-powering. I met Mary Lee Bendolph the next time I visited Gee's Bend. She was at a July 4 picnic that photographer Clarence Williams and I attended, and the three of us hit it off right away. Still, it took a while before I decided to tell the story through her eyes.

Moehringer's *Los Angeles Times* colleague, Barry Siegel, won the Pulitzer in 2002 for a profile of a Utah judge, the distraught father whom the judge sentenced to jail for the wilderness death of a child and the young father's ultimate suicide. Says Siegel:

I found the story the way I usually do, by scrolling through wire stories and local newspaper websites, looking for something that intrigues me. This one came to me via a 15 inch Associated Press story that moved the day after (the father's) suicide and Judge Robert Hilder's anguished public statement. From any perspective, this was an obviously compelling situation, not the least because of the judge's uncommon and very human response. My interest deepened when I asked our library to get me earlier local stories about the case. One of them reported on the sentencing hearing, where Judge Hilder, in explaining why he was sending (the father) to jail, declared that "choices must have consequences." He was, of course, talking about (the father's) choice to leave his son alone in the forest; Hilder could not have known that hours later, his own choice would also have major consequences. It was this parallel narrative—the judge's choice, the father's choice—that I found particularly resonant. I'm often drawn to tales about moral choices and their consequences, and this one seemed to promise a more powerful example of that theme than anything I'd ever before encountered.

Sometimes writers turn to the feature category first. For example, if you want to write an odd-occupation story, you might choose the occupation first and find the specific subject later.

Feature writers also keep their eyes and ears open. They read billboards and advertisements in the Yellow Pages, watch television and listen to the radio, all in quest of ideas. They also tell friends that they're looking for good stories and, often, friends tip them about people, places and things worth writing about.

Invariably, the ideas pour in—some worth investigating, others not, but all requiring focus.

Focusing Ideas

Focus is simply a matter of reducing a potentially large quantity of material into digestible components. When you go to a fast-food restaurant, you don't order a cow. You order a hamburger. When you write a term paper for a world history class, you don't choose a mega-topic such as "The History of Germany." Instead, you focus the topic on something such as "The Political Factors in the Selection of Berlin as Capital of Germany."

And similarly, when you select a feature story topic, you don't begin with an idea such as "missing children." You narrow the topic to a bite-sized chunk such as "teenaged runaways." Then, if you are lucky, you come up with a story about how a mother searched for and found her long-missing teenage daughter.

An unfocused feature wastes the writer's time. For example, suppose you want to write a story about earthquakes. If you wander into a large library and check out or copy everything in stock regarding earthquakes, you'll need a truck to haul off the material and a year to digest it. Even if you have the truck and the year, your organizational chores in writing an unfocused story such as that would be monstrous.

An unfocused feature also wastes the editor's time. If a feature is unfocused, it is usually far too long. Removing unnecessary words, sentences and paragraphs is the editor's job. One editor might send an unfocused story back to the writer for more work. Another more adventuresome editor might hack through the verbiage like an explorer pushing through the Amazon rain forest, removing the bad and occasionally the good with an electronic machete. Yet another editor might simply kill the story, thinking—correctly, perhaps—that it's not worth anyone's rewrite time.

Worst of all, an unfocused feature wastes the reader's time, should it survive editing. In general, if a reader can't figure out what the story is about in the first several hundred words, the reader will desert it for more pleasant experiences.

Focusing, then, is a matter of narrowing. For example, let's suppose you want to write a feature about prisons. Your first focusing decision is easy: Because you're writing for a local newspaper, you should narrow the topic to prisons in your state or immediate locality.

The next narrowing exercise also is easy: Are you going to do a story focused on the keepers—the guards and wardens—or the kept—the inmates? If you narrow the topic to the keepers, you have a number of categorical possibilities, including an explanatory story about a day in the life of a warden or guard, an odd-occupation story about an unusual prison employee such as a tracking-dog handler, a participatory story for which you arrange to be a guard for a day or a profile about a key prison official.

Let's assume you narrow your focus to a profile about a little-known but important prison employee. Whom do you pick? The chief prison administrator? The top prison doctor? A warden?

If you focus on a warden, you have to decide which one. Do you pick the youngest warden? The most experienced warden? The warden who runs the toughest prison in the system? Research will help you narrow your focus still more. For example, if one prison in the system has received heavy news coverage lately because of inmate complaints, the warden of that facility may be your best bet. You should obtain his name from prison officials and check the newspaper's library for background information on him. If he looks like a good candidate, you have successfully focused your story.

While you search for a focus, don't overlook clues to the point of your story. The point, prior to any interviews, is more of a question than an answer. Is the warden's religious faith, courage and perseverance (assuming he has any of those qualities) keeping him sane in his high-pressure position? Is the warden's story even more elemental: good (presumably the warden) versus evil (the inmates)? A definitive point probably will not emerge until after interviews with the warden, colleagues and former inmates, but thinking about what the story may be about before you write it also helps focus your efforts.

Note this, however. On rare occasions, the focus of a story is broadened rather than narrowed. For example, journalist Jim Sheeler's original concept for "Final Salute," the *Rocky Mountain News'* 2006 Pulitzer Prize–winning Veteran's Day article, was to follow a fallen U.S. Marine from the body's arrival to the burial. The story was ultimately refocused and broadened to reveal that Marine Corps casualty team members ritualistically guard their fallen comrades and assist relatives until long after the burials. The story follows a Colorado-based Marine casualty team and its senior officer as they assist families in Colorado, Nevada, South Dakota and Wyoming in dealing with the grief brought on by relatives killed in the Iraq War. The family of a 24-year-old Marine officer is prominently, although not exclusively, featured in the story.

Ideas That Didn't Work

We are told by folklore that the Royal Canadian Mounted Police always get their man. And, like the Mounties, newspaper feature writers usually get their feature once they have accepted an assignment. That's because newspaper feature writers are professionals who understand that news organizations cannot afford to assign too many time-consuming stories that don't pan out. Consequently, professional newspaper feature writers have learned how to turn lemons into lemonade when necessary.

But you're probably a novice journalist. Here are six feature story ideas suggested by beginning journalists like you. The ideas are for 1,500-word stories for a daily newspaper with statewide circulation. The ideas as suggested didn't work. Let's see why.

■ **Feature Idea 1:** A business story about your city's first nonprofit vegetarian restaurant, where lunch is the only meal served, the menu is limited, tipping is prohibited and the employees are hired under a new state development grant. The proprietor is a Buddhist monk.

Problem: Too unfocused. This idea is like an all-you-can-eat restaurant. There are at least three good stories here; if you focus on (or eat, to continue the simile) everything, you will have more than you can comfortably digest. But if you choose one course, you will have a good meal. People are more interesting than things, so a first choice would be a story about the monk who is serving his creator by serving hungry people. An alternative selection would be to interview the employees of this unusual establishment, particularly if they have worked for other restaurants and can provide colorful comparisons. A third choice would be to focus on customers who eschew fast-food hamburgers for the restaurant's boiled beans and curried corn.

■ **Feature Idea 2:** A how-to story about selecting and caring for a puppy.

Problem: This story is unfocused also. Practically everyone loves a puppy (except those who have to clean up after it). And practically everyone values free advice from professionals. So what's wrong with this story idea? Only this: Entire books have been written about selecting puppies. And other books have been written about caring for them. The books about selection suggest that different people want and need different kinds of dogs, so your first task is to focus on a type of recipient. How about preschool children? Then we need to lop off the "caring-for" aspect to keep the feature within acceptable length. Finally, let's add timeliness—a birthday purchase—to let readers know why they are reading this story. Ultimately, then, our story is about selecting a birthday puppy for a preschool child. That kind of keenly focused story will be easier to write and will make more sense to readers.

■ **Feature Idea 3:** An odd-occupation story about a state patrolman on his shift.

Problem: One of the first withdrawals from the idea bank that beginning feature writers make is the "ride-along" story. Many police agencies make provisions for citizens to ride along with officers during a shift, and reporters often take advantage of this opportunity to get to know the community and crank out a feature while they are at it. But the ride-along story has been written so many times, it's a journalistic cliché. There are focusing techniques, however, that you can use to salvage this idea. One is to pick a veteran cop working the toughest shift (that's 11 P.M. to 7 A.M. on a hot weekend night with a full moon) in the roughest part of town. Another is to ride with a specialist, the officer with the most driving-while-intoxicated arrests for the preceding year. Another is to pick the best-educated cop, the one with the doctoral degree in psychology. Focus, focus, focus.

■ **Feature Idea 4:** An overview story about headaches and the various treatments for them, using prominent local neurologists and university medical center physicians as sources.

Problem: Writing a story about headaches is like writing a term paper about "The American Short Story." How about focusing on new nondrug treatments for tension-caused headaches? Or, if you want to focus the topic with laser-beam precision, talk to pediatricians about headaches afflicting children. You'll also want to find some headache sufferers to humanize the story.

■ **Feature Idea 5:** An overview story about children available for adoption in the state.

Problem: Adoption availability usually depends on the age and physical condition of the child. For example, older children with severe handicaps are often readily available for adoption. Healthy babies are not. In addition, children are often available from both state and private agencies, which have different requirements and waiting periods. Then there are the gray and black markets, which operate with yet different rules. So, unless this story is going to be a hundred-part series, narrowing of topic is required. So is humanizing. You could both focus and humanize the story by writing about a couple attempting to adopt a healthy baby from a private adoption agency.

■ **Feature Idea 6:** A profile of a local apartment complex designed for the physically disabled.

Problem: Profiling people is difficult; profiling a place is even more difficult. Are we going to read about the history of the apartment complex or about how living there has made life easier for the residents? If you're going to focus on the residents—and you should—the story will be easier to write and more meaningful if the focus is narrowed to two or three typical residents. And you shouldn't just interview the subjects; you should live their day with them to really get the feel of how the apartment design helps.

Ideas That Worked

As you have read, professional journalists usually succeed in making their feature stories interesting. Experienced journalists don't have a monopoly on good features; they only have a better batting average than beginners. Novices do hit home runs. They succeed by starting with a good idea and focusing it. Here are some well-focused features written by beginners:

- a business story about how the senior carpenter for the state's only casket company builds coffins;
- a commemorative story about a Vietnamese lawyer who fled his homeland and, three decades later, found himself owning a chain of children's clothing stores in the United States;
- an explanatory story about how the clothes for the state's only professional football team are washed to remove grit and grime;
- a first-person story about surviving an attack by a rabid dog;
- an historical story about past patrons of the state's oldest hotel, which is scheduled for demolition;
- a hobbyist story about a local resident who has the country's largest private collection of antique "Climber" automobiles;
- a how-to story explaining a prominent psychologist's tips for handling winter depression;
- an invention story about a local tinkerer struggling to market a revolutionary laser pistol sight;
- a medical story about an ailing 86-year-old college freshman struggling to finish her degree before she dies;
- a number story about how 10 peculiarly named communities in the state got their names;
- an odd-occupation story about the state highway department's only full-time explosives expert;
- an overview story about state efforts to relocate troublesome bears, focusing on a day in the life of one game-and-fish officer charged with capturing and moving the beasts;
- a participatory story about spending a shift as a department-store Santa Claus;
- a profile of a blind fan obsessed with the *Star Wars* motion picture series; and
- an unfamiliar-visitor story about a local university student trapped in Bolivia during a coup.

Getting a solid feature story idea is a little like hitting a home run. Homers are the result of a good pitch, combined with judgment, skill and a little luck on the part of the batter. Often, a large number of balls must cross the plate before the batter sees a potential hit and swings. Like a batter, you should recognize that you will need to explore many ideas before you find one worth developing. If you come up with a dozen ideas and then carefully focus each one, you will have a good chance of scoring.

"Life on the Land: An American Farm Family"

In 1985 John Camp, a reporter for the *St. Paul Pioneer Press,* came to the conclusion that someone in Minnesota needed to write a major article about the economic crisis facing farmers. Joe Rossi, a photographer for the paper, had already reached the same conclusion. The two focused their idea, and the result was a series on the David Benson family, which won Camp the 1986 Pulitzer for feature writing. The series—four stories, each linked to a seasonal activity and summarized by a fifth feature—totals a staggering 20,000 words. A word about words versus column inches: Newspaper feature writers usually size stories by column inches. A column inch is a block of type one-inch deep and one-column wide, or *very* roughly 50 words. Magazine writers usually size articles by the number of words. Thus, 20,000 words converts to about 400 column inches.

This profile uses a simple chronological structure: First, David Benson and his interpretation of the farm crisis are introduced. Then the rural setting is described and the rest of the Bensons are presented. When the people, the place and the problem have been adequately described, Camp recounts a day at the Benson farm, with occasional flashbacks to earlier, harder times.

Camp explains how his five-part series came into focus:

> Rossi knew these people. Not real well, but he knew them because David Benson was kind of a spokesman for a rural humanist ethic. He knew that they were very articulate. At the same time, I was talking to the managing editor and said, "We've got to do something about the farm crisis because it's getting terrible. It's absolutely beyond belief. And having a farm editor is not going to cut it because he's going nuts already." So [the managing editor] said, "What do you want to do?" And I said, "We've got to have two or three reporters working on it." The graphics editor said, "Joe Rossi wants to do a family thing." And I was looking for a cultural thing. In the meantime, they said, "They're [more than 100 miles] away. Let's look for someone in our circulation area." The farm editor got some names together of other farm families, and one by one we kind of eliminated them. This was not an accidental family we were looking for. We were looking for a family that had been on the land for a long time, where there was a multigenerational interest in it. We didn't want a family that was in such deep trouble that they were just gone. We didn't want a family that was so rich that they didn't have any problems. We wanted the struggle in there. We also needed a family that was articulate and that was going to be open with us. So it seemed like Rossi's concept was the best.

Here is the first story of Camp's series, "Life on the Land: An American Farm Family." Note the early use of quotations to summarize the farm crisis and the quick introduction and description of the principal characters. Also note the almost musical rhythm of the writing.

PULITZER PRIZE WINNER

JOHN CAMP

LIFE ON THE LAND: AN AMERICAN FARM FAMILY

PART I—MAY 12, 1985
David Benson sits on the seat of the manure wagon, behind the twin black draft horses, reins in his hands, and he says this:

"Machinery can be intoxicating. You sit there on top of a huge tractor, rolling across those fields, and you feel like God. It's an amazing feeling, and a real one, and I think some people get so they don't feel complete without it.

"That's one of the reasons they keep buying bigger and bigger tractors, these enormous four-wheel-drives, tearing up and down the fields. Tearing up and down. They are incredibly expensive machines; they'll run you $16 an hour in fuel alone, and you can do in one day what used to take you three or four—but then the question arises, are you doing anything useful on the three or four you saved? You buy this gigantic machine with its incredible capability and all of sudden, you're done.

"And you start thinking, 'My God, if I bought another 600 acres I could do that, too.' So you buy it, and then you find if you only had a bigger machine, you could buy even more. At the end of it, you're doing 2,000 acres on this fantastic Star Wars machinery and you're so far in debt that if anything goes wrong—and I mean if they stop eating soy sauce in Ireland—you lose the whole works, including the place you started with.

"And it's not the same as losing in the city. These people are going around asking, Jeez, what did I do wrong? They said this was the American way. You try to get bigger and take a few risks, but nobody ever told me that if I lose they were going to take away everything, my whole way of life and my children's way of life and our whole culture and the whole neighborhood and just stomp us right into the ground.

"My God, you know, people are bulldozing farmsteads so they can plant corn where the houses used to be, because there's nobody to live in these houses anymore. That's happening."

David Benson. He has horses, but he's not a back-to-the-land dabbler, not an amateur, not a dilettante—he has a couple of tractors, and a barn full of machinery. But he finds a use for horses. He likes them.

And unlike a lot of farmers in Minnesota, he's making it. Making it small, but he's making it.

Go down to Worthington. Get off Interstate 90, off the state highway, off the blacktopped country road, and finally go down the gravel track and into the farm land, listening to the power lines sing and the cottonwoods moan in the everlasting wind, watching a red-orange pickup a mile away as it crawls like a ladybug along a parallel road between freshly plowed fields, leaving behind a rising plume of gravel dust, crawling toward the silos and the rooftops that mark the Iowa line. . . .

A MAILBOX ON A POST
The landscape is not quite flat—it's a landscape of tilted planes, fields tipped this way or that, almost all showing the fertile loam of recent plowing. The black fields dominate the countryside, interrupted here and there by woodlots, by pasturage where lambs play in the fading sunlight, by

red-brick or purple-steel silos, Grant Wood barns and Sears-Roebuck sheds, and by the farm-houses.

There's a turn-of-the-century farmhouse here. Gray with white trim, it could be any one of a thousand prairie homes. There's a single rural-route mailbox on a post across the road from the end of the driveway. It says Benson on the side, but the paint has been scoured by the wind and the name is almost illegible.

There is a tire swing hung from a cottonwood with a yellow rope, and a kid named Anton kicking a black-and-white soccer ball in the driveway.

The walk to the porch is guarded by lilacs and lilies of the valley and a patch of violets. A tortoiseshell cat named Yin lounges on the porch, watchfully making way for visitors; a familial tiger-striper named Yang watches from the sideyard. Just before the porch is a strip of iron set in a concrete block: a boot scraper, and well-used.

The door swings open and Sally-Anne Benson is there, navy sweatshirt, blue jeans, tan work boots.

"Hi," she says. "Come in. David is still in the field, with the oats."

From behind her come the kitchen smells of fresh bread and noodles and sauce, and blond Heather is turning to go up the stairs to her bedroom.

"We're going over to Grandpa's to do the chores," Sally-Anne says to Heather.

These are some of the Bensons. The Bensons in this house are David, 38, and Sally-Anne, 35, husband and wife, and their children, Heather, 11, and Anton, 8. Sally-Anne is small with thin wrists and curly brown hair, blue-gray eyes, a quick smile and a tendency to bubble when she's had a few glasses of white wine. She answers to the nickname "Sag" or "Sag-Oh," which is an acronym of her maiden name, Sally-Anne Greeley. David has a red walrus mustache and the beginnings of crows-feet at the corners of his eyes, smile lines at his mouth and a story-teller's laugh. The children are blond; blonder than seems real, or even possible.

RHYTHM OF WORK BLISSFUL

The Bensons in the white house up the road and around the corner on the blacktop are Gus and Bertha Benson, David's parents.

Gus, 82, is mostly retired, though on this day he's been fanning oats—cleaning the oats to be used as seed—for the planting. He has white hair combed straight back, a white stubble on his pink face, and powerful, heavy hands. Bertha is 75. Her hair is a steel brown-gray, she wears plastic-rimmed glasses, and after 56 years of farming, she still can't watch when chickens are butchered. She can pick them, the hens who make the fatal mistake of not laying, but she can't watch them topped with a corn knife.

David and Sally-Anne do the bulk of the heavy farm work now. Gus particularly likes to work with the beef cattle and Bertha keeps house and recently has taken up weaving and rug-making, and cans and freezes produce during the summer; last year she got in 100 quarts of apple sauce. Heather and Anton have their chores. Together they live on 160 acres of the best land God ever made.

And they work it hard. They have the crops, the cattle, a growing flock of sheep, chickens, geese, and a boxful of tiny turkeys on the back porch.

The day started with David getting up at 6:15 A.M. and apologizing for it. "Boy, I got up earlier, and I just couldn't. . . . Oh, boy, I just laid back down and the next thing I knew it was after 6. . . ."

He's planting oats, and has been hard at it for the previous two days, sitting up on top of the John Deere, first disking, then chisel-plowing a small patch of compacted ground, then hook-ing up a grain drill to seed the oats.

(continued)

PULITZER PRIZE WINNER   CONTINUED

"You sit up there, going back and forth, when you're disking, and your mind goes on automatic pilot," he said. "You can think of anything, and sooner or later, you do. It's a liberating experience, really. You put in maybe 400 hours a year on a tractor, and you spend a good part of it just . . . thinking. It's even better when you're working with the horses, because everything moves fairly slowly and you don't have the tractor engine, so it's quiet. There's a rhythm to it. It's almost . . . blissful, is that the word?"

THE LAND COMES FIRST

At noon, Sally-Anne brings out lunch, cheese sandwiches and fresh milk from Bluma, the milk cow, and homemade bread and a chunk of cake. David climbs stiffly off the tractor and drops down into the roadside ditch and leans back into last year's tall brown grass, out of the eternal prairie wind.

"It's just going so well, going so well," he says, looking across the barbed-wire fence toward the field. "Just need to get it in. This is beautiful weather, but I wish the wind would lay off."

He looks up at the faultless blue sky. "And we could use some rain, use some rain. Sure. We sure could."

He lies in the ditch eating, his face covered with dust, alternately eating and explaining: "We'll grow beans and corn and oats and alfalfa for hay, and the alfalfa puts nitrogen back in the soil; of course, we won't grow all those at once, we'll rotate through. You've got to be strict about it, you can't decide to knock off a little extra here and there, or you'll kill it, the land."

He's almost apologetic about the chisel plow. "Normally we don't need it, but last year we brought in some heavy earth-moving equipment to build that terrace down there, and it compacted the ground enough that disking won't do it."

He needed the terrace to correct a drainage problem. "If you don't build water structures you're going to wash ditches, and that's another way you can kill it," he says.

Kill the land. The nightmare. The land must be cared for, the Bensons say. But the land is in trouble right now. Neither David nor Sally-Anne Benson would be considered solemn, but David will sit in his dining room chair after supper, leaning his elbows on the strawberry-patch oilcloth that covers the table, and talk like this:

"The strength of the Midwest culture was that it had a people who were developing an interest in the land, and in developing a community that had some continuity to it. Without that, we have an ethereal culture that just isn't satisfying to most people, and can't be—a people who don't really know what they want.

"We are living in the middle of one of the largest areas of fertile land on the planet. Normally you'd think that people would go to a place like that, would want to live there to form a good rooted culture, where you could form your own ties to the land and to the neighborhood and even to those people you just see driving by, but whose whole lives you know, and they know yours. . . ."

The connections between the people, the land, the crops, the food, the neighborhood, the community—they're impossible to put a hand on, but they are real. Much of its connecting web can be explained in stories of times past, of incidents that somehow hallow a particular patch of ground or even make it a place of humor, or sadness, or dread.

Gus and Bertha sit at their dining room table, at what their children call the home place, and remember it.

"Spring is always the moving time for farmers," says Bertha. "We bought this place in 1938, and we moved here in the spring of 1939, from Stanton, Nebraska. That's where Gus was born, in Stanton, and two of our children—the other two were born here. Gladys and Shirley and Marilyn and David, 17 years apart, the four of them, and we enjoyed every one. . . ."

"When we moved here, we couldn't tell what color the house was, it was so bad, but we were more concerned about the land. When we bought it the land cost $95 an acre, and we were trembling and afraid, because we thought if we did something wrong, we could lose it and lose everything we saved."

They had been married in Nebraska in 1929, and spent the next 10 years as renters, building up a working capital of $3,000. It all went into the new place in Minnesota.

"We moved up here because it was dry in Nebraska for so many years, you couldn't farm. We came up here on a trip and we thought it was so beautiful in Minnesota, so beautiful," Bertha says.

UNFREEZING THE CAR

And it was cold, and windy, and the life was rough. They laugh about it now, Bertha and Gus, but at the time . . .

"When Marilyn was born, it was so cold I had to start a fire with corn cobs in a pan, and put it under the engine to get it warmed up so we could start it," Gus recalls. "She was ready for the hospital, four in the morning, and I can still remember the cold . . ."

"And remember, when we got electricity . . ."

"Oh, yes, when we got the electricity," says Bertha. "That was in when, 1948?"

"1948, that's when it was."

"I remember," says Bertha, a glow in her face. "We got an electrician from Dundee to do the house, all the way from Dundee because all the other electricians were busy. The whole neighborhood went on at the same time. We were one of the last, because we were so close to the Iowa border, we were like in a corner. But I remember how the lights came on, and we sat with all the lights all evening, sat with the lights on us. . . .

"The electricity is the best thing for farm wives. Before that, we took soft water from the cistern, and regular hard water from the well, in a pail. I think I could go back to that way of living, except that I want my hot water. Hot water is the most wonderful thing!"

"Oh, we had a wedding here, too," says Gus.

"One of Shirley's girls, Christina," says Bertha. "They had their wedding in the yard, and dancing in the corncrib, and a hay ride in the afternoon."

"They decorated the corncrib," says Gus. "They cleaned it out and decorated it and danced in there."

"We never thought David would come back," Gus says suddenly. "We thought we'd be the last. We thought he would be an engineer. He was living in San Francisco, and one day he called and said, 'Don't sell the farm, we might come back.' "

David and Sally-Anne have their memories, too—some of their courtship, in Sally-Anne's hometown of Lexington, Mass., and some of San Francisco, where they spent some time when they were in their early 20's, and many, now, of their 14 years on the farm.

MEMORIES GROW FAST

Of walking the beans. Of haying time. Of rebuilding the aging machinery. Of David on the John Deere, dragging plow, Sally-Anne on the David Brown 990 with the disk, the wind whistling across them both, the sun beating down. . . .

Sally-Anne, laughing: "You remember at a party putting those chickens asleep?"

David: "Nothing like it. Hypnotizing chickens. We had one asleep for three or four minutes I think, just stretched stone cold out on the ground . . . a rooster.

"By the way," he says to Sally-Anne, "do you see we've got another transvestite rooster coming along?"

(continued)

PULITZER PRIZE WINNER   CONTINUED

"Oh, I saw that, he's getting big, too, he's almost as aggressive as the top one. . . ."

"Well, not that bad. . . ."

David explains: "We decided to get rid of all our roosters. We ate them, every one, or thought so. Then all of a sudden, here comes this chicken out of the flock. I mean, we thought all along he was a hen, but he starts getting bigger and growing some wattles and pretty soon he's crowing all over the place. He was hiding in there, pretending to be a hen. Now we've got another one coming out of the closet. He's getting bigger. . . .

"I remember when we were kids, we used to chase the chickens down—chickens have got pretty good speed over the short haul, and have pretty good moves. Anyway, you'd get a rock and just chuck it at them, and every once in a while you'd lay it right alongside their heads, just throwing it at them on the run.

"And then you'd be hiding out behind the corncrib, because it'd drop over and you were sure it was dead. But it never was. It'd always get up and walk around like nothing happened. I'm not sure you can hurt chickens, to tell you the truth.

"No kid should grow up without chickens; chickens have got to be good for you. . . ."

SOME MEMORIES DIFFICULT

Some of the memories are funny, like the chickens. Some are not.

Sally-Anne: "One time we had this horse, named Belle, and that year there was an unusual mold that grew on the corn stalks, and Belle ate some of it. It turns out that it destroys your muscle control. She couldn't control the way she moved . . . like polio, in people. Anyway, we had the vet out, and he said that's what it was.

"There was nothing we could do, and David had to shoot her.

"David got the gun and brought her out of the barn, and kept backing away from her so he could get a clean shot and she kept going to him, kept trying to walk up to him, because she trusted him and she didn't know what was wrong with her. . . ."

Sally-Anne shivers as she tells the story. "I didn't want to watch. It was just awful, but finally he got back and shot her. The vet said there was nothing wrong with the meat, so David and a friend skinned her and butchered her . . . it was still pretty bad, but then, after a while, another friend came over and said, 'Ah, Taco Bell, huh?' And that made it better, somehow. God, it was awful."

A farm of 160 acres can't really support six people, and the Bensons know it. They talk about buying more land, of going into debt, the very experience they saw drag down so many of their neighbors.

In the meantime, Sally-Anne teaches at the Worthington Montessori School in the mornings, and David does casual work as a mechanic. Sally-Anne brags that he can fix most things, especially Volvos. "If you live anyplace around Worthington, and own a Volvo, you probably know him," she said.

The life suits them. More land would be nice, but the spectre of debt is overpowering. The Bensons, for now, have no debt—they don't even need spring operating loans. Between grain sales, auto mechanics and Sally-Anne's job, they are self-supporting and self-financed. They're proud of their ability to survive, but there is no sense of victory when they see a neighbor fail.

Instead, there is a sense of loss. It's their community evaporating, the Bensons' along with everyone else's.

"I don't know," says David. "Maybe what we need is some kind of creative financing like they do for home mortgages. Some kind of rent-share program where younger farmers can have a chance, can move into these homesteads and take them over and work them like they should be.

"And if they fail anyway? Well, at least we tried. If we don't try, we're going to kill it, the land."

Strong stuff, deeply felt; but it's hard to stay solemn for too long at the Bensons'.

"When are you coming back?" they ask the visitors at the table. "Three or four weeks? Gee, that'd be just about right time for haying."

Sure would like to see you for haying, yes indeed, they say. Bring a hat. Bring gloves. Bring beer. Love to have you.

Source: © 1985. The *St. Paul Pioneer Press.* Reprinted by permission.

Throughout Camp's five-part series, the story remains sharply focused on the economic woes faced by American farmers during the 1980s. Camp's story begins by explaining the economic realities of farm life through the eyes of the Benson family, then in the second part moves on to the tending of the corn and beans and the hay harvest, moves forward again to the home canning of late summer in the third part and then to the beginning of the harvest and winter on the farm. The story's fifth installment concludes with the big harvest, the beginning of the harsh Minnesota winter, a recap of the year's work and a concluding portrait of the Benson family. Camp sets up the focus in the first four paragraphs of the first part of the story, which you've read, then restates the idea in numerous places in other installments, including this paragraph from the fifth and final part of the feature series:

> "The future of farming is in the hands of the older farmers. The financial system we have right now makes it almost impossible for new farmers to get started. The financing terms are so bad that a new farmer, once he buys his land and equipment, can't afford to make a single mistake, ever. If he does, it's all gone. Everybody makes mistakes. Everybody.
>
> "You don't even have to make a mistake. You can do everything the extension people tell you to do, you can do everything the government wants you to do, then we get a new president and he changes something, and everything is up for grabs. Somebody changes the rules, and what used to be a good practice is now a mistake and you're out of business."

Focus. Throughout all of Camp's 20,000-word series, the focus is easily understood.

"Zepp's Last Stand"

Madeleine Blais, a writer for *The Miami Herald's* glossy Sunday *Tropic* magazine, won the 1980 Pulitzer Prize for feature writing with five stories. As you've read, four stories were freelance articles. Then the magazine hired her and she was assigned to profile Edward Zepp's lifelong battle with the Pentagon. Blais says: "That's the one that I think won the Pulitzer. I think the others they thought were nice, but Zepp's is a much more traditional story."

Like all good feature writers, Blais sharply focuses her stories. In this case, the focus was simple: Tell the story of a man fighting for his day in court, fighting for a principle.

Blais says she also often tries to come to a sort of tentative conclusion about how the story will turn out before she covers it. She explains: "With some stories, I preconceive a lot beforehand, of what I imagine the material will reveal. Usually, if you try to do that, you're right. If you're able to preconceive it, then you probably have a good idea of what's going on."

Here is "Zepp's Last Stand," which took about a month and a half to report and write. Note the overall chronological progression, which is interrupted only occasionally by flashbacks. Notice how Blais slowly builds to the climactic courtroom confrontation. Most of all, study Blais's artful description of Zepp and his surroundings.

PULITZER PRIZE WINNER

MADELEINE BLAIS

ZEPP'S LAST STAND

> *"There was indeed one of us who hesitated and did not want to fall into line. That was Joseph Behm, a plump, homely fellow. But he did allow himself to be persuaded, otherwise he would have been ostracized. And perhaps more of us thought as he did, but no one could very well stand out, because at that time even one's parents were ready with the word 'coward.'"*
>
> —*All Quiet on the Western Front,* Erich Maria Remarque

All his life Edward Zepp has wanted nothing so much as to go to the next world with a clear conscience. So on Sept. 11 the old man, carrying a borrowed briefcase filled with papers, boarded an Amtrak train in Deerfield Beach and headed north on the Silver Meteor to our nation's capital. As the porter showed him to his roomette, Ed Zepp kept saying, "I'm 83 years old. Eighty-three."

At 9 A.M. the next day, Zepp was to appear at the Pentagon for a hearing before the Board for Correction of Military Records. This was, he said, "the supreme effort, the final fight" in the private battle of Private Zepp, Company D, 323rd Machine Gun Battalion, veteran of World War I, discharged on Nov. 9, 1919—with dishonor.

Something happens to people after a certain age, and the distinctions of youth disappear. The wrinkles conquer, like an army. In his old age, Zepp is bald. He wears fragile glasses. The shoulders are rounded. His pace is stooped and slow. It is hard, in a way, to remove 60 years, and picture him tall, lanky, a rebel.

The old man, wearing a carefully chosen business suit which he hoped would be appropriately subdued for the Pentagon, sat in the chair of his roomette as the train pulled out of Deerfield Beach. With a certain palsied eagerness he foraged his briefcase. Before the train reached full speed, he arranged on his lap the relics from his days at war. There were the dog tags and draft card, even his Department of War Risk life insurance policy. There was a letter to his mother written in 1919 in France, explaining why he was in the stockade. His fingers, curled with arthritis and in pain, attacked several documents. He unfurled the pages of a copy of the original court-martial proceedings which found him in violation of the 64th Article of War: failure to obey the command of a superior officer. There was also a copy of the rule book for Fort Leavenworth, where Zepp had been sentenced to 10 years at hard labor.

When Ed Zepp was drafted in 1917, he told his draft board he had conscientious objections to fighting overseas. The draft board told him his objections did not count; at the time only Quakers and Mennonites were routinely granted C.O. (conscientious objector) status. "As a Lutheran, I didn't cut any ice," he said. Zepp was one of 20,873 men between the ages of 21 and 31 who were classified as C.O.'s but inducted nonetheless. Of those, only 3,999 made formal claims once they were in camp. Zepp's claim occurred on June 10, 1918, at Fort Merritt, N.J., the

(continued)

PULITZER PRIZE WINNER   CONTINUED

day before his battalion was scheduled for shipment overseas. Earlier, Zepp had tried to explain his position to a commanding officer, who told him he had a "damn fool belief." On June 10, Zepp was ordered to pack his barracks bag. When he refused, a sergeant—"Sgt. Hitchcock, a real hard-boiled guy, a Regular Army man"—held a gun to his head: "Pack that bag or I'll shoot."

"Shoot," said Zepp, "you son of a bitch."

Conscientious objection has always been a difficult issue for the military, but perhaps less difficult in 1917 than in recent times. Men who refused to fight were called "slackers" and "cowards." By the time the United States entered the war, the public had been subjected to a steady onslaught of "blatant propaganda," according to Dr. Raymond O'Connor, professor of American history at the University of Miami.

The government found ways to erode the spirit of isolationism felt by many Americans, and replace it with a feeling of jubilant hostility against the Germans. It was patriotic to despise the Kaiser. It was patriotic to sing: *Over There; Oh, I Hate To Get Up In The Morning* and *Long Way to Tipperary*. A new recruiting poster pointed out that "Uncle Sam Wants You." The war's most important hero was Sgt. York, a conscientious objector who was later decorated for capturing Germans. They made a movie of Sgt. Alvin York's heroics.

They made an example of Pvt. Edward Zepp, a kid from Cleveland.

Zepp was formally released from the Army 60 years and two days ago.

But Zepp has never released the Army.

At his upcoming hearing at the Pentagon, Zepp was after a subtle distinction, two words really, "honorable discharge," meaningless to anybody but himself. It would be a victory that couldn't even be shared with the most important person in his life, his wife, Christine, who died in 1977.

In 1952, Zepp appeared before the same military board. At that time the Army agreed that he was a sincere C.O. His discharge was upgraded to a "general discharge with honor." He became entitled to the same benefits as any other veteran, but he has never taken any money: "I have lived without their benefits all my life." The board refused to hear his case again; only a bureaucratic snafu and the intercession of Rep. Daniel Mica (D., Palm Beach) paved the way to the hearing scheduled for Sept. 12.

For 41 years Zepp worked as the money raiser for The Community Chest, now called The United Way, in Cleveland. He learned how to get things done, to get things from people.

For years, he has sought his due from the Pentagon. His persistence was not only heroic, but also a touch ornery. Here is a man who refused to fight in World War I but who takes a blackjack with him to ward off potential punks every time he leaves his Margate condominium at night. He talks about how there are just wars, and maybe we should have gone all out in Vietnam, "just like we did in Hiroshima, killing the whole city" and in the next breath he talks about the problems that occur when "the Church starts waving a Flag."

It is impossible to tell how much of his fight is hobby and how much the passion of a man who says he cannot die—he literally cannot leave this earth—until his honor is fully restored.

To some, his refusal to fight meant cowardice; to Zepp, it represented heroism. It is an ethical no-man's-land. War leaves no room for subtle distinctions.

For his day in court, Ed Zepp was not taking any chances. His health is failing; he is at the age of illness and eulogy. He has an understandable preoccupation with his own debilities (proximal atrial fibrillations, coronary heart disease, pernicious anemia). Many of his references, especially his war stories, are to people now gone. At $270 for a round-trip train ticket, the plane would have been cheaper, but Zepp thought flying would be too risky; it might bring on a seizure, a blackout, something worse.

On the train the old man talked obsessively about what happened during the war. He told his story over and over and over—clack clack clack, like the train on the rails. Except for this constant talk, there was nothing about him that revealed his mission. As he hesitantly walked the narrow, shaking corridors, making his way from car to car, he did not have the air of a man headed for the crucial confrontation of his life. He looked like a nicely dressed elderly man who might be taking the train out of a preference for gravity or perhaps in sentimental memory of the glory days of railroading.

"This was the war to end war," Zepp said on the way to the dining car. "The war to make the world safe for democracy. Democracy. They gave me a kangaroo court-martial."

All his life, Zepp has believed he was denied the very freedoms he had been recruited to defend. He has nursed his grievances like an old war injury, which, on one level, is exactly what they are. "They murdered me, you know. They tried to, in a way."

His refusal to fight turned him into a fighter: "I was cursed," he said. "It made a killer out of me, almost."

He said he was seeking only one thing: "My honor. My good name. I don't see how a great nation can stigmatize as dishonorable a person who was following the dictates of his conscience. When I die, I want it said of me, 'Well done, thou good and faithful servant.' "

Ed Zepp turned to the young waiter, in his starched white mess coat, who had been patiently waiting for him to order lunch. He ordered a turkey sandwich: "I can't eat much. My doctor says I should eat lightly. I take enzyme pills to help me digest."

September 1979, Sebring, Fla.: Ed Zepp's light lunch has just been placed before him. September, 1917, Cleveland, Ohio: Ed Zepp's appeals to the draft board have been rejected twice.

During any long trip, there is a distortion of landscape and time; the old man's talk echoed the feeling of suspension that comes with being on the road. The closer he got to the Pentagon, the closer he got to 1917.

Before he was drafted at the age of 21, Zepp had already earned a business degree and worked as a clerk at Johns Manville. At the time, his native Cleveland was heavily industrialized, with much social and political unrest. Socialist Eugene Debs was a frequent visitor; Zepp says the man was "fire." He remembers listening to his speeches and once joined a Debs march, clear across town, to a large hall on the west side. Debs preached workers' rights and counseled against war. So did Zepp's pastor, who was censured by the Lutheran Church for his outspoken views against the war. "War," says Ed Zepp, "was an ocean away."

Zepp's parents were Polish immigrants, Michael and Louise Czepieus. His father was a blacksmith, "not the kind who made shoes for horses, but rather he made all the ironwork pertaining to a wagon." There were five children and all of them were sent to business school and ended up, says Zepp, "in the business world."

"I was a top-notch office man all my life," he says. In any family there is talk about somebody's lost promise, failed opportunity, and in the Zepp family, there was talk, principally among his sisters, about how, with his meticulous mind, he would have been a great lawyer, but for the war, but for what happened over there.

The waiter removed the empty plates from Zepp's table, and the next group of hungry passengers was seated.

(continued)

PULITZER PRIZE WINNER   CONTINUED

Three P.M. Waldo, Fla., in the club car. Ed Zepp is nursing a soda, and on the table in front of him, like a deck of marked cards, are the original court martial proceedings.

Eighty miles an hour.

The train was moving almost as fast as Edward Zepp is old, and he seemed impressed by that. "It is," he said, "a wonderful way to see the countryside." The world passed by in a blur.

Despite his ailments, there is something energetic and alert about Zepp; for two months before the hearing, he swam every day for half an hour to build stamina. Sipping his soda, he wondered whether he had chosen the correct clothes. His suit was brown and orange. He had a color-coordinated, clip-on tie and a beige shirt. "I have another suit that my wife, Christine, picked out for me, but it has all the colors of the rainbow, and I didn't want to show up at the Pentagon looking like a sport in front of all those monkeys. Oops. I'd better be careful. They probably wouldn't like it if I called them monkeys, would they?"

This trip was partly in memory of Christine, Zepp's third wife, whom he married in 1962, shortly before he retired to Florida. His first marriage was brief; during the second marriage he had two children, a son who died in his early 30s ("He served in Korea and he was a teacher.") and a daughter, now 46 years old, a psychiatric social worker who lives near Boston.

"Christine would want me to do this. She was a fighter, she was a real person. She was the only one I cared about. And what happened? She died. All the guys in my condominium thought I would be the first to go, but she passed away on May 1, 1977, two days before my 81st birthday. Do you know what she said to me before she died? 'I want to be buried with my wedding ring on.' I meet other women at the square dances at the senior center. One of them said, 'Ed, let's go to the Bahamas for a week. Get your mind off this. It's too much pressure.' But I couldn't go away. Christine and I are married, even in death."

When Ed Zepp speaks of his third wife, his face sometimes gets an odd look; there is a dream-like minute or so. The voice catches, the blue eyes become rheumy, his words come out in a higher pitch. Just as it seems as if he will break down and sob, composure returns. The same thing often happens when he speaks of what happened during the war.

"Anyone who reads this court-martial," said Zepp, "will acquaint himself with all the vital points of my case: how the draft board refused to listen; how the Army loused it up in Camp Sherman when they failed to inform me of General Order Number 28; how, at Fort Merritt, Sgt. Hitchcock held the gun to my head and forced me to pack, and then they Shanghaied me out of the country on the SS *Carmania,* and in France they gave me a kangaroo court-martial."

General Order Number 28, issued by the War Department on March 23, 1918, was an effort by the government in mid-war to expand the definition of those who qualified for C.O. status. Men who had already been drafted, but had sought C.O. status were supposed to be informed by a "tactful and considerate" officer of their right to choose noncombatant service.

"General Order Number 28 was never read or posted during the time I was at boot camp at Camp Sherman in Chillicothe, Ohio," Zepp maintains. "This was how it was done—gospel truth: 250 of us were lined up in retreat. Lt. Paul Herbert went through the ranks, asking each man, 'Any objections to fighting the Germans?' Well, I thought they were looking for pro-German sympathizers. I wasn't a pro-German sympathizer. My parents were Polish. I did not speak up.

"Then at Fort Merritt, Sgt. Hitchcock, he was a hard-boiled sergeant, put the gun on me. He never told the court-martial about that. He approached me in a belligerent manner; there was no kindly and courteous officer informing me of my rights as specified in General Order Number 28.

"They shipped me overseas against my will, and for two months in France I still didn't know what action would be taken against me for defying Sgt. Hitchcock and Capt. Faxon. They kept me busy with regular military work. I helped erect a machine-gun range, I had rifle practice, I learned how to break a person's arm in close combat.

"During that time, Lt. Herbert propositioned me with a nice soft easy job. He came up to me and he said, 'Zepp, how about calling the whole thing off. I'll get you a nice soft easy job in the quartermaster.' " Zepp repeated Herbert's words in the buttery tone of voice he always uses when he repeats Herbert's words. "He tried to make a deal. But I had no confidence. I smelled a rat. And to prove to you beyond a shadow of a doubt it was not a sincere offer, find one word in the court-martial proceedings that he offered me a job. He was trying to make a deal. It was a trap.

"And then they Shanghaied me out of the country and gave me a kangaroo court-martial. I wasn't even allowed to face my accusers." During Zepp's court-martial many of the basic facts which are part of his litany are mentioned. The sergeant who held a gun to his head testified, but no mention was made of that action. Capt. C.W. Faxon said he believed Zepp had "sincere religious objections." Sgt. Steve Kozman admitted to giving the defendant "a few kicks in the behind" on his way to the SS *Carmania.*

In his testimony, Zepp told about how, the same evening as he refused to pack his barracks bag, "Lt. Paul Herbert came up to me and spoke in a general way about my views and called them pro-German. He also asked me if I had a mother and I said, 'Yes,' and he asked me if I had a sister and I said, 'Yes,' and he said, 'Would you disgrace them by having your picture in the paper?' "

Zepp argued that in light of General Order Number 28 the Army had no right to ship him overseas without first offering noncombatant service. The heart of Zepp's case, as he spoke it before that tribunal long ago, showed his instinct for fine, if quixotic distinctions:

"I did not willfully disobey two lawful orders, but I was compelled to willfully disobey two alleged lawful orders."

Savannah, Ga. 7 P.M. The train had crossed state lines, and Zepp had just entered the dining car for an evening meal of fish and vegetables. His conversation once again crossed the borders of geography and time.

Even at dinner, it was impossible for him to abandon his topic.

"Let me tell you about what happened after the court-martial. They put me in a dungeon; there were rats running over me, the floor was wet, it was just a place to throw potatoes, except they'd all rot. It was later condemned as unfit for human habitation by the psychiatrists who interviewed me. That was a perfect opportunity to act crazy and get out of the whole thing. But I stuck by my conscience. I was not a coward. It's easier to take a chance with a bullet than stand up on your own two feet and defy."

He talked about how the Army discovered he had "office skills" and he spent much of his time as a clerk—"sergeant's work, or at least corporal's."

He said he was transferred to Army bases all over France during the year 1919; the best time was under Capt. John Evans: "I had my own desk, and Captain Evans put a box of chocolates on it, which he shouldn't have, because it turned me into a 250-pounder. I had the liberty of the city, and Capt. Evans gave me an unsolicited recommendation." Zepp quoted it by heart: "Private Zepp has worked for me since Jan. 3, 1919. During this time he has been my personal clerk, and anyone desiring a stenographer will find him trustworthy and with no mean ability."

In August of 1919, as part of his clerical duties, Zepp was "making out service records for boys to return home to the United States, and finally the time came for me to make one out for myself."

In September he arrived in Fort Leavenworth where once again he served as a clerk: "They made me secretary to the chaplain, and I taught the boys how to operate a typewriter.

(continued)

PULITZER PRIZE WINNER   CONTINUED

"Finally on Nov. 9, 1919, they released me. I still don't know why I didn't serve the complete sentence. I never asked for their mercy. I think it must have been my mother, she must have gone to our pastor, and he intervened."

Zepp paused, and his look became distant. There was that catch in his voice; he cried without tears.

Dinner was over.

Ten P.M. Florence, S.C. After nursing one beer in the club car, Zepp decided it was time to get some sleep. As he prepared to leave for his roomette, he said, "They tried to make Martin Luther recant, but he wouldn't. Remember: 'If they put you to shame or call you faithless, it is better that God call you faithful and honorable than that the world call you faithful and honorable.' Those are Luther's own words. 1526."

It was hard to sleep on the train; it rocked at high speeds and it made a number of jerking stops and churning starts in the middle of the night in small towns in North Carolina.

Ed Zepp asked the porter to wake him an hour before the 6 A.M. arrival in Washington, but his sleep was light and he awoke on his own at 4. He shaved, dressed, and then sat in the roomette, briefcase beside him. The train pulled in on time, before sunrise.

Wandering the almost-empty station, Zepp had a tall dignity, eyeglasses adding to his air of alertness. He sat by himself on a bench, waiting for his lawyer who was due at 7. Zepp's lawyer was a young fellow who had read about his client in *Liberty Magazine.* Thirty-four years old, John St. Landau works at the Center for Conscientious Objection in Philadelphia. Landau called the old man in Florida and volunteered his services. They made plans to meet at Union Station, and Zepp told the lawyer, "Don't worry. You'll recognize me. I'll be the decrepit old man creeping down the platform."

Landau, himself a C.O. during the Vietnam War, arrived at the appointed hour. The two men found an empty coffee shop where they huddled at a table for about an hour. Zepp told his lawyer he had not brought his blackjack to Washington, and the lawyer said, smiling, "I take it you are no longer a C.O."

At 8:30 they left to take Metro, Washington's eerily modern subway system with computerized "farecards," to the Pentagon.

Zepp was easily the oldest person on the commuter-filled subway. He did not try to speak above the roar. His was a vigil of silence. When the doors sliced open at the "Pentagon" stop, the hour of judgment was upon him.

"The gates of hell," he said, "shall not prevail."

It would be hard to surmise, given the enthusiasm of his recital, that Zepp was in Washington on not much more than a wing and a prayer. In April, the Pentagon had mistakenly promised him a hearing; it was a bureaucratic bungle. On May 9, he was told there had been an error; there was no new evidence in his case; therefore there should be no new hearing. On May 31, Rep. Mica wrote to the review board requesting a new hearing on the strength of his office. It was granted for Sept. 12, but Zepp had been forewarned in a letter from the Pentagon that just because he was getting his hearing, he should not conclude from this concession that "the department" admits "any error or injustice now . . . in your records."

Just before Zepp was ushered into the small hearing room at 11, he gave himself a pep talk: "I am going to be real nice. Getting even doesn't do anything, punching someone around. I want to do things the Christian way. And I'll use the oil can. When I was at the Community Chest, I called all the women 'darlings' and I would polka with them at the parties. I used the oil can profusely."

Zepp departed for the hearing room.

The fate of the World War I veteran, defended by a Vietnam era lawyer, was to be decided by a panel of five—four veterans of World War II, one veteran of the Korean War. The chairman was Charles Woodside, who also served on the panel that heard the appeal of the widow of Pvt. Eddie Slovik, the first deserter since the Civil War to be executed. Less than a week before Zepp's hearing, newspapers carried a story about how Slovik's widow, denied a pension by the Army, had finally died, penniless, in a nursing home.

Landau stated Zepp's case, saying that the defendant accepted the findings of the 1952 hearing, the findings which concluded Zepp had in fact been sincere: "The reason we're here is that we believe the general discharge ought to be upgraded to an honorable discharge. . . . What we see as the critical issue is the quality of [Mr. Zepp's] service."

The first witness was Martin Sovik, a member of the staff of the Office for Governmental Affairs of the Lutheran Church Council. Like Landau, Sovik had also been a C.O. during Vietnam.

He confirmed that in 1969 the Lutheran Church in America supported individual members of the church, following their consciences, to oppose participation in war. One member of the panel asked Sovik how you can determine whether a person is in fact a C.O.

"That decision is made within a person's mind—obviously you can't know whether a person is a C.O. anymore than whether he is a Yankees' fan or an Orioles' fan except by his own affirmation."

Next, the old man took his turn. The panel urged him to remain seated during the testimony. The old man marshalled the highlights of his military experience: *Shanghaied, nice soft easy job, tactful and courteous officer, hard-boiled sergeant, gun at my head, face my accusers, unfit for human habitation, unsolicited recommendation.* The words tumbled out, a litany.

Every now and then Zepp's composure cracked, stalling the proceedings. "I'm sure it's hard to recall," said Woodside.

"It's not that," said the defendant. "I'm just living it. This was indelibly impressed, it is vivid on my mind, like something that happened yesterday."

At 1, a luncheon recess was called. Woodside promised that he would continue to listen with sympathy when the hearing resumed.

"Govern yourself by the facts," said Zepp. "Then we'll both be happy."

As they were leaving the hearing room, Zepp turned to Landau and Sovik and apologized for breaking down. "You're doing all right, you're doing just fine," said Sovik.

"I can't help it. Every now and then my voice breaks," said Zepp. "It touches me."

Sovik, putting his hand on the old man's arm, said: "It touches us all."

The afternoon was more of the same: *Lt. Herbert was not making me a sincere offer, German sympathizer, disgrace your sisters, sincere religious objections.*

Finally the executive secretary of the Corrections Board, Ray Williams, the man most familiar with Zepp's case, asked the defendant:

"Mr. Zepp, since you received your general discharge under honorable conditions back in 1952 as a result of a recommendation of this board, have you ever applied to the V.A. for any benefits?"

Zepp: "No I haven't."

Williams: "You understand you are entitled to all the benefits of an honorably discharged soldier."

Zepp: "That's right. The one thing that bothers me is my conscience, my allegiance to the Almighty. I have to see this thing through. . . . I don't think that a person who follows the dictates of his conscience and is a true Christian should be stigmatized as a dishonorable person. And I think he shouldn't even get a second-rate discharge."

(continued)

PULITZER PRIZE WINNER   CONTINUED

Williams: ". . . In all good conscience you can say that your discharge is under honorable conditions."

Zepp: "I personally feel it would behoove the United States of America, who believes in freedom of conscience, religion or the Bill of Rights, that a person who follows, truthfully follows, the dictates of his conscience, and you are obligated to follow that because you've got a relationship with God, and I don't think that we should stigmatize anybody like that as being a dishonorable person.

"And the reason I'm here at my advanced age—83, arthritis and all that—my inner self, my conscience, says, 'Now here. You go to the board and make one last effort.' " Zepp paused. He hunched forward and made ready to sling one final arrow: "In view of the fact, Mr. Williams, that there's not much difference, then why not make it honorable? There isn't much difference. Let's make it honorable and we'll all be happy."

Zepp's lawyer closed with this plea:

"The military has come a long way since 1918 in their dealing with these individuals who have religious scruples about continued military service. . . . I would contend that it's in part because of individuals like Mr. Zepp who were willing to put their principles on the line many years ago . . . that it took individuals like that to finally work out a good system of dealing with conscientious objection. And that's what the military has now after many, many years. That, in its own right, is a very important service to the military."

The panel closed the proceedings. A decision was promised sometime within the next month.

Back at Union Station, waiting for the return trip: gone now the derelict emptiness of the early morning hours. In the evening the station was smart with purpose: well-dressed men and women, toting briefcases and newspapers, in long lines waiting for trains. The old man sat on a chair and reviewed the day. He smiled and his eyes were bright.

"I feel very confident. I sensed victory. I put all my cards on the table and I called a spade a spade. Did you see how I went up afterwards and I shook all their hands, just like they were my friends. I even shook the hands of Williams, my enemy, and I leaned over and I said to him, 'I love you, darling.' I acted as if I expected victory and I did not accept defeat. I used the oil can profusely."

He paused. Zepp looked up, seeming to study the ceiling. He cupped his chin with his left hand. The old man was silent. A college girl across from him watched him in his reverie, and she smiled a young smile.

Finally, the old man spoke. He seemed shaken. His voice was soft, filled with fear, the earlier confidence gone. The thought had come, like a traitor, jabbing him in the heart:

"What next?"

"I'll be lonesome without this. Here's my problem. Now that I don't have anything to battle for, what will I do? There's nothing I know of on the horizon to compete with that."

He paused. His face brightened. "Well, I can go swimming. And I can keep square dancing. Something happens to me when I square dance; it's the—what do they call it?—the adrenalin. I am a top form dancer. Maybe I can go back to being the treasurer of the Broward Community Senior Center. I did that before my wife became sick, but I quit to take care of her. I always was a fine office man. Maybe I'll become active in the Hope Lutheran Church. In other words, keep moving. Keep moving. That's the secret.

"All I know is that I could not face my departure from this earth if I had failed to put up this fight."

At 7:20, there came the boom of an announcement over the loudspeaker; the voice was anonymous and businesslike:

"The Silver Meteor, bound for Miami, Florida, scheduled to depart at 7:40, is ready for boarding. All passengers may now board the *Silver Meteor*, with stops in Alexandria . . . Richmond . . . Petersburg . . . Fayetteville . . . Florence . . . Charleston . . . Savannah . . . Jacksonville . . . Waldo . . . Ocala . . . Wildwood . . . Winter Haven . . . Sebring . . . West Palm Beach . . . Deerfield Beach . . . Fort Lauderdale . . . Hollywood . . . Miami."

Edward Zepp boarded the train, located his roomette and departed for home. Within minutes of leaving the station, exhausted by the day's excitement, he fell asleep.

On Tuesday, Oct. 2, 1979, the Pentagon issued the following statement: "Having considered the additional findings, conclusions and recommendation of the Army Board for Correction of Military Records and under the provisions of 10 U.S.C. 1552, the action of the Secretary of the Army on 4 December 1952 is hereby amended insofar as the character of discharge is concerned, and it is directed: (1) That all Department of the Army records of Edward Zepp be corrected to show that he was separated from the Army of the United States on a Certificate of Honorable Discharge on November 1919. (2) That the Department of the Army issue to Edward Zepp a Certificate of Honorable Discharge from the Army of the United States dated 9 November 1919 in lieu of the General Discharge Certificate of the same date now held by him."

"In other words," said Edward Zepp. "I was right all along."

A week later, a copy of the Pentagon's decision arrived at Zepp's Margate condominium. He discovered the decision was not unanimous. One member, James Hise, had voted against him.

"I'm so mad I could kick the hell out of him. A guy like that shouldn't be sitting on the Board. I am going to write to the Pentagon and tell them he should be thrown off the panel. It would be better to have just a head up there loaded with concrete or sawdust than this guy Hise, who doesn't know the first thing about justice. If he can't judge better than that, he should be kicked off. He's a menace to justice in this world.

"I'd like to go up there and bust his head wide open."

Source: © 1979. *The Miami Herald.* Reprinted by permission.

Draw your own conclusions about Zepp. Blais says her initial appraisal was that Zepp was "cantankerous," a quality "he put to good use to get his way. What he is is the classic example of a man who can't be satisfied."

The ending, which telegraphs that feeling, is not accidental, says Blais. "I write the ending first. I remember a long time ago someone said, 'The kicker [or ending] contains the writer's truest feelings about a piece.' I find that that's the way I've been doing things lately. If you know where the story is going—if you can write the ending—you know where you're going.

"That final quote, where he says, 'I'd like to go up there and bust his head wide open,' when he told it to me, I said, 'Oh, wow, that's it.'"

Structurally, the story is largely chronological. After the opening paragraphs—which tell readers why they are reading the story and what Zepp looks like—the narrative moves to the train trip north, pauses occasionally for flashbacks to the incidents leading up to the trip, then moves to the meeting in Union Station, the hearing at the Pentagon and finally back to Florida.

The writing is brilliant. For example, reread Blais's description of Zepp in the third paragraph. Can you picture the man? And note the fourth paragraph: Blais uses military language to describe ordinary activities such as Zepp's briefcase being "foraged" and the pages of the court-martial proceedings being "unfurled."

And like Jon Franklin's Pulitzer-winning story of Mrs. Kelly, the Zepp article uses traditional dramatic unity. Blais begins with an introduction, then provides rising action as Zepp speeds by train toward Washington and tells his story, offers a climax with the board meeting, falling action in the aftermath of the meeting and finally gives the reader a resolution to the story with the vote of the board—and Zepp's reaction.

Blais agrees with Franklin, who says a problem and a solution, or a conflict and a resolution, should be intrinsic to a significant feature. "All good writing is about conflict. If it's not there, it's not good," she says. And certainly "Zepp's Last Stand" is rife with conflict: Zepp in conflict with his draft board in 1917, Zepp in conflict with Sgt. Hitchcock, Zepp in conflict with the Pentagon and, finally, Zepp in conflict with James Hise of the Army Board for Correction of Military Records.

As you have read, feature writers disagree about whether a problem and a solution, or a conflict and a resolution, are required for a successful story. But there's no debate about the necessity for a finely focused idea. Camp's idea was simple: Paint a word portrait of four seasons in the life of a farm family. So was Blais's: Tell the story of a man righting a wrong. Great feature stories are always propelled by such simple ideas.

Tom French also had a simple idea. French, a *St. Petersburg Times* writer, won the 1998 Pulitzer Prize for a feature series about the brutal murders of an Ohio woman and her two daughters who were vacationing in Florida. French explains how a 21-part series proposed for publication over six months ultimately became a simpler seven-part series titled "Angels and Demons."

> I got the idea one day that I wanted to do a narrative where you take a handful of different stories from around Tampa Bay—all set in the same time period—and you weave them together for a collective portrait of America. It's a very simple idea. The simplest way [to explain it] is that I wanted to do a "Canterbury Tales" set at the turn of the millennium. Florida was perfect for it. Sort of this new frontier for America. Everyone comes here. And you have all of these people here from all over the world who have lived through the century. . . . My argument to [the editors] was that we get this opportunity once every 1,000 years. We hadn't had this opportunity since the Gutenberg Bible was printed. It [was] a really wonderful opportunity to do something really audacious. And different. Wholly different.
>
> So what were the stories going to be? We thought of them as threads in a tapestry. What were the threads going to be and how closely interlinked did they have to be for them to hold together? We spent a lot of time at the beginning to try to answer some of those questions because I really needed to know before I could begin looking [for] and picking [threads]. We decided we would use a chain-link approach. Every thread needed to be connected to one of the threads, but not every thread needed to be connected to all of the other threads.
>
> We essentially had [the series] mapped out for 21 days altogether in three separate clusters. . . . So we started picking. We decided to write about the Rogers case for a lot of

reasons. One is the myth of Florida. Three women came down here looking for the myth of Florida and paid for it with their lives. Another is how Florida itself could be used in such a perverse way. [Another is] how God could allow that to happen?

French proposed that the Florida "Canterbury Tales"—three groups of seven stories each—would be interwoven, with each story linked to at least one other story. The common thread connecting all of the stories would be faith. "Angels and Demons," for example, is about faith in justice and emotional recovery by the husband and father of the murdered women, and faith in justice by the tireless Florida police detectives who investigated the murders and the prosecutors who convicted the man who killed the three women. Ultimately, *St. Petersburg Times* editors asked French to reconceive his ambitious "Canterbury Tales" as a series of separate stories including the account of the Rogers murders. But the concept's essential nature—a simple story of faith told well—remains.

CHAPTER THREE

THE MAGAZINE ARTICLE AND ARTICLE IDEA

Pick up a Sunday edition of a major newspaper such as *The Dallas Morning News* or *The Miami Herald* and you'll be holding a bundle of newsprint that exceeds 300 pages in its numerous sections. Dozens of features of all categories and lengths appear in those 300 pages.

For example, on a typical Sunday, *The Dallas Morning News* carried 16 locally written features, in addition to dozens of wire service features and syndicated features. The local feature articles—which averaged about 2,000 words—ranged from a 4,500-word story about a modern Texas wagon train to a 650-word sidebar about survivors of a Dallas airplane crash.

In addition to the feature and news stories, that issue of the *Morning News* was a virtual storehouse of cartoons and crossword puzzles, advice columns, horoscopes, fashion pages, and advertising.

The French word *magasin,* from which the English word *magazine* is derived, in fact means "storehouse." The variety of information and entertainment currently stored in America's bulging Sunday newspapers suggests a question: Are U.S. dailies—especially major Sunday newspapers in our metropolitan areas—becoming more like magazines?

If frequency of publication, format and audience define a magazine, the answer is no. Magazines usually appear weekly, monthly or quarterly on slick paper, saddle-stitched (a type of binding in which signatures of a magazine are inserted, then stapled together through the center fold) or with perfect binding (a type of binding in which pages are stacked, then bound together with flexible glue at the spine), with frequent use of full color. Most daily newspapers are still printed on six columns of cheaper newsprint, folded but not bound, with only spot use of color. Most magazines are national in scope (though some excellent city, regional and state magazines are flourishing), and are targeted to specific audiences, such as skiing enthusiasts or catfish farmers or retirees. Newspapers are usually local or regional in flavor and are aimed at a broad general audience.

But if variety of content defines a magazine, the answer may be affirmative. Many Sunday newspapers do offer a tremendous catalogue of reading material and, in that sense, are like magazines—particularly the old general-interest magazines such as *Life, Look, Saturday Evening Post* and *Collier's.* And, as you've read in an earlier chapter, American newspapers continually become even more diversified and featurized in order to compete with other media forms.

HOW A MAGAZINE ARTICLE DIFFERS
FROM A NEWSPAPER FEATURE

The newspaper feature is clearly a close relative of the magazine article. They are similar in structure. Both begin with eye-catching "showcase" leads. Both have carefully organized bodies with a smooth flow of facts and ideas. Both end strongly. Both are also generally based on solid reporting. Both commonly use quotations and descriptions. And both can range in length from a few hundred to several thousand words, although a newspaper feature tends to be broken up into a multipart series if it exceeds 5,000 words.

That means a good newspaper feature writer should be able to produce equally good magazine articles. Right?

Not necessarily. Although many good writers can write fine features and articles for any market, they still need to pause between articles to shift mental gears. True, there are many similarities between newspaper features and magazine articles, but there are also some distinct differences.

The magazine article has its own character. Two of the most apparent differences in the magazine article are the leisurely approach to subject material and the fact that writers frequently take a subjective stand on what they are writing. Many magazines like a point of view. Newspapers, of course, usually prefer the facts, with a minimum of opinion, in their feature stories.

Alerting the beginning writer to the new green pastures of leisurely writing and subjective viewpoint is a bit like opening Pandora's box. Dangers are inherent in both. Too often, the beginning writer mistakes leisurely writing for sloppy writing, and blithely pounds away at the computer, unleashing a torrent of fatty, top-of-the-head words. Don't. A good magazine writer works harder and writes tighter when developing a leisurely style than at any other time. Every word still counts. The copy must catch and hold the attention of the reader all the way through. It's an attitude the writer is developing, not a gush of meaningless words. At the same time, even the subjective approach must be tempered. Unless you're some nationally known pundit, your opinions—or point of view—should be woven against a fabric of facts. Don't just tell the reader you are against animal research and vivisection. Give the reader a string of dramatic case histories in which animals have needlessly suffered, or medical researchers have shown disregard for the animals. Quote the researchers and animal experts. Give the numbers. Tell the reader how many animals die yearly under the knife. Describe the alternate health research that could as easily settle the medical questions without unnecessary cruelty. Facts are more compelling than opinion. Any reader may reject your point of view, but a point of view solidly constructed on a foundation of fact is harder to ignore. Even better, for the magazines that don't insist on a point of view, give your readers all sides of the argument and let them make up their own minds.

Another obvious difference in magazine articles is in paragraphing. In general, magazine paragraphs are longer and more formal than those in newspaper features. The newspaper's narrow column widths make long paragraphs appear formidable. The average newspaper writer, accustomed to short, punchy paragraphs, sometimes finds it difficult to return to formal paragraphs with topic sentences and full, adequate development. This is not to say that the good magazine article won't have a few punchy one-sentence paragraphs for impact. Many do. But a magazine submission filled with brief, newspaper-style paragraphs dotted down the page is apt to get you a note from the editor calling for rewrites. Or a rejection.

Magazine leads are also often longer than newspaper leads. An anecdotal lead (you'll hear more about these in later chapters) can run 300 to 600 words, easily, before getting to the crux of the subject. Many newspaper features are already half-finished by that point in the material. The reason for this is that most magazines are meant for leisure reading, to be picked up for a story or two, then laid aside until the next moment of leisure. Newspapers are gone over quickly by their readers, who flip from page to page, looking for things that interest them.

Newspaper and magazine approaches to lead writing can be as different as grabbling and fly-fishing. Both newspapers and magazines are after the same catch—readers. But the newspaper feature writer must often yank the reader into the story with one or two well-crafted sentences. The magazine writer has a chance to dangle persuasive bait, to lure the reader into the story with sleight of hand, to have the reader thoroughly hooked before even presenting a statement of theme. If the newspaper feature lead doesn't grab readers quickly, it may never get another chance. The magazine lead must be just as interesting, since it serves the same purpose—as a hook for readers, a showcase that will compel them into the story and keep them reading—but it has more time to tease readers and the assistance of vivid graphic devices to get it started.

STAFF WRITER VERSUS FREELANCER

You will notice that most of the chapters devoted to magazine writing in this book are directed toward freelance writers. That's because another basic difference between newspaper features and magazine articles is in the people who write them. Most newspaper features are generated, assigned, and written by staff members, people actually employed by the newspaper. Consequently, newspapers, except for travel sections and Sunday supplements, are seldom in the market for freelance material. Magazines, on the other hand, rely heavily on freelance writers. Yes, there are magazine staff writers as well, and some very good ones. And there are magazines that generate all their own magazine stories, with no room for or interest in freelance submissions—magazines such as *Time* and *Newsweek* and *U.S. News and World Report* and *Business Week* and dozens, perhaps hundreds, of others. But most magazines are lightly staffed and depend primarily on their ability to attract good freelancers with clever ideas who are willing to write for them on a pay-per-article basis.

Let's look at some typical magazine staffs. A few of the busier magazines, such as *Newsweek,* may list as many as 300 editors and writers and photographers in a staff box. That's a massive information-gathering crew. Writers and editors are trained to work in the *Newsweek* style, writing in committee when necessary, to produce a satisfactory weekly product. But huge magazine staffs are the exception, not the rule. Far more common is the typical trade journal staff. There are thousands of them out there, magazines that might appear monthly, producing 40 to 60 pages of copy, circulating to 40,000 or 50,000 readers, and still operating with staffs of four or five people. It's not at all uncommon to look at a magazine staff box and see a listing for an editor, followed by an associate editor, an art director, an advertising sales manager and a circulation manager. Five people, and three of them completely dissociated from the writing side of the publication. That leaves only two people to determine what will appear in the magazine and to write or edit all copy to conform to the magazine's style. Without freelancers, many such magazines couldn't survive. Even more surprising are the many magazines that operate with only one person at the helm, doing everything: writing, editing, designing, selling ads, keeping up the subscription lists and maybe even sweeping up at the end of the day.

Big staff or little staff, an overwhelming majority of magazines couldn't exist without freelance writers. Nor would they want to. Instead of depending on a small cadre of writers and editors to dream up their article ideas, they can tap the bottomless pool of bright freelancers, all trying to come up with something new enough or different enough to be salable. The bigger, better magazines, by offering better rates and a touch of literary cachet, can attract the best writers in the world. The competition can be murderous. Smaller magazines, paying more modest rates, may be more apt to attract beginning writers, but the ideas must still be sound and the writing must be acceptable. Working your way from low-grade markets to the top markets is a tough training process, just as stringent as the training ground through which each newspaper or magazine staffer must advance. The difference is that staff writers have editors and peers to help them overcome weaknesses, whereas freelancers learn at their own pace and usually alone.

What important differences develop between newspaper features and magazine articles as a result of the freelance input? Aside from technical matters such as paragraph and lead length, as well as attitudinal approaches such as a leisurely writing style and possible subjective treatment, the typical magazine article is often more thoroughly researched than the newspaper feature because of a more generous preparation time. For example, freelance writers may have several months to research various stories while they are checking the markets for an expression of interest. Newspaper feature writers usually have deadlines ranging from hours to perhaps weeks. Like most newspaper staff writers, Nan Robertson, *The New York Times* cultural reporter who won the 1983 feature-writing Pulitzer for her toxic shock syndrome story, usually researches and writes her stories under tremendous pressure. "Most of the stuff is due right away," she explains. "I've never had six months to do a story. I rarely have as much as a month."

Nor does the typical magazine freelancer, of course. The magazine writer who spends six months on a single story before beginning the next will never be very successful. Sales will come too infrequently. But a good freelance magazine writer may easily spend six months on a story while juggling it with a dozen other story ideas. The pressure is off. Unless an editor has responded to a story query with a definite assignment and a specified due date, or unless a story is timely and will lose its impact through delay, there are no deadlines for home-based magazine freelancers, save those they set for themselves.

Consequently, there is no excuse for not researching a subject thoroughly. For one thing, spotty research will show up in the finished product. For another, careful research makes the writing a lot easier. It's always simpler to discard excess research materials that don't fit than it is to go back to the source and dig again through previously turned soil for something you forgot, or decided at the last moment that you couldn't get along without. Pulitzer winner Madeleine Blais of *The Miami Herald,* an excellent example of the writer who can handle both the newspaper and the magazine formats, sums up research this way: "In a magazine piece, you know a lot more than you use, but with a newspaper deadline feature, you use 110 percent of what you have."

Nor is the research completed once the magazine writer—particularly the freelance writer—has finished the story. Unless an editor knows your work well and has confidence in your accuracy, the article will probably sit while someone checks your facts. This may be as simple as a phone check or a letter to ask you for the source of a particular quote or clarification of some questionable piece of data, or it might be as exhaustive as the accuracy checks performed by *Reader's Digest.* The *Digest,* a long-time favorite of freelance writers because of its high rate of pay, employs a huge worldwide staff of researchers to validate facts and quotations. *Digest* editors, determined to keep their pages as free of errors as possible, say they use their researchers to check some 3,500 facts a month with more than 1,500 sources.

THREE NECESSARY SKILLS FOR THE FREELANCE WRITER

Another major difference between newspapers and magazines is the evolution of article ideas. Both newspaper and magazine writers may come up with their own ideas, and often do. But most newspaper feature writers, as you recall, are staffers on salary. Their survival as writers doesn't necessarily depend on their ability to formulate good feature ideas. On smaller newspapers, feature writers usually cover general assignments as well, and may turn out a feature only when an idea presents itself easily or when an editor calls them over and hands them a feature possibility on a platter. Even on larger metropolitan newspapers, where feature writers may be specialists, a good portion of their feature ideas may be generated by editors or in editorial conferences. The same is true of magazine staffers, of course. If you work for a magazine as a salaried staffer, you will probably write a variety of articles, either self-generated or handed to you as an assignment from an editor.

But even if you prefer a magazine staff position, the traditional path to a good magazine staff job is freelance writing. The quickest way to prove to an editor that you can handle a magazine writing position is to show an impressive portfolio of writing credits when you apply for the job. All writing credits help. Freelancing credits may be best of all. If you can show an array of freelance articles from good magazines bearing your byline, it not only will prove you are a competent writer, but also will show you have initiative and imagination. Adam Ballinger, publisher of several successful Southern agricultural magazines, is one of the many magazine specialists who worked their way up through freelance writing. "I put myself through college writing freelance magazine articles," explains Ballinger. "During my junior and senior years, I wrote and placed more than 60 pieces. Not only was the money handy, but my clip book was a terrific door-opener when I started job hunting."

University students are in an enviable position for freelancing. When an economics professor talks about some new pet business theory or a health teacher discusses interesting causes and effects of hypothermia, the student freelancer's ears will come to a point, and he or she will follow it up. A bit of time on the computer. Library research.

Perhaps a talk with the professor during office hours. Then a quick search for possible markets. With luck and a good query letter, the student may get a green light to do an article. The rewards are numerous. A check in the mail to help with college expenses, a nice writing credit for his or her portfolio, contact with a new editor for later assignments and—this doesn't hurt, either—a professor who is suitably impressed by the student's enterprise.

You may decide to try freelancing as a route to a staff job, or you may prefer freelance writing as a career in itself. Either way, many magazines depend heavily on freelance writers for articles. But ideas may not be as easy to come by for the freelancer as they are for newspaper and magazine staffers. Freelance writers can't rely on an amenable editor to put them on the trail of a good article idea. Those first article ideas and sales often come hard. Editors are always on the lookout for good new writers, but they don't know you. You'll have to prove yourself to them.

To become a successful freelancer, you must master three, equally important facets of the magazine writing profession:

1. You must be able to come up with good story ideas.
2. You must know the magazines and what they want.
3. You must be able to write a cogent, well-organized article.

Please take special note: You must master all three. Not one or two. If you come up with super ideas and know exactly where to send them, but you can't write—you're dead. Or if you have excellent ideas and you write your articles superbly, but you don't know what magazines might be interested in them—your articles will languish on shelves, drawing dust. By the same token, if you're a master writer with a solid knowledge of the markets, but you have no ideas, you could spend a freelance career staring unprofitably at your computer.

Ideas can be elusive, but anyone can be trained to think in terms of magazine article ideas if he or she is willing to make the necessary mental adjustment. Marketing stories can be equally tricky, as well as time consuming and frustrating, but again, anyone can learn to study magazines and analyze the types of articles they run. This chapter and others will give you pointers to set you in the right direction. Writing is more difficult. Neither this book nor any other can teach you to write. Writing is learned only one way, through the fingertips, with practice. The book can give you techniques and shortcuts, and point out some of the more obvious errors to be avoided (and will, in later chapters), but you must teach yourself to become a superior writer—through analysis, through imitation if necessary, and certainly through long, hard application at the keyboard of your computer.

The first step in becoming a successful freelance magazine writer is learning to generate ideas. Freelancers get ideas in much the same way as non-deadline newspaper feature writers. They often work harder for them, since they seldom have friendly editors or cooperative co-workers to slide good article hints onto their desks. And the ideas themselves will cover a dazzling array of interests, since the range of available markets is almost unlimited. Virtually everything under the sun is grist for the freelancer's mill.

But you must learn to recognize the materials when they present themselves. The beginning writer is often awed by the crazy-quilt variety of subjects unearthed by the professional writer. Don't be. Article materials exist all around you. In the columns of your local newspaper. In the Yellow Pages of your phone book. In university classes. In stores and shopping centers. On street corners as you drive or walk along. Pay attention to what your eyes see. Learn to listen more alertly. You must train yourself to look at every new person you meet, every event you attend, every small adventure or unexpected encounter, with a new awareness, constantly testing each person, place or thing for magazine article potential.

This may sound a peculiar way to go through life, forever watchful, obsessed with scouting out possible magazine article ideas. It really isn't like that. For the beginner, true, it takes conscious effort, and you may bore your friends for a time, always talking about possible magazine ideas. But it soon becomes second nature, and the possibilities will filter through your mind on an almost subconscious level, being categorized and accepted or rejected without really breaking into your normal flow of action and thought.

Even though the search for ideas goes on at a subterranean level, the good freelancer will adopt one eccentricity that will remain obvious. Always carry a small notebook, or have one easily accessible. When the mind goes *ping,* and tells you it has encountered a ripe article idea, stop and write it down. Record your sudden brainstorms. Jot down the phrase or make a note of the scene that tripped your mental circuits. Don't take the chance of forgetting either the idea or your original spark of creative interest. A busy freelancer has a busy mind, and sudden inspiration can be too easily crowded out. A handy notebook can be indispensable.

Stalking the Elusive Article Idea

There are different approaches to the search for ideas. Some writers seek the idea first, then look for a suitable market. Say a prominent restaurant owner in your city buys a very expensive, very old bottle of wine, paying $15,000 for it at an auction sale. He then donates the bottle to a charity organization, which holds a wine-tasting party at his restaurant. City nabobs shell out $100 each for the privilege of sipping the expensive wine, downing a few wedges of cheese and showing off their evening finery. An alert freelancer would ponder the event. For the investment of a few hours of research and on-site interviews, the freelancer could turn the material into at least three magazine articles. Because the wine is unique, very old and very fine, the freelancer should check out magazines for wine connoisseurs, offering them an unusual story of an excellent vintage that may, through the charity connection, have done something to help relieve human suffering. Then, still thinking of the charity connection, the freelancer could offer another story to a charity-oriented magazine, suggesting a new fund-raising approach. And finally, because the restaurant owner is involved, the freelancer may query restaurateur magazines, proposing an article that will show how much goodwill and local publicity can come to a man who is willing to donate his money and facilities to a good cause.

A number of successful freelance writers work in just the opposite direction. First they seek markets that interest them, and then they go on the prowl for suitable story ideas to offer to those markets. John Simpson, a retired Navy officer who took up freelancing because he was bored, makes a steady practice of working this way. Simpson scours the market guides and haunts the periodical room at the library, looking for little-known markets. The pay-per-word is lower, he says, but the writing competition is considerably less fierce. Many of the smaller magazines are starving for material. When he runs across a new grocery magazine that deals with the production, packaging and merchandising of food staples, he checks the local phone book for food plants that might be of interest to the grocery magazine readers. He then makes a couple of quick phone calls, gathering enough information to write an intelligent query letter. When the magazine responds with an expression of interest, he drives to the food plant with notepaper and camera (he has taught himself to shoot all his own pictures) and conducts his interviews. He has sold hundreds of trade-magazine articles this way.

Still other writers work with clip files. They develop their ideas slowly, over a period of time. They are constantly reading, looking for newspaper and magazine articles that speak to them. Novelist Barbara Moore, who occasionally writes magazine articles for top-level consumer magazines, never reads a newspaper without scissors and pen at her elbow. She says:

> I like to write about things that interest me, so I keep an active file system going. From a typical newspaper, I might pull a story about unexplained animal mutilation in the mountains of Colorado, a nicely written feature about Navajo jewelry, and a piece on genetically altered bacteria. I write the name of the newspaper and the date at the top of each clip. The date is especially important. There's nothing worse than pulling a file folder when you're ready to start work on a query letter and discovering that half of the clips are undated. You can never remember whether something is fresh or too old to be trustworthy.

Moore then files her clips in manila folders under general headings. The mutilation story would probably go in a file marked "Animals." The jewelry feature would find a home under "Native Americans." The genetically altered bacteria, which catches her attention for an entirely different reason, is placed in a well-thumbed folder called "Possible Book Plots." Moore says she allows the folders (she currently has 74 active folders in her file system, each representing a different broad topic of general interest) to accumulate clips until they start to get fat, then she pulls them and sorts through them for potential article ideas. She usually finds three or four in each folder. She then looks for some unusual angle on which to pin her story, and does a market search, looking for the right magazine to which it might be submitted. The clips in the folder act as preliminary research, giving her enough material to write a persuasive query. Once an editor says yes, she gears up for the much heavier research and information-gathering process that lies ahead.

Matching Ideas to Markets

The magazine article writer must also narrow a story to a workable focus, just like the newspaper feature writer. But the process is a bit more complicated for the magazine writer. The newspaper feature writer is usually working for one publication, his or her employer, with the same audience and style and interests. Focus is often predictable. The magazine writer, however, is faced with a numbing array of magazines, each with its own fragmented audience, its own writing style, its own special interests. Focus must match those audiences and interests. Writing style, or voice, must also match.

Suppose you want to write an article about trendsetting women spies. You have the research and interviews done, and you're ready to tackle the markets. If you write for a women's magazine, you might approach the subject with a tone of admiration, prepared to show that women are courageous, effective and superior to their bumbling male counterparts. For an action-oriented men's magazine, you might be more likely to put a sneer into your voice and write in a macho language about "sexpionage," accenting the female spy's ability to beguile and deceive. For a senior citizen's magazine, you might narrow your focus to historical spies, from the infamous Mata Hari to Confederate agent Christine Ford, for whom a gallant Abraham Lincoln is said to have ordered a jail cell door unlocked by Union guards so she could escape. Dozens of approaches to the same general material are possible, and the cautious freelancer will stake out a market before settling on a potential focus. What's more, the focus should remain fluid. If an editor says no to the idea, closing off one market, the writer should be prepared to change the focus to suit another market. This is why few successful freelancers ever bother to write the finished article until they have a definite assignment or statement of interest from an editor.

So how do you match a potential idea to a market? The process is done in four steps. First, turn to a book like *Writer's Market* to scan publications that might be interested in your idea. Second, study at least three or four issues of each targeted magazine. Next, check a reference source such as *Reader's Guide to Periodical Literature* to make certain your targeted publications and their major competition haven't already published a story too similar to your own. Finally, formulate a persuasive letter—called a "query"—to the most appropriate magazine, telling the editor about your proposed article.

Let's look at these four steps in slightly more detail.

Finding Your Market. First, you need to stalk your game. The game is identified in a number of publications, but *Writer's Market,* a 1,200-page annual publication that lists thousands of magazines interested in buying freelance articles, is particularly handy to use. If you want to check some of the others, you might try looking at the *Standard Rate & Data Service* directories, or the *Gale Directory of Publications and Broadcast Media.* You might also want to check the yearly Bacon's publications (Volume 1 of *Bacon's Publicity Checker* lists trade magazines, and *Bacon's Media Alerts* will give you advance information on any special issues being planned by a number of magazines).

Until you get deeply involved in freelancing, *Writer's Market* will probably provide most of the information you will need, and it's easy to put your hands on. You can usually find a copy at your local library, and most bookstores will order a copy to sell to you if you want permanent access. Once you get serious about freelancing, you'll probably want to buy the newest edition every year. Remember, as you skim through the market listings, you should pick at least half a dozen potential markets in case your idea is as good as you think it is and the first two or three editors you contact fail to recognize its value.

A hint to the wise: Market listings take time to collect and to put through the publishing process. Even if you are using the most recent copy of *Writer's Market,* by the time it reaches you some editors may have been replaced. It happens. So always check a recent issue of your target magazine or the magazines official Web site to make sure the same editor is still listed. No point in offending a new editor by addressing your correspondence to a predecessor. Furthermore, it automatically marks you as someone who doesn't read the magazine. And that's a psychological strike against you. As Rebecca Greer, articles editor at *Woman's Day,* once told an audience of writers at New York University, "If you can't be bothered to buy the magazine and look up the editor's name and the proper spelling, how can I trust you to get cancer statistics right?"

Greer and many other good editors often appear at writers' conferences to discuss techniques and markets. Another hint to the wise: Go to as many writers' conferences and authors' symposia as you can afford. And make notes. The panelists are usually pros and will give you expert advice based on their accumulated experience. You can absorb quickly things that might take years of trial and error on your own.

Getting to Know Your Market.   Reading the magazine is important. The easiest way to determine if a particular magazine will be interested in your cunning and cleverly focused idea is to study the magazine itself. Try your local libraries for current issues. Failing that, you'll have to buy copies, sometimes from the publisher if the magazine is one not customarily found on newsstands. If your proposed market is a small magazine designed primarily for a select audience, such as a trade magazine for druggists or a hobby publication for quail hunters, then you will probably have to write directly to the magazine's home office. Some magazines will cheerfully send you free copies to acquaint you with their style. Others charge for sample copies, at least until they know you are a serious freelancer and a likely source for material.

Here's another hint: While you're busy talking to the druggist or the quail hunter, gathering your interview notes, ask each what he or she reads regularly that is relevant. If you're having trouble finding a good drugstore magazine or quail-hunting publication to which you might submit your finished article, it makes sense to find out what kinds of trade and hobby magazines appeal to your subjects. The druggist may well be able to furnish you with copies of pertinent druggist journals or retail magazines. The quail hunter will probably have copies of any good quail-hunting magazines or outdoor magazines that deal even peripherally with quail hunting. Not only will this give you a good line on potential markets, but you may be able to borrow and examine the magazines without having to buy copies or write away for copies.

And you need the copies. Reading the magazine for which you intend to write will give you many hints about subject requirements, treatment and length of articles. How long are the paragraphs? Does the magazine use lots of anecdotes? Direct quotes? Do the editors seem to prefer third-person articles with direct address to involve the readers? Do they permit the use of first person? What's the tone of the writing? Is it light? Serious? Dry? Every question you ask and every answer you derive through careful analysis will have a bearing on the way you treat your own material. Some answers may come hard and require meticulous analysis. Other answers will come easily. For example, if you're planning a 3,000-word article stuffed with dramatic anecdotes and authoritative quotes, and your target magazine uses mainly 1,500-word how-to pieces with step-by-step movements spelled out for the reader, you probably need to revise your plans. Or find a new market.

Learning to analyze good feature stories and magazine articles is an important step in the writing process. More than important, it's vital. That's why there are so many excellent examples in this book. Teach yourself to analyze structure, to check length, to count anecdotes. Look for transitional devices. Study the writing techniques. In effect, you want to strip away the flesh and stare at the bones. That's the best way to prepare yourself when you're dealing with a new editor or a new market. But it's also a good way to pick up tricks of the trade. If a technique works for some other professional writer, it should work for you.

In the meantime, while you're studying the target magazine, don't confine yourself to analysis of the articles. There are other lessons to be learned. For instance, if you have your own camera and are hoping to sell pictures with your article, you can study the pictures in the magazine and decide whether your photographic skills are up to the standards of a particular publication. While you're at it, check the names of the writers against the names listed in the masthead or the staff box. If the same names appear over the stories and in the staff box over the course of two or three issues, you may conclude that the magazine is a poor freelancer's market because staff members are doing most of the writing. You can also get a leg up on an audience analysis by checking out the ads in the magazine. Diaper and baby food ads usually indicate young parents. Advertisements for investment opportunities and retirement plans usually suggest an older, more settled audience. A preponderance of cosmetic and beauty soap ads signify a probable female audience. Commercial spreads for rock records, prep schools and zit removers tell you that the target audience is still in its teens. Become aware of audiences. The composition of a particular reading audience may well dictate the language you use when you write your article.

Checking for Duplication. The third step in researching a market and matching your idea to it is to make certain that your target magazine hasn't recently published an article too similar to yours. Since you can't afford to buy every issue of a magazine for the past few years just to check for duplicate articles, you need to conduct a library search. Good libraries have several tools for doing this—including computerized searches and automated microfilm readers that whisk the researcher to the right topic—but the most commonly used reference is *Reader's Guide to Periodical Literature.* And yes, no matter how convenient it is to look things up at home on your computer, when you're ready to do some heavy research, you'll probably have to go to the library. The *Reader's Guide* is a good case in point. You can look it up on your computer, but it'll cost you about $400 to buy into the electronic database. And the problems don't end there. *Reader's Guide* indexes only the articles that appear in the most popular consumer magazines, so if your target is something esoteric like *Southern Motor Cargo* or *Whittler's World,* you may have to check with the reference librarian or some other form of index. Nearly all of these computerized indexes come with a fee. While libraries regularly pay such fees, most freelancers can't afford them. You'll read more about computer and library research in the next chapter.

While you're browsing through *Reader's Guide,* you should make a note of major articles that have already been written on your subject. Too many articles on the same topic may suggest that you're too late with your idea, even if you have a very unusual approach to offer. No articles at all can mean that you're ahead of the trend or, unfortunately, that very few people are interested in your topic. Remember also that this search is doing double duty for you. Not only can you get an idea of the timeliness or untimeliness of your idea, or whether your particular target publication has already run a similar piece, but the articles you locate may also be useful later as background research for the story you hope to write.

Getting Ready to Query. Finally, once you've narrowed your field of potential markets, you'll want to consider contacting the magazines for specific writer's guidelines to help you in the formulation of your query letter. Some magazines post these guidelines on their Web sites. Others prefer contact by mail. Either way, these editorial hints can be extremely helpful, whether they range from a single page of notes offered by publications such as *Americana* or *AARP The Magazine,* all the way to the generous pages of instructions offered by the editors of *Guideposts Magazine.* Typically, these guidelines offer information about readers and appropriate subject matter, article lengths, treatments, photographic needs and payment for articles and pictures. Some of this same material is offered in brief form in *Writer's Market,* so you may be able to skip this step, depending on your skill as a freelancer and your ability to judge what a magazine is seeking. For the novice, however, the fuller version of guidelines can be very useful.

Furthermore, most sets of writer's guidelines will give you additional information about the magazine's specific audience, since editors want you to know precisely who will be reading materials published in their pages. Let's make an assumption. No matter how carefully you might analyze the magazine, the editor of that magazine knows the readers better than you do. That's because the publication has probably spent a great deal of money on demographic studies in order to show potential advertisers what kind of audience they'll be reaching. *Cosmopolitan* magazine, for example, says its readers are mostly well-educated, working, single women, between 18 and 34 years old, who live in urban areas. *Signature* magazine is directed toward Diner's Club and Carte Blanche members—executives and professionals who are affluent, well traveled and about 43 years old. *AARP The Magazine,* mentioned above, goes to people in the 50-plus market and claims to serve "the interests and needs of America's fastest growing market segment." We can assume that to be an accurate assessment. *AARP The Magazine* currently boasts the largest magazine circulation in the world.

The editors of these and other magazines also know that people tend to read material with which they agree and to avoid material that takes an opposing view. The editor doesn't want his or her special readers to throw the magazine down in disgust, so material that doesn't suit the editor's view of the typical reader simply isn't purchased, no matter how brilliant the concept or clever the wording. That's why it's important to acquaint yourself with the magazine and its audience before you write your query letter.

You'll study the query letter later, but first, let's discuss the value of analysis.

Reading and Analyzing for Technique and Market Needs.   Certainly, writing satisfies a personal compulsion in most writers. Writers need to write. They're often obsessive about it. But what they write must also inform, entertain, and otherwise hold the interest of the reader. If they fail in that, they might as well be writing diaries or personal journals never intended for publication.

So how do they train themselves to approach writing as a craft? Basically, they do it by studying and analyzing the writing forms used by other successful writers to put their ideas across. In effect, they learn to imitate. Not to copy. Not to take someone else's ideas or language. But to study and analyze technique and structure. If you can't figure out how to structure an overwhelming mass of fact and research into a smooth, readable article, you should study someone else's organization for hints and ideas. If you don't know how many direct quotes to use, you should take a close look at the magazine you are writing for to see how much of the material is in direct quotes and how much is paraphrased. In short, you should teach yourself to imitate the form and technique of articles already published in your target market.

Article analysis is especially important for beginning feature and article writers because their experience quotient is low. They haven't written and placed many articles yet. They need to polish their techniques, to learn structure and organization, to sharpen their flow from one thought to the next.

But whether you are a beginner or a published professional, no matter how long you continue to write or how experienced you become, you will always continue to read and analyze articles. As long as you are writing for a variety of markets, you will need to read and analyze in order to meet the needs of those markets.

Let's analyze two prize-winning articles, one from a city magazine, *The Washingtonian,* and the other from New York's weekly newspaper, *The Village Voice,* to show differences and similarities in structure, language and technique.

At present, magazines have no separate Pulitzer category in which they can compete, but they do have a variety of important magazine competitions. These include national honors for writing, such as the William Allen White Editorial Awards, administered by the University of Kansas for city and regional magazines; the Jesse H. Neal Awards for business writing, funded and administered by the Business Press Educational Foundation; and the most prestigious magazine competition of all—the annual National Magazine Awards, established by the American Society of Magazine Editors and administered by the Columbia University Graduate School of Journalism.

The article that follows, Katie McCabe's "Like Something the Lord Made," is an inspirational profile of Vivien Thomas, a black laboratory technician who, without formal scientific training, became a pioneer in cardiovascular medicine and heart surgery. McCabe's piece, painstakingly researched and submitted for publication to *The Washingtonian,* the city magazine in the nation's capital, won the coveted National Magazine Award for feature writing in 1990. McCabe's beautifully written article was later turned into an HBO movie that aired for the first time in 2004. And that's another plus. Good magazine articles can lead to all kinds of lucrative spin-offs.

McCabe is a freelancer from Bethesda, Maryland, who has written frequently for *The Washingtonian.* She first heard about the legendary Thomas while working on a medical story in Washington, D.C. She was interviewing Dr. Judson Randolph, chief of surgery at Children's Hospital, when the doctor suggested a story about a man who had trained many of the country's top surgeons. McCabe, busy with several projects at the time, filed the information for later consideration. Months later, while at Johns Hopkins Hospital, she asked about Thomas and discovered he had died the very day Randolph first told her about him.

McCabe almost gave up on the story, but later she discovered a copy of Vivien Thomas's autobiography and the transcript of a 1967 interview. She decided to delve deeper and try a posthumous profile. She visited hospitals, talked to top surgeons and interviewed Thomas's family and co-workers. Some of her best material came from his former students, many of whom had become famous.

The McCabe piece offers many lessons for the beginning writer. Note the lead, for example. By the ease with which she sets up interviews with such famous names in medicine as Dr. Denton Cooley, the Houston heart specialist, she assures the reader that her subject is revered and highly worthwhile. This impels the reader onward.

Here, then, is McCabe's article:

NATIONAL MAGAZINE AWARD WINNER

KATIE McCABE

LIKE SOMETHING THE LORD MADE

Say his name, and the busiest heart surgeons in the world will stop and talk for an hour. Of course they have time, they say, these men who count time in seconds, who race against the clock. This is about Vivien Thomas. For Vivien they'll make time.

Dr. Denton Cooley has just come out of surgery, and he has 47 minutes between operations. "No, you don't need an appointment," his secretary is saying. "Dr. Cooley's right here. He wants to talk to you now."

Cooley suddenly is on the line from his Texas Heart Institute in Houston. In a slow Texas drawl he says he just *loves* being bothered about Vivien. And then, in 47 minutes—just about the time it takes him to do a triple bypass—he tells you about the man who taught him that kind of speed.

No, Vivien Thomas wasn't a doctor, says Cooley. He wasn't even a college graduate. He was just so smart, and so skilled, and so much his own man, that it didn't matter.

And could he operate. Even if you'd never seen surgery before, Cooley says, you could do it because Vivien made it look so simple.

Vivien Thomas and Denton Cooley both arrived at Baltimore's Johns Hopkins Hospital in 1941—Cooley to begin work on his medical degree, Thomas to run the hospital's surgical lab under Dr. Alfred Blalock. In 1941 the only other black employees at the Johns Hopkins Hospital were janitors. People stopped and stared at Thomas, flying down corridors in his white lab coat. Visitors' eyes widened at the sight of a black man running the lab. But ultimately the fact that Thomas was black didn't matter, either. What mattered was that Alfred Blalock and Vivien Thomas could do historic things together that neither could do alone.

Together they devised an operation to save "Blue Babies"—infants born with a heart defect that sends blood past their lungs—and Cooley was there, as an intern, for the first one. He remembers the tension in the operating room that November morning in 1944 as Dr. Blalock rebuilt a little girl's tiny, twisted heart.

He remembers how that baby went from blue to pink the minute Dr. Blalock removed the clamps and her arteries began to function. And he remembers where Thomas stood—on a little step stool, looking over Dr. Blalock's right shoulder, answering questions and coaching every move.

"You see," explains Cooley, "it was Vivien who had worked it all out in the lab, in the canine heart, long before Dr. Blalock did Eileen, the first Blue Baby. There were no 'cardiac experts' then. That was the beginning."

A loudspeaker summons Cooley to surgery. He says he's on his way to do a "tet case" right now. That's tetralogy of Fallot, the congenital heart defect that causes Blue Baby Syndrome. They say that Cooley does them faster than anyone, that he can make a tetralogy operation look so simple it doesn't even look like surgery. "That's what I took from Vivien," he says, "simplicity. There wasn't a false move, not a wasted motion, when he operated."

But in the medical world of the 1940s that chose and trained men like Denton Cooley, there wasn't supposed to be a place for a black man, with or without a degree. Still, Vivien Thomas made a place for himself. He was a teacher to surgeons at a time when he could not become one. He was a cardiac pioneer 30 years before Hopkins opened its doors to the first black surgical resident.

Those are the facts that Cooley has laid out, as swiftly and efficiently as he operates. And yet history argues that the Vivien Thomas story could never have happened.

In 1930, Vivien Thomas was a nineteen-year-old carpenter's apprentice with his sights set on Tennessee State College and then medical school. But the Depression, which had halted carpentry work in Nashville, wiped out his savings and forced him to postpone college. Through a friend who worked at Vanderbilt University, Thomas learned of an opening as a laboratory assistant for a young doctor named Alfred Blalock—who was, in his friend's words, "hell to get along with." Thomas decided to take a chance, and on February 10, 1930, he walked into Blalock's animal lab.

Out came Blalock, a Coke in one hand, cigarette in the other. A remote cousin of Jefferson Davis, Blalock was in many ways a Southern aristocrat, flashing an ebony cigarette holder and smiling through clouds of smoke. But the 30-year-old surgeon who showed Thomas into his office was even then, Thomas said, "a man who knew exactly what he wanted."

Blalock saw the same quality in Thomas, who exuded a no-nonsense attitude he had absorbed from his hard-working father. The well-spoken young man who sat on the lab stool politely responding to Blalock's questions had never been in a laboratory before. Yet he was full of questions about the experiment in progress, eager to learn not just "what" but "why" and "how." Instinctively, Blalock responded to that curiosity, describing his experiment as he showed Thomas around the lab.

Face to face on two lab stools, each told the other what he needed. Thomas needed a job, he said, until he could enter college the next fall. Blalock, well into his groundbreaking work on shock—the first phase of the body's reaction to trauma—needed "someone in the lab whom I can teach to do anything I can do, and maybe do things I can't do."

Each man got more than he bargained for. Within three days, Vivien Thomas was performing almost as if he'd been born in the lab, doing arterial punctures on the laboratory dogs and measuring and administering anesthesia. Within a month, the former carpenter was setting up experiments and performing delicate and complex operations.

Blalock could see Thomas had a talent for surgery and a keen intellect, but he was not to see the full measure of the man he'd hired until the day Thomas made his first mistake.

"Something went wrong," Thomas later wrote in his autobiography. "I no longer recall what, but I made some error. Dr. Blalock sounded off like a child throwing a temper tantrum. The profanity he used would have made the proverbial sailor proud of him . . . . I told him he could just pay me off . . . that I had not been brought up to take or use that kind of language . . . . He apologized, saying he had lost his temper, that he would watch his language, and he asked me to go back to work."

From that day on, said Thomas, "neither one of us ever hesitated to tell the other, in a straightforward, man-to-man manner, what he thought or how he felt. . . . In retrospect, I think that incident set the stage for what I consider our mutual respect throughout the years."

For 34 years they were a remarkable combination: Blalock the scientist, asking the questions; Thomas the pragmatist, figuring out the simplest way to get the answers. At their black-topped workbench and eight animal operating tables, the two set out to disprove all the old explanations about shock, amassing evidence that connected it to a decrease in blood volume and fluid loss outside the vascular bed.

(continued)

NATIONAL MAGAZINE AWARD WINNER   CONTINUED

In a few years, the explanations Blalock was developing would lead to massive applications of blood and plasma transfusion in the treatment of shock. Methodically, from their lab at "that school down in the backwoods"—as Blalock called Vanderbilt—he and Thomas were altering physiology.

All that was inside the laboratory. Outside loomed the Depression. In a world where "men were walking the streets looking for jobs that didn't exist," Thomas watched his own college and medical-school plans evaporate. "I was out of school for the second year," he wrote, "but I somehow felt that things might change in my favor . . . . But it didn't happen." With each passing month, Thomas's hopes dimmed, something not lost on Blalock. The two men discussed it, and Thomas finally decided that even if he someday could afford college, medical school now seemed out of reach. By 1932, Thomas had made his peace. "For the time being," he said, "I felt secure in that, at least, I had a job. Things were getting to the point that it seemed to be a matter of survival."

But the young man who read chemistry and physiology textbooks by day and monitored experiments by night was doing more than surviving. For $12 a week, with no overtime pay for sixteen-hour days and no prospect of advancement or recognition, another man might have survived. Thomas excelled.

Coached by Blalock's young research fellow, Dr. Joseph Beard, Thomas mastered anatomy and physiology, and he plunged into Blalock's round-the-clock research. At 5 P.M., when everyone else was leaving, Thomas and "The Professor" prepared to work on into the night—Thomas setting up the treasured Van Slyke machine used to measure blood oxygen, Blalock starting the siphon on the ten-gallon charred keg of whiskey he kept hidden in the laboratory storeroom during Prohibition. Then, as they settled down to monitor all-night shock experiments, Blalock and Thomas would relax with a whiskey-and-Coke.

Blalock and Thomas knew the social codes and traditions of the Old South. They understood the line between life inside the lab, where they could drink together in 1930, and life outside, where they could not. Neither one was to cross that line. Thomas attended Blalock's parties as a bartender, moonlighting for extra income. In 1960 when Blalock celebrated his 60th birthday at Baltimore's Southern Hotel, Thomas was not present.

Within the lab, they functioned almost as a single mind, as Thomas's deft hands turned Blalock's ideas into elegant and detailed experiments. In the verbal shorthand they developed, Thomas learned to translate Blalock's "I wonder what would happen if" into step-by-step scientific protocols. Through hundreds of experiments, Blalock wondered and Thomas found out, until in 1933 Blalock was ready to challenge the medical establishment with his first "named lecture."

Almost overnight, Blalock's shock theory became "more or less Gospel," as Thomas put it. By 1935, a handful of other scientists had begun to rethink the physiology of shock, but no one besides Blalock had attacked the problem from so many angles. No one else had compiled such a mass of data on hemorrhagic and traumatic shock. No one else had been able to explain such a complex phenomenon so simply. And no other scientist had a Vivien Thomas.

In his four years with Blalock, Thomas had assumed the role of a senior research fellow, with neither a PhD nor an MD. But as a black man doing highly technical research, he had never really fit into the system—a reality that became painfully clear when in a salary discussion with a black coworker, Thomas discovered that Vanderbilt classified him as a janitor.

He was careful but firm when he approached Blalock on the issue: "I told Dr. Blalock . . . that for the type of work I was doing, I felt I should be . . . put on the pay scale of a technician, which I was pretty sure was higher than janitor pay."

Blalock promised to investigate. After that, "nothing more was ever said about the matter," Thomas recalled. When several paydays later Thomas and his coworker received salary increases, neither knew whether he had been reclassified as a technician or just given more money because Blalock demanded it.

In the world in which Thomas had grown up, confrontation could be dangerous for a black man. Vivien's older brother, Harold, had been a school teacher in Nashville. He had sued the Nashville Board of Education, alleging salary discrimination based on race. With the help of an NAACP lawyer named Thurgood Marshall, Harold Thomas had won his suit. But he lost his job. So Vivien had learned the art of avoiding trouble. He recalled: "Had there been an organized complaint by the Negroes performing technical duties, there was a good chance that all kinds of excuses would have been offered to avoid giving us technicians' pay and that leaders of the movement or action would have been summarily fired."

Thomas had family obligations to consider, too. In December 1933, after a whirlwind courtship, he had married a young woman from Macon, Georgia, named Clara Flanders. Their first child, Olga Fay, was born the following year, and a second daughter, Theodosia, would arrive in 1938.

The satisfaction of making a public racial statement was a luxury Thomas would not have for decades, and even then he would make his point quietly. Meanwhile, he worked hard, making himself indispensable to Blalock, and in so doing he gained a powerful ally within the system. When they confronted discrimination again, they confronted it together.

The test of their partnership was not long in coming. In 1937, Blalock received an offer of a prestigious chairmanship from Henry Ford Hospital in Detroit. As surgeon-in-chief there, he could run his own department, train his own men, expand his research.

He and Thomas were a package deal, Blalock told the powers at Henry Ford. In that case, the answer came back, there would be no deal. The hospital's policy against hiring blacks was inflexible. So was his policy on Vivien Thomas, Blalock politely replied.

The two bided their time, teaching themselves vascular surgery in experiments in which they attempted to produce pulmonary hypertension in dogs. The hypertension studies, as such, "were a flop," Thomas said. But they were one of the most productive flops in medical history.

By 1940, Blalock's research had put him head and shoulders above any young surgeon in America. When the call came to return to his alma mater, Johns Hopkins, as surgeon-in-chief, he was able to make a deal on his own terms, and it included Thomas. "I want you to go with me to Baltimore," Blalock told Thomas just before Christmas 1940. Thomas, always his own man, replied, "I will consider it."

Though Blalock would take a pay cut, the move to Hopkins offered him prestige and independence. For the 29-year-old Thomas and his family, it meant leaving the home they had built in Nashville for a strange city and an uncertain future.

In the end, it was World War II that caused Thomas to "take his chances" with Blalock. If he were drafted, it would be to his advantage to be at Hopkins, Thomas decided, because he would probably be placed with a medical unit. Always the family man, he was thinking practically. So Blalock, with everything to gain, and Thomas, with "nothing to lose," as he put it, made their move together.

When they came to Hopkins, they brought with them solutions to the problems of shock that would save many wounded soldiers in World War II. They brought expertise in vascular surgery that would change medicine. And they brought five dogs, whose rebuilt hearts held the answer to a question no one yet had asked.

(continued)

NATIONAL MAGAZINE AWARD WINNER   CONTINUED

When Blalock and Thomas arrived in Baltimore in 1941, the questions on most people's minds had nothing to do with cardiac surgery. How on earth was this boyish professor of surgery going to run a department, they wondered. With his simple questions and his Georgia drawl, Blalock didn't sound much like the golden boy described in his letters of reference. Besides, he had brought a *colored man* up from Vanderbilt to run his lab. A colored man who wasn't even a *doctor.*

Thomas had doubts of his own as he walked down Hopkins's dimly lit corridors, eyed the peeling green paint and bare concrete floors, and breathed in the odors of the ancient, unventilated structure that was to be his workplace: the Old Hunterian Laboratory. One look inside the instrument cabinet told him that he was in the surgical Dark Ages.

It was enough to make him want to head back to Nashville and take up his carpenter's tools again. After a day of house-hunting in Baltimore, he thought he might have to. Baltimore was more expensive than either he or Blalock had imagined. Even with a 20 percent increase over his Vanderbilt salary, Thomas found it "almost impossible to get along." Something would have to be done, he told Blalock.

Blalock had negotiated both of their salaries from Nashville, and now the deal could not be renegotiated. It seemed that they were stuck. "Perhaps you could discuss the problem with your wife," Blalock suggested. "Maybe she could get a job to help out."

Thomas bristled. His father was a builder who had supported a family of seven. He meant to do at least as well for his own family. "I intend for my wife to take care of our children," he told Blalock, "and I think I have the capability to let her do so—except I may have the wrong job."

If neither Hopkins nor Thomas would bend, Blalock would have to find another way to solve the problem. Blalock was not wealthy, but he had an ally at Hopkins, world-renowned neurosurgeon Dr. Walter Dandy, who was known for his generosity. That afternoon Blalock presented his situation to Dandy, who responded immediately with a donation to the department—earmarked for Thomas's salary.

So Thomas ordered his surgical supplies, cleaned and painted the lab, put on his white coat, and settled down to work. On his first walk from the lab to Blalock's office in the hospital across campus, the Negro man in a lab coat halted traffic. The hospital had segregated restrooms and a back entrance for black patients. Vivien Thomas surprised Johns Hopkins.

Inside the lab, it was his skill that raised eyebrows. What he was doing was entirely new to the two other Hopkins lab technicians, who were expected just to set up experiments for the medical investigators to carry out. How long had he been doing this, they wanted to know. How and where had he learned?

Then, one morning in 1943, while Johns Hopkins and Vivien Thomas were still getting used to each other, someone asked a question that would change surgical history.

For this part of the story, we have Thomas's own voice on tape—deep, rich, and full of soft accents. In an extensive 1967 interview with medical historian Dr. Peter Olch, we meet the warm, wry Vivien Thomas who remains hidden behind the formal, scientific prose of his autobiography. He tells the Blue Baby story so matter-of-factly that you forget he's outlining the beginning of cardiac surgery.

For once, it wasn't Blalock who asked the question that started it all. It was Dr. Helen Taussig, a Hopkins cardiologist, who came to Blalock and Thomas looking for help for the cyanotic babies she was seeing. At birth these babies became weak and "blue," and sooner or later all died. Surely there had to be a way to "change the pipes around" to bring more blood to their lungs, Taussig said.

There was silence. "The Professor and I just looked at each other. We knew we had the answer in the Vanderbilt work," Thomas says, referring to the operation he and Blalock had worked out at Vanderbilt some six years earlier—the "failed" experiment in which they had divided a major artery and sewn it into the pulmonary artery that supplied the lungs. The procedure had not produced the hypertension model they had sought, but it had rerouted the arterial blood into the lungs. It might be the solution for Taussig's Blue Babies.

But "might" wasn't good enough. Thomas first would have to reproduce tetralogy of Fallot in the canine heart before the effectiveness of their "pipe-changing" could be tested.

Off he went to the Pathology Museum, with its collection of congenitally defective hearts. For days, he went over the specimens—tiny hearts so deformed they didn't even look like hearts. So complex was the four-part anomaly of Fallot's tetralogy that Thomas thought it possible to reproduce only two of the defects, at most. "Nobody had fooled around with the heart before," he says, "so we had no idea what trouble we might get into. I asked The Professor whether we couldn't find an easier problem to work on. He told me, 'Vivien, all the easy things have been done.'"

Taussig's question was asked in 1943, and for more than a year it consumed Blalock and Thomas, both by then working in the Army's shock research program. Alone in the lab, Thomas set about replicating the Blue Baby defect in dogs and answering two questions: Would the Vanderbilt procedure relieve cyanosis? Would babies survive it?

As he was working out the final details in the dog lab, a frail, cyanotic baby named Eileen Saxon lay in an oxygen tent in the infant ward at Johns Hopkins Hospital. Even at rest, the nine-pound girl's skin was deeply blue, her lips and nail beds purple. Blalock surprised Eileen's parents and his chief resident, Dr. William Longmire, with his bedside announcement: He was going to perform an operation to bring more blood to Eileen's lungs.

Overnight, the tetralogy operation moved from the lab to the operating room. Because there were no needles small enough to join the infant's arteries, Thomas chopped off needles from the lab, held them steady with a clothespin at the eye end, and honed new points with an emery block. Suture silk for human arteries didn't exist, so they made do with the silk Thomas had used in the lab—as well as the lab's clamps, forceps, and right-angle nerve hook.

So complete was the transfer from lab to operating room on the morning of November 29, 1944, that only Thomas was missing when Eileen Saxon was wheeled into surgery. "I don't think I'll go," he had said to chemistry technician Clara Belle Puryear the previous afternoon. "I might make Dr. Blalock nervous—or even worse, he might make me nervous!"

But Blalock wanted Thomas there—not watching from the gallery or standing next to the chief resident, Dr. William Longmire, or the intern, Dr. Denton Cooley, or next to Dr. Taussig at the foot of the operating table. Blalock insisted Thomas stand at his elbow, on a step stool where he could see what Blalock was doing. After all, Thomas had done the procedure dozens of times; Blalock only once, as Vivien's assistant.

Nothing in the laboratory had prepared either one for what they saw when Blalock opened Eileen's chest. Her blood vessels weren't even half the size of those in the experimental animals used to develop the procedure, and they were full of the thick, dark, "blue" blood characteristic of cyanotic children. When Blalock exposed the pulmonary artery, then the subclavian—the two "pipes" he planned to reconnect—he turned to Thomas. "Will the subclavian reach the pulmonary once it's cut off and divided?" he asked. Thomas said it would.

Blalock's scalpel moved swiftly to the point of no return. He cut into the pulmonary artery, creating the opening into which he would sew the divided subclavian artery. "Is the incision long enough?" he asked Thomas. "Yes, if not too long," the reply came.

In and out of the arteries flashed the straight half-inch needle that Thomas had cut and sharpened. "Is this all right, Vivien?" Blalock asked as he began joining the smooth inner linings of the two arteries. Then, a moment later, with one or two sutures in place: "Are those bites close enough together?"

(continued)

NATIONAL MAGAZINE AWARD WINNER   CONTINUED

Thomas watched. In such small arteries, a fraction of a millimeter was critical, and the direction of the sutures determined whether the inside of the vessels would knit properly. If Blalock began a suture in the wrong direction, Thomas's voice would come quietly over his shoulder: "The other direction, Dr. Blalock."

Finally, off came the bulldog clamps that had stopped the flow of blood during the operation. The anastomosis began to function, shunting the pure blue blood through the pulmonary artery into the lungs to be oxygenated. Underneath the sterile drapes, Eileen turned pink.

"You've never seen anything so dramatic," Thomas says on the tape. "It was almost a miracle."

Almost overnight, Operating Room 706 became "the heart room," as dozens of Blue Babies and their parents came to Hopkins from all over the United States, then from abroad, spilling over into rooms on six floors of the hospital. For the next year, Blalock and Longmire rebuilt hearts virtually around the clock. One after another, cyanotic children who had never been able to sit upright began standing at their crib rails, pink and healthy.

It was the beginning of modern cardiac surgery, but to Thomas it looked like chaos. Blue Babies arrived daily, yet Hopkins had no cardiac ward, no catheterization lab, no sophisticated apparatus for blood studies. They had only Vivien Thomas, who flew from one end of the Hopkins complex to the other without appearing to hurry.

From his spot at Blalock's shoulder in the operating room, Thomas would race to the wards, where he would take arterial blood samples on the Blue Babies scheduled for surgery, hand off the samples to another technician in the hallway, return to the heart room for the next operation, head for the lab to begin the blood-oxygen studies, then go back to his spot in the OR.

"Only Vivien is to stand there," Blalock would tell anyone who moved into the space behind his right shoulder.

Each morning at 7:30, the great screened windows of Room 706 would be thrown open, the electric fan trained on Dr. Blalock, and the four-inch beam of the portable spotlight focused on the operating field. At the slightest movement of light or fan, Blalock would yell at top voice, at which point his orderly would readjust both.

Then the perspiring Professor would complete the procedure, venting his tension with a whine so distinctive that a generation of surgeons still imitate it. "Must I operate all alone? Won't *somebody* please help me?" he'd ask plaintively, stomping his soft white tennis shoes and looking around at the team standing ready to execute his every order. And lest Thomas look away, Blalock would plead over his shoulder, "Now you watch, Vivien, and don't let me put these sutures in wrong!"

Visitors had never seen anything like it. More than Blalock's whine, it was Thomas's presence that mystified the distinguished surgeons who came from all over the world to witness the operation. They could see that the black man on the stool behind Dr. Blalock was not an MD. He was not scrubbed in as an assistant, and he never touched the patients. Why did the famous doctor keep turning to him for advice?

If outsiders puzzled at Thomas's role, the surgical team took it as a matter of course. "Who else but Vivien could have answered those technical questions?" asks Dr. William Longmire, now professor emeritus at UCLA's School of Medicine. "Dr. Blalock was plowing new ground beyond the horizons we'd ever seen before. *Nobody* knew how to do this."

"It was a question of trust," says Dr. Alex Haller, who was trained by Thomas and now is surgeon-in-chief at Hopkins. Sooner or later, he says, all the stories circle back to that moment when Thomas and Blalock stood together in the operating room for the first Blue Baby. Had

Blalock not believed in Thomas's lab results with the tetralogy operation, he would never have dared to open Eileen Saxon's chest.

"Once Dr. Blalock accepted you as a colleague, he trusted you completely—I mean, *with his life,*" Haller says. After his patients, nothing mattered more to Blalock than his research and his "boys," as he called his residents. To Thomas he entrusted both and, in so doing, doubled his legacy.

"Dr. Blalock let us know in no uncertain terms, 'When Vivien speaks, he's speaking for me,'" remembers Dr. David Sabiston, who left Hopkins in 1964 to chair Duke University's department of surgery. "We revered him as we did our professor."

To Blalock's "boys," Thomas became the model of a surgeon. "Dr. Blalock was a great scientist, a great thinker, a leader," explains Denton Cooley, "but by no stretch of the imagination could he be considered a great cutting surgeon. Vivien was."

What passed from Thomas's hands to the surgical residents who would come to be known as "the Old Hands" was vascular surgery in the making—much of it of Thomas's making. He translated Blalock's concepts into reality, devising techniques, even entire operations, where none had existed.

In any other hospital, Thomas's functions as research consultant and surgical instruction might have been filled by as many as four specialists. Yet Thomas was always the patient teacher. And he never lost his sense of humor.

"I remember one time," says Haller, "when I was a medical student, I was working on a research project with a senior surgical resident who was a very slow operator. The procedure we were doing would ordinarily have taken an hour, but it had taken us six or seven hours, on this one dog that had been asleep all that time. There I was, in one position for hours, and I was about to die.

"Well, finally, the resident realized that the dog hadn't had any fluids intravenously, so he called over to Vivien, 'Vivien, would you come over and administer some I-V fluids?' Now, the whole time Vivien had been watching us out of the corner of his eye from across the lab, not saying a word, but not missing a thing, either. I must have looked white as a ghost, because when he came over with the I-V needle, he sat down at my foot, tugged at my pants leg, and said, 'Which leg shall I start the fluid in, Dr. Haller?'"

The man who tugged at Haller's pants leg administered one of the country's most sophisticated surgical research programs. "He was strictly no-nonsense about the way he ran that lab," Haller says. "Those dogs were treated like human patients."

One of the experimental animals, Anna, took on legendary status as the first long-term survivor of the Blue Baby operation, taking up permanent residence in the Old Hunterian as Thomas's pet. It was during "Anna's era," Haller says, that Thomas became surgeon-in-residence to the pets of Hopkins's faculty and staff. On Friday afternoons, Thomas opened the Old Hunterian to the pet owners of Baltimore and presided over an afternoon clinic, gaining as much prestige in the veterinary community as he enjoyed within the medical school. "Vivien knew all the senior vets in Baltimore," Haller explains, "and if they had a complicated surgical problem, they'd call on Vivien for advice, or simply ask him to operate on their animals."

By the late 1940s, the Old Hunterian had become "Vivien's domain," says Haller. "There was no doubt in anybody's mind as to who was in charge. Technically, a non-MD could not hold the position of laboratory supervisor. Dr. Blalock always had someone on the surgical staff nominally in charge, but it was Vivien who actually ran the place."

As quietly as he had come through Hopkins's door at Blalock's side, Thomas began bringing in other black men, moving them into the role he had first carved out for himself. To the black technicians he trained—twenty of them over three decades—he was "Mr. Thomas," a man who

(continued)

represented what they themselves might become. Two of the twenty went on to medical school, but most were men like Thomas, with only high school diplomas and no prospect of further education. Thomas trained them and sent them out with the Old Hands, who tried to duplicate the Blalock-Thomas magic in their own labs.

Perhaps none bears Thomas's imprint more than Raymond Lee, a former elevator operator who became the first non-MD to serve on Hopkins's cardiac surgical service as a physician's assistant. For the Hopkins cardiac team headed by Drs. Vincent Gott and Bruce Reitz, 1987 was a year of firsts, and Lee was part of both: In May, he assisted in a double heart-lung transplant, the first from a living donor; in August, he was a member of the Hopkins team that successfully separated Siamese twins.

Raymond Lee hasn't come into the hospital on his day off to talk about his role in those historic 1987 operations. He has come "to talk about Mr. Thomas," and as he does so, you begin to see why Alex Haller has described Lee as "another Vivien." Lee speaks so softly you have to strain to hear him above the din of the admitting room. "It's been almost 25 years," he says, "since Mr. Thomas got a hold of me in the elevator of the Halsted Building and asked me if I might be interested in becoming a laboratory assistant."

Along with surgical technique, Thomas imparted to his technicians his own philosophy. "Mr. Thomas would always tell us, 'Everybody's got a job to do. You are put here to do a job 100 percent, regardless of how much education you have.' He believed that if you met the right people at the right time, and you can prove yourself, then you can achieve what you were meant to do."

Alex Haller tells of another Thomas technician, a softspoken man named Alfred Casper: "After I'd completed my internship at Hopkins, I went to work in the lab at NIH. I was the only one in the lab, except for Casper. He had spent some time observing Vivien and working with him. We were operating together on one occasion, and we got into trouble with some massive bleeding in a pulmonary artery, which I was able to handle fairly well. Casper said to me, 'Dr. Haller, I was very much impressed with the way you handled yourself there.' Feeling overly proud of myself, I said to Casper, 'Well, I trained with Dr. Blalock.'

"A few weeks later, we were operating together in the lab for a second time, and we got into even worse trouble. I literally did not know what to do. Casper immediately took over, placed the clamps appropriately, and got us out of trouble. I turned to him at the end of it and said, 'I certainly appreciated the way you solved that problem. You handled your hands beautifully, too.'

"He looked me in the eye and said, 'I trained with Vivien.'"

Alfred Blalock and Vivien Thomas: Their names intertwine, their partnership overshadowing the individual legacies they handed down to dozens of Hallers and Caspers. For more than three decades, the partnership endured, as Blalock ascended to fame, built up young men in his own image, then became a proud but reluctant bystander as they rose to dominate the field he had created.

As close as Blalock was to his protégés, they moved on. It was Thomas who remained, the one constant. From the first, Thomas had seen the worst and the best of Blalock. Thomas knew the famous Blue Baby doctor the world could not see: a profoundly conscientious surgeon, devastated by patient mortality and keenly aware of his own limitations.

In 1950, six years after he and Blalock had stood together for Blue Baby One, Blalock operated on Blue Baby 1,000. It was a triumphant moment—an occasion that called for a Yousuf Karsh portrait, a surprise party at the Blalock home, gifts of Scotch and bourbon, and a long evening of reminiscing with the Old Hands. Thomas almost wasn't there.

As Blalock was laying plans for his 1947 "Blue Baby Tour" of Europe, Thomas was preparing to head back home to Nashville, for good. The problem was money. There was no provision in Hopkins's salary classification for an anomaly like Thomas: a non-degreed techni-cian with the responsibilities of a postdoctoral research fellow.

With no regret for the past, the 35-year-old Thomas took a hard look at the future and at his two daughters' prospects for earning the degrees that had eluded him. Weighing the Hopkins pay scale against the postwar building boom in Nashville, he decided to head south to build houses.

"It's a chance I have to take," he told Blalock. "I don't know what will happen if I leave Hopkins, but I know what will happen if I stay." He made no salary demands, but simply announced his intention to leave, assuming that Blalock would be powerless against the system.

Two days before Christmas 1946, Blalock came to Thomas in the empty lab with Hopkins's final salary offer, negotiated by Blalock and approved by the board of trustees that morning. "I hope you will accept this," he told Thomas, drawing a file card from his pocket. "It's the best I can do—it's all I can do."

The offer on the card left Thomas speechless: The trustees had doubled his salary and cre-ated a new bracket for non-degreed personnel deserving higher pay. From that moment, money ceased to be an issue.

Until Blalock's retirement in 1964, the two men continued their partnership. The harmony between the idea man and the detail man never faltered. Blalock took care of patients, Thomas took care of research. Only their rhythm changed.

In the hectic Blue Baby years, Blalock would leave his hospital responsibilities at the door of the Old Hunterian at noon and closet himself with Thomas for a five-minute research update. In the evenings, with Thomas's notes at one elbow and a glass of bourbon at the other, Blalock would phone Thomas from his study as he worked on scientific papers late into the night. "Vivien, I want you to listen to this," he'd say before reading two or three sentences from the pad in his lap, asking, "Is that your impression?" or "Is it all right if I say so-and-so?"

As the hectic pace of the late '40s slowed in the early '50s, the hurried noon visits and evening phone conversations gave way to long, relaxed exchanges through the open door between lab and office.

Along the way, Thomas and Blalock grew old together, Thomas gracefully, Blalock more reluctantly. Sidelined by deteriorating health, Blalock decided in the early 1950s that cardiac sur-gery was a young man's field, so he turned over the development of the heart-lung machine to two of his superstars, Drs. Henry Bahnson and Frank Spencer. Today Bahnson is chairman emer-itus of the department of surgery at the University of Pittsburgh Medical Center, and Spencer chairs the department of surgery at New York University.

Blalock told Thomas, "Let's face it, Vivien, we're getting older. These young fellows can do a much better job than I can. There's no point in my beating myself out with them around. They're good."

But fifteen years at center stage had made it hard for Blalock to be a bystander. At the end of the 1950s, he fumed as pilot projects fizzled and he and Thomas fell to philosophizing about problems instead of solving them. "Damn it, Vivien," he complained, "we must be getting old. We talk ourselves out of doing anything. Let's do things like we used to and find out what happens."

"You were lucky to have hit the jackpot twice," Thomas answered, remembering that the good old days were, more often than not, sixteen-hour days. Besides, it was Blalock, 60 years old, recently widowed and in failing health, who was feeling old, not Thomas, then only 49. Per-haps Blalock was remembering what it had been like when he was 30 and Thomas 19, juggling a dozen research projects, working into the night, trying to "find out what happens." By including Thomas in his own decline, Blalock was acknowledging something deeper than chronology: a common beginning.

(continued)

NATIONAL MAGAZINE AWARD WINNER   CONTINUED

From beginning to end, Thomas and Blalock maintained a delicate balance of closeness and distance. A few weeks before Blalock's retirement in 1964, they closed out their partnership just as they had begun it—facing each other on two lab stools. It was Thomas who made the first move toward cutting the ties, but in the act of releasing Blalock from obligation he acknowledged how inextricably their fortunes were intertwined.

"I don't know how you feel about it," he said as Blalock mulled over post-retirement offers from around the country, "but I'd just as soon you not include me in any of those plans. I feel as independent as I did in our earlier years, and I want you to be just as free in making your plans."

"Thank you, Vivien," Blalock said, then admitted he had no idea where he would go or what he would do after his retirement. "If you don't stay at Hopkins," he told Thomas, "you'll be able to write your own ticket, wherever you want to go."

"Thanks for the compliment," Thomas smiled, "but I've been here for so long I don't know what's going on in the outside world."

Weeks after the last research project had been ended, Blalock and Thomas made one final trip to the "heart room"—not the Room 706 of the early days, but a glistening new surgical suite Blalock had built with money from the now well-filled coffers of the department of surgery. The Old Hunterian, too, had been replaced by a state-of-the-art research facility.

By this time, Blalock was dying of ureteral cancer. Wearing a back brace as a result of a disc operation, he could barely stand. Down the seventh-floor hallway of the Alfred Blalock Clinical Sciences Building they went: the white-haired Professor in his wheelchair; the tall, erect black man slowly pushing him while others rushed past them into the operating rooms.

Just before they reached the exit from the main corridor to the rotunda where Blalock's portrait hung, he asked Thomas to stop so that he could get out of his wheelchair. He would walk out into the rotunda alone, he insisted.

"Seeing that he was unable to stand erect," Thomas recalled later, "I asked if he wanted me to accompany him to the front of the hospital. His reply was, 'No, don't.' I watched as with an almost 45-degree stoop and obviously in pain, he slowly disappeared through the exit."

Blalock died three months later.

During his final illness Blalock said to a colleague: "I should have found a way to send Vivien to medical school." It was the last time he would voice that sense of unfulfilled obligation.

Time and again, to one or another of his residents, Blalock had faulted himself for not helping Thomas to get a medical degree. Each time, remembers Dr. Henry Bahnson, "he'd comfort himself by saying that Vivien was doing famously what he did well, and that he had come a long way with Blalock's help."

But Thomas had not come the whole way. He had been Blalock's "other hands" in the lab, had enhanced The Professor's stature, had shaped dozens of dexterous surgeons as Blalock himself could not have—but a price had been paid, and Blalock knew it.

Blalock's guilt was in no way diminished by his knowing that even with a medical degree, Thomas stood little chance of achieving the prominence of an Old Hand. His prospects in the medical establishment of the 1940s were spelled out by the only woman among Blalock's "boys," Dr. Rowena Spencer, a pediatric surgeon who as a medical student worked closely with Thomas.

In her commentary on Thomas's career, published this year in *A Century of Black Surgeons,* Spencer puts to rest the question that Blalock wrestled with decades earlier. "It must have been said many times," Spencer writes, "that 'if only' Vivien had had a proper medical education he might have accomplished a great deal more, but the truth of the matter is that as a black physician in that era, he would probably have had to spend all his time and energy making a living among an economically deprived black population."

What neither Blalock nor Thomas could see as they parted company in June 1964 in the seventh-floor hallway of the Blalock Building was the rich recognition that would come to Thomas with the changing times.

It was the admiration and affection of the men he trained that Thomas valued most. Year after year, the Old Hands came back to visit, one at a time, and on February 27, 1971, all at once. From across the country they arrived, packing the Hopkins auditorium to present the portrait they had commissioned of "our colleague, Vivien Thomas."

For the first time in 41 years, Thomas stood at center stage, feeling "quite humble," he said, "but at the same time, just a little bit proud." He rose to thank the distinguished gathering, his smiling presence contrasting with the serious, bespectacled Vivien Thomas in the portrait.

"You all have got me working on the operator's side of the table this morning," he told the standing-room-only audience. "It's always just a few degrees warmer on the operator's side than it is on his assistant's when you get into the operating room!"

Thomas's portrait was hung opposite The Professor's in the lobby of the Blalock Building, almost 30 years from the day in 1941 that he and Blalock had come to Hopkins from Vanderbilt. Thomas, surprised that his portrait had been painted at all, said he was "astounded" by its placement. But it was the words of hospital president Dr. Russell Nelson that hit home: "There are all sorts of degrees and diplomas and certificates, but nothing equals recognition by your peers."

Five years later, the recognition of Vivien Thomas's achievements was complete when Johns Hopkins awarded him an honorary doctorate and an appointment to the medical-school faculty.

Thomas's wife, Clara, still refers to her husband's autobiography by Vivien's title, *Presentation of a Portrait: The Story of a Life,* even though when it appeared in print two days after his death in 1985, it bore the more formal title of *Pioneering Research in Surgical Shock and Cardiovascular Surgery: Vivien Thomas and His Work with Alfred Blalock.* It is to her that the book is dedicated, and it was in her arms that he died, 52 years after their marriage.

Clara Thomas speaks proudly of her husband's accomplishments, and matter-of-factly about the recognition that came late in his career. "After all, he could have worked all those years and gotten nothing at all," she says, looking at the Hopkins diploma hanging in a corner of his study. "Vivien Theodore Thomas, Doctor of Laws," it reads, a quiet reminder of the thunderous ovation Thomas received when he stood in his gold-and-sable academic robe on May 21, 1976, for the awarding of the degree. "The applause was so great that I felt very small," Thomas wrote.

It is not Thomas's diploma that guests first see when they visit the family's home, but row upon row of children's and grandchildren's graduation pictures. Lining the walls of the living room, two generations in caps and gowns tell the story of the degrees that mattered more to Thomas than the one he gave up and the one he finally received.

At the Thomas home, the signs of Vivien's hands are everywhere: in the backyard rose garden, the mahogany mantelpiece he made from an old piano top, the Victorian sofa he upholstered, the quilt his mother made from a design he had drawn when he was nine years old.

The book was the last work of Vivien Thomas's life, and probably the most difficult. It was the Old Hands' relentless campaign that finally convinced Vivien to turn his boxes of notes and files into an autobiography. He began writing just after his retirement in 1979, working through his illness with pancreatic cancer, indexing the book from his hospital bed following surgery, and putting it to rest, just before his death, with a 1985 copyright date.

(continued)

NATIONAL MAGAZINE AWARD WINNER   CONTINUED

Clara Thomas turns to the last page of the book, to a picture of Vivien standing with two young men, one a medical student, the other a cardiac surgeon. It was the surgeon whom Clara Thomas and her daughters asked to speak at Vivien's funeral.

He is Dr. Levi Watkins, and the diplomas on his office wall tell a story. Watkins was an honors graduate of Tennessee State, the first black graduate of Vanderbilt University Medical School, and Johns Hopkins's first black cardiac resident. Levi Watkins Jr. is everything Vivien Thomas might have been had he been born 40 years later.

That was what he and Thomas talked about the day they met in the hospital cafeteria, a few weeks after Watkins had come to Hopkins as an intern in 1971. "You're the man in the picture," he had said. And Thomas had smiled and invited him up to his office.

"He was so modest that I had to keep asking him, 'What did you do to get your picture on the wall?' " says Watkins of his first meeting with a man who was for fourteen years "a colleague, a counselor, a friend."

"Even though I only knew him a fraction of the time some of the other surgeons did, I felt very close to him. From the very beginning, there was this deeper bond between us: I knew that he had been where I had been, and I had been where he could not go."

Both men were aware that their differences ran deep: Watkins, whose exposure to the early civil-rights movement as a parishioner of the Reverend Martin Luther King Jr. had taught him to be "out front and vocal about minority participation"; and Thomas, whose upbringing in Louisiana and Tennessee in the early years of the century had taught him the opposite.

"I think Vivien admired what I did," says Watkins, "but he knew that we were different. There was a generation's difference between Vivien and me, and it was a big generation. Survival was a much stronger element in his background. Vivien was a trailblazer by his work."

Watkins holds part of Thomas's legacy in his hand as he speaks, a metal box called an Automatic Implantable Defibrillator. No larger than a cigarette package, Watkins's AID is deceptively simple-looking. From inside a patient's body, it monitors the heartbeat, shocking the heart back into normal rhythm each time it fibrillates.

"It was Vivien who helped me to work through the problems of testing this thing in the dog lab," says Watkins, turning the little half-pound "heart shocker" in his hand and running his fingers along its two electrode wires. "It was my first research project when I joined the medical faculty, and Vivien's last." Only months after Thomas's retirement in 1979, Watkins performed the first human implantation of the AID, winning a place in the long line of Hopkins cardiac pioneers.

But more than science passed from man to man over fourteen years. In the 60-year-old Thomas, the 26-year-old Watkins found a man with the ability to transcend times and the circumspection to live within them. In their long talks in Thomas's office, the young surgeon remembers that "he taught me to take the broad view, to try to understand Hopkins and its perspective on race. He talked about how powerful Hopkins was, how traditional. He was concerned with my being too political and antagonizing the people I had to work with. He would check on me from time to time, just to make sure everything was all right. He worried about my getting out there alone."

It was "fatherly advice," Watkins says fondly, "from a man who knew what it was like to be the only one." When Thomas retired, one era ended and another began, for that was the year that Levi Watkins joined the medical-school admissions committee. Within four years, minority enrollment quadrupled. "When Vivien saw the number of black medical students increasing so dramatically, he was happy—*he was happy,*" says Watkins.

Always one for gentle statements, Thomas celebrated the changing times on the last page of his book: Thomas is shown standing proudly next to Levi Watkins and a third-year medical student named Reginald Davis, who is holding his infant son. According to the caption, the photograph was taken in 1979 in front of the hospital's Broadway entrance. But the true message lies in what the caption does not say: In 1941, the Broadway entrance was for whites only.

Had the photograph been taken eight years later, it might have included Thomas's nephew, Koco Eaton, a 1987 graduate of the Johns Hopkins Medical School, trained as a sub-intern in surgery by the men his uncle had trained a generation earlier. Thomas did not live to see his nephew graduate, but he rejoiced at his admission. "I remember Vivien coming to me in my office," says Watkins, "and telling me how much it meant to him to have all the doors open for Koco that had been closed to him."

Up and down the halls of Hopkins, Koco Eaton turned heads—not because he was black, but because he was the nephew of Vivien Thomas.

It was on a summer afternoon in 1928 that Vivien Thomas says he learned the standard of perfection that won him so much esteem. He was just out of high school, working on the Fisk University maintenance crew to earn money for his college tuition. He had spent all morning fixing a piece of worn flooring in one of the faculty houses. Shortly after noon, the foreman came by to inspect.

"He took one look," Thomas remembered, "and said, 'Thomas, that won't do. I can tell you put it in.' Without another word, he turned and left. I was stung, but I replaced the piece of flooring. This time I could barely discern which piece I had put in. . . . Several days later the foreman said to me, 'Thomas, you could have fixed that floor right in the first place.' I knew that I had already learned the lesson which I still remember and try to adhere to: Whatever you do, always do your best. . . . I never had to repeat or redo another assignment."

So it went for more than half a century. "The Master," Rollins Hanlon called him the day he presented Thomas's portrait on behalf of the Old Hands. Hanlon, the surgeon and scholar, spoke of Thomas's hands, and of the man who was greater still; of the synergy of two great men, Thomas and Blalock.

Today, in heavy gilt frames, those two men silently look at each other from opposite walls of the Blalock Building, just as one morning 40 years ago they stood in silence at Hopkins. Thomas had surprised The Professor with an operation he had conceived, then kept secret until healing was completed. The first and only one conceived entirely by Thomas, it was a complex but now common operation called an atrial septectomy.

Using a canine model, he had found a way to improve circulation in patients whose great vessels were transposed. The problem had stymied Blalock for months, and now it seemed that Thomas had solved it.

"Neither he nor I spoke for some four or five minutes while he stood there examining the heart, running the tip of his finger back and forth through the moderate-size defect in the atrial septum, feeling the healed edges of the defect. . . . We examined the outside of the heart and found the suture line with most of the silk still intact. This was the only evidence that an incision had been made in the heart.

"Internal healing of the incision was without flaw. The sutures could not be seen from within, and on gross examination the edges of the defect were smooth and covered with endocardium. Dr. Blalock finally broke the silence by asking, 'Vivien, are you sure you did this?' I answered in the affirmative, and then after a pause he said, 'Well, this looks like something the Lord made.'"

Source: © 1989. *The Washingtonian.* Reprinted by permission of the author.

As magazine articles go, McCabe's piece is fairly long, running almost 9,500 words. But when one considers that the article covers a time span of over 50 years, the length is hardly excessive. With so much material to choose from, the writer's selectivity presents an unusual opportunity to study how such choices are made effectively.

What McCabe chooses to leave out is as interesting as what she leaves in. "Like Something the Lord Made" follows Thomas's professional life from 1930, when he was 19, to his death in 1985, and it gives almost no information about his formative years. The reader is left to wonder what motivated an economically disadvantaged youth in the tough times of the 1920s and 1930s to aspire to work his way through college and medical school. Indeed, even to hope. Like much excellent writing, the article leaves this and other questions unanswered, thereby leaving the reader wanting to know more. But McCabe wasn't writing a book-length biography; she was writing an article, and her focus stays steadily on Thomas's career.

Take another example: The reader learns from a casual reference in the article's ninth paragraph that Thomas's lab specialty was canine vivisection—as this chapter has indicated, a topic that is highly controversial. The final anecdote, from which the article's title was taken, describes a surgical procedure called atrial septectomy, which Thomas invented in the lab and presented to Blalock only after a healed heart could be carefully examined.

Okay, whose heart? That of a "canine model," the reader is told. How was the heart made available to Blalock for examination? Elementary, dear Watson. Thomas used a dog for surgical experimentation, allowed it time to heal, then killed it and removed the heart for Blalock to look at. Some dog owners may cringe at reading about it, but McCabe refuses to get sidetracked from her main topic. She's not writing about animal-rights activists or the ethics of using animals in the heart research that has led to saving human lives. She's writing about one extraordinary person, and she sticks to the point, telling the reader as little about "Annie," a lab dog, as she does about "Eileen," the first baby on whom Thomas's new surgical techniques were tried. Space limitations and maintenance of focus help guide such decisions about selectivity.

Much of writing is a nuts-and-bolts process, and other technical points in McCabe's article are well worth pointing out. Why, for example, run up the word count in the lead by describing a mere telephone interview? Throughout the article, why interweave comments about the late Mr. Thomas from other notable surgeons? Because this warm praise assures the reader not only that Vivien Thomas was an unusual person, but also that Thomas's teachings remain highly influential. Note also McCabe's initial use of the present tense, to which she reverts throughout the article when she quotes other people who knew Thomas, although most of the story of his life is given chronologically in the past tense. The present tense would not have been chosen by many writers, but they would have sacrificed the emphasis such a tense permits on Thomas's ongoing influence, not to mention the sense of immediacy that present tense just naturally lends to article writing.

One other technical point is also worth noticing—the use of Thomas's name. Custom, consistency and avoidance of reader confusion prompt most writers to use their subjects' full names on first reference, then refer to them by last names thereafter. On first reference, of course, McCabe uses Vivien Thomas. Yet on second reference, she uses Vivien, and refers to him as Thomas when she starts describing his life. All three usages thread through the copy. Just sloppy writing? Hardly. The triple name choice allows

McCabe's interviewees to refer to Thomas as they habitually did, without confusing the readers.

Although savvy use of technical points is an important part of writing, another element is inspiration. As McCabe says, writing about Vivien Thomas was "a labor of love." In her *Washingtonian* article, she introduced to a wide public the life of a person who was largely unknown outside the field of medical science—and what an inspiring life it was.

The next article is also a posthumous profile, but it contrasts starkly in subject matter with McCabe's article. Watch how it's developed.

Although it has been suggested in this chapter that the typical magazine article differs from its newspaper cousin in a number of ways—including longer paragraphs, leisurely leads, more extensive research, brighter polish and wider scope—no dramatic line is drawn to delineate the two journalistic forms. In fact, many newspaper features could easily appear in magazines, and many magazine articles could just as easily appear in newspapers.

An excellent example of this crossover is the article "Death of a Playmate," written by Teresa Carpenter about the shocking death of Dorothy Stratten, a *Playboy* favorite. It was one of three stories that, as a package, won Carpenter the 1981 Pulitzer feature-writing award. "Death of a Playmate" and the other two stories—one dealing with the murder of a Long Island housewife and the other with the killing of a prominent politician—were all written for New York City's weekly newspaper *The Village Voice.*

"Death of a Playmate" required about four weeks for information gathering, Carpenter says, then some break time to digest the material and another week to write. Like the Vivien Thomas story, facts were hard to gather. Playmate Dorothy Stratten and her husband, Paul Snider, were dead. The other principals were guarded or not talking at all. Still, Carpenter persevered and drew her materials together, including a critical coroner's report, and interviewed those who could and would talk.

"I try to take stories with the idea of doing them whether the principals will cooperate or not," Carpenter says. "Generally, you can do a good profile of someone who refuses to cooperate simply by talking to everyone around. You might do a better profile than relying exclusively upon a single source. So access is a tricky thing."

Once she got the coroner's report, she says, access became somewhat easier. "That's when I got the Hugh Hefner interview. Things started to fall into place."

Carpenter's splendidly crafted "Death of a Playmate" is a newspaper feature. It's also a magazine article—an excellent magazine article that happens to have been published in a newspaper. Studying it will help explain the nature of a magazine article and may illuminate the crossover similarities between the two journalistic forms.

A word of warning: "Death of a Playmate" contains some strong language and some graphic writing. It is not a story for the delicate in nature. If your tolerance level is low, you may wish to skip on to the next entry. For those of you hardy enough to read on, your rewards will be numerous. Carpenter's Prize-winning "Death of a Playmate" is at once grotesque, disquieting, repellent, shocking—and utterly fascinating.

PULITZER PRIZE WINNER

TERESA CARPENTER

DEATH OF A PLAYMATE

It is shortly past four in the afternoon and Hugh Hefner glides wordlessly into the library of his Playboy Mansion West. He is wearing pajamas and looking somber in green silk. The incongruous spectacle of a sybarite in mourning. To date, his public profession of grief has been contained in a press release: "The death of Dorothy Stratten comes as a shock to us all. . . . As Playboy's Playmate of the Year with a film and television career of increasing importance, her professional future was a bright one. But equally sad to us is the fact that her loss takes from us all a very special member of the Playboy family."

That's all. A dispassionate eulogy from which one might conclude that Miss Stratten died in her sleep of pneumonia. One, certainly, which masked the turmoil her death created within the Organization. During the morning hours after Stratten was found nude in a West Los Angeles apartment, her face blasted away by 12-gauge buckshot, editors scrambled to pull her photos from the upcoming October issue. It could not be done. The issues were already run. So they pulled her ethereal blond image from the cover of the 1981 Playmate Calendar and promptly scrapped a Christmas promotion featuring her posed in the buff with Hefner. Other playmates, of course, have expired violently. Wilhelmina Rietveld took a massive overdose of barbiturates in 1973. Claudia Jennings, known as "Queen of the B-Movies," was crushed to death last fall in her Volkswagen convertible. Both caused grief and chagrin to the self-serious "family" of playmates whose aura does not admit the possibility of shaving nicks and bladder infections, let alone death.

But the loss of Dorothy Stratten sent Hefner and his family into seclusion, at least from the press. For one thing, Playboy has been earnestly trying to avoid any bad national publicity that might threaten its application for a casino license in Atlantic City. But beyond that, Dorothy Stratten was a corporate treasure. She was not just any playmate but the "Eighties' first Playmate of the Year" who, as Playboy trumpeted in June, was on her way to becoming "one of the few emerging film goddesses of the new decade."

She gave rise to extravagant comparisons with Marilyn Monroe, although unlike Monroe, she was no cripple. She was delighted with her success and wanted more of it. Far from being brutalized by Hollywood, she was coddled by it. Her screen roles were all minor ones. A fleeting walk-on as a bunny in *Americathon*. A small running part as a roller nymph in *Skatetown U.S.A.* She played the most perfect woman in the universe in an episode of *Buck Rogers in the 25th Century* and the most perfect robot in the galaxy in a B-grade spoof called *Galaxina*. She was surely more successful in a shorter period of time than any other playmate in the history of the empire. "Playboy has not really had a star," says Stratten's erstwhile agent David Wilder. "They thought she was going to be the biggest thing they ever had."

No wonder Hefner grieves.

"The major reason that I'm . . . that we're both sittin' here," says Hefner, "that I wanted to talk about it, is because there is still a great tendency . . . for this thing to fall into the classic cliche of 'small-town girl comes to Playboy, comes to Hollywood, life in the fast lane,' and that somehow was related to her death. And that is not what really happened. A very sick guy saw his meal ticket and his connection to power, whatever, etc. slipping away. And it was that that made him kill her."

The "very sick guy" is Paul Snider, Dorothy Stratten's husband, the man who became her mentor. He is the one who plucked her from a Dairy Queen in Vancouver, British Columbia, and pushed her into the path of Playboy during the Great Playmate Hunt in 1978. Later, as she moved out of his class, he became a millstone, and Stratten's prickliest problem was not coping with celebrity but discarding a husband she had outgrown. When Paul Snider balked at being discarded, he became her nemesis. And on August 14 of this year he apparently took her life and his own with a 12-gauge shotgun.

It is not so difficult to see why Snider became an embarrassment. Since the murder he has been excoriated by Hefner and others as a cheap hustler, but such moral indignation always rings a little false in Hollywood. Snider's main sin was that he lacked scope.

Snider grew up in Vancouver's East End, a tough area of the city steeped in machismo. His parents split up when he was a boy and he had to fend for himself from the time he quit school in the seventh grade. Embarrassed by being skinny, he took up body building in his late teens and within a year had fleshed out his upper torso. His dark hair and mustache were groomed impeccably and women on the nightclub circuit found him attractive. The two things it seemed he could never get enough of were women and money. For a time he was the successful promoter of automobile and 'cycle shows at the Pacific National Exhibition. But legitimate enterprises didn't bring him enough to support his expensive tastes and he took to procuring. He wore mink, drove a black Corvette, and flaunted a bejeweled Star of David around his neck. About town he was known as the Jewish Pimp.

Among the heavy gang types in Vancouver, the Rounder Crowd, Paul Snider was regarded with scorn. A punk who always seemed to be missing the big score. "He never touched [the drug trade]," said one Rounder who knew him then. "Nobody trusted him that much and he was scared to death of drugs. He finally lost a lot of money to loan sharks and the Rounder Crowd hung him by his ankles from the 30th floor of a hotel. He had to leave town."

Snider split for Los Angeles where he acquired a gold limousine and worked his girls on the fringes of Beverly Hills. He was enamored of Hollywood's dated appeal and styled his girls to conform with a 1950s notion of glamour. At various times he toyed with the idea of becoming a star, or perhaps even a director or a producer. He tried to pry his way into powerful circles, but without much success. At length he gave up pimping because the girls weren't bringing him enough income—one had stolen some items and had in fact cost him money—and when he returned to Vancouver some time in 1977 Snider resolved to keep straight. For one thing, he was terrified of going to jail. He would kill himself, he once told a girl, before he would go to jail.

But Paul Snider never lost the appraising eye of a pimp. One night early in 1978 he and a friend dropped in an East Vancouver Dairy Queen and there he first took notice of Dorothy Ruth Hoogstraten filling orders behind the counter. She was very tall with the sweet natural looks of a girl, but she moved like a mature woman. Snider turned to his friend and observed, "That girl could make me a lot of money." He got Dorothy's number from another waitress and called her at home. She was 18.

Later when she recalled their meeting Dorothy would feign amused exasperation at Paul's overtures. He was brash, lacking altogether in finesse. But he appealed to her, probably because he was older by nine years and streetwise. He offered to take charge of her and that was nice. Her father, a Dutch immigrant, had left the family when she was very young. Dorothy had floated along like a particle in a solution. There had never been enough money to buy nice things. And

(continued)

PULITZER PRIZE WINNER   CONTINUED

now Paul bought her clothes. He gave her a topaz ring set in diamonds. She could escape to his place, a posh apartment with skylights, plants, and deep burgundy furniture. He would buy wine and cook dinner. Afterwards he'd fix hot toddies and play the guitar for her. In public he was an obnoxious braggart; in private he could be a vulnerable, cuddly Jewish boy.

Paul Snider knew the gaping vanity of a young girl. Before he came along Dorothy had had only one boyfriend. She had thought of herself as "plain with big hands." At 16, her breasts swelled into glorious lobes, but she never really knew what to do about them. She was a shy, comely, undistinguished teenager who wrote sophomoric poetry and had no aspirations other than landing a secretarial job. When Paul told her she was beautiful, she unfolded in the glow of his compliments and was infected by his ambitions for her.

Snider probably never worked Dorothy as a prostitute. He recognized that she was, as one observer put it, "class merchandise" that could be groomed to better advantage. He had tried to promote other girls as playmates, notably a stripper in 1974, but without success. He had often secured recycled playmates or bunnies to work his auto shows and had seen some get burnt out on sex and cocaine, languishing because of poor management. Snider dealt gingerly with Dorothy's inexperience and broke her in gradually. After escorting her to her graduation dance— he bought her a ruffled white gown for the occasion—he took her to a German photographer named Uwe Meyer for her first professional portrait. She looked like a flirtatious virgin.

About a month later, Snider called Meyer again, this time to do a nude shooting at Snider's apartment. Meyer arrived with a hairdresser to find Dorothy a little nervous. She clung, as she later recalled, to a scarf or a blouse as a towline to modesty, but she fell quickly into playful postures. She was perfectly pliant.

"She was eager to please," recalls Meyer. "I hesitated to rearrange her breasts thinking it might upset her, but she said, 'Do whatever you like.'"

Meyer hoped to get the $1000 finder's fee that *Playboy* routinely pays photographers who discover playmates along the byways and backwaters of the continent. But Snider, covering all bets, took Dorothy to another photographer named Ken Honey who had an established track-record with *Playboy*. Honey had at first declined to shoot Dorothy because she was underage and needed a parent's signature on a release. Dorothy, who was reluctant to tell anyone at home about the nude posing, finally broke the news to her mother and persuaded her to sign. Honey sent his set of shots to Los Angeles and was sent a finder's fee. In August 1978, Dorothy flew to Los Angeles for test shots. It was the first time she had ever been on a plane.

Even to the most cynical sensibilities, there is something miraculous about the way Hollywood took to Dorothy Hoogstraten. In a city overpopulated with beautiful women—most of them soured and disillusioned by 25—Dorothy caught some current fortune and floated steadily upward through the spheres of that indifferent paradise. Her test shots were superb, placing her among the 16 top contenders for the 25th Anniversary Playmate. And although she lost out to Candy Loving, she was named Playmate of the Month for August 1979. As soon as he learned of her selection, Paul Snider, by Hefner's account at least, flew to Los Angeles and proposed. They did not marry right away but set up housekeeping in a modest apartment in West Los Angeles. It was part of Snider's grand plan that Dorothy should support them both. She was, however, an alien and had no green card. Later, when it appeared her fortunes were on the rise during the fall of 1979, Hefner would personally intervene to secure her a temporary work permit. In the meantime, she was given a job as bunny at the Century City Playboy Club. The Organization took care of her. It recognized a good thing. While other playmates required cosmetic surgery on breasts or scars, Stratten was nearly perfect. There was a patch of adolescent acne on her forehead and a round birthmark on her left hip, but nothing serious. Her most troublesome flaw was a tendency to get plump, but that was controlled through passionate exercise. The only initial change Playboy deemed necessary was trimming her shoulder-length blond hair. And the cumbersome "Hoogstraten" became "Stratten."

Playboy photographers had been so impressed by the way Dorothy photographed that a company executive called agent David Wilder of Barr-Wilder Associates. Wilder, who handled the film careers of other playmates, agreed to meet Dorothy for coffee.

"A quality like Dorothy Stratten's comes by once in a lifetime," says Wilder with the solemn exaggeration that comes naturally after a tragedy. "She was exactly what this town likes, a beautiful girl who could act."

More to the point she had at least one trait to meet any need. When Lorimar Productions wanted a "playmate type" for a bit role in *Americathon,* Wilder sent Dorothy. When Columbia wanted a beauty who could skate for *Skatetown* Wilder sent Dorothy, who could skate like an ace. A happy skill in Hollywood. When the producers of *Buck Rogers* and later *Galaxina* asked simply for a woman who was so beautiful that no one could deny it, Wilder sent Dorothy. And once Dorothy got in the door, it seemed that no one could resist her.

During the spring of 1979, Dorothy was busy modeling or filming. One photographer recalls, "She was green, but took instruction well." From time to time, however, she would have difficulty composing herself on the set. She asked a doctor for a prescription of Valium. It was the adjustments, she explained, and the growing hassles with Paul.

Since coming to L.A., Snider had been into some deals of his own, most of them legal but sleazy. He had promoted exotic male dancers at a local disco, a wet underwear contest near Santa Monica, and wet T-shirt contests in the San Fernando Valley. But his chief hopes rested with Dorothy. He reminded her constantly that the two of them had what he called "a lifetime bargain" and he pressed her to marry him. Dorothy was torn by indecision. Friends tried to dissuade her from marrying, saying it could hold back her career, but she replied, "He cares for me so much. He's always there when I need him. I can't ever imagine myself being with any other man but Paul."

They were married in Las Vegas on June 1, 1979, and the following month Dorothy returned to Canada for a promotional tour of the provinces. Paul did not go with her because Playboy wanted the marriage kept secret. In Vancouver, Dorothy was greeted like a minor celebrity. The local press, a little caustic but mainly cowed, questioned her obliquely about exploitation. "I see the pictures as nudes, like nude paintings," she said. "They are not made for people to fantasize about." Her family and Paul's family visited her hotel, highly pleased with her success. Her first film was about to be released. The August issue was already on the stands featuring her as a pouting nymph who wrote poetry. (A few plodding iambs were even reprinted.) And she was going to *star* in a new Canadian film by North American Pictures called *Autumn Born.*

Since the murder, not much has been made of this film, probably because it contained unpleasant overtones of bondage. Dorothy played the lead, a 17-year-old rich orphan who is kidnapped and abused by her uncle. Dorothy was excited about the role, although she conceded to a Canadian reporter, "a lot [of it] is watching this girl get beat up."

While Dorothy was being pummeled on the set of *Autumn Born,* Snider busied himself apartment hunting. They were due for a rent raise and were looking to share a place with a doctor friend, a young internist who patronized the Century City Playboy Club. Paul found a two-story Spanish style stucco house near the Santa Monica Freeway in West L.A. There was a living room upstairs as well as a bedroom which the doctor claimed. Paul and Dorothy moved into the second bedroom downstairs at the back of the house. Since the doctor spent many nights with his girl-friend, the Sniders had the house much to themselves.

(continued)

PULITZER PRIZE WINNER   CONTINUED

Paul had a growing obsession with Dorothy's destiny. It was, of course, his own. He furnished the house with her photographs, and got plates reading "Star–80" for his new Mercedes. He talked about her as the next Playmate of the Year, the next Marilyn Monroe. When he had had a couple of glasses of wine, he would croon, "We're on a rocket ship to the moon." When they hit it big, he said, they would move to Bel-Air Estates where the big producers live.

Dorothy was made uncomfortable by his grandiosity. He was putting her, she confided to friends, in a position where she could not fail without failing them both. But she did not complain to him. They had, after all, a lifetime bargain, and he had brought her a long way.

As her manager he provided the kind of cautionary coaching that starlets rarely receive. He would not let her smoke. He monitored her drinking, which was moderate at any rate. He would have allowed her a little marijuana and cocaine under his supervision, but she showed no interest in drugs, save Valium. Mainly he warned her to be wary of the men she met at the Mansion, men who would promise her things, then use her up. Snider taught her how to finesse a come-on. How to turn a guy down without putting him off. Most important, he discussed with her who she might actually have to sleep with. Hefner, of course, was at the top of the list.

Did Hefner sleep with Dorothy Stratten? Mansion gossips who have provided graphic narratives of Hefner's encounters with other playmates cannot similarly document a tryst with Dorothy. According to the bizarre code of the Life—sexual society at the Mansion—fucking Hefner is a strictly voluntary thing. It never hurts a career, but Hefner, with so much sex at his disposal, would consider it unseemly to apply pressure.

Of Stratten, Hefner says, "There was a friendship between us. It wasn't romantic. . . . This was not a very loose lady."

Hefner likes to think of himself as a "father figure" to Stratten who, when she decided to marry, came to tell him about it personally. "She knew I had serious reservations about [Snider]," says Hefner. "I had sufficient reservations . . . that I had him checked out in terms of a possible police record in Canada. . . . We didn't get anything. . . . I used the word—and I realized the [risk] I was taking—I said to her that he had a 'pimp-like quality' about him."

Like most playmate husbands, Snider was held at arm's length by the Playboy family. He was only rarely invited to the Mansion, which bothered him, as he would have liked more of an opportunity to cultivate Hefner. And Stratten, who was at the Mansion more frequently to party and roller-skate, was never actively into the Life. Indeed, she spoke disdainfully of the "whores" who serviced Hefner's stellar guests. Yet she moved into the circle of Hefner's distinguished favorites when it became apparent that she might have a real future in film.

Playboy, contrary to the perception of aspiring starlets, is not a natural conduit to stardom. Most playmates who go into movies peak with walk-ons and fade away. Those whom Hefner has tried most earnestly to promote in recent years have been abysmal flops. Barbi Benton disintegrated into a jiggling loon and, according to Playboy sources, Hefner's one time favorite Sondra Theodore went wooden once the camera started to roll.

"Dorothy was important," says one Playboy employee, "because Hefner is regarded by Hollywood as an interloper. They'll come to his parties and play his games. But they won't give him respect. One of the ways he can gain legitimacy is to be a star maker."

There is something poignant about Hefner, master of an empire built on inanimate nudes, but unable to coax those lustrous forms to life on film. His chief preoccupation nowadays is managing the playmates. Yet with all of those beautiful women at his disposal, he has not one Marion Davies to call his own. Dorothy exposed that yearning, that ego weakness, as surely as she revealed the most pathetic side of her husband's nature—his itch for the big score. Hefner simply had more class.

Dorothy's possibilities were made manifest to him during *The Playboy Roller Disco and Pajama Party* taped at the Mansion late in October 1978. Dorothy had a running part and was tremendously appealing.

"Some people have that quality," says Hefner. "I mean . . . there is something that comes from inside. . . . The camera comes so close that it almost looks beneath the surface and . . . that magic is there somehow in the eyes . . . That magic she had. That was a curious combination of sensual appeal and vulnerability."

After the special was aired on television in November, Dorothy's career accelerated rapidly. There was a rush of appearances that left the accumulating impression of stardom. Around the first of December her *Fantasy Island* episode appeared. Later that month, *Buck Rogers in the 25th Century.* But the big news of the season was that Hefner had chosen Dorothy Playmate of the Year for 1980. Although her selection was not announced to the public until April, she began photo sessions with Playboy photographer Mario Casilli before the year was out.

Her look was altered markedly from that of the sultry minx in the August issue. As Playmate of the Year her image was more defined. No more pouting, soft-focus shots. Stratten was given a burnished high glamour. Her hair fell in the crimped undulating waves of a '50s starlet. Her translucent body was posed against scarlet velour reminiscent of the Monroe classic. One shot of Stratten displaying some of her $200,000 in gifts—a brass bed and a lavender Lore negligee—clearly evoked the platinum ideal of Jean Harlow. Dorothy's apotheosis reached, it seemed, for extremes of innocence and eroticism. In one shot she was draped in black lace and nestled into a couch, buttocks raised in an impish invitation to sodomy. Yet the cover displayed her clad in a chaste little peasant gown, seated in a meadow, head tilted angelically to one side. The dichotomy was an affirmation of her supposed sexual range. She was styled, apparently, as the Compleat Goddess for the '80s.

By January 1980—the dawning of her designated decade—Dorothy Stratten was attended by a thickening phalanx of photographers, promoters, duennas, coaches, and managers. Snider, sensing uneasily that she might be moving beyond his reach, became more demanding. He wanted absolute control over her financial affairs and the movie offers she accepted. She argued that he was being unreasonable; that she had an agent and a business manager whose job it was to advise her in those matters. Snider then pressed her to take the $200,000 from Playboy and buy a house. It would be a good investment, he said. He spent a lot of time looking at homes that might suit her, but she always found fault with them. She did not want to commit herself. She suspected, perhaps rightly, that he only wanted to attach another lien on her life.

This domestic squabbling was suspended temporarily in January when it appeared that Dorothy was poised for her big break, a featured role in a comedy called *They All Laughed* starring Audrey Hepburn and Ben Gazzara. It was to be directed by Peter Bogdanovich, whom Dorothy had first met at the roller disco bash in October. According to David Wilder, he and Bogdanovich were partying at the Mansion in January when the director first considered Stratten for the part.

"Jesus Christ," the 41-year-old Bogdanovich is supposed to have said. "She's perfect for the girl. . . . I don't want her for tits and ass. I want someone who can act."

Wilder says he took Dorothy to Bogdanovich's house in Bel-Air Estates to read for the role. She went back two or three more times and the director decided she was exactly what he wanted.

Filming was scheduled to begin in late March in New York City. Paul wanted to come along but Dorothy said no. He would get in the way and, at any rate, the set was closed to outsiders. Determined that she should depart Hollywood as a queen, he borrowed their housemate's

(continued)

PULITZER PRIZE WINNER   CONTINUED

Rolls Royce and drove her to the airport. He put her on the plane in brash good spirits, then went home to sulk at being left behind.

The affair between Dorothy Stratten and Peter Bogdanovich was conducted in amazing secrecy. In that regard it bore little resemblance to the director's affair with Cybill Shepherd, an escapade which advertised his puerile preference for ingenues. Bogdanovich, doubtless, did not fancy the publicity that might result from a liaison with a 20-year-old woman married to a hustler. A couple of days before the murder-suicide, he spoke of this to his close friend Hugh Hefner.

"It was the first time I'd seen him in a number of months because he'd been in New York," says Hefner. "He was very very up. Very excited about her and the film. . . . I don't think that he was playing with this at all. I think it was important to him. I'm talking about the relationship. . . . He was concerned at that point because of what had happened to him and [Cybill]. He was concerned about the publicity related to the relationship because of that. He felt in retrospect, as a matter of fact, that he . . . that they had kind of caused some of it. And it played havoc with both of their careers for a while."

Stratten, as usual, did not advertise the fact that she was married. When she arrived in New York, she checked quietly into the Wyndham Hotel. The crew knew very little about her except that she showed up on time and seemed very earnest about her small role. She was cordial but kept her distance, spending her time off-camera in a director's chair reading. One day it would be Dickens's *Great Expectations;* the next day a book on dieting. With the help of makeup and hair consultants her looks were rendered chaste and ethereal to defuse her playmate image. "She was a darling little girl," says makeup artist Fern Buckner. "Very beautiful, of course. Whatever you did to her was all right."

Dorothy had headaches. She was eating very little to keep her weight down and working 12-hour days because Bogdanovich was pushing the project along at a rapid pace. While most of the crew found him a selfish, mean-spirited megalomaniac, the cast by and large found him charming. He was particularly solicitous of Dorothy Stratten. And just as quietly as she had checked into the Wyndham, she moved into his suite at the Plaza. Word spread around the set that Bogdanovich and Stratten were involved but, because they were discreet, they avoided unpleasant gossip. "They weren't hanging all over one another," says one crew member. "It wasn't until the last few weeks when everyone relaxed a bit that they would show up together holding hands." One day Bogdanovich walked over to a couch where Dorothy sat chewing gum. "You shouldn't chew gum," he admonished. "It has sugar in it." She playfully removed the wad from her mouth and deposited it in his palm.

Bogdanovich is less than eager to discuss the affair. His secretary says he will not give interviews until *They All Laughed* is released in April. The director needs a hit badly and who can tell how Stratten's death might affect the box office. *Laughed* is, unfortunately, a comedy over which her posthumous performance might throw a pall. Although the plot is being guarded as closely as a national security secret, it goes something like this:

Ben Gazzara is a private detective hired by a wealthy, older man who suspects his spouse, Audrey Hepburn, has a lover. In following her, Gazzara falls in love with her. Meanwhile, Gazzara's sidekick, John Ritter, is hired by another wealthy older man to follow his young bride, Dorothy Stratten. Ritter watches Stratten from afar—through a window as she argues with her husband, as she roller skates at the Roxy. After a few perfunctory conversations, he asks her to marry him. Hepburn and Gazzara make a brief abortive stab at mature love. And Gazzara reverts to dating and mating with teenyboppers.

Within this intricate web of shallow relationships Dorothy, by all accounts, emerges as a shimmering seraph, a vision of perfection clad perennially in white. In one scene she is found sitting in the Algonquin Hotel bathed in a diaphanous light. "It was one of those scenes that could make a career," recalls a member of the crew. "People in the screening room rustled when they saw her. She didn't have many lines. She just looked so good." Bogdanovich was so enthusiastic about her that he called Hefner on the West Coast to say he was expanding Dorothy's role—not many more lines, but more exposure.

Paul Snider, meanwhile, was calling the East Coast where he detected a chill in Dorothy's voice. She would be too tired to talk. He would say, "I love you," and she wouldn't answer back. Finally, she began to have her calls screened. Late in April, during a shooting break, she flew to Los Angeles for a flurry of appearances which included the Playmate of the Year Luncheon and an appearance on *The Johnny Carson Show.* Shortly thereafter, Dorothy left for a grand tour of Canada. She agreed, however, to meet Paul in Vancouver during the second week of May. Her mother was remarrying and she planned to attend the wedding.

That proposed rendezvous worried Dorothy's Playboy traveling companion, Liz Norris. Paul was becoming irascible. He called Dorothy in Toronto and flew into a rage when she suggested that he allow her more freedom. Norris offered to provide her charge with a bodyguard once they arrived in Vancouver, but Dorothy declined. She met Paul and over her objections he checked them into the same hotel. Later, each gave essentially the same account of that encounter. She asked him to loosen his grip. "Let the bird fly," she said. They argued violently, then both sank back into tears. According to Snider, they reconciled and made love. Dorothy never acknowledged that. She later told a friend, however, that she had offered to leave Hollywood and go back to live with him in Vancouver, but he didn't want that. In the end she cut her trip short to get back to the shooting.

Snider, by now, realized that his empire was illusory. As her husband he technically had claim to half of her assets, but many of her assets were going into a corporation called Dorothy Stratten Enterprises. He was not one of the officers. When she spoke of financial settlements, she sounded like she was reading a strange script. She was being advised, he suspected, by Bogdanovich's lawyers. (Dorothy's attorney, Wayne Alexander, reportedly represents Bogdanovich too, but Alexander cannot be reached for comment.) Late in June, Snider received a letter declaring that he and Dorothy were separated physically and financially. She closed out their joint bank accounts and began advancing him money through her business manager.

Buffeted by forces beyond his control, Snider tried to cut his losses. He could have maintained himself as a promoter or as the manager of a health club. He was an expert craftsman and turned out exercise benches which he sold for $200 a piece. On at least one occasion he had subverted those skills to more dubious ends by building a wooden bondage rack for his private pleasure. But Snider didn't want to be a nobody. His rocket ship had come too close to the moon to leave him content with hang-gliding.

He tried, a little pathetically, to groom another Dorothy Stratten, a 17-year-old check-out girl from Riverside who modeled on the side. He had discovered her at an auto show. Patty was of the same statuesque Stratten ilk, and Snider taught her to walk like Dorothy, to dress like Dorothy, and to wear her hair like Dorothy. Eventually she moved into the house that he and Dorothy shared. But she was not another Stratten, and when Snider tried to promote her as a playmate, Playboy wanted nothing to do with him.

Paul's last hope for a big score was a project begun a month or so before he and Dorothy were married. He had worked out a deal with a couple of photographer friends, Bill and Susan Lachasse, to photograph Dorothy on skates wearing a French-cut skating outfit. From that they would print a poster that they hoped would sell a million copies and net $300,000. After

(continued)

PULITZER PRIZE WINNER   CONTINUED

Dorothy's appearance on the Carson show, Snider thought the timing was right. But Dorothy had changed her mind. The Lachasses flew to New York the day after she finished shooting to persuade her to reconsider. They were told by the production office that Dorothy could be found at Bogdanovich's suite at the Plaza.

"It was three or four in the afternoon," says Lachasse. "There had been a cast party the night before. Dorothy answered the door in pajamas and said, 'Oh my God! What are you doing here?' She shut the door and when she came out again she explained 'I can't invite you in. There are people here.' She looked at the photos in the hallway and we could tell by her eyes that she liked them. She took them inside, then came out and said, 'Look how my tits are hanging down.' Somebody in there was telling her what to do. She said, 'Look, I'm confused, have you shown these to Paul?' I said, 'Dorothy, you're divorcing Paul.' And she said, 'I don't know, I just don't know.'"

When Lachasse called the Plaza suite the following week a woman replied, "We don't know Dorothy Stratten. Stop harassing us."

"Paul felt axed as in every other area," says Lachasse. "That was his last bit of income."

During the anxious spring and early summer, Snider suspected, but could not prove, that Dorothy was having an affair. So as the filming of *They All Laughed* drew to a close in mid-July, he did what, in the comic world of Peter Bogdanovich, many jealous husbands do. He hired a private eye, a 26-year-old freelance detective named Marc Goldstein. The elfish Goldstein, who later claimed to be a friend of both Dorothy and Paul, in fact knew neither of them well. He was retained upon the recommendation of an unidentified third party. He will not say what exactly his mission was, but a Canadian lawyer named Ted Ewachniuk who represented both Paul and Dorothy in Vancouver claims that Snider was seeking to document the affair with Bogdanovich in order to sue him for "enticement to breach management contract"—an agreement Snider believed inherent within their marriage contract. That suit was to be filed in British Columbia, thought to be a suitable venue since both Snider and Stratten were still Canadians and, it could be argued, had only gone to Los Angeles for business.

Goldstein began showing up regularly at Snider's apartment. Snider produced poems and love letters from Bogdanovich that he had found among Dorothy's things. He instructed Goldstein to do an asset search on Dorothy and to determine whether or not Bogdanovich was plying her with cocaine.

Even as he squared off for a legal fight, Snider was increasingly despairing. He knew, underneath it all, that he did not have the power or resources to fight Bogdanovich. "Maybe this thing is too big for me," he confided to a friend, and he talked about going back to Vancouver. But the prospect of returning in defeat was too humiliating. He felt Dorothy was now so completely sequestered by attorneys that he would never see her again. Late in July his old machismo gave way to grief. He called Bill Lachasse one night crying because he could not touch Dorothy or even get near her. About the same time, his roommate the doctor returned home one night to find him despondent in the living room. "This is really hard," Paul said, and broke into tears. He wrote fragments of notes to Dorothy that were never sent. One written in red felt-tip marker and later found stuffed into one of his drawers was a rambling plaint on how he couldn't get it together without her. With Ewachniuk's help, he drafted a letter to Bogdanovich telling him to quit influencing Dorothy and that he [Snider] would "forgive" him. But Ewachniuk does not know if the letter was ever posted.

Dorothy, Paul knew, had gone for a holiday in London with Bogdanovich and would be returning to Los Angeles soon. He tortured himself with the scenario of the successful director and his queen showing up at Hefner's Midsummer Night's Dream Party on August 1. He couldn't bear it and blamed Hefner for fostering the affair. He called the Mansion trying to get an invitation to the party and was told he would be welcome only if he came with Dorothy.

But Dorothy did not show up at the party. She was keeping a low profile. She had moved ostensibly into a modest little apartment in Beverly Hills, the address that appeared on her death certificate. The apartment, however, was occupied by an actress who was Bogdanovich's personal assistant. Dorothy had actually moved into Bogdanovich's home in Bel-Air Estates. Where the big producers live.

Several days after her return to Los Angeles, she left for a playmate promotion in Dallas and Houston. There she appeared radiant, apparently reveling in her own success. She had been approached about playing Marilyn Monroe in Larry Schiller's made-for-TV movie, but she had been too busy with the Bogdanovich film. She had been discussed as a candidate for *Charlie's Angels* although Wilder thought she could do better. She was scheduled to meet with independent producer Martin Krofft who was considering her for his new film, *The Last Desperado*. It all seemed wonderful to her. But Stratten was not so cynical that she could enjoy her good fortune without pangs of regret. She cried in private. Until the end she retained a lingering tenderness for Paul Snider and felt bound to see him taken care of after the divorce. From Houston she gave him a call and agreed to meet him on Friday, August 8, for lunch.

After hearing from her, Snider was as giddy as a con whose sentence has been commuted, for he believed somehow that everything would be all right between them again. The night before their appointed meeting he went out for sandwiches with friends and was his blustering, confident old self. It would be different, he said. He would let her know that he had changed. "I've really got to vacuum the rug," he crowed. "The queen is coming back."

The lunch date, however, was a disaster. The two of them ended up back in the apartment squared off sullenly on the couch. Dorothy confessed at last that she was in love with Bogdanovich and wanted to proceed with some kind of financial settlement. Before leaving she went through her closet and took the clothes she wanted. The rest, she said, he should give to Patty.

Having his hopes raised so high and then dashed again gave Snider a perverse energy. Those who saw him during the five days prior to the murder caught only glimpses of odd behavior. In retrospect they appear to form a pattern of intent. He was preoccupied with guns. Much earlier in the year Snider had borrowed a revolver from a friend named Chip, the consort of one of Dorothy's sister playmates. Paul never felt easy, he said, without a gun, a holdover from his days on the East End. But Paul had to give the revolver back that Friday afternoon because Chip was leaving town. He looked around for another gun. On Sunday he held a barbecue at his place for a few friends and invited Goldstein. During the afternoon he pulled Goldstein aside and asked the detective to buy a machine gun for him. He needed it, he said, for "home protection." Goldstein talked him out of it.

In the classifieds, Snider found someone in the San Fernando Valley who wanted to sell a 12-gauge Mossberg pump shotgun. He circled the ad and called the owner. On Monday he drove into the Valley to pick up the gun but got lost in the dark. The owner obligingly brought it to a construction site where he showed Snider how to load and fire it.

Dorothy, meanwhile, had promised to call Paul on Sunday but did not ring until Monday, an omission that piqued him. They agreed to meet on Thursday at 11:30 A.M. to discuss a financial settlement. She had been instructed by her advisers to offer him a specified sum. During previous conversations, Paul thought he had heard Dorothy say, "I'll always take care of you," but he could not remember the exact words. Goldstein thought it might be a good idea to wire Snider's body for sound so that they could get a taped account if Dorothy repeated her promise to provide for him. They could not come up with the proper equipment, however, and abandoned the plan.

(continued)

PULITZER PRIZE WINNER   CONTINUED

On Wednesday, the day he picked up the gun, Snider seemed in an excellent mood. He told his roommate that Dorothy would be coming over and that she had agreed to look at a new house that he thought might be a good investment for her. He left the impression that they were on amicable terms. That evening he dropped by Bill Lachasse's studio to look at promotional shots of Patty. There, too, he was relaxed and jovial. In an off-handed way, he told Lachasse that he had bought a gun for protection. He also talked of strange and unrelated things that did not seem menacing in the context of his good spirits. He talked of Claudia Jennings, who had died with a movie in progress. Some playmates get killed, he observed. Some actresses are killed before their films come out. And when that happens, it causes a lot of chaos.

Bogdanovich had somehow discovered that Dorothy was being trailed by a private eye. He was furious, but Dorothy was apparently not alarmed. She was convinced that she and Paul were on the verge of working out an amicable agreement and she went to meet him as planned. According to the West Los Angeles police, she parked and locked her 1967 Mercury around 11:45 A.M., but the county coroner reports that she arrived later, followed by Goldstein who clocked her into the house at 12:30 P.M. Shortly thereafter, Goldstein called Snider to find out how things were going. Snider replied, in code, that everything was fine. Periodically throughout the afternoon, Goldstein rang Snider with no response. No one entered the house until five when Patty and another of Paul's little girlfriends returned home, noticed Dorothy's car and saw the doors to Snider's room closed. Since they heard no sounds, they assumed he wanted privacy. The two girls left to go skating and returned at 7 P.M. By then the doctor had arrived home and noticed the closed door. He also heard the unanswered ringing on Snider's downstairs phone. Shortly before midnight Goldstein called Patty and asked her to knock at Paul's door. She demurred, so he asked to speak to the doctor. The latter agreed to check but even as he walked downstairs he felt some foreboding. The endless ringing had put him on edge and his German shepherd had been pacing and whining in the yard behind Paul's bedroom. The doctor knocked and when there was no response, he pushed the door open. The scene burnt his senses and he yanked the door shut.

It is impolitic to suggest that Paul Snider loved Dorothy Stratten. Around Hollywood, at least, he is currently limned as brutal and utterly insensitive. If he loved her, it was in the selfish way of one who cannot separate a lover's best interests from one's own. And if he did what he is claimed to have done, he was, as Hugh Hefner would put it, "a very sick guy."

Even now, however, no one can say with certainty that Paul Snider committed either murder or suicide. One of his old confederates claims he bought the gun to "scare" Bogdanovich. The coroner was sufficiently equivocal to deem his death a "questionable suicide/possible homicide." One Los Angeles psychic reportedly attributes the deaths to an unemployed actor involved with Snider in a drug deal. Goldstein, who holds to a theory that both were murdered, is badgering the police for results of fingerprintings and paraffin tests, but the police consider Goldstein a meddler and have rebuffed his requests. The West LAPD, which has not yet closed the case, says it cannot determine if it was Snider who fired the shotgun because his hands were coated with too much blood and tissue for tests to be conclusive.

And yet Snider appears to have been following a script of his own choosing. One which would thwart the designs of Playboy and Hollywood. Perhaps he had only meant to frighten Dorothy, to demonstrate to Bogdanovich that he could hold her in thrall at gunpoint. Perhaps he just got carried away with the scene. No one knows exactly how events unfolded after Dorothy entered the house that afternoon. She had apparently spent some time upstairs because her purse was found lying open in the middle of the living room floor. In it was a note in Paul's handwriting explaining his financial distress. He had no green card, it said, and he required support. Dorothy's offer, however, fell far short of support. It was a flat settlement of only $7500 which, she claimed, represented half of her total assets after taxes. "Not enough," said one friend, "to put a nice little sports car in his garage." Perhaps she had brought the first installment to mollify Paul's inevitable disappointment; police found $1100 in cash among her belongings, another $400 among his. One can only guess at the motives of those two doomed players who, at some point in the afternoon, apparently left the front room and went downstairs.

It is curious that, given the power of the blasts, the little bedroom was not soaked in blood. There was only spattering on the walls, curtains, and television. Perhaps because the room lacked a charnel aspect, the bodies themselves appeared all the more grim. They were nude. Dorothy lay crouched across the bottom corner of a low bed. Both knees were on the carpet and her right shoulder was drooping. Her blond hair hung naturally, oddly unaffected by the violence to her countenance. The shell had entered above her left eye leaving the bones of that seraphic face shattered and displaced in a welter of pulp. Her body, mocking the soft languid poses of her pictorials, was in full rigor.

No one, least of all Hugh Hefner, could have foreseen such a desecration. It was unthinkable that an icon of eroticism presumed by millions of credulous readers to be impervious to the pangs of mortality could be reduced by a pull of the trigger to a corpse, mortally stiff, mortally livid and crawling with small black ants. For Hefner, in fact, that grotesque alteration must have been particularly bewildering. Within the limits of his understanding, he had done everything right. He had played it clean with Stratten, handling her paternally, providing her with gifts and opportunities and, of course, the affection of the Playboy family. Despite his best efforts, however, she was destroyed. The irony that Hefner does not perceive—or at least fails to acknowledge—is that Stratten was destroyed not by random particulars, but by a germ breeding within the ethic. One of the tacit tenets of the Playboy philosophy—that women can be possessed—had found a fervent adherent in Paul Snider. He had bought the dream without qualification, and he thought of himself as perhaps one of Playboy's most honest apostles. He acted out dark fantasies never intended to be realized. Instead of fondling himself in private, instead of wreaking abstract violence upon a centerfold, he ravaged a playmate in the flesh.

Dorothy had, apparently, been sodomized, though whether this occurred before or after her death is not clear. After the blast, her body was moved and there were what appeared to be bloody handprints on her buttocks and left leg. Near her head was Paul's handmade bondage rack set for rear-entry intercourse. Loops of tape, used and unused, were lying about and strands of long blond hair were discovered clutched in Snider's right hand. He was found face-down lying parallel to the foot of the bed. The muzzle of the Mossberg burnt his right cheek as the shell tore upward through his brain. The blast, instead of driving him backwards, whipped him forward over the length of the gun. He had always said he would rather die than go to jail.

Goldstein arrived before the police and called the Mansion. Hefner, thinking the call a prank, would not come to the phone at first. When he did he asked for the badge number of the officer at the scene. Satisfied that this was no bad joke, Hefner told his guests in the game house. There were wails of sorrow and disbelief. He then called Bogdanovich. "There was no conversation," Hefner says. "I was afraid that he had gone into shock or something. [When he didn't respond] I called the house under another number. A male friend was there to make sure he was [all right]. He was overcome."

Bogdanovich arranged for Stratten's cremation five days later. Her ashes were placed in an urn and buried in a casket so that he could visit them. Later he would issue his own statement:

(continued)

PULITZER PRIZE WINNER   CONTINUED

DOROTHY STRATTEN WAS AS GIFTED AND INTELLIGENT AN ACTRESS AS SHE WAS BEAUTIFUL, AND SHE WAS VERY BEAUTIFUL INDEED—IN EVERY WAY IMAGINABLE—MOST PARTICULARLY IN HER HEART. SHE AND I FELL IN LOVE DURING OUR PICTURE, AND HAD PLANNED TO BE MARRIED AS SOON AS HER DIVORCE WAS FINAL. THE LOSS TO HER MOTHER AND FATHER, HER SISTER AND BROTHER, TO MY CHILDREN, TO HER FRIENDS AND TO ME IS LARGER THAN WE CAN CALCULATE. BUT THERE IS NO LIFE DOROTHY'S TOUCHED THAT HAS NOT BEEN CHANGED FOR THE BETTER THROUGH KNOWING HER, HOWEVER BRIEFLY. DOROTHY LOOKED AT THE WORLD WITH LOVE, AND BELIEVED THAT ALL PEOPLE WERE GOOD DOWN DEEP. SHE WAS MISTAKEN, BUT IT IS AMONG THE MOST GENEROUS AND NOBLE ERRORS WE CAN MAKE.

PETER BOGDANOVICH

Bogdanovich took the family Hoogstraten in tow. They were stunned, but not apparently embittered by Dorothy's death. "They knew who cared for her," Hefner says. Mother, fathers—both natural and stepfather—sister, and brother flew to Los Angeles for the service and burial at Westwood Memorial Park, the same cemetery, devotees of irony point out, where Marilyn Monroe is buried. Hefner and Bogdanovich were there and after the service the family repaired to Bogdanovich's house for rest and refreshments. It was all quiet and discreet. Dorothy's mother says that she will not talk to the press until the movie comes out. Not until April when Stratten's glimmering ghost will appear on movie screens across the country, bathed in white light and roller skating through a maze of hilarious infidelities.

Playboy, whose corporate cool was shaken by her untimely death, has regained its composure. The December issue features Stratten as one of the "Sex Stars of 1980." At the end of 12 pages of the biggest draws in show business—Bo Derek, Brooke Shields, etc.—she appears topless, one breast draped with a gossamer scarf. A caption laments her death which "cut short what seasoned star-watchers predicted was sure to be an outstanding film career."

Hype, of course, often passes for prophecy. Whether or not Dorothy Stratten would have fulfilled her extravagant promise can't be known. Her legacy will not be examined critically because it is really of no consequence. In the end Dorothy Stratten was less memorable for herself than for the yearnings she evoked: in Snider a lust for the score; in Hefner a longing for a star; in Bogdanovich a desire for the eternal ingenue. She was catalyst for a cycle of ambitions which revealed its players less wicked, perhaps, than pathetic.

As for Paul Snider, his body was returned to Vancouver in permanent exile from Hollywood. It was all too big for him. In that Elysium of dreams and deals, he had reached the limits of his class. His sin, his unforgivable sin, was being small-time.

Source: © 1980. Teresa Carpenter and *The Village Voice*. Reprinted by permission.

"Death of a Playmate" is unlike newspaper features in many ways. First, it's about the same length as McCabe's magazine piece—over 9,000 words. And incorporated into that length is the kind of complex, extensive reporting readers don't commonly expect to find in newspaper features. Paragraph length is also excessive. Many newspaper editors would turn red in the face at the sight of Carpenter's 110-word first paragraph.

The lead is long, too. In the average newspaper feature, the point of the story is often obvious within the first 100 words. In fact, a good rule of thumb for most newspaper features is that the readers should know by the end of the first paragraph why they're reading the story. Certainly they should know by the time they reach the third or fourth paragraph. In Carpenter's story, however, the point isn't fully clear until the end of the seven-paragraph lead block, about 700 words into the story. Paul Snider, the dead woman's husband, isn't mentioned until the final paragraph of the lead, yet he is an integral part of the web so carefully woven here for the reader.

The slow summary approach to the story was a deliberate choice by Carpenter. She says "Death of a Playmate" and her other two Pulitzer Prize stories were similar to the extent that they were reconstructions of very complicated stories. "My lead in each of those three is essentially a prologue laying out the story so that the reader knows what to expect and then essentially saying, 'Okay, reader, now I am going to deliver.' "

After the lead, Carpenter takes the reader through Stratten's discovery by Snider, her marriage to him, her ascent in the Playboy organization, her friendship with filmmaker Peter Bogdanovich, her impending divorce from Snider, the shotgun slaying and suicide and, finally, the reactions of Bogdanovich and Hefner.

"There is a beginning of the story in earnest in the second section, and then there is a slow arc over the story to the end," Carpenter says. "It's basically chronological. It's not a trick. It's just good story telling. I have found that format to be very effective in making sense to a reader."

Chronological narrative is a standard literary device, and often, as in Carpenter's "Death of a Playmate," it can be extremely dramatic and compelling. But since you are analyzing techniques that can be copied, here is a word of caution. Chronology doesn't work for everything. Remember "Mrs. Kelly's Monster"? Suppose the story had been written with the leisurely chronological approach, leading the reader through Mrs. Kelly's early childhood, marriage and the eventual development of the aneurisms that led her to Dr. Ducker's operating table. The story would still have been important, but it would have put most readers to sleep. The literary key to chronology, one that Carpenter knows well, is the ability to separate chronology that is gripping from chronology that is boring.

"If you're a good storyteller, then you'll be a literary journalist," Carpenter says. "A literary journalist can't invent. In that case, he's a writer of fiction. But short of that, a literary journalist can realize the overall arc of a story and tell a story to bring the reader along in a way so he appreciates the intrinsic drama in the material. That's just good story telling, but you'd be amazed at how many people can't tell a story."

Look closely at one more Carpenter technique. You will have noticed that there are very few direct or partial quotes in "Death of a Playmate." Even though she taped virtually all of the story's interviews and then painstakingly transcribed her tapes, she used direct quotations only about a dozen times in the final writing process. The rest is paraphrasing. "That's my style," Carpenter says.

> Some reporters' day is made when they have a good quote, but I've always been suspicious of them. You can become so intoxicated with a single good quote that you ignore the basic substance of what the subject has said. I find that it's difficult to integrate spoken language into a well-written piece because the level of language is different. I think that there is a wide

latitude for distortion when you quote someone. I know that not every journalist agrees with me on this, but it's just been my experience that unless you recreate the context very carefully and accurately, someone can be misrepresented by his own words. If someone tenders an impious expression ironically, then the burden is on you to capture the ironic context or you misrepresent them. I think a lot of young and inexperienced journalists will hear an incendiary quote and say, "Whoopee, there's my story." Well, it's not your story unless you can recreate the context.

She goes on to say, "There are exceptions. I will quote when the expression is so unique, either in terms of substance or style, that it reveals something about a speaker that a paraphrase wouldn't. But for an intelligent writer, it's much easier to keep control of the material and represent the material accurately if you are paraphrasing."

Taking the Next Step

At this point, you are well embarked. You know what a newspaper feature story is and how feature writers develop ideas. You've learned in this chapter how a magazine article differs from a newspaper feature, and you've also learned, as with "Death of a Playmate," that distinctions between the two journalistic genres are sometimes blurred.

You've read about magazine article writers and how they develop their ideas in much the same way as newspaper feature writers, though with distinct differences and always with an eventual market in mind. You've learned the four steps for researching a market and matching your ideas to an appropriate magazine, and you've begun to study successful published pieces with an eye toward learning techniques and divining the needs of a specific market. Now you're ready to bring your ideas into sharp focus and make a sales pitch to an editor, right?

No, not yet. Before you can write a persuasive query letter (which you will examine in Chapter 8) to your favorite editor, you must be sure you know enough about the topic to make a persuasive query. And that often means it's time to begin the research necessary to put together both the query letter and the eventual finished article.

CHAPTER FOUR

RESEARCHING FOR NEWSPAPER FEATURE STORIES AND MAGAZINE ARTICLES

Research shows. When a writer has boned up well on a subject, maybe only half or a third of the researched material will be used in the finished product. Maybe less. But the certainty that comes from knowing your topic will permeate all of your copy.

Skimping on research is a common temptation. You can over-research, too, and get so intrigued with the process of tracking down elusive facts that you spend more time on it than is really required by the piece you are working on. The trick is to hit a workable balance.

Ignorance—your own ignorance—is the best starting point for research. Although writers must become "temporary experts" on the wide array of subjects they're called upon to cover, few writers have more than a couple of areas of real expertise. Even if you double-majored in college in journalism and anthropology and can nod smilingly when the archaeologist you're interviewing mentions *Australopithecus africanus,* you don't just keep nodding if he or she rambles on about *Australopithecus robustus* and *Australopithecus boisei* unless you know those terms, too. The time to ask for clarification is while you're interviewing. As Pulitzer winner Peter Rinearson of *The Seattle Times* has put it, "One thing I learned early on as a reporter, that it's a lot better looking stupid to your sources than looking stupid to your readers." Writer and TV-documentary producer Lee Hays made the same point at an Author's Guild Symposium in New York: "No matter how well researched you are, the subject frequently has expertise or knows things you couldn't possibly be privy to. They will assume sometimes that you know it. I think at times like that you really have to stop them and say, 'Hey, explain that.'"

It takes courage to say to an interviewee, "I don't understand." Even the best of pros can hesitate to admit gaps in their knowledge, as you'll learn at the end of this chapter from Pulitzer winner Saul Pett. But filling in gaps in the middle of an interview can save hours of research work later. Some interviewees gain confidence in you if you level with them. They don't want to sound dumb in the article, and they'll want to be sure you've got the facts straight.

When you're interviewing, you're simultaneously conducting visual research. What kind of shirt is the film star wearing? What is the specific type of Persian rug on which the model is strolling barefoot? While many interviews must take place in a hotel or an office, a subject's home gives interesting opportunities for visual research. Author Gael Greene suggests, not wholly tongue in cheek, "Check the medicine chest, look into the refrigerator, so you can pick up details they are not going to tell you. . . . I always look in the medicine chest. And, in fact, I arrange my medicine chest in case anyone looks in mine." All writers look over book titles on a subject's coffee table or in a subject's library. Visuals are research, of a very telling kind.

NEWSPAPER REFERENCE ROOMS

Time is of paramount importance to the newspaper reporter. When you do background research for a short newspaper feature, you rarely have time to do more than check your newspaper's computer archives, or pop into the newspaper's library and go with whatever you find there.

The reference room library is often sufficient. You probably won't find this year's *Statistical Abstract of the United States* or *Dictionary of Canadian Biography,* but you won't be surprised to find a fairly recent *Who's Who in America.* You'll find a good collection of crisscross directories and telephone directories and atlases and almanacs and yearbooks pertinent to the circulation area. You'll find at least one good, big dictionary, probably *Random House* or *Webster's Third,* perhaps even the older but classic *Webster's Second.* Or, if your newspaper library has enough shelf space, you might be able to use the daddy of them all, the exhaustive (and fascinating) *Oxford English Dictionary.* Most newspaper reference rooms also run to a good American encyclopedia or a recent *Encyclopaedia Britannica.* But, of course, the true wealth of the newspaper library or database archives lies in the thoroughness of its clip files.

Organized by name and subject, a newspaper's paper and electronic clip files are the irreplaceable history of all major news events, plus a lot of minor events, that the paper has covered. The term "morgue" has given way to "library" or "reference room" on most papers, but unless the newspaper has keyed all its holdings into a computer database, the morgue-like image remains: a drab, windowless room with overhead lighting, lined with big shelves for bound volumes of the newspaper going back through time and filled with row upon row of cabinets bulging with photos and clips. These a reporter examines only under the steely eye of the newspaper librarian, for fear some precious clip could disappear and cripple the work of other reporters for decades to come. Times change. A head librarian now often has numerous helpers. Microfilm or microfiche may have replaced bound volumes, and a quick punch-up on a computer might replace leafing through yellowing clips. However, the essential nature of a newspaper's back files remains the same.

A quick search of newspaper clip files, whatever their form, gives the reporter a launching pad. A prominent citizen dies and you must write a front-page obit. An historic building is to be rejuvenated or demolished, and you're to write a feature. Or you're assigned yet another holiday feature and want to avoid taking the same angles that have been used in years before.

But use your head before you automatically rush to clip files for background checks. There is no point in digging through piles of old clippings or scanning innumerable computer entries just to locate someone's date of birth if the information is readily available in the nearest copy of *Who's Who* or some other reference book. There's already a world of information waiting for you if you know where to look.

MAGAZINE REFERENCE RESOURCES

Magazine reference sources available to staffers cover a wide range. At one end of the scale are operations such as those of *Time,* which employs a whole stable of researchers—often young college grads hoping to work their way up to the status of writers—to call upon for the onerous chore of running down statistics or double-checking facts. Through the years, *Time* not only has accumulated more than a half million folders of clippings to use for background material, but also has access to numerous computerized databases, many filled with more information than a small city library.

At the other end of the scale is the small magazine whose "reference" holdings consist of a collection of back issues stacked on shelves. The magazine relies on freelancers, and the freelancers in turn rely on either home-based computer research or "hands-on" searches of public libraries and university libraries.

It seems the world has busily replaced slow, dusty library research with a few well-phrased questions to a computer. Newsrooms and magazine offices have discarded their old Underwood typewriters and switched entirely to computers and computer-assisted cold-type production systems. Not only has the writing process been affected, but so has the information-gathering process. Writers can now research many stories without ever leaving their terminals. They can even use their computers to locate and interview expert sources.

Does this mean libraries are becoming obsolete? If so, why bother to learn library skills? After all, computers are not only convenient, they offer incredible speed. A two-decade bibliographic database can be searched in a couple of minutes, compared with hours spent in the stacks of a library. How can libraries possibly match that?

Don't be in a hurry to throw away your library card. Most successful writers still spend time prowling through dusty library stacks, and so should you. Not only do library computers have access to valuable resources you can't get at home, but the process of digging through the library's carefully organized card files, Dewey-decimal–classified book shelves and chronologically catalogued periodical stacks will provide excellent training in the proper approach to research. Scanning book titles and flipping pages of old magazines may trigger new directions for focus, or even suggest new article ideas. Working with a keyboard and a modem will nearly always provide bundles of information more quickly and easily, but it often rules out the lucky, serendipitous finds.

Historical library material is usually more thorough, as well. Remember, the earliest electronic databases were largely bibliographic, meaning that although computer researchers might have found important book citations and article references, they still had to go to a library to find copies of the printed material. Computer research has changed and improved with the passage of time, of course. Now it's easier to find "full-text" databases that provide the complete text of articles, as well as speeches and documents. Most databases also allow researchers to search for any word or combination of words, since articles are indexed not only by specific key words, but also by every single word contained in the article.

Even if you can afford all the database fees, libraries are still important. Remember, the oldest extant book dates back to A.D. 868, more than 1,100 years ago. Once Johann Gutenberg introduced moveable, reusable type and created modern mechanized printing techniques, book publication began to burgeon. Newspapers and magazines came along shortly thereafter. By the 1990s, American publishing firms were cranking out 50,000 new book titles a year. Americans also print more than 9,000 newspapers, 1,500 of them on a daily basis, as well as some 11,000 magazines and journals. That's a mind-numbing amount of printed material coming off American presses every single year. Not to mention all the books and newspapers and magazines published annually in Europe and Asia and the rest of the world.

Furthermore, the world has been publishing those books and newspapers and magazines for centuries. Millions and millions of them. Computers may give you access to recently printed materials, but what happens when you really need to dig through those massive piles of older publications?

Computers can't take you that deeply into the past, as yet. Remember, the sale of electronic information is still a relatively new industry. The first databases appeared back in the 1960s, when every tidbit of information had to be entered laboriously into the system by keypunch operators. It was a slow, tedious process. Technology eventually improved, and by 1969 most information could go directly into a database without human intervention. The elimination of the slower keypunch process is commonly cited as the starting point for most modern databases. But until technology takes that next step and makes it possible to retrieve easily and cheaply the full 1,100 years of printed materials that preceded databases, writers will be forced to take computer printouts of many bibliographic citations to the nearest good library in order to look up some of the material they need.

If you like working your way through card catalogs and printed materials and microfilm machines, you must at least learn to do your prowling efficiently. You'll need an adequate working knowledge of hands-on research tools. And you'll learn to improve your skills as you continue stalking the stacks.

Many freelancers start at that standard source, *The Reader's Guide to Periodical Literature.* But they don't stop there. *Reader's Guide* indexes only about 160 general periodicals. With the general periodicals as a starting point, freelancers can usually discover whether the topic they're contemplating has been covered often before and what has been written about it, but they won't turn up much fresh material for a new piece. The thousands of small or specialized magazines not covered by *Reader's Guide* might not be indexed anywhere by anyone, or they might be covered only by their own internal indices, run every few months within the magazine. And as you move, for example, from the humanities or finance to sociology and the hard sciences, you move each time into entirely different reference sources.

When in doubt on a research project, remember that hesitancy in admitting your own ignorance makes you your own enemy. A good shortcut is to throw yourself on the mercy of the research librarian. A good research librarian knows far more about research than you'll ever need to learn. But don't just charge up to somebody who's checking out books and blurt out your question, unless it's a very basic one, such as "Where is the card catalog, please?" (For that matter, many libraries have more than one card catalog.) The research librarian, who is thoroughly familiar with the library's holdings, is the person you want. Then, as with all research, you must be specific in formulating exactly what you're looking for, or you can waste hours floundering in a sea of irrelevant material.

Without the proper subject heading for printed references or descriptor words for computer research, you're in much the same position as trying to get into Fort Knox without the proper key. You'll save time in a library by preparing a list of alternate key phrases, and you'll save even more time by checking the *Library of Congress Subject Headings.* Best yet, read the highly recommended *Finding Facts Fast,* by Alden Todd, and familiarize yourself with such basic library holdings as *Guide to Reference Books* and *Subject Guide to Reference Books.* You'll learn how to navigate the library maze and get quickly to the subject that interests you.

You'll also find an amazing list of specialized encyclopedias, directories, dictionaries, and atlases in each new edition of *Books in Print* (another useful reference work). You'll discover such esoteric titles as *The World Encyclopedia of Comics, The Complete Prime Time Network TV Shows 1946–Present, The Mariner's Dictionary, Dictionary of World and Phrase Origins, The American Thesaurus of Slang, Nature Atlas of America, Rand McNally Atlas of the Body* and *Index to Women of the World from Ancient to Modern Times.* Pages could be spent listing samplings of odd and useful books to be found in most libraries. Whatever your sphere of interest, you will probably find it has been covered.

Each new subject will lead you into a different galaxy of research sources, and for each you will have to start the search for information anew. But the time you spend learning to make a search on one topic won't be wasted, even if you never write about the same topic again. You're mastering the technique of researching in detail. Luckily for writers, it's an interesting occupation—and it ends only when you stop writing.

COMPUTERIZED RESEARCH

Even if we recognize the continued value of library research, we must also embrace the ready assistance of the computer as a research tool. Modern search engines and directories make computer research exceptionally convenient. Think of the advantages. All types of written and graphic data are available, either free or at modest cost. Materials are usually current—new information can be online within moments of composition. And best of all, if you know where and how to look for it, you can research almost any topic without ever leaving your desk.

Unfortunately, there's also a negative side to this abundance of data. Where massive amounts of information can be found, one is also likely to find misinformation. You will encounter people with their own political agendas, religious beliefs, special interests and conflicting arguments, waiting to persuade you to their points of view. With all the nuts and kooks out there, who do you believe? What can you trust?

Remember that an open democracy requires a pluralism of voices. If you are to make informed decisions, you need to examine all sides of an equation. Some points of view may be supported by fact. Others may rely on pure emotion. Experience will eventually teach you to sift through the garbage. Until then, unlimber your personal salt shaker and sprinkle copious grains of salt on everything you read. When Web sites offer conflicting sides to an issue, don't swallow the first argument you encounter. Wait until you've studied all viewpoints.

Oddly, the presence of nuts and kooks on the Internet may have brought us full circle to the formative days of our democratic society. When the early deep thinkers (from Britishers John Milton and John Locke to the Colonial framers of our American Constitution) pleaded for a free and uncensored press, they were suggesting that anyone with an idea should have access to the public. And the system worked fine in the beginning. Anyone could start a newspaper cheaply enough, and if they didn't have time to put out a regular newspaper, they could always commit ideas to paper, publish a pamphlet and watch it, like Thomas Paine with his "Common Sense," change the course of history. Unfortunately, as America grew more sophisticated over the next 200 years, media became more complex, too expensive for the average citizen. Only the wealthy and well organized could afford to launch a new newspaper or begin broadcasting from a new radio or television station.

Then, in 1969, along came the early stages of the Internet. Sort of. The first computer web to connect various users was called ARPAnet (named for the Defense Department's "Advanced Research Projects Agency"), and, in the beginning, it was just as elitist as any other medium. Spawned by the Cold War and hostilities in Vietnam, it linked heavy-duty computers at about a dozen universities. Over the next 15 years, several hundred additional universities joined ARPAnet, but it remained elitist until technological improvements in 1984 made the process a whole lot cheaper and easier to use. By 1989, thousands of scientists, government researchers and independent users had climbed aboard, and high telephone costs began to drop.

That was only the start. The Internet, as we know it, came through the explosive growth of the 1990s. Sure, those original scientists can still exchange information and visit their research compatriots. But now, true to the pioneering hopes of our original "free press" supporters, almost anyone can construct his or her own Web site on the 'Net and offer ideas, conceits, opinions and firmly held beliefs. And that brings us back to our warning. If you prowl the Internet as a researcher, looking for treasures of information, you will no doubt find nuggets of truth, flashes of rich data and even an occasional mother lode of solid, factual information. But you're also going to dig up a few slag heaps, toxic dumps and sparkly lumps of fool's gold, as useless as they are attractive.

This wide range of ideas will make your research both easier and more difficult. The Internet may be the single most valuable research tool invented in our technology-driven age, filled with fun and fertile ideas and factual resources, but its very accessibility also means it will have its share of conspiracy idiots, militia hotheads, UFO crackpots, garbage minds and people with half-baked notions. If you plan to use the Internet as a research tool, learn to exercise good judgment. Don't fall for every rumor, religious rant, partial truth, bit of drivel, nutty idea or outright lie. Check further. Look for confirmation in sensible quarters. Even if you go to a site that one might reasonably expect to be honest, use your brain. Who set up the site? What hidden agendas might they be expected to have? If you're writing an article on diamond harvesting, and you decide to check native living conditions by visiting the embassy pages of a small African diamond-producing nation called Batango, don't expect to find negative information. The job of Batango's information counselor is to make his country look good, not list its faults. So be careful out there.

Okay, so you've been warned and warned again. Now how do you tap into this grand new research device? And how do you call up just the right information?

USING SEARCH ENGINES AND DIRECTORIES

You'll find hundreds of millions of Web sites floating out there on the Internet, filled with all kinds of information, flashy graphics, photographs, animations, video clips and links to other sites. In fact, estimates suggest that the Internet may contain close to two billion colorful, indexable pages. That's two billion! Two thousand million. And growing all the time.

So if you're looking for information on panic attacks or sleep apnea, how do you cut through all those millions upon millions of pages to access just what you need? Obviously, you turn to one or more of several existing search mechanisms that have been designed to cut through the chaos and bring you some semblance of order.

A search engine is a program designed to prowl the Internet and seek out information on various computer systems, whether they be as extensive as the World Wide Web, or more narrowly focused corporate or proprietary networks. In effect, these engines send out swarms of electronic robots that search ceaselessly through the Internet, seeking and categorizing information. You can then sit at your keyboard and type in a key word or phrase and get an almost instantaneous list of references that come close to matching your criteria.

And search engines are relatively new. The first, called Archie (from the word archive, without the v), was created in 1990 by a student at McGill university. Archie could search a wide territory for file names, but it couldn't scan the contents. It was followed quickly by Gopher, Veronica and Jughead, search devices that could index plain text documents. These early devices were fine while the Internet was still in its infancy, but the Web was growing too fast for them. As Internet content grew, search engines became commercially viable. By 1994, Allweb, Lycos and Infoseek were all competing for attention.

Then in 1998, Google joined the fray. It was a small outfit when it started, the brainchild of two young Stanford Ph.D. candidates named Larry Page and Sergey Brin. They added a couple of new wrinkles like ranking pages and the popularity of links to Google's listings. And it worked. By the year 2001, the Google search page had become a favorite launching pad for webheads. It's especially handy for writers, many of whom choose the Google site as their home page, allowing them to seek research materials with a minimal waste of time.

How successful is Google? Wall Street insiders currently estimate Google's corporate value to be about $100 billion, making it one of the largest media businesses in the world. Not bad for the pair of 30-year-olds who founded it and still run it with the help of some 6,000 employees. In fact, Google has so dominated the search field in the last few years that it has become a part of our language—a verb meaning to look up something or someone. You say to a friend, "Hey, I googled our professor last night. Did you know he was once an exotic male dancer?"

So Google is now one of several 800-pound gorillas in the search business, along with the other major rival search engines, like Yahoo!, MSN Search, Gigablast and Teoma, all trying to out-innovate each other. And they're free, thanks to advertising—those little sponsored links that appear, for example, on the right-hand side of Google's search results. You'll like these big general search engines, and you'll use them often. You'll probably also use the smaller, more subject-specific search engines. Some of these engines respond to questions rather than key words, like Ask.com, Answerbag, Brainboost and Lycos iQ. Others specialize in distant corners of the world, like Accoona and Baidu for China, Rambler and Yandex for Russia, In.gr for Greece and UK Pages for the United Kingdom. You can also find search engines that specialize in job openings, shopping bargains, medical information, blogs, property, charities and even people. All these search engines have their strong points. Try them and use those that are best for your areas of interest.

You'll never have to worry about a shortage of material. No matter how esoteric your search topic may be, the engines will dig up plenty. Perhaps too much. And the amounts will vary from day to day and engine to engine. For example, on the morning this material was written, Yahoo! and Google were asked to look up "computer research." Yahoo! provided links to 216 million hits (related Web pages) in 0.19 seconds. The Google engine came back with 285 million related pages (as an example of how the Internet is growing and search engines are improving, the same key words, entered four years ago when a previous edition of this textbook was written, brought up only about four million hits, more than 280 million fewer than the new search). So what do you do with 285 million hits? You could go through them and check out each page, but it might take a few lifetimes. Luckily, most search engines these days rank their hits, with the most likely matches coming first. It doesn't always work, but if you're looking for a particular bit of information, and you ask for it properly, you may well find it within the first 10 to 50 offerings, surely within the first 100.

So learn to refine your search. If you have a nasty headache, you don't call the nearest pharmacy and ask for "medication." That could get you anything from bunion pads to a dose of that hacking-sneezing-barfing-so-you-can-get-some-rest stuff. If you know the specific medication you want, ask for it. Otherwise, dig up key words and say, "Head, throbbing, help me." The clerk should get the idea.

Okay, now we can do an "index" search through a directory's hierarchical listings. Using the word "headache," we can also conduct a "key word" search. If we don't have a specific key word, we can try a "concept" search, offering one or more related words. And there are many other forms of search out there. We can do phrase searches, title searches or author searches. On occasion, if we don't know the exact spelling of a name or word, we'll try a "fuzzy" search, using a search engine that allows bad spelling. Google, for example, will accept your misspelled Shakspear and give you results, but it will also ask you at the top of the first page of results, "Did you mean Shakespeare" with a link that will take you on. It works, with typos, too. We purposely typed in printers with an "m," like priMters. Google asked its usual "Did you mean printers," but gave us 15,000 hits for primters. The link to the correctly spelled printer totaled 191 million hits.

But if we really want to get specific, we might try using plusses and minuses. If we're looking for information on corporate accounting scandals, we could just enter "corporate scandals." (As this paragraph was written, those two words called up nearly five million hits on Google, too many for our purposes. We could refine and try "+corporate +accounting +scandals." Plusses don't make a difference on all search engines, but when they do, they require that a document contain all three words. In our test, that brings us down to a little over three million hits, still an overly hefty amount. If we don't insist on coverage of the Enron fiasco, heavily covered by the media in 2002, we could add "–enron" to our key word search. Now we should get pages on corporate hanky panky, but excluding references to Enron.

Another form of the plus-and-minus search is called the Boolean search, named after George Boole, a nineteenth-century mathematician, except that this algebraic search calls for the use of words rather than math symbols. If you call for stock market scandals and you want all three words to appear in each document, you enter "corporate AND accounting AND scandals." If you want only scandals that have nothing to do with Enron, you enter "corporate AND accounting AND scandals AND NOT enron."

There are lots of tricks to online research, and you'll learn them all as you dig deeper. You'll discover advanced searches with refined catalogs and word filters, metasearch services that will check several search engines at the same time, adult filters that will block the inclusion of any porn pages and language adjustments that allow you to search in one or several languages.

ELECTRONIC MAGAZINES

While we're on the subject of computers and magazine research, it may be useful to mention an entirely new set of growing writing markets. One of the surprises on the blossoming Internet is the explosive growth of electronic magazines. Called online "Zines," "e-zines," or even "webzines," these burgeoning markets run the gamut from dinky, atrociously written newsletters to huge, polished professional news vehicles that rival the slickest print publications. Try some of the Web sites that list online magazines. You'll find from two to four thousand in operation at any given moment, ranging from "ABBA" to "ZigZag." They cover fiction, culture, personals, politics, religion and a whole gamut of peculiar topics. Plus most print publications (as well as broadcast markets) now also have online versions to carry greater detail than limited print space often allows.

Let's take one narrow field as an example. Computer games. From simple arcade games to hardcore shooters and colorful dungeon-and-dragon adventures, computer games have become a prime filler of America's wired leisure time, so popular that dozens of print magazines exist just to keep gamers current on what's good and what's coming next. If you do your playing on a PC, you can visit your local newsstand and find such magazines as *PC Gamer, Games for Windows* or *Computer Games*. If you prefer Macintosh games, check out *MacAddict* or *MacHome Journal*. There are even magazines for console games—*PlayStation Magazine, Game Informer* or *Electronic Gaming Monthly*. You'll hear more about these magazines in Chapter 9, when we get to reviews and opinion writing.

But print-based magazines are only a dimple when compared with the many electronic gaming magazines. You can find them easily enough by using the search directories mentioned earlier. Just go down the hierarchy. Click computer games, then publications, then start testing the links. A partial list will include slick electronic magazines such as *GameSpot, Games Domain, Adrenaline Vault, Pawprint Press* and dozens of other powerful examples. You'll also find scores of smaller fan sites, many poorly written, some started purely to satisfy a gaming fan's zeal, others with an eye toward collecting free review copies. And they all need fresh material.

A word of warning, however. Electronic publishing is still in flux. Internet magazines come and go on an almost daily basis. Those that last any length of time are usually hungry for writers, and will tell you so on their home pages. Some pay well. Most don't. If you're eager to add to your portfolio of writing credits, these electronic magazines will provide a rich magnet for your work. But if you want to pick up spare change while writing, be careful which markets you choose.

TURNING RESEARCH INTO THE FINISHED ARTICLE

Research is the name of the game in this chapter, so let us examine an excellent article that demonstrates the value of exhaustive research. Saul Pett, an Associated Press Newsfeatures writer who died in 1993, won a feature-writing Pulitzer in 1982 for a massively researched feature on the federal bureaucracy. "A four-pound story," he called it. The feature, one of the six or seven pieces Pett normally produced for the AP each year, is a staggering 10,000 words long, but he managed to take his giant array of facts and structure them into a fascinating article.

Pett, like many newspaper feature writers, had flexible deadlines. Based in New York, Pett said that despite open-ended deadlines, his editor often suggested a completion date.

"If he likes it and I like it, we go," Pett explained. "We try to guess about whether it will be long or short. We try to guess at whether it can be told in a justifiable length. There isn't a deadline in the sense of a newspaper deadline, but frequently there's a vaguer type of deadline where you want the story to appear before something happens. There's an implied deadline, where it shouldn't be worth any more time." Pett said one to two months was typical for most of his features.

The idea for "The Bureaucracy: How Did It Get So Big?" came from Jack Cappon, Pett's editor. Pett didn't like the story idea at first and resisted taking the assignment. It was too massive, and the research requirements were too overwhelming.

> I kept saying it wasn't practical. How the hell are you going to do a feature on something as big and shapeless as the federal government? It kept coming up, however. He kept bringing it up. Finally, I agreed it ought to be done, but I didn't know how to do it. If you figured out some kind of shape to it, it would take a lot of people working on it. Originally, we thought we'd do it as a team. Then he charmed me into at least trying it, starting it. The idea of starting it was to look into it enough so that I could come up with a notion of what needed doing, an outline. I started, and I kept getting in deeper and deeper and deeper. Then I did it myself. It

was a case of really kind of groping your way. We started with certain questions. How did this big government of ours get so big? What were the things in history—the needs, the political forces—that caused it to grow so? How big is it? How good is it? How ridiculous is it? How much irritation does it cause? How does it compare to bureaucracies abroad?

At any rate, I got into it. I started talking to people and reading. The talks with people were most important when they directed me to something worthwhile to read. That's what I did—read and interviewed and talked to people.

Much to my dismay, I couldn't find a single book on the subject, which struck me as extraordinary. I couldn't find a single magazine piece on the whole subject of the federal bureaucracy. You find any number of pieces or books on parts—fragments—but never the whole thing. Nobody else was insane enough to try to take on the whole thing. And I can see why.

The feature took about four to six months to complete, including three weeks' writing time, Pett said.

PULITZER PRIZE WINNER

SAUL PETT

THE BUREAUCRACY: HOW DID IT GET SO BIG?

WASHINGTON—We begin with the sentiments of two Americans two centuries apart but joined in a symmetry of indignation.

One said this: "He has erected a multitude of new offices and sent hither swarms of officers to harass our people, and eat out their substance."

The other said this: "The government is driving me nuts. The forms are so complicated I have to call my accountant at $35 an hour or my lawyer at $125 an hour just to get a translation."

The latter opinion belongs to Roger Gregory, a carpenter and small contractor of Sandy Springs, Md., a man of otherwise genial disposition.

The first statement was made by Thomas Jefferson of Monticello, Va., in the Declaration of Independence, in the bill of particulars against the king of England that launched the American Revolution.

It is one of the ironies of history that a nation born out of a deep revulsion for large, overbearing government is now itself complaining, from sea to shining sea, about large, overbearing government.

Somewhere between Thomas Jefferson and Roger Gregory, something went awry in the American growth hormone. And now in our 40th presidency, Ronald Reagan is trying to saddle and tame a brontosaurus of unimaginable size, appetite, ubiquity and complexity.

In designing a government, James Madison said, "The great difficulty is this: you must first enable the government to control the governed and, in the next place, oblige it to govern itself." Has it?

One is often told that in a democracy the people get the government they deserve. In the process, do they also get more government than they want? Does anybody recall voting for the regulations which resulted in three years of litigation between the city of Los Angeles and the U.S. Department of Labor over whether the city was guilty of discrimination against the handicapped by refusing to hire an assistant tree-trimmer with emotional problems?

The government of the United States is so big you can't say where it begins and where it ends. It is so shapeless you can't diagram it with boxes because, after you put the president here and Congress there and the judiciary in a third place, where in the hell do you put the Ad Hoc Committee for the Implementation of PL89–306? Or the Interagency Bird Hazard Committee? Or the Interagency Task Force on Inadvertent Modifications of the Stratosphere? Or the Interdepartmental Screw Thread Committee? Or the Interglacial Panel on the Present?

The government of the United States is so unstructured it is owned by everybody and owned by nobody and run by nobody. Presidents run only a part of it. Presidents can't even find and sort out the separate parts.

Jimmy Carter tried. On the crest of promises to streamline and make sense out of the federal bureaucracy, he began by looking for the blueprint. He appointed a panel and the panel looked everywhere, in the drawers, in the closets, in the safe, but they couldn't find it.

"We were unable," the panel concluded, "to obtain a single document containing a complete and current listing of government units which are part of the federal government. We could find no established criteria to determine whether an organizational unit should be included or excluded in such a list."

President Carter never did find out what he was president of. As a candidate, he had flayed the "horrible, bloated bureaucracy." As president, he managed to reduce one or two minor horrors but added to the bloat.

Other presidents have found the bureaucracy an immoveable yeast. Franklin Roosevelt ran into so much resistance from the old departments, he created a flock of new agencies around them to get action. Harry Truman complained the president can issue an order and "nothing happens." He tried to reorganize the bureaucracy with the help of Herbert Hoover but not much changed. John Kennedy said it was like dealing with a foreign power.

It was all much easier when Mr. Jefferson was president. Then, the entire federal establishment throughout the nation, civilian and military, numbered fewer than 10,000. They wouldn't fill half the Pentagon today.

Since 1802, the population of the United States has multiplied 55 times while the population of government has grown 500 times. Since 1802, and most especially in the last 50 years, the government has been transformed, far beyond the ken of the men who started it, in size, power and function. The capital of capitalism now subsidizes rich and poor, capital and labor.

The number of civilian personnel (2.8 million) and military personnel (2.1 million) employed by the federal government has remained fairly constant in recent years. But federal programs have brought vast increases in state and municipal personnel.

Thus, government in the United States on all levels now employs 18 million people. One out of six working Americans is on the public payroll. Government on all levels now costs more than $832 billion a year. Clearly, it is the nation's largest single business and the least businesslike.

None violates Polonius' advice to Laertes more severely than Uncle Sam. He is both a borrower and a lender. He borrows in cosmic amounts and lends on a celestial scale. He lends at less interest than he borrows. And every year, billions slip through his fingers and disappear into the sinkholes of waste, mismanagement and fraud.

But governments are rarely designed for efficiency, especially democratic governments, and most especially this one. This one has grown spectacularly as people demanded more and more of it and as politicians and bureaucrats saw or stimulated those demands. This government was designed for accommodation and consensus. It began on the docks of Boston, not the other side of town, at the Harvard Business School.

Poor old Uncle. He does many essential things that only government can do. He is capable of great change, a necessity for governments that would survive. He has held the place together 205 years in more freedom and comfort than history ever knew. But he is a creature of diverse forces. He gets it on all sides and is perceived in many ways.

A big, bumbling, generous, naive, inquisitive, acquisitive, intrusive, meddlesome giant with a heart of gold and holes in his pockets, an incredible hulk, a "10-ton marshmallow" lumbering along an uncertain road of good intentions somewhere between capitalism and socialism, an implausible giant who fights wars, sends men to the moon, explores the ends of the universe, feeds the hungry, heals the sick, helps the helpless, a thumping complex of guilt trying mightily to make up for past sins to the satisfaction of nobody, a split personality who most of his life thought God helps those who help themselves and only recently concluded God needed help, a malleable, vulnerable colossus pulled every which way by everybody who wants a piece of him, which is everybody.

(continued)

PULITZER PRIZE WINNER   CONTINUED

In one lifetime, the cost of all government in the United States has become the biggest single item in our family budgets, more than housing, food or health care. Before World War II the average man worked a month a year to pay for it; now it takes four months. Now it consumes a third of our Gross National Product. In 1929, it took a tenth.

Our federal income tax began in 1913 but it didn't begin to bite until Pearl Harbor. At that, we have been spared the irony that befell Mother England. Her income tax began as a "temporary war measure" in 1799, to fight Napoleon.

It is in the nature of government measures to achieve immortality. Few die. Governments expand in war and contract slightly in peace. They never go back to their previous size. Peacetime emergencies also have a way of becoming permanent. The Rural Electrification Program was set up in 1935 to bring electricity to American farms. Today more than 99 percent of farms are electrified but the REA goes on, 740 people spending $29 million a year.

When we were kids, the word trillion seemed a made-up word like zillion. Now it's for real. Last year, the federal government owed $914.3 billion. Next year it will owe $1.06 trillion. It is owed $176 billion in direct loans. It has also guaranteed loans for $253 billion. If Chrysler and the others default, the government debt would rise to nearly $1.5 trillion. Like the man said, it all mounts up.

If you would begin to visualize the physical presence of the government, you must brace yourself for more statistics. The government of the United States now owns 413,042 buildings in the 50 states and abroad, excluding military installations abroad. That cost nearly $107 billion. It also leases 227,594,942 square feet of space at an annual rental near $870 million. It owns 775,895,133 acres of land, one-third the land mass of the United States. Uncle is big in real estate.

The government of the United States is so big it takes more than 5,000 people and $210 million a year just to check part of its books. The government is the nation's largest user of energy. A check by a House committee found the government was saving less energy than much of the nation and the Department of Energy, itself, had an "abysmal" record of conservation. The government uses enough energy to heat 11 million homes. It owns 449,591 vehicles. It leases others.

Among others, the government finds it needs the services of 67,235 clerk-typists, 65,281 secretaries, 28,069 air traffic controllers, 27,504 computer specialists, 13,501 internal revenue agents, 5,771 economists, 5,479 voucher examiners, 3,208 psychologists, 16,467 general attorneys, 38 undertakers, 519 non-military chaplains, 1,757 microbiologists, 658 landscape architects, 3,300 librarians, 62 greenskeepers, 16 glassblowers, 8,092 carpenters, 66 saw sharpeners, 4 bicycle repairers, 6 tree fellers, 5 swineherds, and 15 horse wranglers.

"The government is driving me nuts," says Ruby Beha of "Ruby's Truck Stop" on U.S. 50 near Guysville, Ohio. "And the more you make, the more they take."

She complains of high taxes and government forms which require half her waking life, she says, to fill out. She couldn't agree more with Alexis de Tocqueville, the 19th-century French observer of governments, who said, "The nature of despotic power in democratic ages is not to be fierce and cruel but minute and meddling."

Unlike King George, King Sam sends hither swarms of officers with bundles of money and oodles of regulations. In his great urge to protect everybody from everything, from disaster and discrimination, from pestilence and pollution, he sends money with strings attached.

In this, he is damned if he does, and damned if he doesn't. If he sends money without regulation, he risks monumental larceny. If he sends it with regulations, he risks an outraged citizenry.

He has an outraged citizenry. More than the size of bureaucracy, Americans who complain about government complain they are up to their esophagus in indecipherable forms, choking red tape, maddening detail and over-zealous bureaucrats.

In Janesville, Wis., an inspector from the U.S. Department of Agriculture cites a small meat-packing plant for allowing the grass to grow too high outside the plant. What, one cries to the heavens, does that have to do with the meat inside?

"I guess," says Dan Wiedman, the man in charge of sanitation at the plant, "he feels that if the outside isn't neat, the inside isn't sanitized."

In New York, the president of Columbia University says that among the sums he must raise is $1 million a year for government paperwork.

In Sheldon, Iowa (population 4,500), the mayor has to fill out 27 feet of government forms, in quadruplicate, every year, most of them concerning minority employment. Sheldon has no minorities.

In Cambridge, Mass., the president of Harvard says that the federal government, with the strings it attaches to federal funds, tries to decide "who may teach, what may be taught, how it should be taught, and who may be admitted to study."

In Hanover, Wis. (population 200), three men operate a small junkyard called Hanover Auto Salvage. One man is the owner but all three work 60 hours a week and all three draw equal amounts for income from the business every week. The Department of Labor says the two non-owners should be paid overtime. They didn't ask for the overtime. Why, they ask, should they be paid more than the owner for the same work?

In Baltimore, Md., Stefan Graham, director of the zoo, is told by the U.S. Department of Agriculture he must do something about the high bacteria count in a pool occupied exclusively by three polar bears.

The bears have been there a long time. They have lived longer than your average polar bear. They are in good health. The man from Agriculture agrees but regulations are regulations. How, asks the zoo keeper, do you get bears to change their personal habits to keep the bacteria count down? Dunno, says Agriculture, but comply or get rid of the polar bears.

In New York, Mayor Ed Koch is told that unless he installs elevators for the handicapped in subway stations, he risks losing federal funds for mass transit. The elevator system would be so expensive, says Koch, it would mean that each subway ride by each handicapped person would cost the city $50. It would be cheaper to transport them by limousine or cab.

In North Carolina and other places in the South where blacks can now attend white colleges, the Department of Education threatens to withhold federal funds unless black colleges are made more attractive to whites.

In Washington, D.C., Sen. Daniel Patrick Moynihan (D.-N.Y.) complains that for the better part of a year his staff had to negotiate with the Senate Ethics Committee over whether the senator had used the letter "I" more times than the franking privilege rules allow.

"Personally phrased references . . . shall not appear more than five times on a page," according to Section 3210 (a) (5) (c) of the rules. "The essence of the argument," says the senator, "was whether the term we, as in 'we New Yorkers,' implied the term I."

In Janesville, Wis., a small banker complains that since they ask the same questions every year, why can't federal and state bank examiners share the answers and eliminate one of the inspections?

In New York, a long investment prospectus from Merrill Lynch Pierce Fenner and Smith includes this cautious paragraph:

"Section 13. Masculine Pronouns. Masculine pronouns, whenever used herein, shall be deemed to include the feminine, and the use of the masculine pronoun shall not be deemed to

(continued)

PULITZER PRIZE WINNER   CONTINUED

imply any preference for it or any subordination, disqualification or exclusion of the feminine."

God forbid anybody should think that the mighty Wall Street firm was so male chauvinist, so illegally macho, they wouldn't accept money from female investors.

The men (there were no sex discrimination laws then) who wrote the Constitution of the United States were deliberately imprecise. They left room for growth and change. Their descendants often are compulsively detailed.

Somebody in Washington gets an idea. Wouldn't it be nice, especially since there is a lobby of the handicapped, if street curbs had ramps for people in wheelchairs at intersections? Simple? No.

The word goes forth from Washington across the land, whenever federal funds are involved in road construction, that ramps be installed at intersections, each to be a specific width, length, pitch and non-slip material.

The first thing that happens is that in a heavy rain the water running along the gutter is diverted by the ramps and deposits its debris, not in sewers, but out in the street. The second thing that happens is that in the winter, snow plows rip up the protruding grades. The third thing that happens is that blind people relying on canes complain that the ramps confuse their perception of where the curb ends and the street begins.

Washington's passion for detailed regulation has its ironic inconsistencies. For example, the government asks fewer questions of a man buying a Saturday night special than it does of a man importing a salami from Italy. And the man who buys a gun is allowed to leave with his purchase before his answers are verified.

Washington was far more cautious when the city of Des Moines planned to build a viaduct over a railroad in 1971. The estimated cost then was $1.3 million and the feds would put up half in matching funds. But it took five years for the city to persuade Washington that its regulations about environment and noise would be satisfied. By then the viaduct cost $4.1 million. It would have been faster and cheaper if the city had built the viaduct itself, footing the entire bill.

The federal government is easily ridiculed for its bureaucratic excesses, its stifling regulations, its intrusive Big Brotherism. But against that, one needs to recall it was the federal government, not the states or private industry or private charity or the free marketplace, that sustained the country in the Great Depression and saved it from revolution. It was the federal government that ended slavery in the South and had to come back 100 years later with "swarms of officers" to make that liberation real.

It is the federal government that insists management pay labor overtime for overtime work, that cushions the shock of dismissal and prevents child labor. It is the federal government that keeps the poor and the aged out of county poor farms and back attics. It is the federal government that keeps Wall Street honest, makes bank deposits safer, makes the air and the water cleaner, reduces deaths in the mine shafts of Pennsylvania, keeps horrors like thalidomide from disfiguring our babies, makes American airways the safest among the world's busiest, and keeps chaos out of our airwaves by controlling shares to the small Citizen Band owner and the big television networks.

It is the federal government and its loans which keep many small and large business men in business, many farmers on the family farm, many students in college. It is the federal government which injected new life into many downtown areas of the dying cities, with money for new hotels, parking garages, civic centers and open plazas. It is the federal government that gave Detroit its Renaissance Center and Baltimore a revitalized harbor.

"I have no apologies for the federal government being interested in people, in nutrition, education, health and transportation," Hubert Humphrey once said. "Who's going to take care of the environment and establish standards? You? Me? Who's going to work out our transportation problems? The B & O railroad?"

Others ask, who would do all this with better planning and greater efficiency? Chrysler? Lockheed? The New York Central Railroad?

Elmer Staats, as head of the General Accounting Office, spent 15 years ferreting out waste, fraud and sloppy management in Washington. He found plenty. He is not naive about the bureaucracy. He says:

"Americans have come to expect more and more from government while trusting it less. Many of the same individuals who bemoan the growth of government are the first to seek its help when their own interests are involved. They decry the government bureaucrats but are unwilling to accept positions in government because the salaries are too low or the ethical requirements too high. They speak out at every opportunity against the encroachment of government but fail to speak up when asked to volunteer for community endeavors. They most often assert demands or speak of rights rather than duty, obligation or responsibility. They see nothing inconsistent with pleading for tax reduction yet expecting public services to remain the same.

"The once prized characteristic of American society of hard work and self-reliance too often has given way to the view that 'someone else should do it' or someone else should pay the bill, that someone else being government."

The men who created our government were suspicious of government. They feared any restrictions of individual liberty. They were more interested in preventing the accumulation of power than in promoting its efficient use. Thus, they gave us a government of checks and balances and separation of powers in a design that built in tension, competition, even mutual suspicion between branches of government. It was not a blueprint for a smoothly coordinated team.

James Madison, the "father of the Constitution," said that under the document the states would be more powerful than the central government and the federal taxing powers would not be "resorted to except for supplemental purposes of revenue." He said federal powers were "few and defined" while state powers were "numerous and indefinite." Federal powers would be "exercised principally on external objects . . . war, peace, negotiation and foreign commerce." State powers would extend "to all the objects which . . . concern the lives, liberties and properties of the people."

When Mr. Jefferson was in the White House in 1802, the entire federal establishment in Washington numbered 291 officials; the entire executive branch, 132 people. Congress consisted of 32 senators and 106 representatives, all of whom had to get along with a total staff of 13 among them (Congress has 3,500 today). The Supreme Court had six justices, one clerk among them.

The business of national government then was defense, minting money, conducting foreign relations, collecting revenue, maintaining lighthouses for navigation and running the postal service, which in those days belonged to the Treasury Department and—would you believe?—turned a profit.

Almost all the things that government does that affect the lives and fortunes of its citizens were done by the state and local governments, and that wasn't much. Then and for decades after, the national government got along on customs and excise taxes.

The chief proponents of a strong central government then were business leaders and they wanted it only strong enough to protect commerce, provide a nation-wide free home market and a sound currency and banking system.

(continued)

PULITZER PRIZE WINNER   CONTINUED

The public attitude toward the poor reflected the young country's sense of rugged individualism, reliance on family and a strong work ethic. The poor were thought to be poor because of personal failure.

From the Revolution to the Great Depression a century and a half later, help for the needy came mostly from family, charity, or local government. Local public relief bore a stigma.

The federal government grew slowly in its first 150 years. On the expanding frontier, it was involved in territorial jurisdiction and land grants for public education, roads, flood control, drainage, canals and railroads. Until 1893, federal money largely went to pensions, public buildings and river and harbor improvements. There were short-term federal deficits, because of the Civil War, the recession of 1890 and World War I, but nothing like what would come later.

The first federal regulation of the private sector came in 1863 with the creation of the Office of the Comptroller of the Currency as part of the national banking system. In the next 40 years, only two regulatory agencies were added—the Interstate Commerce Commission and the Animal and Plant Health Inspection Service.

Generally, the federal government remained aloof from most domestic affairs. Generally, it was a quiet time and presidents were not overworked. Grover Cleveland could take afternoons off, riding in his Victoria drawn by a matched pair. While the citizenry tipped their hats and said, "Good afternoon, Mr. President."

If it were possible to chart the American dream, you would have a steadily climbing line from 1776 to 1860, a sharp drop for the Civil War and then again a rising line with minor dips, rising, rising, rising to a pinnacle in 1929. We were prosperous. We were buoyant. We were supremely confident.

Then the wheels fell off.

Suddenly, 12 million Americans, one out of four of the country's breadwinners, were looking for jobs that didn't exist. More than 5,000 banks failed and 86,000 businesses went out of business and, in 1932, alone, 273,000 families were evicted from their homes.

In the spreading hunger and deepening humiliation, middle-class neighbors knocked on back doors for handouts. Some people ate weeds and some people fought over leftovers in the alleys behind restaurants and rioting farmers dumped cans of milk rather than sell for two cents a quart and in many places people talked of revolution from the left or the right and across the land nobody seemed to be able to do anything about anything. With all the property foreclosures, with tax revenues way down, the state and city governments were virtually helpless to help, private charities dried up, and the whole blessed country seemed at a dead stop.

Only the federal government had the resources to help and under Franklin Roosevelt it did. This was the watershed, the great turn in history in which laissez-faire died and the basic philosophy of American government was profoundly altered.

Federal Emergency Relief, Social Security, Unemployment compensation. The Civilian Conservation Corps. The National Labor Relations Act. The Securities and Exchange Commission. The Agricultural Adjustment Administration. The Tennessee Valley Authority. The Work Progress Administration.

The cartoons showed men leaning on shovels but it was WPA, or a form of it, that built 10 percent of the new roads, 35 percent of the new hospitals, 70 percent of the new schools. Denver was given a new water supply system; Brownsville, Tex., a port; Key West, the roads and bridges that connect it to the Florida mainland.

WPA built the Lincoln Tunnel between New York and New Jersey, the Camarillo Mental Hospital in California, the canals of San Antonio, the Fort Knox gold depository in Kentucky, Dealey Plaza in Dallas and Boulder Dam in the Colorado River.

Franklin Roosevelt made the economic welfare of Americans a federal commitment. In his turn, Lyndon Johnson took the ball and ran with it—ran away with it, some say.

The '60s were a time of high employment and great economic growth. Every American, it was thought, could be assured a job, a minimum standard of living, adequate diet, decent housing and sufficient health care.

Everything looked possible if you threw enough money and expertise at it—the moon, Vietnam, the policing of the world in our image, the end of poverty, racial injustice, decay of the cities and the sliding quality of life. Thus, we got:

More aid to the poor. More foreign aid. Supreme Court decisions to ensure the rights of minorities and the accused. Food stamps. Medicare. Affirmative Action. Job training. Child care. School lunches. Housing and rent subsidies. Corporate subsidies. Educational aid. Urban renewal. Consumer programs. Wars on poverty and cancer and pollution. Projects to combat heart disease, reduce mental illness, raise reading scores, reduce juvenile delinquency.

All of it, part of what seemed like an unquestioning national momentum to take the risk and inequity out of life, in ghettos and board rooms, in factories and farms, in schools and homes. And people voted for the candidates who made government bigger, Republican as well as Democratic, and before long Washington was into everything from the number of Hispanic teachers in Waukegan to the number of prongs in the electric plugs of a bakery in West Warwick, R.I.

The cost of domestic social programs rose from 17 to 25 percent of the Gross National Product between 1964 and 1974. Defense outlays grew, too, but as a slice of the federal budget domestic programs became twice as large as defense.

Much was attempted, much was accomplished, much ended up a mess. Where failure resulted, it usually was attributed, in retrospect, to an excessive confidence in what government could do. The war on poverty fed and housed the poor but largely failed to make them self-sufficient. Subsidized housing provided better housing but no less crime in the disrupted neighborhoods. Federal efforts to improve student learning fell far short of their spectacular promises.

Ed Koch was a congressman who voted with the flood tide of federal largesse, a fact he now regrets as the mayor of New York swamped in federal regulations.

"The bills I voted for came to the floor in a form that compelled approval. After all, who can vote against clean air and water or better access and education for the handicapped?

"As I look back, it is hard to believe that I could have been taken in by the simplicity of what Congress was doing and by the flimsy empirical support—often no more than a carefully orchestrated hearing record or a single consultant's report offered to persuade members that the proposed solution could work throughout the country."

While the rapid growth of the federal government began in the '30s, it is since 1960 that its restrictive effects have deepened profoundly on individuals, business and lesser governments. Between 1961 and 1973, Washington sprouted 141 new agencies, more than a third of the current total, and none disappeared.

Twenty years ago, federal money going to the state and local governments was slightly more than $7 billion. Now there are nearly 500 programs that cost $88 billion. Then, there were few regulations tied to the money. Now there are 1,260 sets of rules. Then, federal aid went almost entirely to the 50 states. Now it also goes directly to 65,000 cities, towns and wide bends in the road.

A commission appointed by Congress last year concluded that the constitutional system of shared and separate powers among federal, state and local governments is "in trouble."

"The federal government's influence," the commission said, "has become more pervasive, more intrusive, more unmanageable, more ineffective, more costly and, above all, more unaccountable. The intergovernmental system today is a bewildered and bewildering maze of complex, overlapping and, often, conflicting relationships."

(continued)

PULITZER PRIZE WINNER   CONTINUED

Governor Bruce Babbitt of Arizona, a Democrat, aimed his shaft directly at Congress:

"It is hard to see why a national Congress, responsible for governing a continental nation, should be involved in formulating programs for rat control, humanities grants for town hall debates on capital punishment, educating displaced homemakers, training for use of the metric system, jellyfish control, bike paths and police disability grants.

"It is long past time for Congress to . . . ask with the shades of Jefferson and Madison, 'Is this a truly national concern?' Congress ought to be worrying about arms control and defense instead of the potholes in the streets. We just might have both an increased chance of survival and better streets."

Almost since he yawned, stretched and left the cave to get organized, man has made bureaucracy a part of his history.

Julius Caesar levied a 1 percent general sales tax. He also levied an inheritance tax, which contained history's first and most picturesque tax loophole. Close relatives of the deceased were exempt.

It is because of bureaucracy that we think of Bethlehem at Christmas, not a suburb.

"And it came to pass in those days that there went out a decree from Caesar Augustus that all the world should be taxed. And all went to be taxed, everyone into his own city. And Joseph went up to Bethlehem . . . to be taxed with Mary, his espoused wife, being great with child."

Long before Ronald Reagan, there was a Roman historian, Tacitus, who viewed bureaucracy with gloom and doom. "The closer a society is to ruin," he said, "the more laws there are."

If true, we are not alone. In recent years, in most places of the world, small government has grown large and large government has grown larger. The rising tide of paternalism from national capitals has been nearly universal.

Sweden, where someone calculated a new law or ordinance was passed every eight hours of the last decade, now spends more than half of its national income on government. Other countries which spend relatively more on government than we do include the United Kingdom, France, Belgium, Canada, West Germany, Austria, Holland, Denmark, Norway and Italy. Among the major powers, only Japan spends less than we do; it has virtually no military establishment and meets welfare needs through the private business sector.

We are not alone in our irritation.

In Italy, it took Giuseppe Grottadauria two-and-a-half years to get his residence papers switched from Messina to Rome, without which he couldn't vote, buy a car or register his son's birth.

In Italy, it can take four hours in a line at the post office to pay a phone bill. It can take years to get a phone installed and months to register in a university, by which time the new student is taking final exams.

In Sweden, the government intruded on a national pastime. It decreed that people picking and selling wild berries must be registered for income tax. The result was that for two years Sweden had to import berries while thousands of tons rotted in the forests.

In Nanking, China, the requisitioning of 1.3 acres of land took three months and the signatures of 144 officials in 17 different organizations on 46 documents.

In Japan, Mihoko Yokota returned from eight years in the United States and applied for a driver's license. She was asked for proof of residence. She tried to register her new address in Kamakura but was told she needed a form from her last address in Japan. She asked her mother in Hiroshima to send the form by special delivery but when she went to the Kamakura post office to register her new address in order to receive the mail she was told she needed proof of residence which she could not get from the Kamakura city office until her mother in Hiroshima sent the form which could not be delivered until the post office had the form from the Kamakura city hall which finally meant that the form from Mihoko's mother had to be hand-carried by a friend travelling between the two cities. And if you're wondering what yamemasho means, it is the closest the Japanese come to saying, to hell with it.

Students of sanity know there are two ways to react to the Catch-22 situations, the claustrophobic red tape, the sins, excesses and sheer idiocy of big government. One way is to react with indignation; the other, with humor. A carefully calibrated combination of both comes highly recommended for dealing with the following:

The Pentagon's XMI tank program, costing $13 billion, produces a tank which can't run in any but dust-free conditions like those in the lab.

The National Aeronautic and Space Administration asks Congress for $1.1 billion for a new telescope. Turns out NASA made a small bookkeeping error. It will cost $2.2 billion.

The Department of Health, Education and Welfare (now the Department of Health and Human Services) estimates that in fiscal 1979 it blew $2 billion in overpayments or payments to ineligibles in three major welfare programs. Ideally, it says, it hopes to reduce this slippage to 4 percent. That's still $1.1 billion.

Various federal agencies do nothing about $2.5 to $3 billion owed the government by contractors and grantees for questionable payments. Nobody knows the complete total because of poor bookkeeping. One tiny part of HEW blew $1.5 million by letting the statute of limitations expire before trying to recover improper charges.

The government has 12,000 computers. The General Accounting Office spot-checks the payroll computer at the Department of Housing and Urban Development. It feeds the computer fictitious names. Turns out the infernal machine would have paid Donald Duck.

By one estimate, the government spends $9 billion a year on consultants. Two-thirds of the contracts are reportedly let without competing bids. Many of the consultants are former officials of the agency seeking the consultation. Many of the resulting studies end up in drawers and are never used.

One consultant is paid $440 for working September 31, 1978. (Thirty days hath September.) The Environmental Protection Agency pays $360,000 for a study which shows, among other things, that the average speed of trucks in Manhattan is 68 mph.(!)

The new Department of Education pays $1,500 a week for six weeks to a consultant (a former Education official) to design an office layout for its top executives. The Energy Department consults outsiders to explain an act of Congress (the Civil Service Reform Act). Another department hires a consultant to find out how many consultants it has.

A bureaucrat in the Bureau of Labor Statistics makes one mistake in computing used car prices nationally, which pushes up the Consumer Price Index by two-tenths of 1 percent, which increases benefits for millions of people getting regular checks based on the Index.

The General Accounting Office estimates that in the past five years it saved taxpayers nearly $21 billion that otherwise would have gone down the drain because of waste, bad management and uncollected bills. Since the GAO makes only special checks at the behest of Congress, that figure has to be regarded as the tip of an iceberg colored red.

Horrendous as that is, there are those who suspect that private industry is in no position to look down its corporate nose at government.

Clark Clifford, the Washington attorney who has dealt with both for years, says he has also seen "scandalous waste" in the private sector. Paul O'Neill, a former high official of the Office of Management and Budget and now a senior vice president of International Paper Company, adds, "The steel and auto industry made huge mistakes. If you put the Washington press corps on the back of industry you'd find equal stupidity."

(continued)

PULITZER PRIZE WINNER   CONTINUED

With a couple of differences. Private industry has a bottom line: profit. A widget that saves money is highly prized and rewarded.

Government has no bottom line and money becomes an abstraction, as if it belonged to nobody. In government, if your department spends less this year, you're apt to get less from Congress next year. A bureaucrat who finds he can get by with fewer people may find his own grade and salary reduced.

Also, private industry generally can still fire people. The government of the United States generally can't. Once in, federal employees are tough to get out, like headless nails.

An agency fired an employee for beating his supervisor with a baseball bat. The Federal Employees Appeals Authority ordered the culprit reinstated in the same job under the same supervisor with eight months back pay. Reason: the employee was given insufficient notice of dismissal.

It took a Commerce Department manager 21 months and mounds of paper work to fire a secretary who consistently failed to show up for work for reasons of health which proved phony. The manager had to devote so much time to the case his own work suffered and he received a reprimand.

In New York, a postal worker was fired for shooting another man in the stomach during a difference of opinion. The attacker went to jail but appealed for dismissal. He won reinstatement and $5,000 in back pay on the grounds that the papers were filled out wrongly. So they filled them out rightly and this time the firing stuck but the postal gunslinger kept the $5,000.

Nearly all federal employees are protected by Civil Service or other rigid umbrellas. They are also represented by 78 labor unions and associations. Civil Service was begun in 1883 to replace the old spoils system by which all federal workers could be fired every four years. Merit replaced politics as a condition of employment.

But by 1919, a congressman was complaining on the floor of the House about all the "clinkers" in government who couldn't be purged: "They are in all departments, killing time, writing answers to letters that do not answer, stupidly pretending to do work that live employees must do over again."

Fifty-nine years later, President Carter complained to Congress: "It is easier to promote and transfer incompetent employees than to get rid of them. It may take as long as three years to fire someone for just cause. . . . You cannot run a farm that way, you cannot run a factory that way, and you certainly cannot run a government that way."

Added to the Civil Service complications were the difficulties created by equal opportunity legislation. An administrator would have to think hard about firing a member of a minority for incompetence. If the incompetent countered with a discrimination suit, the administrator would have to hire his own lawyers to defend himself. If the decision went against him, he could lose pay or position.

In 1978, out of 2.8 million people on his payroll, Uncle Sam managed to fire 119 for "inefficiency." Later that year, Carter got some civil service reform out of Congress and in the next go-round 214 employees were sacked for the same reason. Not exactly a spectacular leap forward. There remained a huge permanent core entrenched in concrete and beyond the reach of presidents to touch.

Low-level federal workers are said to be paid somewhat more than their counterparts in the private sector. Many higher levels are paid much less than they could earn on the outside.

Federal pensions are generally better than private ones and in recent years, along with cost of living increases, 99 percent of federal employees were given annual merit raises. Were there really that many that good?

In the Carter administration, Carol Foreman headed food inspection and consumer services in the Agriculture Department. "I have a staff of 10,000," she once said. "A few are very dedicated, a few are very talented, and then there are the others."

The goof-offs and foul-ups in government obviously get more attention than the people doing their job. Few Americans were aware of the calibre of Foreign Service officers until the hostages came back from Iran. Few are aware of the young lawyers who pass up golden offers from big firms to work in legal aid for the poor. The doctors in public health get no attention every day they prevent epidemics until the day they fail. The men and women who leave fat corporate jobs to work much harder for much less in government get no space in the papers until one of their number is caught with his hand in the till.

Most students of government agree that the trouble with government is not the bureaucrats, good, bad or indifferent, but that chaotic system that incubates and nourishes them.

What we have is a big, implausible, ramshackle house, distorted by random additions, by corridors that go nowhere and rooms that don't connect, a house loosely expanded through the years for numberless children, most of them unexpected. There was no family planning. There was no architect.

"Congress has the power but not the incentive for coordinated control of the bureaucracy while the president has the incentive but not the power," said Morris P. Fiorina, a political scientist, speaking generically.

Congress can create, change or kill an agency through its funding power. Presidents can only hope to mobilize public opinion. Presidents seek re-election and a place in history. Members of Congress seek re-election but, each being one of 535, cannot count on immortality. Congressmen get re-elected, not for the broad strokes of history, but for the post offices or sewage systems or dams they bring their constituents.

And back there, everybody is for saving money in general but not in particular. The taxpayer in Colorado may not shed a tear over cuts in urban renewal funds for New York, but don't touch his water projects. And vice versa, the taxpayer in New York. And the rural congressman, who couldn't care less about a Model Cities program, votes for Model Cities in a trade for a vote for farm subsidies from the urban congressman. "A billion here, a billion there," said Everett Dirksen. "Pretty soon, you're talking about real money."

Even the pure in heart can't escape the swelling effect of politics. Two powerful Republican senators (Jesse Helms and Robert Dole) had candidates for the job of assistant agriculture secretary for governmental and public affairs. The Reagan administration solved the dilemma by splitting the job between the two choices but not the salary. Each will be paid $52,750 a year . . .

There is, we are told, a constituency for every dollar in the federal budget. Everyone seems to have a compelling reason and consistency is not always the rule of the day.

The American Medical Association, which once opposed Medicare as socialized medicine, now opposes cuts in Medicare on which many doctors depend heavily for their income.

In 1978, the snow was so heavy that cities in Michigan asked for federal money to help with the snow removal. In 1979, the snow was so light the ski areas in Michigan asked for federal aid. Rain or shine, Uncle Sam often finds himself in a no-win situation.

If he insists on taking more time to examine the eligibility of people asking for welfare, does he risk causing some of them to starve or freeze? If he doesn't guarantee a loan for Chrysler, will he be responsible for throwing thousands of auto workers out on the street? If he sends a mother to jail for food stamp fraud, won't he have to feed her children in a foster home at greater cost? If he cuts subsidies for the merchant marine and airlines, will he have enough ships and planes in the next war?

Presidents come, presidents go, but in Washington there remains a permanent bureaucracy with its own ideas, momentum, inner resources, cozy ties with key members of Congress and

(continued)

PULITZER PRIZE WINNER   CONTINUED

ingenious ploys for survival. Nothing evokes the fancy footwork of a bureaucrat so much as a presidential attempt to cut his budget.

Ask Amtrak to cut the fat out of its operation and it comes back with a dandy plan to eliminate railroad routes going through the home districts of powerful committee chairmen in Congress who would never tolerate it. Ask Interior to save money and it proposes to close the national parks earlier or shut down the elevators in the Washington Monument, neither of which the public would take lying down.

Generals are very good at this, although lately they haven't had to be. Ask a general in the Pentagon to cut and he goes dutifully before an appropriations committee, with whose chairman he is secretly wired, and he says, loyally, yes, he can oblige the president. But on further questioning, his expression grows more pained until finally, in all candor, he lets it be known in hushed tones, that the proposed reduction would leave the entire East Coast of the United States defenseless.

Deeply embedded in the inner workings of the permanent government, like the wheels and timing mechanism of a bank vault, there are "iron triangles" of power and expertise which continue to hum, quietly and smoothly, regardless of the passing sounds of elections.

At the three corners, there are the bureaucrats running a given program, the key congressmen favoring it and the special interest groups benefiting from it. They are welded together for mutual self-interest and survival. They can defy presidents.

Bryce Harlow, who has been around Washington almost as long as the Monument, who worked on the Hill and served in high places in the Eisenhower and Nixon administrations, likens the triangles to complexes of bees.

"They form like bees around a flower, and they stroke it and milk it and make it give forth its honey. They are in all departments of the government and they don't much care who is president or who is the cabinet member in charge. To a large extent, America is governed by these complexes.

"Let's begin with an administrative under-secretary in, say, the Agriculture Department. We'll call him Jack Brown . . ."

Jack knows everybody. He knows the key people in his department who are dependent on him. He knows John Doe and Horace Smith in the Office of Management and Budget. They have been working together for years on agricultural budgets. They socialize together.

Jack Brown also knows Bill Gordon, a veteran member of the professional staff of the House subcommittee on farm appropriations. Jack and John and Horace and Bill and their wives go to the same conventions together, to meetings of the cotton council, the soybean council, the Grange, the Farm Bureau.

"Everybody knows everybody and they all get on well together," Harlow concludes, "and they are all milking the same flower."

More and more professional bureaucrats are people who were trained in specialized sciences and technologies and seek to apply their expertise in government. They have counterparts on the staffs of Congress and in state and local governments. They form a network of experts on which presidents, Congress, governors and mayors rely. They speak their own language. They sometimes agree more with each other than with the people they work for.

It used to be, says Senator Daniel Moynihan, who was an assistant secretary of labor under Kennedy, that "when the Labor Department needed a policy, it sent out for one, you might say, from the AFL-CIO." Now it gets policy from in-house experts.

Samuel Beer, a professor of government at Harvard, maintains that most of the Great Society programs began with the professionals in government, not with the public demanding them.

"In the fields of health, housing, urban renewal, highways, welfare, education and poverty, it was in very many cases people in government service, acting on the basis of specialized and technical knowledge, who conceived the new programs, initially urged them on the attention of the president and Congress, and, indeed, went on to lobby them through to enactment."

Whether the programs begat the constituents or the constituents begat the programs, whichever came first, the chicken or the egg, we now have a lot of chickens in Washington. And they all know how to lobby. They all know how to bring pressure for and against.

It used to be, someone said, that politics was about a few things; now it's about everything. It used to be that major power blocs which shaped government were business, labor and agriculture. Now power is fragmented into a thousand insistent voices, which have to be heard and reconciled.

They are highly organized for the annual fight over the federal pie and fight frequently for their slice with the help of interested bureaucrats. They have become so effective as to cause some students of government to fear that power in this country has shifted from the people and their elected representatives to organized interest groups and bureaucrats.

E. Pluribus Unum is in trouble. If ever we were one out of many, we are now many out of one. John Gardner, founder of Common Cause, calls the centrifugal forces of special interest groups a "war of the parts against the whole."

The parts multiply like the denizens of a rabbit warren on New Year's Eve. Everybody, it seems, wants something or opposes something and, in the melee, bureaucracy grows larger and more shapeless and threatens to become, in itself, a government of too many people, by too many people, for too many people.

Source: © 1981. The Associated Press. Reprinted by permission of the Associated Press.

There you have it. An enormous amount of primary research (interviews, documents, government reports and news stories) and secondary research (books, summaries and popularizations) went into Pett's piece, almost too much to handle. But Pett managed it remarkably. Structurally, the story uses a problem-and-solution format, like a mystery story. Why has the bureaucracy grown so large? the story asks, and answers.

Like any good writer, Pett was alert to any offshoots or secondary trails while conducting his interviews and research. Take a look at the lead, for example. In this story, the lead is eight paragraphs (or, if you prefer, 11 sentences) long. It contrasts two statements, one old and one modern, then with graphic imagery and lively language brings the reader to the jackpot question: Has the government learned to govern itself?

Pett explained how the lead came about.

One of the people I interviewed was a bureaucrat down in Tennessee. He was a good observer of bureaucracy at work. As we were talking and he was throwing a lot of bureaucratic language at me, which was putting me to sleep, he asked me a question: "Surely you're familiar with the part of the Declaration of Independence that complains about British bureaucracy." And I kind of nodded my head knowingly, ashamed to admit that I didn't. He quoted it. I couldn't wait to get my own copy of the Declaration. I read it and found that passage [in the second paragraph] in which Thomas Jefferson is speaking of King George. Now I knew I had the lead. It gave the story a shape. Then I recalled what Roger Gregory had said, and I put the two together: one man speaking for now and the other for 200 years before. And they both seemed to come to the same conclusion. And both conclusions led me to the fact that an awful lot of people in this country were complaining about large, overbearing government.

But there was a problem with using Gregory. Pett, writing his story in a cabin in Virginia, met Gregory, who was doing contracting work for Pett's friends who owned the cabin. "I got to know Roger, and he asked me what I was working on. I told him. That's when he said what he said about the government," Pett explained.

"Roger lives in Maryland, right across the river, but he does work for these friends in Virginia. I thought he would be a good one to match with a fellow named Jefferson. Another reason I liked Roger's quote was because at the time I assumed he was a Virginian because I met him in Virginia. I said, 'Wouldn't that be nice? To say something in my lead about the sentiments of two Virginians.' Then I discovered that he wasn't, and that almost broke my heart."

Still, the lead works, thanks to Pett's skill.

The body of the feature is orderly. After the lead introduces the problem, the reader learns through carefully researched facts and anecdotes how big the government really is, what problems that bigness causes, how the bigness isn't necessarily bad, how the government got so big, how other governments compare to the U.S. bureaucracy, why the government is still growing and what probably caused all that bigness—and still causes it. Thus, the problem is introduced, examined in both historical and contemporary perspective and explained.

Such a long story could easily have been boring. Pett's secret for retaining reader interest was to use quotes, anecdotes and superior writing to illustrate points. For example, when he described red tape, he provided graphic language and anecdotal detail, complete with a quotation.

> More than the size of bureaucracy, Americans who complain about government complain they are up to their esophagus in indecipherable forms, choking red tape, maddening detail and over-zealous bureaucrats.
>
> In Janesville, Wis., an inspector from the U.S. Department of Agriculture cites a small meat-packing plant for allowing the grass to grow too high outside the plant. What, one cries to the heavens, does that have to do with the meat inside?
>
> "I guess," says Dan Wiedman, the man in charge of sanitation at the plant, "he feels that if the outside isn't neat, the inside isn't sanitized."

The bureaucracy story was well received by Associated Press members. Pett said,

> It did very well, despite the length. We indicated that if [newspapers] wanted to use it in sections, we could show them how to break it up. It is written in sections. Very few did. Most of them used it in one big gulp. For a long time, I've clung to the idea that if you've got a good subject, and it requires a lot of space, I prefer to write it and I prefer to read it in one piece rather than a series. I detest series. Lot of wasted words in there. You end one and you have to kind of summarize. When you start another one, it's repetitious. I like the idea of being able to get a certain momentum going.

The momentum continued when the story went before the Pulitzer panel of judges, who gave it one of journalism's highest accolades. But none of it—wide use by AP member newspapers, momentum, or Pulitzer Prize—would have been possible without Pett's superior foundation of research.

CHAPTER FIVE

INTERVIEWING FOR NEWSPAPER FEATURE STORIES AND MAGAZINE ARTICLES

KINDS OF INTERVIEWS

Newspaper feature and magazine article interviews are similar. The only important difference is that the typical newspaper feature interview may be somewhat less thorough because the newspaper writer frequently faces an imminent deadline.

Interviews for newspapers or magazines can be conducted in person, by telephone, in a group or by electronic mail or letter. Each category of interview has a unique purpose, as well as distinct advantages and disadvantages.

For example, the skillfully conducted *personal* interview—the cornerstone of the story—should yield good quotations, accurate description and insight into the issues and individuals in the story.

The disadvantage of the personal interview is that it takes time—time to arrange, time to gain the confidence of the subject, time to get the necessary information and time to disengage from the interview.

If the personal interview is like a full meal, the *telephone* interview is a fast-food sandwich because it serves a purpose but in a minimal way.

The advantage of the telephone interview, usually used for a story's secondary figures or for re-interviews of primary subjects, is its quickness, like fast food.

One disadvantage of using the telephone is that you can't see the interviewee, which means you can't describe him or her. The main disadvantage is that you can't establish much rapport with the interviewee because of the impersonality of the telephone. To mitigate this disadvantage, work on your telephone manners and also provide verbal reinforcement for interviews, such as an occasional "Uh-huh" or "I understand."

When *Los Angeles Times* writer Barry Siegel needed to re-interview a busy Utah judge for Siegel's 2002 Pulitzer Prize–winning story about a trial involving a young father who later committed suicide, telephone interviews were the logical solution. Siegel says: "I spent four months on this project. This included a week-long trip to Utah. Back in Los Angeles, I spent a good deal of time reading through, annotating and organizing the huge pile of documents I had. I also spent a good deal of time on the phone, doing follow-up interviews with Judge Hilder after I returned from Utah. Hilder wasn't regularly available during the work week, but on weekends, he was busy at home, occupied with a house remodeling project. So on Saturdays and Sundays, he would turn on his speakerphone and talk to me for hours as he painted and sanded."

The third category of interview is the *group* session, often with a subject whose spouse or friend is present. A variation is an interview with a company employee in the presence of one or more corporate public relations representatives.

The only advantage to the group interview is that it's better than no interview at all. Its disadvantage is that everyone in the room may want to answer your question, or—in the case of a PR representative overseeing the interview—the subject's answers may be tainted.

To get the most out of a group interview, code your notebook so that you can ascertain who said what, or use an audio recorder. Also, make arrangements to contact the prime interviewee later by telephone for additional comments.

Occasionally a writer is unable to reach a source in person or by telephone. In that case, a *written* list of questions is an alternative to no interview at all. For example, if you repeatedly fail to reach a key executive in a major corporation, try submitting questions by e-mail. If you conduct an interview by e-mail, treat the electronic communication as a formal business letter: Be professional and make certain there are no misspellings or grammatical mistakes. If you have published material that is posted on the Internet, provide links so that the interviewee can verify your credentials. Also use a subject heading that will differentiate your e-mail from unsolicited advertising. The executive may respond by e-mail or by letter, and may even telephone you, thus upgrading the quality of the interview.

The advantage to the written interview is that, like the group interview, it's better than nothing. Its disadvantages are numerous: You can't establish rapport with the subject; your source has ample opportunity to ignore or to be unresponsive to your questions; you have no opportunity for clarification or elaboration; and what you cannot see you cannot describe.

GETTING READY TO INTERVIEW

Who to Interview

All article interviews begin with a question: Who will be interviewed?

That sounds like an easy question, but the answer often can be elusive. For example, assume you're a newspaper feature writer and you want to write an odd-occupation story about a thus far unselected professor at the state university because you've learned that more than half of the nation's university professors supplement their income with outside activities. These activities range from consulting in their field to operating businesses, you've been told.

You call the university's media liaison office and ask for help. The media representative provides you with three names: A broadcasting professor has a half-interest in a radio station; a business teacher does consulting for Fortune 500 companies; and an English professor writes paperback romance novels.

Then the media liaison recalls that an education professor has recently quit his tenured post to buy and operate a bowling alley a few miles from campus. His customers call him "Doctor Strike," the media representative tells you. Bingo. With that, you've found your main *who* and, in the process, refocused your story, which will now be about university teachers who leave teaching, personified by Doctor Strike.

Your interviewee list isn't complete, of course. You'll need to talk to Doctor Strike's former department chairperson and a few colleagues and students. You'll also want to talk to some of his customers and employees and perhaps his wife. For perspective, you'll need other examples of professors from the state's colleges who have junked their teaching careers. And you'll need to find at least one expert who can explain why professors leave teaching. (If you were freelancing this to a national general-interest magazine, you could still focus on the professor, but you probably would need to draw your other examples from universities across the country to give the story national scope.)

As you can see, the focus of your story should lead you to a key *who*. But the right *who* also can change the focus of the story. Finally, except for the most superficial newspaper features, your *who* really should be a list rather than a single name.

Jacqui Banaszynski, a *St. Paul Pioneer Press* writer, used a somewhat similar process for her 1988 Pulitzer Prize–winning feature series, "AIDS in the Heartland." Banaszynski, who wanted to humanize the AIDS crisis for Minnesota readers, explains:

> I started covering AIDS . . . when I worked at the Minneapolis *Star Tribune*. I covered the women and minorities beat there and I defined the gay community as a minority because politically they are. When I came [to the *Pioneer Press*], one of the things I brought with me was an interest and contacts with the gay community. So as AIDS stories began to develop here, I would pick them up. Our medical reporter tended to do the baseline stuff [and] I was writing about the human condition. We sat down in late 1985—the medical reporter, myself and our assignment editor—and said, "What are we going to do about AIDS? This is getting bigger and we have got to do something." We brainstormed for an hour and came up with 50 to 55 story ideas. One of the stories was the diagnosis-to-death story, which was not novel. We knew it had been done, but that didn't particularly bother me because it hadn't been done for our readers. From there, however, it took a full year to find somebody. . . .
>
> I was very determined that we needed to find a gay man who had AIDS [rather than a heterosexual] because in Minnesota [most] AIDS patients are gay men. That would give me the opportunity to explore what AIDS is really about—which is about discrimination and oppression and homophobia. We stumbled onto several people who seemed good, but for one reason or another they rejected us or we rejected them. Usually it had to do with the fact that they didn't want to go public. In a couple of cases, I didn't think their story was compelling enough.

A source suggested that Banaszynski contact Dick Hanson, a farmer and political activist who lived northwest of St. Paul. More than one year after the brainstorming session, Banaszynski found her *who*—Hanson and, to a lesser extent, his partner, Bert Henningson Jr. In the process, the focus of Banaszynski's story changed from that of a simple profile of Hanson to the far more complicated story of two AIDS sufferers in a homosexual relationship who are battling a deadly disease and an unsympathetic society.

> [Photographer Jean Pieri and] I went out to the [Hanson] farm . . . and I came away thinking that what we had was one straightforward profile about Dick Hanson—a public figure who

had a lot of political connections, and had an interesting history that was fairly well known in Minnesota—who was dying of AIDS. I didn't think we had more than that. In part, that was because I didn't think we had the luxury of time because Dick was pretty sick. The other reason was because the first time out there I wasn't seeing anything that was that compelling and that different. On a subsequent trip Dick and Bert became more comfortable with us and started talking more. They started talking about the family, about financial issues. And so I left the farm that time and put the editors off and said I needed to go back one more time. I went back the third time [and] we went out to dinner and that's when these guys started to really tell a story. Dick was away from the table for a few minutes and I was talking to Bert about their relationship and that's when I started to see this incredible love story. I also realized that these two men were extremely articulate about the things going on in their lives, and had thought about them a lot.

Isabel Wilkerson, the Chicago bureau chief for *The New York Times* who won a feature-writing Pulitzer in 1994 for her profile of a 10-year-old Chicago boy burdened with a man's obligations, knew the characteristics of the child she wanted to interview but struggled for months to find the ideal candidate. Wilkerson explains the process she used to find Nicholas Whitiker, who would be featured in the *Times* as one of 10 children growing up in extremely challenging circumstances in various parts of the United States:

How the Nicholas story came to be is a story unto itself, and how I found Nicholas is the basis of workshops that I have done all over the country because it just ended up being this journey that I could not have expected.

What (*Times* reporters and editors) ended up doing was we spent almost a year—we spent about eight months (in 1992)—talking. It was editors and reporters coming together in New York. The national editor and metro editor had decided to (see) what would be the best way to combine resources to tell the story in a way it had not been told before. So reporters and editors came together and we talked and reporters were saying, "We've done profiles before. We've tried to write the story when it breaks. . . ." We all were feeling a sense of frustration. "What is it that we can do?" We actually brought in some young people themselves from the neighborhoods and we interviewed them . . . searching for what would be the best way to tell it. One of the editors came up with the idea of what about grabbing the reader's attention with one story a day for 10 days about a single child. One child a day for 10 days—on the front page.

So we had the go-ahead to begin looking for people to fill this 10-part series. Once it had been decided that this would be the format in which we would tell the story, each reporter was then told to write down the general themes that (he or she) thought should be the approach. If we had 10 kids, how would we distinguish each child from another? How would we avoid repetition and duplication in the story-telling? People came up with something that you would expect—drugs and crime and gangs and schools and the usual. . . . In mine I did some of those things and I also I came up with some others. And one of the things I came up with was family.

I had done many stories about children in one way or the other, and the experiences that I had in doing stories about children told me that I wanted to inform my search to find this child. . . . What kind of person do I want? . . . I was thinking, everybody has a family. The family itself is a vague and all encompassing term that means everything and nothing. It was so broad.

I figured out several things that I wanted to consider. I didn't want an extreme. I wanted a child that anyone could relate to. . . . I wanted someone who would be universal in his general character and circumstance. I also decided that I wanted a child who had siblings so that these siblings could play off of one another and off of the main character (and) supporting characters, so to speak. I had had a lot of experience . . . interviewing children and I found that there was a particular age—that some ages were better than others. I wanted a child between the ages of nine and 12. And that ended up being critical to finding (Nicholas). It turns out that if I had changed the age limit by even one year, I would not have found (Nicholas).

Wilkerson considered searching for her child in schools, welfare offices and gang intervention programs, but rejected those venues.

I ended up deciding to go in the back door and that was to find a parent who would allow me access to his or her child. That made it all the more complicated and added an additional layer. It made it a far more time-consuming search because it was an oblique, indirect way to find the child that I wanted.

I decided that I wanted a parent who had been on the edge but who was trying to climb out of this, someone who had been in a cave or in a tunnel but who was just emerging from it. I thought that would be the best point in which to find someone because they would be more reflective about their experience but they would also have been through something that would have some drama and conflict. I also thought it would end up being more hopeful and not quite so dreary as so many of these stories can be.

I went to all of the places that I thought parents would go when they were trying to pull themselves up. I went to night school classes, I went to adult education classes, I went to data processing classes, typing classes, GED classes, court reporting classes. I basically combed the Chicago area for all of the places where people who had been on the edge might go to improve themselves and pull themselves out of their situation. This took a great deal of time just to set this up. I'd have to call and find which class would be the best one for me to go to, where the teacher wouldn't mind me coming in and making an announcement at the beginning of the class. . . .

I would go in and I would tell them: "I'm a reporter with *The New York Times* and I'm writing a story about families, talking about how difficult it is to raise children in the cities today. And I'd like to talk with as many of you as I can and talk with you about your experiences raising children. And those of you who have children between the ages of 9 and 12, I'd like you to sign up and I would like to give you a call later. . . ."

I spent as much time searching as I did with the family itself. . . . If you (find) the right person, everything else falls into place. If you end up with the wrong person, it is very difficult to recover from that. Wrong person in many different ways. Someone who is not quite ready for the commitment that is involved. Someone who really does not want to tell the story. Someone who wants to do this for a reason that is not going to be helpful to the story: They want to get publicity for their child or maybe are trying to use the child for some other purpose. What you are hoping for is that you'll find the person where your interest fits their motivations, which ultimately are in the best interests of the story. It's very difficult to do that.

I felt like the Dr. Seuss character that used to go up to every living creature and ask, "Are you my mother?" I had come so close to what I thought was the ideal and it had just evaded my grasp.

After weeks of announcements and meetings with dozens of parents, Wilkerson found Angela Whitiker.

I made my spiel . . . and this woman came in late and had not heard what I had said. By this time, the sign up sheet had been moving about the room from woman to woman. And when it came to her, someone told her, "You're supposed to sign this if you have a child between the ages of 9 and 12." And she reflexively signed her name. Nicholas was 9 at the time. If I had said 10 to 12, she would not have signed and I would never have met Nicholas. And there would be times when I would go in and say 10 especially after I had had (a negative) experience with very young children and I thought I should up it.

She was very open, very honest. And I later found out that she was at the perfect juncture in life where she had emerged from a horrible situation, and because she had she was almost a proselyte for a new kind of life. She was like a reformed smoker who can't wait to go out and tell others about what you need to do to kick the habit. She was just at that right moment, right for telling her story.

When Wilkerson met Nicholas and the other four Whitiker children, she knew she had found her subjects. The story idea had taken more than a year to refine. The search had taken a month. The interviewing and reporting would take another month.

Angelo Henderson of *The Wall Street Journal* wrote an early version of his story about the Detroit pharmacist who killed an armed robber that was based largely on interviews with the druggist. When Henderson's editor read the story, the editor said, "'I don't know how sorry I should feel for the dead guy,'" Henderson explains. Henderson renewed his efforts to learn more about the armed robber. A police public information officer gave Henderson the information he needed to see a death certificate. The death certificate provided a link to Chicago, where Henderson located the funeral home that provided services for the dead man. The funeral home wouldn't provide family information, but did provide an obituary, which gave the cemetery location. At the cemetery, Henderson learned the address of the family responsible for the plot. Henderson went to the home and found the robber's family. The final version of the story—the one that won the 1999 Pulitzer Prize for feature writing—provided profiles of both the druggist and the armed robber.

Asking for the Interview

The next step is to ask for the interview. Getting an interview is sometimes difficult because studies show that many people are wary of the press. For example, first-time interviewees may picture themselves confronted with questions such as, "Do you still beat your mother?"

The best way to ask for interview time is to explain quickly and clearly who you are, why you want the interview and how much time you will need. Ask for enough time to complete the interview but allow more time in your schedule in case the interview goes beyond the allotted period.

You also may have to explain to the interviewee how the story you want to write differs from investigative reporting and what the interview will be like.

Remember that no one (except perhaps government employees responding to questions about their work) owes you an interview. Everyone else who agrees to talk to you is performing a courtesy. To be sure, giving you an interview is not an act of pure altruism. The interviewee can benefit from the experience in numerous ways, including recognition and the excitement of a new experience.

Many of America's best newspaper and magazine writers agree that asking for the interview is worrisome. Pulitzer winner Madeleine Blais of *The Miami Herald* says: "It's the convincing that I dread the most." Her approach is "to convey confidence that this story is worth doing."

Banaszynski says she dreaded asking Dick Hanson for permission to write about him because she couldn't bear to ask him "if I could watch him die."

> I was terrified. My stomach was a mess. I said [to Dick], "You know this means that I'm asking permission to stay with this story to the end."
>
> At this point, Dick still felt that there was some hope, that he would beat AIDS. Dick looked at me—he kind of winced—and said this was a story of life and hope. I looked at him and said, "Dick, I know that you think that this is going to work out and if it does, I want to be there because I've got the best story in the universe: the first person to beat AIDS. But if it doesn't work out, I want to be there, too."
>
> Dick shrugged and said, "Of course."
>
> I looked at him and said, "Wait a minute. You're making this decision too quickly. I want you and Bert to talk about this because it's going to mean a lot of things." We talked about all of the time it was going to take. I said, "You're going to get sick of me, real tired of my face, real tired of having a camera in your face when you're just feeling awful. You're going to get real tired of sharing your time. Your family is going to come down on you real hard. You're going to get letters. This is going to be a big drain."
>
> Dick and Bert had a two-minute conversation and approved the idea. This was Dick's last way to do something productive with his life.

Teresa Carpenter, who won the feature Pulitzer in 1981, says asking for an interview is also complicated by the unpredictability of interviewees. "One problem I get into when I have a long story and a raft of interviews to set up is trying to second-guess who will and will not talk. You can do that within limits but, in fact, some people you think would never talk to you respond to a simple, direct request—and other people who you think would have a lot to gain by talking to you, won't.

"So the thing to do is not think it through too much and just start making calls. Just make calls as quickly as you can," Carpenter advises.

Delays in scheduling interviews are common. For example, Blais notes that she was asked to "audition" before a boy who was to be subject of a medical feature. "I was being tested because the mother had said that although the boy wouldn't mind being interviewed, he wanted to meet the person first. I was being auditioned and I was auditioning the subject matter," Blais explains. On the other hand, Sheryl James, the *St. Petersburg Times* reporter who won the Pulitzer in 1991 for her story about the Florida woman who abandoned her newborn baby in a box next to a trash dumpster, spent nearly seven months trying to convince the baby's mother to talk to her.

Sometimes the writer initiates the delay after asking for the interview. Alice Steinbach, the Baltimore *Sun* journalist who won the 1985 feature Pulitzer for a story about a blind boy named Calvin Stanley, says letting time pass before starting a story is often a good idea. Steinbach says:

> I really had to try to slow [the Stanleys] down. When I went to interview them and Calvin, I knew when I met Ethel [Calvin's mother] and Calvin and Calvin Stanley [the father] that

these were people who could verbalize the story, and who were insightful enough about themselves and about the situation to tell me what a good story needs. You can have a great story but if people can't tell you [about it], you can't write it.

But I also knew that we would get to be very intimate and personal. I wanted them to know exactly what they were getting in for. And so, I spoke to them about this, and I spoke to Calvin about it. I let them know that I was going to be hanging around a lot, that there'd be a photographer at the school, that I'd be at the school, that I would be asking them intimate questions, painful questions, and that I did not want them to do it unless they felt they could handle that. I explained to Calvin and to his parents that it might make the other kids jealous, that there might be some feedback that would be negative when the story came out.

I gave them articles that I had written so that they could get a sense of the kinds of questions I would be asking. I said, "Take these articles. Think about it. Talk about it. And I will call you in two weeks." And they immediately said, "We really want to do it," and I said, "No, I'd rather we do it this way." When I called them, they agreed.

I really laid the groundwork very carefully. By the time I started the story, I really felt we all knew what we were in for, and that made a big, big difference.

Persuading People Who Don't Want to Talk

If you have trouble convincing the subject to help you, there are some time-tested techniques you may wish to consider.

If you suspect the subject might reject your request, find a mutual acquaintance beforehand and ask that person whether your subject would make a good story. Then, assuming your acquaintance agrees with your judgment, contact your interviewee and say: "Your (best friend, boss, minister, wife or attorney, depending on who gave you the individual's name) suggested that I call you for an interview because what you've done would make an interesting story." This approach combines a little flattery with credibility by association. The subject probably won't want to offend the friend by refusing your request and, in addition, will assume you're reliable because you know his or her friend.

If you detect reluctance on the part of the subject, try to find out what's bothering the potential interviewee. If the problem is something you can correct, correct it. For example, if the subject is concerned about the kind of story you intend to write, send a sample of a previous story you've written.

Finally, there's pleading, a less dignified though occasionally acceptable approach. Or you might try an alternative last-ditch variation that Pulitzer Prize winner Banaszynski uses on rare occasions.

I have gone so far in some interviews as to tell people [who are not public figures], "Look, I want to do this interview. I know you don't want to do this story. Let me come and talk to you and [if you're unhappy] at the end of this session, I'll give you my notebook." I've never had to give up my notebook and I've gotten three or four great stories that way that other reporters couldn't get.

When and Where to Interview

You need to plan your interview with the thoroughness of a physician contemplating surgery. And, like the surgeon, you must guide the process because you have a limited time to accomplish a large number of goals. Finally, as with the surgeon, if the interview fails, it may be because of your lack of skill.

Exercising control means planning when and where to interview key subjects. For example, if you interview "Doctor Strike" on a Saturday night—his busiest time—you can expect a short session. Instead, find out when his slowest day is, and make your appointment then.

And if you interview him in his busy little office at the bowling alley, the ringing telephone and the thunder of gutter balls will probably sabotage thoughtful answers to your questions. Instead, arrange to talk to him over a prolonged cup of coffee at a restaurant down the street, or in his home.

James stresses controlling the interview environment. She explains:

> To me, the secret of good feature interviewing is in establishing a zone of rapport with the subject. This requires making sure you control the physical situation of the interview—never catch someone on the fly, between classes, before a speech. Be patient: Wait to set up an interview with them, preferably in their habitat, and speak to them alone. I avoid interviewing two people at one time, unless the story drama dictates it.

Banaszynski particularly favors home interviews. She explains:

> I always try to interview people at their homes for two reasons: It puts them at ease and it tells me a hell of a lot about them. To see how someone and where someone lives tells a lot. You also tend to get more time that way. . . . People are very reluctant to kick you out of their homes. They let you stay and they usually feel they have to do something gracious like get you some coffee. And so the interview process tends to extend on and on and they get much more casual.

If you are writing an in-depth profile and have the time, consider the advice of writer Gael Greene. Greene says:

> In a profile, the ideal way for me to interview is practically to live with the person for two or three days, if possible. I have a list of questions and I have done as much research as I can, have talked to all their friends and ex-lovers and mates and so on. It's productive just to move in and sit there until they stop being aware of my presence and are just being themselves. Then at some point, at lunch or dinner, I might ask a few questions—the soft, easy questions, and let them say the things they want to say.

In short, use common sense. If you're interviewing an executive who can tell his secretary to hold his calls, the office probably is a good place for the session. On the other hand, if you're interviewing a factory worker, the workplace would be a poor location because it wouldn't be private or quiet. Instead, meet the person at home, assuming you can have a private discussion there.

Researching the Interviewee

When you're granted the interview, you'll need to research both the interviewee and the topic of the interview. As you read in the previous chapter, serious research means a visit to a newspaper archive, a city or academic library, an electronic database or to a combination of all of these sites.

But your library research should be supplemented with calls to people who know your interviewee and understand the topic of your article. Prepare your interviewee for this by telling him or her what you're going to do and—if the story is personal—by asking the interview for the names of two or three close friends. (You can get names of enemies later.)

In the case of Doctor Strike, you should ask for a *curriculum vitae,* which is an academic resume. In addition, some portions of the university's personnel file on Strike will be open for your inspection under your state's freedom of information law. (If your subject works for a large company, the company public relations office might provide you with a biography, but they are not required to do so.)

With these sources, you should be able to piece together lots of information before you even talk to Doctor Strike. You'll discover information such as his full name, age, address, academic degrees and title, previous employment record, how much money he earned at the university and perhaps his memberships in civic and professional associations.

In addition, a check of Strike's business license or corporate records—on file with the city or state and thus open to public inspection—may reveal something about partners and the extent of his business interests. And don't overlook other public record possibilities, which can reveal marriages and divorces and legal problems.

Of course, any information you plan to use should be verified in the interview.

The point of all this is that if you enter an interview armed with detailed information about your interviewee, you'll be able to spend the interview time more effectively and you'll also be likely to flatter the subject with your thoroughness.

CONDUCTING THE PERSONAL INTERVIEW

Making Friends

Effective interviewing—the practice of getting another person to talk freely—is largely an exercise in human relations. To be successful at it, you must be part used-car salesman, part psychiatrist and part FBI agent. You'll use some of this human relations skill in asking for the interview and in conducting research. But most of that effort should be directed toward the interview itself—particularly the first few minutes of the session.

Professional writers say the secret to an effective interview is to make friends, and the sooner the better. Research has shown that the first four minutes of an interview sets the tone for the rest of the meeting, which means that you have about 240 seconds to establish a working relationship with the subject, or be left with an interviewee who may be unconcerned about your needs, unwilling to help and perhaps even hostile to your presence.

The interviewee will be sizing you up during those first four minutes, researchers say. For that reason, you need to be aware of your appearance, body language, voice and word choice.

Let's take appearance first, which experts say makes up about half of the first impressions. Dress appropriately. If you're interviewing a bank president in his office, blue jeans would be inappropriate attire. On the other hand, if you're interviewing a factory worker in a blue-collar tavern, a business suit won't help your cause.

Watch body language. Head nodding is friendly and reinforcing. A blank stare may be threatening. A slouch says you're lazy. Erect posture says you're alert.

Voice and word choice count for the other half of the impression, experts say. If you're used to speaking loudly, soften your voice in an intimate office setting—or expect the interviewee to try to get rid of you at the earliest opportunity. If you mispronounce a word or use poor grammar, the interviewee has every reason to suspect you're likely to misquote him or her in the article.

In short, the interviewee is deciding whether he or she likes what you look like and how you speak at the same time that he or she is sizing up what you're saying and how you're saying it.

Dale Carnegie, the Missouri farm boy who wrote a best-seller half a century ago about making friends and influencing people, pointed out that six simple techniques will help people like you—assuming you haven't shot yourself in the foot with inappropriate attire and elocution.

Carnegie wasn't talking about writers courting interviewees, but his suggestions are still applicable. First, be interested in your subject, Carnegie suggested. Second, smile while you talk and listen. Third, use the interviewee's name (correctly, if you please). Fourth, be a good listener. Fifth, talk in terms of the other person's interests and with the other person's terminology. Finally, make the interviewee feel as though he or she is the most important person in the world by paying close attention while you're with him or her.

Professional writers use Carnegie's techniques—whether or not they're aware of them—on a daily basis.

For example, journalist Barbara Walters uses Carnegie's most fundamental premise when conducting interviews with political figures and celebrities. Walters says: "There isn't anyone who doesn't respond to being liked. So if I show you I like you, you're going to like me."

And Mort Weisinger, who has sold more than 300 articles to top consumer magazines, uses a Carnegie-based technique to get cold-fish interview subjects started. He says:

> Whenever I sense that the interview isn't going very well, and I'm stuck with an unresponsive interviewee, I drop back and ask a question that always seems to work. I say, "Excuse me, Mr. Smith. I wonder if you would describe to me what you do on a typical day, from the moment you wake up until you go to bed at night?" It nearly always works. Not only do you get them talking, but you can get some excellent anecdotal material for your article.

New York Times journalist Nan Robertson, who won the 1983 Pulitzer Prize for feature writing, says that if she sees "that a person is resistant and sort of withdrawn," she tries to find something she has in common with the subject, such as books or sports.

Then she "will ask them nuts and bolts questions—about where they came from and what their parents were like and what they did. Biographical stuff. Everybody loves to talk about themselves. What you do is make them feel at home. Ask them things that they can answer. That kind of totally nonthreatening question that both tells you about the background of the subject and makes them feel comfortable."

She adds:

> I've found that actually touching people makes them feel better, if you are in a position to be next to one another. If you're consoling a grieving widow, the best thing to do is to touch her. If you establish tactile contact, it's reassuring—if you're not a threatening person. I am physically demonstrative and I naturally do that with people. Smiling, looking people in the eyes, touching briefly—any of these things that work with human beings work in terms of reporting.

Robertson also says the interview setting is important to making friends. "I don't like to have what I call a 'lateral interview,' with both of us sitting side by side on a sofa or a restaurant bench. I like to face anyone I'm talking with."

For that matter, don't sit across the room from your subject. Distance makes a psychological statement. On the other hand, don't invade the interviewee's private space (which is about four feet for most Americans of European descent). If you're too far away from your subject or on top of your subject, move your chair.

Wilkerson of *The New York Times* faced multiple interview challenges for her profile of Nicholas Whitiker. She had to make friends not only with Nicholas's mother, but with Nicholas, his brothers, sisters, and extended family, and school officials as well. She explains:

> The mother was perfectly fine letting me spend time with the children. She was generous and wonderful about that. She allowed (me) to take them on outings almost from the very beginning—to take them to McDonalds, to take them driving around—which was a stunning thing for her to do. It said a lot about the rapport we seemed to have from the beginning.
>
> (But) I had to establish rapport with all the children *and* the extended family. It ended up that you couldn't talk with them without hearing about cousins and kids in school and grandmothers, and your initial response as a reporter is to sort of block all that out and say, "I am focusing on you." But I found that you could not really do that because this was so essential to their being and you wanted to become a part of their world. You wanted to blend with their world. Not stand out as an outsider. So what that meant was that I could not disregard all of these other people that they were talking about. In fact, I had to memorize the names and Nicholas' opinions of these 14 cousins and all the siblings, aunts, and uncles and four fathers. . . . And I had to know not only their names but their character and what he (Nicholas) thought of them so that I could be on the same page with him wherever he was going.
>
> I (also) needed to get access to him in school. I think a lot of reporters could relate to the experience of trying to win over the school. . . . I took them to school the first day. . . . It became apparent that I was going to have to talk to the principal as soon as I walked in. . . . I was directed to the principal's office. The principal was naturally skeptical and concerned that I was there to do a story or expose about the school. I had to listen patiently as he talked about . . . (the improvements in the school). It felt like a two hour interval with a man I knew was not central to the story, but I patiently listened and asked questions. . . . Knowing that I was being auditioned and screened. . . . I tried to impress upon him what my interest was. And after that dual audition—my auditioning him and him auditioning me—he agreed that I would be able to go with Nicholas to school every day and would be able to have access to the school. Even though I had been given the approval of the principal, the teacher then was wondering . . . if I was there to assess how she handled the classroom. I don't know that she ever quite fully felt comfortable with me, but she permitted me to be in the classroom.

I knew I was really accepted (by the children) when I would sit next to one of them and they were doing multiplication tables and one would discreetly push her little math book over toward me so that I would be able to see that seven times eight was 56. . . . The lesson of all this is that when you enter a foreign environment, people cannot stay at a fever pitch forever. After a certain point, you are accepted as a part of the environment. People just cannot view you as an outsider forever. Over time, their defenses fall and they begin to accept you. And that was what eventually happened with these children.

Asking Questions

Think about your questions before you ask them. Most newspaper and magazine writers—even professionals of long standing—jot down their questions beforehand. Of course, you should be flexible about those questions. If you have 99 good questions but the subject says something stunning in the middle of the third answer, be prepared to follow that lead and spontaneously create new questions pursuing the new angle.

As you phrase the questions—whether in your mind or on paper—scrutinize how you ask each one, because questions come in a variety of styles, each with its own effect. Here are four useful types of questions.

■ The *open-ended question* allows the respondent a broad range in the answer. If the question is unfocused, the answer is useless. Let's assume you're interviewing students at the state university for a newspaper feature. Here's an unfocused open-ended question you might—but shouldn't—ask.

Example: "What's your opinion of the university?"

Opinion of what? the interviewee will think. The bookstore? Dormitory conditions? Cafeteria food? Academic quality? Here is a more focused and useful version of the open-ended question.

Example: "How do you think the university's advising system can be improved?"

■ The *closed question* asks for a more narrow reply.

Example: "Which academic departments at the university have you heard positive things about?"

Example: "Which professors teaching general education courses would you recommend to a freshmen entering the university?"

■ The *probe question* asks for amplification of an unresponsive or incomplete answer.

Example: "Why do you recommend Professor Schmutz's basic psychology course?"

■ The *mirror question,* by repeating part of the interviewee's answer, forces the respondent to amplify his or her answer and also gives you time to finish writing down the original answer. The mirror question often is coupled with a probe question.

Example: Writer—"Why do you recommend Professor Schmutz?"

Interviewee—"Because he's fair, has knowledge of his subject and never wears a tie."

Writer—"You say you like him because he's fair, knows his subject and never wears a tie? Why is the lack of a tie important?"

In general, the writer should use focused open-ended, closed and probe questions, followed by an occasional mirror question, to slow down the interviewee and to clarify quotations.

The writer should specifically try to avoid three question types: yes-or-no, leading and loaded questions. Hypothetical queries may sometimes be used. Here are examples.

■ The *yes-or-no question,* which allows the interviewee to answer in only one of two ways, is virtually useless for the feature or magazine writer because it doesn't yield a detailed answer (unless it is followed by a probe question).

Example: "Do you think Professor Schmutz is a good teacher?"

■ The *leading question* is considered unethical by many writers and editors because it strongly suggests the "right" answer to an interviewee.

Example: "Everyone I've interviewed says Professor Schmutz is an outstanding teacher. What's your opinion?"

■ The *loaded question,* designed to antagonize an interviewee, is equally manipulative.

Example: "You're a Palestinian. Professor Schmutz has said in his political science class that the only way to solve the Palestinian problem is imprison all politically active Palestinians. What's your reaction to this?"

■ A final type of question that occasionally may be used is the *hypothetical query,* which allows the interviewee to think about and comment on coming developments. You must be careful to pose hypothetical questions only about situations that are, in fact, able to occur. The following is an example of a question type that would produce a response that bears no relationship to what is likely to happen.

Example: "It's been suggested that one way to improve the academic quality of the university might be to do away with the football program and channel all of that money into instructional supplies and faculty salaries. What's your opinion about that suggestion?"

In summary, you should structure your questions carefully. And when you structure the questions, you should build them along the lines of focused open-ended, closed, probe and mirror queries.

Alas, most interviews require that the writer ask some "difficult" questions. Difficult questions are hard to define. If you're writing a profile, the difficult question could be something like, "How much money do you make?" or "Weren't you arrested in 1984?" Be sure to ask these questions at the end of the interview so that if the session ends abruptly, you will still have enough material to write your story.

Wilkerson had to ask many difficult questions during the reporting of the Nicholas Whitiker story. Wilkerson says her most difficult question came during an interview with the man who was living with the Whitiker family: She had to ask him about allegations that he disciplined the children too severely. She explains:

> The most difficult part of the reporting was having to deal with the allegations of physical abuse at the hands of the boyfriend. That was the most sensitive part of the piece. Obviously, it had to be dealt with before the story could be run. I had basically written the story by the time I confronted this matter with the boyfriend. . . . He worked evenings. He left for work around five or six o'clock at night and he wouldn't get back until two in the morning. He had the evening shift at his job. . . . During the day he slept. . . . I never saw him because he just was never around. He was either asleep or at work. . . . And so the children would tell me the things going on and they would show up sleepy and unable to hold their heads up in school on certain days. They would be irritable and they would tell me what he had done to them. But I never really ran into him. . . . The kids talked it up such (so) much . . . that I could not avoid it and (I) had to obviously make reference to it in the piece and if I did I had to talk with him as well. Because I had never naturally run into him . . . I had to make a formal appointment to interview him. I was quite concerned going in as to what would be the outcome of such an interview. . . . Angela (Whitiker) was there and he was there. There was mythology surrounding this almost frightening figure in their lives.
>
> This was the very last thing I did. This was after the story had even been edited. . . . The beginning was a cordial, professional, matter-of-fact interview asking him where he was born. Where did you go to school? How long have you lived here? When did you meet Angela? Those kinds of things just to warm up. Then I had to ask the tough question. He was cooperative—not friendly, but not angry. Just was fairly matter of fact in his demeanor in answering of questions. I had to ask him about the beatings that I've been told have occurred. . . . He said, "Yes, I've done all those things. I'm the family enforcer." So he admitted it. He was matter of fact about it. He was unapologetic (and not) defensive. He acted like it was just a normal, everyday thing.
>
> It ended up not being as controversial and life-endangering as I anticipated.

The next step in the interview process depends on the difficult question having been asked. If you have asked a difficult question, you should be prepared to help the subject recuperate from the trauma of being frank—or angry—with you.

Police officers have a standard technique for dealing with this problem. After a confession, police officers may offer reassurance. By saying they understand a culprit's dilemma, they may lessen the chance that the criminal will recant the confession.

Your interviewees will not usually be criminals and you are not a police officer, but the act of suggesting that something just said will not sound as awful as the subject thinks it will is, in fact, effective human relations.

More Tips on Questioning.   Robertson believes a writer's personality will set the tone for the interview. She explains:

> Journalistic techniques really grow out of the kind of person you are. I think that hostile people will be hostile reporters and friendly people will be friendly reporters. An interview is a conversation with slightly more questions than ordinary. . . . If you are friendly, that comes over. If you are hostile and paranoid, that comes over.

For example, investigative reporters tend to be paranoid. An investigative reporter once said to me: "We investigative reporters are all proctologists. You look up there and you expect to see something dirty and you do." That's what make them so great. I'm basically trusting. I'd never make a really great investigative reporter. What I'm good at is getting total strangers to really sort of open their hearts to me. My whole instinct is to make people like me. I really do like people. I'm simply fascinated by them. I truly enjoy going out in the world and meeting strangers.

Robertson offers six interviewing tips most writers follow:

Don't come into the interview with your mind made up about the interviewee.
Keep your ego out of the interview: Your subject is the subject—not you. Don't argue.
Listen; don't keep talking.
Don't interrupt if the answer is not going the way you want it, unless you don't have time and must guide it quickly to a conclusion.
Assume nothing. [For instance: how a name is spelled.]
Never be ashamed of saying, "I don't understand" or "What does that mean?" or "Put it in layman's language, please." Neophytes are often so scared of looking stupid that they don't pursue matters as far as they should. But to ask is to learn, and to help your readers learn. To me, the only stupid question is the unasked question.

Robertson adds:

There's nothing [during the interview] that can be done by the book—nothing—except perhaps ask the really "hairy" question at the end. That's one of the reasons I never write down a list of questions; the conversation becomes stilted and you are forcing it in your direction. I have two or three questions in mind to start a conversation.

As Robertson asks questions, she observes the interviewee's physical reactions.

I think people, whether they know it or not, can tell an awful lot from your body English, as I can tell from theirs and from their facial expressions. I have spent my professional life making fast appraisals of people and they're usually accurate. All reporters have to do this. It's not technique so much as instinct. All of this is based on gut feeling. There are ways of telling when a person's lying; the brief hesitations, the people who are loath to make eye contact. All these are clues.

The intensity of the questioning will vary with the writer. For example, Blais, who has flexible deadlines, likes to take her time with interviews. She initially spends perhaps an hour with an interviewee, then builds to longer sessions. She explains:

I try to hang out a lot, with all types of subjects, sometimes not even taking notes. I always work from the less significant to the more significant questions, until you know what you want to ask.

Blais says she uses the time to ask and re-ask questions, listening for nuances and speech patterns.

Steinbach uses a similar interviewing approach. In "A Boy of Unusual Vision," she explains that she

> interviewed his mother first. Then I interviewed his father. Then I went to the school and I spent a number of days [there]. Then I spent days at the house with the parents and with Calvin and a photographer. Then I went back at night and spent time with Calvin alone in his room. I went out with Calvin when he played.
>
> After a while, it gets to be a process where you forget you're interviewing and they forget you're interviewing. I can remember a day when I was there—with a photographer—and there was a baseball game in the backyard and by the end of the day we were catching and pitching. It becomes that kind of process. They forget. And that's when you get your best stuff, of course.

Carpenter often has tighter deadlines than do Blais and Steinbach and consequently gets down to business more quickly. Her first interview is serious, but she adds: "You'll find that second and third interviews, after the initial . . . interview, will produce wonderful information. That's when the breakthroughs seem to come."

Attribution Guidelines

During practically every interview, you can expect the interviewee to say at least once, "Hey, don't put that in the story" or "I'll answer your question if you agree not to use the information in the story." When that happens, you're being confronted with one of the most vexing problems facing the writer—what to do about the "off-the-record" request.

When an off-the-record request is made (whether it's in regard to something said or as yet unsaid), you have three choices: You can agree to keep the remark secret, you can absolutely deny the subject's request, or you can bargain to use some or all of the information in your story. Off-the-record comments and information withheld by the subject are of little use, so most writers refuse requests to keep information secret and attempt to bargain.

To understand how you can change the subject's off-the-record request into a usable quotation, it's helpful to know the etiquette under which most newspaper and magazine writers operate. First, any comment made during an interview is on-the-record unless the comment is granted off-the-record status by the writer. Professional etiquette requires you to keep your word only if you've actually given it. An interviewee's admission of cannibalism *followed* by a plea "not to print a word of that" should fall on deaf ears. On the other hand, you are required to keep your word if you agree not to print an interviewee's information *prior* to being told that information.

Successful bargaining requires understanding how quotations can be restricted. Typically, quotation agreements can be divided into five categories.

■ The first category is *for-direct-quotation.* Here, whatever the subject tells you can be used as a direct quote, a partial quote or an indirect quote. Here's an example of a direct quotation.

> "The state has a cash-flow crisis," treasurer Harrison Jones said today.

Remarks made during most personal and telephone interviews, of course, are always on-the-record and for direct quotation, unless the subject advises you otherwise prior to making the remark.

■ Proceeding along a continuum of progressively less acceptable restrictions, the next category is *not-for-direct-quotation.* Here, you can identify the source and repeat the quote, but not within quotation marks.

> The state is broke, treasurer Harrison Jones said today.

The purpose of this technique is largely to allow the source to claim having been misquoted if he or she is in hot water after the interview appears. Even though politicians enjoy using this approach, you should avoid it because it casts a shadow on your credibility should the subject deny having made the statement.

■ *Not-for-attribution* comes next. The lack of attribution forces you to connect a quote to a generalized source.

> The sewers of Miami are swarming with alligators, according to a sewer department source.

This kind of attribution—sometimes called *background* attribution—obviously has less credibility than a direct quotation or even a not-for-direct-quotation statement.

Occasionally there are variations on this restriction. For example, when reporter Steve Twomey of *The Philadelphia Inquirer* asked for permission to board the aircraft carrier *America* to spend three days observing and interviewing service personnel, the Navy was delighted. However, when Twomey arrived on the *America,* he discovered that he was required to keep the names and hometowns of most interviewees secret. In order to get the story, Twomey agreed to the restriction. Writing the story using generalized attributions presented problems, but Twomey's article still won the 1987 Pulitzer Prize for feature writing.

■ *Deep background* often refers to information given to a writer on the basis that it not be attributed to the source in any way. Usually the writer can get another source to corroborate the background information and then can attribute that information to the new source. Deep background is frequently used in news analysis articles.

■ The last, and worst, category is, of course, *off-the-record,* where you promise not to reveal either the information or the source.

Much of this is a tempest in a teapot because often interviewees want to restrict information in which you have little interest: They pledge you to secrecy and then tell you something that is irrelevant to the story.

In summary, the plan is to assume anything you're told in an interview is for-direct-quotation unless you agree to an exception. If you agree to an exception, try to move the request along the continuum from off-the-record to at least not-for-direct-quotation or, at worst, not-for-attribution. Agreeing to hear important information on an off-the-record basis is a waste of your time.

Peter Rinearson, a *Seattle Times* reporter and a 1984 Pulitzer feature winner, has to deal with more than his share of off-the-record requests.

> If they want to go off-the-record, I say, "How about not-for-attribution?" If they have any doubt, I explain the ground rules. Sometimes I refuse to go off-the-record. It all depends on the situation. The reality is that on a beat there are various kinds of sources you use for various kinds of things. Certain sources [have] value to you as background. These are sources where you got to get information. They come to trust you and know that they are going to lose their job—I mean literally—if this stuff is used. This is only for a certain class of source—not for a company executive, for instance. I am not talking about the textbook way you learn journalism. I'm talking about the actual practicality, the way it really works.

Jon Franklin, the Pulitzer Prize–winning feature writer who wrote "Mrs. Kelly's Monster," specializes in stories about brain chemistry and faces problems similar to Rinearson's. Getting substantive interviews from scientists is difficult, Franklin notes. Franklin's experts

> don't want to be quoted. You'll notice that I don't use that many quotes. They don't want to go on the line. These folks aren't philosophers, they're scientists. The scientific macho is that "We don't speculate." Also, people are very secretive about what they're doing because it's such a hot field.
>
> Science writing is sort of in its age of yellow journalism. The public doesn't know much about science and the scientists don't know much about the media. Most scientists think I can write anything I want in the newspaper, and suspect I may do so, as a matter of fact. They demand to see quotes. They don't understand why they can't write it, why they can't take back quotes. They don't know what off-the-record means, what background means. They're very suspicious.

In addition to off-the-record requests, some subjects demand to see their quotations or even the entire story as a condition of the interview. Their requests are usually rejected.

Magazine writers and editors sometimes verify quotations by reading key selections to a source by telephone. Most newspaper feature writers refuse all such requests. Blais explains: "A lot of people ask to see the piece and you always have to say, 'No.' I say that it's not allowed and the reason that it is not allowed is that somebody might try to sue to stop the piece. I tell the truth."

Gathering Material

Note-taking Tips.   Researchers say that even if you're a careful listener, you will miss 50 percent of what a speaker—in this case, an interviewee—has to say. And if you don't record that information quickly, you will lose 50 percent of what you did hear. For that reason, note taking is critical unless you routinely depend on tape recorders.

First, use the correct tools. Writers have found that taking notes on standard $8\frac{1}{2} \times$ 11-inch paper slows down writing. Use a reporter's notepad, which typically is about 4 inches wide by 8 inches long. In a pinch, fold in half a dozen sheets of $8\frac{1}{2} \times$ 11-inch paper.

Most American newspaper and magazine writers—unlike their European counterparts—don't know shorthand. However, most American writers do use some form of self-taught shorthand, which is another tool. At its simplest, that shorthand involves using numbers for words ("4" instead of "for") and dropping articles (such as "the") and other nonessential words. Still, note taking in this manner is an inexact art and depends on the writer's getting to a computer as quickly as possible to reconstruct the language of the interviewee. So—assuming you're not using a recorder and you don't know true shorthand—don't try to take down every word. Instead, rely on good notes for direct and partial quotations and on your memory to reconstruct the gist of what the subject said in indirect quotation.

An especially fast-talking interviewee may cause you to fall far behind in note taking, despite your reporter's notepad, self-taught shorthand, and excellent memory. If that happens, consider asking your speeding subject to slow down, suggests Pulitzer winner Banaszynski, who filled 27 notepads while working on "AIDS in the Heartland." She explains: "I've noticed that people are perfectly comfortable . . . with me telling them, 'Hey I need you to slow down because I can't write as fast you you talk.' They have to help you out a little, but that's fine because people like to help."

Finally, be as inconspicuous as possible about your note taking. Keep your notes out of the line of sight of the interviewee. In fact, avoid letting the subject even see when you've stopped writing. (This gives you the option of ignoring inane comments while taking copious notes of important ones.)

Robertson explains: "If your subject is skittish and says something controversial, stop taking notes. Then take it down later, when they're saying something bland."

Steinbach used both notes and tape for her Pulitzer Prize story. "When I did the interviews where I was sitting face to face with a teacher or with the parents, I would tape it. That was a good thing, because the voice inflections, particularly [the mother's], were very important. Then when we were doing things outside or at the school, I always had a notebook with me. I didn't try to get it all down, but you instinctively know" what to note, she says.

Audio Recorder Techniques.   To record or not to record, that is the question, with due credit to William Shakespeare.

Most American newspaper reporters facing daily deadlines seldom use recorders. Replaying and transcribing material takes too much time, the reporters say.

On the other hand, magazine writers—especially freelance writers—use recorders frequently. So do newspaper feature writers who don't face short deadlines.

While there's disagreement among journalists about the value of recorders, all agree that if you use an audio recorder, you should use a good one.

The ideal machine, which should be small so that it won't distract the interviewee, ought to have a built-in microphone with an automatic gain control. The built-in mike will lessen the obtrusiveness of the machine; the gain control will automatically adjust the recording level for varying conditions. Recording should be indicated by a tiny light so you can check whether the machine is working properly. All are common features.

The machine also should have a counter and an audible forward cue so that you can locate specific segments of the recording later. The counter reading can be noted during the interview so you can later find the general location of important quotations, and the cue will allow you to play the recording back at faster than normal speed to pinpoint those quotations quickly. These are common features, too.

A warning signal, to let you know when you're out of memory or tape, is an important but less common feature. So is a voice-activated recording system, which means the machine will record only when someone is talking, thus saving memory or tape.

Even with all of this technology, it's a good idea to take notes as though the recorder did not exist. This will protect you in case the recorder fails and will also provide a table of contents for the recording.

Robertson says the use—or nonuse—of recorders by writers at *The New York Times* is "a generational thing. The younger reporters use recorders more often than the older reporters do."

Robertson doesn't use recorders.

> I think tape recording is very cumbersome. I would rather edit in my mind as an interview is going on. Also, I can write almost as fast as anyone can talk. I learned speed writing way back in my career and it almost ruined me because I was recording everything with my notes rather than listening. To me, an interview is . . . a conversation between two people and you must listen. I am very accurate in my note taking. Once in my life someone has said he was misquoted by me, which is pretty good in 38 years of reporting. I read my notes to him and he backed down.

The New York Times's Rick Bragg also generally eschews recorders. Bragg, for example, says that recording Oseola McCarty, who gave her life savings to the University of Southern Mississippi, would have been a waste of time:

> I wouldn't have gotten anything with a tape recorder. There were such long periods when I was doing the talking (that) it would have basically been a tape of me talking. I guess I probably took a half notebook of notes. Not even that many. It's funny. When she did say something, it was worth writing down. It wasn't one of those times when you can dismiss much of what people say. . . . She spoke in very short sentences, very slowly, very clearly. There wasn't any danger of missing anything. . . . If she said something, it was worth writing down.

However, Bragg says he does use his recorder on rare occasions: "For instance, I . . . interviewed a guy who had been charged in a bond fraud case and I don't know a damn thing about bonds. I don't know a damn thing about fraud. So I took a tape recorder just so that I knew I would understand it and get it right later. . . . I just don't do that many (of those kinds of) stories. I don't even know where my tape recorder is. It'd take me a half a day to find it."

Banaszynski, Dave Curtin of the *Colorado Springs Gazette Telegraph,* Angelo Henderson of *The Wall Street Journal,* Jim Sheeler of the *Rocky Mountain News* and *The Philadelphia Inquirer*'s Twomey and David Zucchino—all relatively young writers and all Pulitzer winners—also avoid using recorders if possible. So do veteran *Washington Post* reporter George Lardner, who won the Pulitzer in 1993 for a story about the murder of his daughter, seasoned *St. Petersburg Times* writer Thomas French, who won the Pulitzer in

1998 for a story about the murder of three Ohio women, and Barry Siegel, *The Los Angeles Times* writer who won in 2002 for the story of a Utah judge who sentenced a young father who ultimately committed suicide. Banaszynski sums up a widely held attitude:

> I have [numerous] problems with tape recorders. One is that I don't like to be interrupted in the middle of the interview to flip the tape around.
>
> I don't trust machines. I'm not a high-tech person.
>
> I don't like to transcribe tapes.
>
> [Recorders] make me a real lazy listener. When I have a tape recorder on, my tendency has been to sort of relax a little too much and rely on that recorder. . . . If I have to rely on my notes, I become very concentrated and very focused and very intense and very intent and I come out with what I need, and I don't let myself get lazy during that process.
>
> And for some reason, I've had several people say, "No, I don't want to be taped." Even though I think it's an assurance for them, they get nervous about it. I find people very at ease with me when I'm using my notebook and I think what happens is that when you're writing in a notebook you're looking at the pages quite a bit and you're not staring at this person and they're able to not have to look in your eyes, which is intimidating.

Los Angeles Times writer J. R. Moehringer, who wrote the graceful story about Gee's Bend, Alabama, and Mary Lee Bendolph and its other residents, says he prefers to use a recorder, "but typically I don't have time. Transcribing takes forever, and most newspaper stories have to be turned out quickly. For 'Gee's Bend,' however, there was no deadline. And really there was no choice (about using a recorder): Mary Lee's language was so remarkable, so poetic and nuanced, her winding sentences so symbolic of the river itself, that I didn't want to miss a single word."

Wilkerson of *The New York Times* also uses recorders selectively. For example, she used a recorder on occasion with her subjects in the Nicholas Whitiker story. She used a recorder to capture the children's discussion in her car while she was driving them to school or to a restaurant. She also used a recorder to underscore the serious nature of her note taking in conversations with Nicholas's mother, Angela Whitiker. Wilkerson explains: "I had lunch with her and made sure the tape recorder was right there so she would be aware that while we had talked a great deal and that it had been in an often comfortable setting, (she needed to) be aware of what she was saying about these very sensitive topics."

Many other Pulitzer Prize–winning feature writers, however, do use recorders more or less routinely, including Franklin, Carpenter, Rinearson, Steinbach, John Camp of the *St. Paul Pioneer Press,* James, Howell Raines of *The New York Times* and Tom Hallman of *The Oregonian* in Portland.

Franklin says he likes "the British system where—in order to get into a journalism school—you have got to show proficiency with shorthand." But Franklin says recorders—especially high-quality recorders—make sense for writers without shorthand.

> I don't really know what I'm going to use and what I'm not. When you're looking for a pattern, you poke around in a story for two or three months. . . . If you take notes, the chances are that you didn't take the notes you needed for that story. If you've got everything on a tape recorder, you can go dig it out. In the beginning, it's a real problem, but what you do is learn to use a tape recorder and diffuse it—mostly by forgetting [material].

I use a tape recorder that costs about $400. I went out and bought that thing after a two-hour interview with [a brain chemistry researcher who said] . . . some of the things I worked for years to get him to say. When I got back . . . what I had on that tape was mostly static. It just blew me away. These tape recorders take a real beating and a tape recorder has to be able to do that.

Carpenter, who records "virtually everything," says the

sensitive moment is when you first bring the recorder out and put it on the table. I find that instead of asking a subject, the thing to do is take it out as a matter of course, put it on the desk. If they bridle, then you deal with it. And my tactic is to generally say, "Well, if the recorder makes you very uncomfortable, then I won't tape, but it really allows me to be much more accurate, have a total record for protection of you." And there have been very few instances where people haven't allowed themselves to be taped.

It's an advantage in a sensitive interview because you don't have to be bobbing up and down in and out of your notebook. If the subject is on a sensitive tack, he or she may be put off by your scribbling in the notebook, and think, "Oh, it's obviously something that I ought to be careful about addressing," where if it's on tape . . . you make a mental note to go back to it.

Rinearson says he doesn't use recorders on his aerospace beat, but he did use them while interviewing for his Pulitzer series.

"It's real difficult to get time with some people, and I could use time three times as effectively if I had a tape recorder going. The tape recorder is not really very efficient in *your* time, but it is in interview time. The first thing it does is that it lets you get more accomplished in a given amount of time. The second thing it does is that it lets you be more informal, more relaxed."

Rinearson, unlike many writers who use recorders, takes few notes during a taped interview. He says he asks interviewees "if I can tape it, [then] I put the tape recorder on the table and I don't have to worry about the recorder for an hour. When the tape runs out, it'll beep and tell me.

"I am able to use my mind to phrase questions rather than worry about word order in the quotes. As far as I'm concerned, it's just like a word processor or even a pen and paper. It's just another tool."

Steinbach notes:

Obviously, it's much faster if you don't use one because typing up your notes is horrendous. But I'm a great believer in tape recorders for several reasons. First of all, I realize—having been interviewed myself—how easily reporters don't get the correct words down. They think they've got the correct words down, but they don't. I've read interviews I've given, and it's not what I've said. That's a very chastening experience. You cannot write that fast if a person is talking in a normal way.

Secondly, a tape recorder frees you to really listen to the other person and gauge interaction with them. You can look at them. They can look at you. They're not looking at the top of your head. That is disconcerting. The tape recorder gives the interviewer a chance to really respond to what the interviewee is saying, to think about it. Plus the fact that when you get back and have to listen to all of this again, it's really very helpful because you hear things you didn't hear at first, and inflections, pauses.

Some people say, "Oh, but aren't people put off when you stick a tape recorder in front of them?" I've found it's quite the opposite. You get it out of the way. There's no notebook, no top of the head, no "Wait-a-minute. I-didn't-get-that," which completely ruins the spontaneity. It's just ludicrous when somebody is explaining their deepest philosophy to you or is in the middle of an emotional statement and you say, "Wait-a-minute. Let-me-get-that-down." Well, you've ruined it. But I understand there are times you can't use them, when you don't have time.

For James, who used a recorder to gather information for her Prize-winning series about a mother who abandoned a baby in Florida, the increased interaction with interview subjects provided by recording is worth the time spent transcribing. She explains:

I find tape recorders invaluable not only in helping to establish and maintain eye-to-eye contact with my sources, but also in capturing unique language and voice. The aunt in this series, for example, spoke country-style plain and simple—yet she was so eloquent. It was a voice that I had to preserve. The italicized segments representing her thoughts in the story are literally word-for-word transcriptions of my interviews with her.

Some reporters argue against using tape recorders. They can malfunction, tapes take time to transcribe, and taping encourages laziness on the part of the reporter. All of these points are worth considering. But tape recorders can be tested right before and during an interview. For instance, my tape recorder's red light indicates it is recording. I check it frequently. I also check the actual recording during lulls in my interviews if I can. My tape also has an end-of-tape-signal. It is a lifesaver. As for transcribing, I have one major piece of advice: Buy a full-fledged transcribing machine, with headset and foot pedal. Don't try to "transcribe" with your handheld tape recorder. It wears the machine down, and it is extremely inefficient—like trying to use a telegraph instead of a telephone. Using a transcriber at my computer, I can transcribe very rapidly. The extra details and information I preserve—not to mention observations on my interviewing skills—are worth the extra time.

Still, recorders fail, as Franklin notes.

Carpenter recalls an instance. "I just did 10 hours of interviewing on a book I'm doing and there was just a horrible machine buzz above everything. It's a problem when you're dealing with tape. I do make notes when I tape, but it's not the same as having the full text."

Steinbach had a similar experience.

I've had one experience where I had a very long gripping interview with a woman about a murder case she was involved in. I was with her for a long time. When I got home [and listened to the tape], something had happened. I could just barely hear her voice. She was still in town [but] she was leaving for the airport. I called her back and said "Can I drive you to the airport and can we recreate the interview?" and she was very nice about it. But ever since then, what I've done—and I don't like doing it—is to say, "Excuse me, but I just want to double-check that this is working," and play back a little bit of the tape. And of course, I always test it before I go in for the interview.

Henderson, *The Wall Street Journal* reporter who wrote about a Detroit pharmacist who killed a robber, had a machine failure early in his career that limited his enthusiasm for recorders.

I generally don't use tape recorders. Sometimes when you tape, you don't listen as carefully as you would otherwise and your notes aren't as good. When I was in college, I interviewed a University of Kentucky budget director in depth, and taped the entire interview. When I got back to the (student newspaper) newsroom and pushed "play," all I could hear was a "huu-ummm." I had to do the interview again.

A final note: If you record *telephone* interviews, obey your state law. Currently, about three dozen so-called single-party states require that only one person—presumably you—approve of the recording. The other states require that both parties be aware of the recording. Because laws change, it's a good idea to inform the interviewee if you're recording the conversation.

Fixing Quotes

Inexperienced writers often worry about what they should do when they encounter poor grammar, off-color remarks or inaccuracies during an interview session. Should the material go into the story?

Let's take grammar first. Problem: Suppose you're interviewing a commercial fur trapper who—in reference to using modern trapping techniques—says, "I don't pay no never-mind to those dang-fooled fancy trappin' ways." Solution: Most writers would use the quote as uttered because it reflects the character of the interviewee.

On the other hand, if a high school teacher made a grammatical slip—using "mc" rather than "I," for example—most writers would correct the error because they're aware that spoken English is usually more informal than written English and the high school teacher would be embarrassed by the slip while the trapper would not.

Banaszynski sums up the view of most feature writers:

> If their language is ungrammatical to the point it becomes idiom or street jive, I leave it in if it's appropriate to their culture. I know that's been a big controversy with people from certain parts of the country and from certain socioeconomic groups because they claim we're making them look stupid, but I think the way a person talks says a lot and it doesn't have to be a negative thing.
>
> If someone just tends to do things like not connect subjects and pronouns properly or not match subject tense and verb tense, I fix that. I [also] fix a quote if it's necessary to make what the person is saying understandable because often as we talk we are not as careful with our grammar as we are when we write. So if someone refers to "he" and later in the sentence refers to another "he" and it's not clear which one they're talking about, I may put in a person's name. [Even so] I don't alter quotes very much.

Bragg, whose Pulitzer Prize–winning feature package included the story of Oseola McCarty's $150,000 gift to her local university, says *The New York Times* tends to automatically repair quotes and he must argue to keep colorful language in the story. Bragg explains:

> Quite frankly, you didn't have to [fix Mrs. McCarty's quotes]. She was very well spoken. [But] we do it. . . . I do it all the time. I wish we had some [industry] guideline on that because quite frankly it troubles me. We fix some people and we don't fix others. . . . To be real honest with

you, I don't know what our *policy* is. I'm like a cork bobbing on that particular [issue]. . . . [But] *The Times* as a paper [uses] virtually no dialect of any kind. . . . They did let me quote a Cajun man one time in dialect because it was kind of necessary to the story. If someone says, "I ain't got no . . ." they change it to "I don't have any . . ." [or] to an indirect quote. . . .

Camp offers a view on the issue of off-color or potentially embarrassing comments. He explains: "I don't fix quotes. I'll just leave things out. Sometimes people say things to you in kind of unwatched moments. There is one news theory that this is kind of a true picture of the guy's mind. And there are other people who say if [the subject] doesn't mean that and is a serious person, [reporting] this one unguarded moment" will cause unnecessary injury. "I tend to lean more to the side of 'Let's report what the person means.' I try to represent people as accurately as I can, and I'm not going to pick up on some anomaly."

Inaccuracies are another matter. If an interviewee says that former President Clinton resigned from office—President Richard M. Nixon actually holds that distinction—you need to stop the interviewee in his tracks and get him to correct his misstatement, assuming you know that he made a misstatement. The problem here is that an inaccuracy may be libelous and if you repeat a libel, you're as culpable as the interviewee. Another option, of course, would be to delete the inaccuracy later.

Description

Feature and magazine articles usually require description. Description requires keen observation. Sometimes keen observation requires participation.

For example, Franklin interviewed Edna Kelly, her doctor and others for "Mrs. Kelly's Monster," but Franklin's description of the brain operation was pivotal to the story's success. And Franklin had to participate in the operation in order to observe it adequately. Similarly, Blais had to participate in Edward Zepp's trek to Washington in order to observe his battle with the Pentagon. And Hallman of *The Oregonian* spent 10 months with 14-year-old Sam Lightner and his family, including two trips to distant medical facilities, as they sought relief for Sam's disfiguring birth defect.

There are numerous approaches to describing people, places, and events. What works in describing people is usually also effective for describing places and events. Let's look at the ways a few Pulitzer Prize–winning writers described their subjects. A writer's most common approach is simple *physical description.* Of the subject of the 2001 Pulitzer Prize–winning "The Boy Behind the Mask," Hallman wrote:

> Like all teens, Sam's perception of how others saw him would determine how he saw himself.
> And when strangers looked at Sam, they first fixated on the left side of his face, a swollen mass that looked like a pumpkin left in the fields after Halloween. His left ear was even more abnormal, a purple mass the size and shape of a pound of raw ground beef. His jaw, twisted. His teeth, crooked. His tongue, shoved to the side. His left eye, nearly swollen shut.
> When he walked to school each morning, he stopped at the crosswalk on Northeast Sandy Boulevard and watched passengers in cars and buses stare at him. When he walked through the neighborhood, he heard laughter and comments.

Once, a neighbor boy led his friends over to Sam's house and knocked on the front door so the others could see Sam's face.

Here's how J. R. Moehringer, a 2000 Pulitzer Prize–winning *Los Angeles Times* correspondent, described Camden, Alabama, the community that was across the river from Mary Lee Bendolph and her long-isolated, largely African American neighbors in Gee's Bend, Alabama:

Camden was the kind of town where the newspaper got its start in the early 1800s, printing ads for slave-catchers. It was the kind of town where the manager of the Wilcox Hotel would tell a government worker in 1941, "A nigrah is a nigrah. And if you go and try to fix 'em up, make somethin' out of 'em, put 'em to livin' like white folks and try to treat 'em decent, you don't do anything but make a mean nigger out of 'em that somebody will eventually have to kill." It was the kind of town ruled for a third of this century by a pear-shaped sheriff named Lummie Jenkins, whose pastimes included hunting quail and tormenting Benders. His thick glasses, Mary Lee recalls, turned his black eyes into burnt corn kernels.

Blais uses multiple techniques to describe Zepp. Here's one approach:

Something happens to people after a certain age, and the distinctions of youth disappear. The wrinkles conquer, like an army. In his old age, Zepp is bald. He wears fragile glasses. The shoulders are rounded. His pace is stooped and *slow.* [Italics added.]

Physical description can be risky because Blais's "slow" might be another writer's "leisurely." There are several solutions to this problem. Some writers describe only what is not arguable. Other writers ask interviewees for *self-description,* which can be physical or even psychological. Here is Zepp's self-description addressed to his lawyer:

Don't worry. You'll recognize me. I'll be the decrepit old man creeping down the platform.

Interviewees also can be described *by other people,* a technique commonly used in profiles.

An interviewee's *style of language* can provide description. For example, when Zepp learned that one member of the Pentagon board voted against his honorable discharge, Blais, quoting Zepp, wrote:

I'm so mad I could kick the hell out of him. A guy like that shouldn't be sitting on the Board. I am going to write the Pentagon and tell them he should be thrown off the panel. It would be better to have just a head up there loaded with concrete or sawdust than this guy.

An interviewee can also be described by his *surroundings:*

Zepp was easily the oldest person on the commuter-filled subway. He did not try to speak above the roar. His was a vigil of silence. When the doors sliced open at the "Pentagon" stop, the hour of judgment was upon him.
    "The gates of hell," he said, "shall not prevail."

An interviewee also can be described by his *mental processes,* a tricky technique but one possible through intensive interviewing. Here is Franklin's description of surgeon Tom Ducker as he encountered Mrs. Kelly's monster:

> The neurosurgeon stares intently at the veins, surprised, chagrined, betrayed by the X-rays.

Obviously, Franklin didn't read Ducker's mind. He interviewed him after the operation and used that information to re-create the doctor's thoughts.

An interviewee can be described by how he *responds* to situations, too. Here, Franklin showed how Ducker dealt with Mrs. Kelly's death:

> It is 1:43, and it's over.
>> Dr. Ducker bites, grimly, into the sandwich.
>> The monster won.

During interviews, try to gather enough information to use a variety of descriptive techniques. If you're writing the story and find you lack crucial information, interview the subject by telephone.

No matter how carefully you describe a subject, however, there's a potential for a negative reaction. Blais explains: "Even if it's complimentary, there's always one little thing that they hated. You just can't predict. My husband always quotes a reporter who went out and wrote a story about an embezzler, a murderer, an all-around reprobate. And you describe him as all of those things plus wearing an ugly brown tie. And the guy calls up the next day and says, 'How can you say that about my tie?'"

Wilkerson had a similar experience with Angela Whitiker, the mother of 10-year-old Nicholas Whitiker. In her story about Nicholas's life, she wrote the following paragraph:

> So Nicholas and his siblings usually head straight home. They live in a large, barren apartment with chipped tile floors and hand-me-down furniture, a space their mother tries to spruce up with her children's artwork.

After the story was published, Angela Whitiker expressed surprise about one part of the paragraph. Wilkerson explains:

> People often are sensitive about things that you would never expect nor would you even care about. (When the story was printed, Angela said) "I never thought of our floors as being cracked." That was not her fault at all. It was the landlord's problem. The landlord wasn't taking care of the apartment. It wasn't a criticism of her. Here her entire life was laid bare, basically. None of that seemed to faze (her) at all. She said, "I never noticed my floors being cracked." That was all she said and that is basically how she said it.

Closing the Session

If you've done a good job interviewing your subject, closing the session may be difficult because the subject, who probably has enjoyed the experience immensely, will want to prolong the interview. You must persuade him or her that the time has come to end the interview.

The best way to close the interview is to explain that the time you've asked for has long been up and you have another appointment. You should also add that you may have other questions (and the chances are good that, indeed, you will) and you would like to be able to telephone. The interviewee will usually be willing to continue the relationship and will probably insist that you call if you have the slightest question. With that, you should smile, thank the interviewee and leave.

THE INTERVIEW STORY

Now let's see how all of this comes together in a profile.

Ed Weathers was an editor for *Memphis,* a city magazine. Cybill Shepherd, a movie and television actor, is a Memphis native. Shepherd was a logical subject for *Memphis* magazine, and Weathers drew the assignment to interview her.

Weathers made an appointment for the interview, then researched the actor's career. So far so good.

Then, unpredictably, something went wrong. At the appointed time, Weathers went to Shepherd's Memphis apartment. The actor appeared for the interview in a bikini, and Weathers made a polite effort not to notice her swimsuit attire. Shepherd took Weathers's apparent detachment as hostility, and at the conclusion of the first interview, called Weathers's editor and asked that he be replaced with another writer who would be less unfriendly.

A rocky beginning like that has wrecked many stories. But Weathers got his story, and a good one: Weathers's editor was able to convince Shepherd that it was a misunderstanding and she agreed to the second interview.

As you read "Cybill Shepherd," note how Weathers quickly paints a word portrait of Shepherd and asks the central question of the story: Who is she? Then look for the two places in the first half of the story where Weathers stops the chronological story of her career to bring the reader forward in time to observe her. Also look for the break between the two interviews and note how the second half of the story is less a recounting of career moves and more a discussion of the actor's future. Finally, recalling Blais's notion that the final paragraphs of a story often provide a clue to the writer's real feelings about the subject, study the final four paragraphs for insight into Weathers's view of Shepherd.

ED WEATHERS

CYBILL SHEPHERD

> *. . . To be born woman is to know—*
> *Although they do not talk of it at school—*
> *That we must labour to be beautiful.*
> —*Adam's Curse,* William Butler Yeats

When Cybill Shepherd materializes on the deck of her apartment overlooking the Mississippi this late spring day, she is wearing a "Memphis Country Club Member-Guest 1982" visor, aviator sunglasses, and a black bikini that would be right at home on the Côte d'Azur.

"Hi!" she says, with barely a trace of Southern accent. She offers her visitor a surprisingly firm handshake, comments on the terrific view of the river and Mud Island, measures the height of the midday sun, and, after arranging for ice water all around, stretches out on a lounge chair to bask in the rays of her hometown.

Memphis sunshine, it seems, suits Cybill Shepherd, and on this day she is trying to get as much of it as possible before she has to return to Los Angeles to film a TV movie for CBS—before she has to go back to her career.

Her attire—the visor and sunglasses, the bikini—seems almost symbolic: it offers high visibility, but little revelation. The grey-blue eyes, in fact most of her famous face, are hidden. The shimmering blond hair is tied up behind her neck. She wears no apparent make-up, no fingernail polish, no jewelry. The tall, trim, healthy body acts in a strange way as a strategy of misdirection, a kind of beautiful woman's head fake. She is there, she is definitely, almost defiantly there for all to see, but the person behind the persona remains concealed. Even in her hometown—perhaps most of all in her hometown—Cybill Shepherd, whose natural phenomenon of a countenance once graced the cover of *Glamour* magazine a record eight times in one year and has been called by movie critics "one of the screen's most glorious faces," remains something of an unknown quantity.

She drapes a towel across her legs and begins to rub suntan lotion on her shoulders. "Sometimes, from what I read, I believe nobody knows anything about me in Memphis," she says. Then she waves to a workman on the next roof. "Who is this guy up there?" she asks, half pleased, half contemptuous. "I hope he's enjoying the view." Clearly, he is, though he doesn't seem to know just whom he's ogling. In that, he could be seen to represent the whole city.

Like the hero in her movie, *The Heartbreak Kid,* Memphis has at times been so bedazzled by Cybill Shepherd's beauty that it has forgotten to ask just who she is. For she is not just another pretty face. She is not even just another *beautiful* face. When it comes to Cybill Shepherd, cover girl/movie star/television celebrity, beauty is at the center of things, to be sure, but there's also something else—something that starts to become apparent when she says, "Why did I get all those roles? Because I have certain physical attributes. Why did I get them when there are so many other good-looking blondes? Because I'm smarter than most of the other good-looking blondes. That's very important in the bitch-goddess, that she be intelligent."

The bitch-goddess. The Cool American Blonde. The ultimate WASP princess. Cybill Shepherd's film characters have been called all those things, and it is how many movie-goers, lacking any other knowledge of her, presume her to be in real life.

Shepherd herself, though she is careful to distinguish her real self from her roles and protests that each role has been different, calls her typical character "an archetype." It reached the point in the mid-Seventies that when Martin Scorsese was looking for someone to play a beautiful, blonde, intelligent, hot-and-cold, slightly distant foil to Robert DeNiro's obsessive crazy in *Taxi Driver,* he took to calling it "the Cybill Shepherd role." Going for the real thing, he finally cast Shepherd herself.

With her roles in *The Last Picture Show, The Heartbreak Kid, Daisy Miller,* and *Taxi Driver,* this beautiful, blonde, intelligent, warm-and-cool, slightly distant Memphian clearly struck some archetypal chord for Hollywood in the 1970s. And in real life she *does* seem somehow to contain the archetype—"It's no good if the role is not a part of me," she says—but she also seems to contain a lot more. Despite the bikini, there's more to Cybill Shepherd than meets the eyes.

Still, it was what Cybill Shepherd does for the eye, of course, that first made her famous and kept her distant from Memphis for so long. She has made a lifetime of being beautiful, but it hasn't always been easy.

Cybill Lynne Shepherd was born February 18, 1950, to Mr. and Mrs. W.J. Shepherd of Memphis. She was named after her grandfather, Cy Shobe, and her father, Bill. She attended East High from elementary through high school, where she made her mark as, among other things, an athlete. "I'm very athletic," she says, recalling that she set the district record in the long-jump—14'7" inches—when she was fourteen, later captained a city-champion girls' basketball team as a roving guard, and was a competitive diver. Her summers were spent water-skiing in Florence, Alabama, which she calls "her second home."

Shepherd sang in the Holy Communion Church choir, and studied singing with well-known local voice teacher Sara Beth Causey. She dated "mostly college boys" while in high school, was known to climb out her bedroom window at night to meet a boyfriend, wrote poetry, flunked gym and got kicked off the cheerleading squad for sassing the gym teacher, won first prize in the East High Science Fair, and was named Most Attractive in her senior yearbook. Just about all she didn't do was act; Shepherd wasn't even in the school play—or the Thespian Society.

In 1966, when Cybill was 16, a cousin entered her in the Miss Teenage Memphis Contest. She won, and was later named Miss Congeniality in the Miss Teenage America Contest, although she didn't make the finals. ("The girl who won did the *hula* as her talent!" she recalls disdainfully.)

Before long she was doing some local modeling, and New York agents began noticing her work. The next year they invited her to go to New York and enter the Model of the Year Contest, a national competition for professional print-media models. She said she wanted to wait until she finished school, in June of 1968. In the summer of 1968, however, her grandparents gave her a trip to Europe as a graduation present, and she discovered art. "Touring Italy and learning about the Italian Renaissance was a rebirth for me, too," she says. She told the modeling people to forget her; she was going to Louisiana State University to study the history of art, hoping to go to Florence, Italy, during her junior year abroad.

But New York was persistent. "Stewart Cowley of Stewart Models in New York said, 'Well, you're a lot closer to Florence, Italy in New York than you are in Baton Rouge, Louisiana.' " She says, "And that made sense." Cowley also told her she had terrific potential as a model—if she'd just lose 15 pounds. "So I lost ten pounds," she says. "It was horrible."

(continued)

CONTINUED

But it worked. In September of 1968, on a Saturday night, Cybill Shepherd won the national Model of the Year Contest against the best professional faces in the country. The following Tuesday she had her first paying job, with Ship'n'Shore blouses. Soon came work from *Vogue,* then ads for Ultra Bright, Coca Cola, Cover Girl, and Revlon.

Glamour, however, was a tougher cover to crack. She'd been on four or five "go-sees" to the magazine, to show her portfolio, and had never been used. Then, in the spring of 1969, she happened to be in the *Glamour* offices when one of the models scheduled for a shoot in Key West called in sick. "So," she says, "the photographer looked at me and said, 'She'll do.'"

She ended up on the cover of that issue and in 101 photos—that's right, 101—inside. In the next year, she did seven more covers for *Glamour.* "I had an enormous amount of exposure," she says now. "Even to this day many people know me from the modeling."

She attributes part of her success to having the right figure at the right time: "Normally, one is never beautiful enough or thin enough to be a model," she says. "But I have always been a healthy-sized (5'9", 125 pounds, about her current weight from all appearances), regular-looking person. And that was one of the reasons I was so successful—the natural look was just coming into fashion." So was Cybill, still a teenager. Before long she was making over $500 a day in front of the cameras.

The warm Memphis sun seems to be making Shepherd languid as she recounts her early history. Now and then she stops to yawn. At one point she looks up at the high-rise across the way to wave pleasantly to some admiring businessmen who are staring at her out of their office windows. She also waves to a police helicopter that flies by overhead at an unusually low altitude. "Hello," she says to it uselessly.

Myrtle Boone, a strong-faced black woman who helped raise Cybill and is now helping Shepherd with her four-year-old daughter, Clementine, interrupts at one point with a phone call. Shepherd takes the call on the deck. It has something to do with airline flights to New York, and she reads out the flight numbers as her visitor writes them down. "Great! Great!" she says into the phone. After she hangs up, the visitor hands her a piece of paper with the flight numbers. "I'm going to lose this," she says, with mock innocence. "Where am I supposed to put this now?" Finally, grinning, she deposits it in the top of her bikini.

Then she frowns. "Why do I have this rash all over my legs?" she asks, referring to some invisible affliction. "It must be the towel. This is horrible." She pronounces "horrible" with a French accent: "orreebluh." She lies back in the chair.

Closing her eyes against the sun, she returns to her early career.

"I always found anything to do with fashion to be unbelievably boring," she says. "I didn't find it pleasant. I never made a friend of a girl who was a model, nor of a photographer. . . . Basically, you were a hanger to hang clothes on, and a canvas to paint make-up on. It's a well-paying job—that's the best thing I can say for it. And you get to travel. And the people are all right—they just don't talk to you like a human being."

But she soon moved beyond modeling. Hollywood beckoned.

"I started having movie offers after I'd been in New York for six months," she says. "But most people that interviewed me for movies were so incredibly sleazy and disgusting that I developed this kind of disdain. Yucch." One exception was French director Roger Vadim, who had made Brigitte Bardot, Catherine Deneuve, and Jane Fonda sex symbols early in their careers. Shepherd did a screen test for the "very gentlemanly" Vadim, but financing for the film for which she auditioned fell through. Vadim then wanted to cast her in *Pretty Maids All In A Row,* but Shepherd turned him down: "I think I would have been killed off in the first ten minutes, in some grisly death in a toilet in the high-school restroom, and I didn't need that."

Then, of course, there was Peter Bogdanovich. Best known at the time as a film critic and writer, Bogdanovich was casting for his first film as a director. It was to be called *The Last Picture Show;* it would be set in a small town in Texas. He was looking for someone to play the role of Jacy Farrow, described by one critic as "the prettiest, richest, bitchiest girl in town."

In 1969, Bogdanovich saw Shepherd on the cover of *Glamour* and flew to New York. "He saw over 200 girls for the role," she says, "including Sissy Spacek and Lauren Hutton. Sissy wasn't pretty enough, and Lauren was too old. I was just right. I had the right quality." The movie was a big hit, and the critics heaped praise on everyone in it. Cybill Shepherd, twenty years old, was a star.

Picture Show came out in 1971. Then came *The Heartbreak Kid,* directed by Elaine May, in 1972; Shepherd also received fine reviews for her role as the WASP tease in that film. That was followed with the title role in Bogdanovich's version of *Daisy Miller,* the Henry James story, in 1974. Her performance as the heroine, an ingenuous but strong-minded American girl abroad, stirred some controversy, one critic saying that while it was one of the "most beautiful performances I have seen this year," he "couldn't tell whether Cybill Shepherd was Daisy, or whether Cybill Shepherd was just Cybill Shepherd."

Then, in 1975, came the infamous *At Long Last Love,* Bogdanovich's attempt to do a 1930s musical comedy, starring Shepherd and Burt Reynolds. The critics panned the film and the performances, including Shepherd's singing, a fact which must have hurt her as much as any criticism of her acting. The film flopped at the box office. Worse than that, it allowed the Hollywood snipers to come out of hiding and to start taking public shots at Shepherd and Bogdanovich.

During the making of *The Last Picture Show* in 1970, Shepherd and Peter Bogdanovich, who was still married at the time, had begun a love affair that was to last for nearly eight years. He got divorced, and they lived in his Bel-Air mansion, where, Shepherd estimates, they watched up to 1,000 movies a year in his screening room, giving her what she calls "a real film education." Among their frequent houseguests was Orson Welles.

According to most accounts, some of the Hollywood crowd took an instant, jealous dislike to Shepherd as far back as 1970, snubbing her at parties and so forth. One writer said she was being called "Eliza Doolittle to [Bogdanovich's] Professor Higgins . . . a nobody-know-nothing to his somebody-so-something." Glitter critic Rex Reed quoted Bogdanovich as saying, "Cybill was an itch and I scratched it." A less sensationalistic writer had Bogdanovich giving a more thoughtful appraisal of her during the same period: "The camera really loves her," he said. "It is difficult to take a bad picture of her. In person there is also a lot of what she projects on the screen, plus a lot of things you don't know about. She is extremely intelligent, and sensitive, and she understands things very quickly, almost intuitively, and she is also very healthy in her attitude towards life."

While Shepherd was making hit movies and getting good reviews, the gossips were forced to speak in whispers. But with the failure of *At Long Last Love,* they began to cackle out loud.

Shepherd herself downplays the roughness of her treatment in the early Hollywood days, preferring to avoid the subject. Asked how she was treated, she simply says, "Oh, fine. I never went to many Hollywood parties. They're awful." As for the bad reviews and the accusation that she was simply Bogdanovich's protégée, she says, "A lot of my press at the time acted like all I had done was pictures with Peter. They still do. That's still a problem. . . . Our relationship was being reviewed instead of the movies."

Her success in *Taxi Driver* (1976) recouped Shepherd's acting reputation among most of the critics, but despite that success, her movie career never quite got back on the fast track. Her next four films—*Special Delivery* (1976), *Silver Bears* (1978), *The Lady Vanishes* (1979), and

(continued)

CONTINUED

The Return (1980)—were widely ignored. Since 1980, Shepherd has not made a feature film, primarily, she says, because the roles she's been offered have been so bad. One commentator said that Shepherd became "pretty poison" in Hollywood following *At Long Last Love.*

In 1978, her live-in relationship with Bogdanovich ended, as well, and a stage of Cybill Shepherd's career—for better or worse—was over.

> Cybill Shepherd is looking at the Memphis sky. "The swallows are out," she says mildly.
>
> She begins a digression about the places she has travelled. Learning that her visitor has been to the Netherlands, she grows animated. "The Rijksmuseum is my favorite museum in the world!" she says. "The Vermeer room there was one of the greatest experiences of my life. The Dutch are a very warm people. I can't wait to go back."
>
> Clementine and Cybill's brother, Bill (she also has a sister, Terry), come outside to say that they are going for a walk. Clementine, a brown-haired, blue-eyed heartbreaker, is wearing a bright green sundress and grey-and-pink Nike running shoes. Bill, slim and tanned, has been entertaining her in the nearly bare apartment which his sister has just moved into. Clementine shows her mother a piece of paper on which she has been writing numbers. "Hi, Sweetie!" says Cybill. "Oh, look at all the numbers you did! A nine, and an eight, and that looks like a six, and a two. Wonderful! I'm very impressed." A hug and a kiss, and Clementine is on her way.

Cybill Shepherd did not just sit around waiting for Hollywood to take her back to its fickle bosom. Instead, she launched a series of new career moves.

In 1975 she had done *A Shot In the Dark* on stage in Norfolk, Virginia, the first of many regional stage appearances during the late Seventies and early Eighties, including *Last of the Red Hot Lovers, Seven Year Itch,* a production of *Picnic* at Memphis State in 1980, and the lead in *Lunch Hour,* a Jean Kerr comedy that toured the New England "Straw Hat" circuit in 1982. Also in 1982 she began taking her first acting lessons at the Actor's Studio and with Stella Adler in New York. "Orson Welles once said an actor or actress is either getting better or getting worse, so you'd better make sure you're getting better," she says by way of explanation.

She had also begun a singing career. Encouraged by Bogdanovich, she recorded an album of Cole Porter tunes called *Cybill Does It* in 1975; later she did an album with jazz great Stan Getz called *Mad About the Boy* (1976); her last album, *Vanilla* (1979), was recorded with Memphis piano great Phineas Newborn Jr. and a group of other Memphis musicians. The albums got progressively better receptions. In 1981, when she began visiting New York to sing in small jazz clubs, she often got enthusiastic reviews from surprised critics.

Finally, and perhaps most important of all, in 1978 Cybill Shepherd returned to Memphis. She had been gone for ten years. "If this article is really going to have anything to do with who I am, you're going to have to account for the fact that I made a conscious decision to make Memphis my home," she says. "I came back here and made some new friends and fell in love with the place all over again." The regional theatre, the singing, and the renting of a Memphis apartment confirmed a break, albeit not final, with her Hollywood past. "I decided to do theatre everywhere but Los Angeles and New York. And I was getting experience singing in jazz clubs," she recalls. "It meant I wasn't making any money, but I was getting a lot of experience. But when you do something like that, everyone in Los Angeles and New York thinks, well, you might just as well be dead."

Shortly after her return to Memphis, Shepherd met David Ford, who worked for a local car dealership; they were married in November of 1978. "I saw him at Blues Alley," she says about their courtship. "He was in there and I was in there, and the rest is history." The next year Clementine was born. For the next several years, commuting from Memphis to New York, and the theatre circuit, usually with Clementine in tow, Cybill Shepherd left her screen career on hold. In 1982, she and Ford were amicably divorced.

The next stage in her career came in 1983, when another acting role finally came along that Cybill Shepherd wanted. NBC was putting together a new TV series called *The Yellow Rose,* something in the tradition of *Dallas, Dynasty,* and other prime-time soaps. The network was casting for the female lead, a strong, independent young widow on a Texas ranch. "It was a great part," says Shepherd. "I knew I was so perfect for the role, I was near tears." The producers put her through three readings before they, too, admitted she was perfect.

The critics gave *The Yellow Rose* modest praise, noting that it was a notch above the heavy breathing of the other p-t soaps. But the TV public turned to other pastures. After 22 episodes, the show was cancelled. "The only thing I regret about not doing the show anymore is that the character was a strong woman, independent," she says. "Men were constantly telling her, 'Colleen, you can't go out and do that!' and she'd go out and do it anyway. There aren't too many women like that on television."

As this first interview, long and hot, comes to an end under the waning afternoon sun, Cybill Shepherd has shifted basking positions. She is lying prone on the wooden deck, and is clearly growing tired. Her answers are getting shorter, frequently mumbled into the towel supporting her head, and her yawns more frequent. She has been interrupted several times by business calls. "Well, the only thing is, I'm not going to come back until I have to go to work . . . I'm really enjoying this here. I'm relaxing . . . Yeah, because I don't like the idea of a business cover, anyway . . . Okay, baby . . . Wonderful . . . Bah-bah." (It becomes clear that she can turn a thick Memphis accent off and on like a soda-fountain syrup machine.)

Bill and Clementine have returned, and Clementine has made several trips to the deck to check on her mother. She is sent back inside with a gentle reminder to close the sliding door. Cybill is still concerned about the invisible problem with her immaculate skin. ("I think I'm going to have a rash all over my body. Must have been something I ate.") Her only lapse of languor comes when a wasp makes an appearance on the deck, causing her to jump up and run inside: "I'm terrified of bees," she says.

Finally, with one last check of her complexion ("This is very red right here. This rash! I'm getting a rash all over my body!"), she is ready to end the interview. "I can only do so much a day and I get tired," she says, heading inside.

Her apartment is furnished with little more than a few directors' chairs (one labeled "Cybill Shepherd"), some rolled-up oriental rugs, a dhurrie rug on the dining room floor, a kilim rug on the living room floor, and a small dining room table. A painting of a woman vamping on the beach in a sun hat leans against one wall (it is by Norris Mailer, Norman Mailer's wife), several mountain bikes are propped against another wall, some Japanese tatami mats are on the dining room floor, and a portable phonograph/tape recorder is next to the mats, with tapes—Willie Nelson, John Anderson—scattered about on the floors.

While Cybill has gone inside to put on a robe, Clementine greets her mother's guest.

"Are you leaving?" she says.

"Yes, I think so."

"Yes, but when?"

"In a couple of minutes."

"Bye." Clementine departs in a cloud of glory.

Her mother returns in a sun robe. Complimented on her child, she says, with proud modesty, "She is a good person." On her way to the door, she agrees to another interview the following week, one designed to catch the world up on the life of Cybill Shepherd today.

(continued)

CONTINUED

A week later, Cybill Shepherd is running a few minutes late for her noon appointment, and she's not at home when her visitor arrives. A radio is playing KIX, a country-and-western station, loudly inside her empty apartment. The sounds of Crystal Gayle and Mickey Gilley fill the hallway. Through the hall window can be seen a crane delivering dirt to fill the planters on her apartment deck.

At 12:20, the elevator door opens and Cybill Shepherd emerges pushing a Puch Pic-Nic mountain bicycle, which resembles a hi-tech dirt bike.

"Hi!" she says, this time in a thick Southern accent. ("Haaah!") She apologizes for being late and explains that it was such a nice day she decided to go biking on Mud Island. "It's wonderful!" She exults, about both the exercise and the island. She is proud of the bike. "Eighteen gears, all-terrain tires," she says.

She is wearing a visor, a "Great Mississippi River Race" T-shirt, red bermuda shorts, purple socks, and tennis shoes. She looks, as usual, healthy, glowing, terrific. She explains that she only has a few more days in Memphis before heading off to L.A., and wants to make the most of what is mostly a vacation for her.

It's clear that free time is at a premium these days for Cybill Shepherd, who has at least eighteen gears and all-terrain resilience herself. Her career, Hollywood be damned, is rolling once again.

Inside her apartment she calls out to a downtown eatery and charms them into delivering lunch, even though they're overloaded with customers this afternoon. Then she sits down at the dining room table, sips a glass of ice water, and begins to describe the life of Cybill Shepherd of 1984.

"I get up real early in the morning," she says, adding that her schedule will change if she's shooting a movie. "The early morning is a working period for me. That's my sharpest time of day. It's the quietest time of day, especially if I can get up before my daughter gets up." She laughs. "One thing I learned real quickly having a child: no matter what time you go to bed at night, you have this wonderful little alarm clock to get you up in the morning."

Clementine, she explains, "lives with me and travels with me. If I do location work, she will always visit me on location for a certain period of time." In Memphis, Myrtle Boone helps take care of Clementine; in Los Angeles there is another governess for the four-year-old. "And my ex-husband is very, very good with her," she adds. "He has always done a lot more parenting than most fathers do. Even from the first diaper. I've just had a lot of help with Clementine."

Three days a week, Shepherd works out at the Peabody Health Club. On the other days, she says, she either swims at the Shrine Building or rides her bike. The rest of most Memphis days is taken up with phone calls, lunches, interviews, and career business.

These days, most of Cybill Shepherd's career business is involved with three things: television movies, singing, and her first effort at producing a feature film.

As she is being interviewed this June day, her NBC movie *Trick Eyes* is already in the can and she will be leaving for L.A. soon to make the CBS movie *Seduced,* which will be filmed in L.A., Toronto, and the Virgin Islands. "You know, television stars make more than movie stars," she says. "Recently my agent said to me, 'Well, you're at the place in your career where you have to decide whether you want to be a movie star or a television star.' I said, 'You mean, I have to decide if I want to do movies or television?' He said, 'Yes,' I said 'I'm not going to make that decision.' The medium is not important. What's important is the part. And the fact that I like to work. I enjoy my work."

In fact, the kind of work Shepherd does these days in those early morning hours often comprises reading scripts, working out roles, and rewriting parts. "I've rewritten every part I've ever done," she says. She scribbles notes all over her scripts and reads them aloud to herself. "Learning the words is really nothing compared to the work of preparing the role," she says. "Figuring out who this person is, why they are doing what they're doing, what did they do before, what the subtext is, what the relationship of the characters are—all that's a complicated process."

The singing part of her career is also gaining momentum. "I've been preparing an album for five years," she says. "Actually, I'm really preparing two albums. One is a country-and-western album. The other is more jazz-oriented."

Shepherd's interest in music is obvious. She is likely to leave the radio on during an interview, and during lulls in the conversation she often sings along with whoever's on. (She stops everything to sing "Shine On" with the radio in mid-interview.) "I was a singer before I was anything else," she says. "I'll always be a singer, whether I'm performing or not."

Lunch arrives. It is delivered by a pleasant older man in a three-piece suit—apparently the owner of the restaurant. He is a bit embarrassed. "Hello!" she says, as if greeting an old friend. "Look at you! Can I get you a glass of water?" She gives him a tour of her apartment, takes him out on the deck, engages in a conversation with the workers delivering the dirt. Everyone is introduced to everyone in the best Southern style. "Thank you so much!" she says to the man who delivered the lunch as he leaves. It is a brief *tour de force* of Southern hospitality.

Finally, as she dives into her lunch of fried catfish and lima beans, Shepherd describes the project which has her most excited these days: this month, she will begin filming *September, September,* the 1950s novel written by Memphian Shelby Foote. She will be writer, executive producer, and star.

Shepherd has written the first draft of the screenplay, and novelist Larry McMurtry of *The Last Picture Show* fame, is helping with revisions. Columbia Pictures is backing it through the Carson Company, which did the hit, *The Big Chill.* As of July, the director had not yet been chosen. *September, September* will be filmed on location in Memphis.

"The reason I'm doing *September, September* is that I was getting all these terrible offers of parts," Shepherd says. "I mean the money was there. If I wanted to do 'em I could have done them. But I said, 'I've got to develop my own properties.' You know, necessity is the mother of invention. I said, 'Okay, if I'm going to get a good part, I'm going to have to go out, buy the book, option the book'—I certainly don't have the money (to do all that)—but I had to figure out a way to do these things. I cannot wait for people." Flashing the script, she says, "This is going to win me an Academy Award, not only as best actress but for best picture." She is grinning, but she doesn't seem to be joking.

Beyond *September, September* Cybill Shepherd's plans remain up in the air. She says she'd like to do a film in which her athletic abilities come into play, and she's looking into developing another property that would do that. "I don't know if I want to tell you about it or not," she says. "It's about a women's professional softball team, and it's very funny." She adds that she has been approached to do the life story of jazz singer Anita O'Day, either as a TV movie or a feature ("They'll do it either way I want"), and that she's considering doing *The Best Little Whorehouse in Texas* at Memphis State. "I would love to do that," she says. "I really enjoyed working at Memphis State. It's a beautiful facility."

In fact, when Cybill Shepherd discusses her dreams for the future, she more often than not detours into a discussion of her hopes for her hometown. She says that one of her dreams is for Memphis to have its own music institute, where young people could be introduced to all kinds of music, especially the blues. She calls Mud Island "extraordinary" and "spectacular." She gets excited about Beale Street, calling it "the best thing in Memphis" and expressing regret that her original plans to open a club there fell through several years ago. And she looks to the days when

(continued)

CONTINUED

the Orpheum Theatre will be the focus of an arts complex that will be "the Lincoln Center of Memphis" and more local performers can get paid for their efforts.

As for her own long-term plans, she says she'd like to continue developing films and maybe take up directing ("when I'm in my forties"). Beyond that, she says, "I would like to have the opportunity to continue to grow in what I do and to become better at what I do, and also a chance to see my daughter grow and develop. I don't have the ultimate wisdom about what's best for me, so what I think I want to do may not be the best thing. My father always used to say to me, 'Be careful, or you may get what you want.' "

It is several days later, and Cybill Shepherd has just finished a two-hour photo session in connection with this story. She has been more than good-natured during the entire long evening, waiting patiently, making jokes, flirting with crew members, as the photographer perches her on the ledge of her deck and arranges her in various poses, set against the river, the Memphis-Arkansas bridge, and the ebbing sunset. Then there has been a series of indoor shots in her apartment.

Now, wearing her glasses ("Lord knows, I need them") and, if possible, looking even prettier because of them, she has offered beers all around to the crew and warned everybody to hurry out to the deck to catch the sunset. "We don't want to miss the sun," she says. She sings along with Mickey Gilley on the radio. "But you don't know me," she sings, clear and strong.

Out on the deck, everyone grows quiet at the solemnity of the river, the sky, the lowering sun. "You know what I want on my epitaph?" she says softly, looking with mock seriousness toward the horizon. "I want it to say on my epitaph: 'We'll make this a comedy yet.' " She laughs.

The sky turns a deeper purple, and Shepherd turns contemplative. "You know," she says. "I regret every sunset I miss here." And as she gazes across the Mississippi, the Memphis sun disappears, headed toward L.A.

Source: © 1984. *Memphis* magazine. Reprinted by permission of the author.

Let's look at the story in more detail. First, there's the effective structure. In the first five paragraphs, Weathers puts Shepherd in time and place, describes her, lets her speak and asks the key question of the story. Then Weathers begins a chronological retelling of Shepherd's story, beginning with her birth and concluding with her current film and television work. In between, two breaks bring the reader to the present, offering observation and trivia, providing breathing space in what might otherwise have been a deadening biography. Then there's a third return to the present, followed by a transition to the second interview, which is primarily about Shepherd's upcoming activities. A final break occurs at the end of the story when Shepherd sits for the magazine's photographer. In summary, the lesson is clear: A profile is more than a running biography; it is a story that should be told with pacing and rhythm. The structure also illustrates that serious profiles are rarely written as the result of one interview.

The story reflects significant research in paragraphs like this, where three sources are cited.

According to most accounts, some of the Hollywood crowd took an instant, jealous dislike to Shepherd as far back as 1970, snubbing her at parties and so forth. One writer said she was being called "Eliza Doolittle to [Bogdanovich's] Professor Higgins . . . a nobody-know-nothing to his somebody-so-something." Glitter critic Rex Reed quoted Bogdanovich as saying, "Cybill was an itch and I scratched it." A less sensationalistic writer had Bogdanovich giving a thoughtful appraisal of her during the same period: "The camera really loves her," he said. "It is difficult to take a bad picture of her. In person there is also a lot of what she projects on the screen, plus a lot of things you don't know about. She is extremely intelligent, and sensitive, and she understands things very quickly, almost intuitively, and she is also very healthy in her attitude towards life."

Weathers also reinforces and personalizes his research by injecting Shepherd's answers to his questions at appropriate points. For example, in a narrative paragraph about Shepherd's participation in the Miss Teenage America Contest, Weathers quotes her:

> ("The girl who won did the *hula* as her talent!" she recalls disdainfully.)

Note, too, that Weathers avoids using the first person, an approach beginning writers love and most editors detest. In "Cybill Shepherd," the interviewer is barely mentioned and when he is, it is in a vague, third-person voice, as in this sentence from the second paragraph.

> She offers her visitor a surprisingly firm handshake, comments on the terrific view of the river and Mud Island, measures the height of the midday sun, and, after arranging for ice water all around, stretches out on a lounge chair to bask in the rays of her hometown.

"Her visitor" is, of course, a little obtrusive, but much less so than "me," which is probably what a less skilled writer would have used.

But it is Weathers's use of at least seven descriptive techniques that brings "Cybill Shepherd" to life. For example, within the story, he uses physical, psychological and self-description, description of Shepherd by other people, description of Shepherd by the style of language she uses, description by her surroundings and description by her response to various situations.

There is a footnote to this profile of Cybill Shepherd. You may have guessed that Weathers interviewed Shepherd as her career was flagging. Shepherd's career, however, reignited with a hit television series called "Moonlighting with actor Bruce Willis." As a result, Weathers interviewed the actress a second time—six years later. From that interview came a second article, "Cybill at Forty." In that story, he brings readers up to date, chronicling Shepherd's professional and personal successes and failures. Shepherd, by the way, starred in a second popular television series, appropriately titled "Cybill," from 1995 until 1998. After the television series, Shepherd hosted several more television talk shows and appeared in more theatrical and television movies, including made-for-television movies in 2003 and 2005 about controversial publishing and television diva Martha Stewart. Weathers has yet to write part three of the Cybill Shepherd story, but perhaps that's because she said it all with her frank paperback autobiography: *Cybill Disobedience: How I Survived Beauty Pageants, Elvis, Sex, Bruce Willis, Lies, Marriage, Motherhood, Hollywood, and the Irrepressible Urge to Say What I Think.*

Successful writers like Weathers create successful stories from good ideas, good reporting—which includes research, interviews and observation—and good writing. Experienced newspaper and magazine writers know that a superb idea can easily be sabotaged by poor reporting or writing. And expert reporting, of which interviewing is a component, can be scuttled by a poorly developed idea or weak writing. And, of course, even extraordinary writing can't save a story flawed by a weak idea or sloppy reporting.

In short, the feature or article is like a three-legged stool. All of the legs need to be in place if the stool is to serve its purpose. The next four chapters are devoted to that third leg—writing the newspaper feature and magazine article.

CHAPTER SIX

WRITING THE NEWSPAPER FEATURE STORY

BEGINNING THE PROCESS

As you've learned, newspaper feature writers face deadlines ranging from a few hours to months. Approaches to writing the feature obviously vary with the amount of time available. For example, a general-assignment reporter such as Helen Garcia, from Chapter 1, has only hours to research, interview, organize, write, and rewrite her story. In all likelihood, Garcia's feature writing could not equal the quality of the work of Pulitzer feature winners Jon Franklin, Madeleine Blais, Teresa Carpenter, Saul Pett, Nan Robertson, Peter Rinearson, Alice Steinbach, John Camp, Steve Twomey, Jacqui Banaszynski, David Zucchino, Dave Curtin, Sheryl James, Howell Raines, George Lardner Jr., Isabell Wilkerson, Ron Suskind, Rick Bragg, Lisa Pollak, Thomas French, Angelo Henderson, J. R. Moehringer, Tom Hallman, Barry Siegel, Sonia Nazario, Julia Keller, Jim Sheeler and others. Those writers are all journalists of considerable experience and had much more time to complete their winning stories.

But whether a story is finished in an hour or a month, the process is similar. First, there's a focused idea, followed by reporting, which is a combination of research, interviews and observation. Then the writer sifts through the accumulated information and outlines the story in search of structure. After the story structure is clarified, the writing begins.

Or, as author and writing consultant Peter Jacobi puts it in his seminars: "Think before you write. Gather facts before you write. Organize before you write. Writing is easier (hard as it always shall be) if an idea precedes research" which precedes structuring which precedes writing.

Organizing practices vary. Some feature writers formulate stories in their mind. Others make an outline on paper. Pett, an AP special correspondent, had a relaxed deadline for his 10,000-word story on the federal bureaucracy, so he made a detailed outline.

> Before I write, I go through a very tedious process in which I try to outline my material. That's not to outline the story, that's outlining the material.

In a project like that, I come back with a dozen little notebooks. Then I've got a stack of articles, chapters in books. It gets to be quite a pile. I try to outline by categories. For example, one of the categories would have been comparisons with other bureaucracies. Everything in my material referring to that would be put in an outline saying "International Comparisons." And the outline would very briefly describe what there is to say about that phase of the subject, and who said it, and where I'll find it. Was it in a *New York Times* editorial, a text by somebody or whatever?

What has the growth of the federal bureaucracy done to state government? That's a big aspect all by itself.

Another one is examples of ridiculousness—senseless and excessive spending by the federal government.

The historical facts of it: How did it get to be what it is?

All that has to lend itself to some sort of organization. If I cut up my notebooks and the articles I had and made piles by subjects, that's what I'd have. Some writers have their little piles.

I do it in an outline. The outline takes forever. It's dull work and I hate it but when it's done and you start writing, you're glad you did it. Frequently, I don't have to stop and look up something. If I do, I know where to find it, as a result of the outline. And it helps in your thinking. The outline of the material gives you a good idea of the major segments of the story, and you have a better idea what it all adds up to.

And that makes it possible for you to figure out how you want to start the story.

Village Voice reporter Carpenter, who profiled the life and death of Playmate Dorothy Stratten, says she's still "wrestling with the best way of processing information."

However, Carpenter notes that she made a "long outline" and then let a week pass before writing the Stratten story. She explains: "When you're embroiled in the reporting, everything seems important. Some facts you have worked so hard to get, you just can't bear to give them up. When you research intensely, every little detail seems important. But if you give yourself distance, the truly important ones stand out."

Twomey, a reporter for *The Philadelphia Inquirer* who won a Pulitzer for his feature about the military value and strategy of using aircraft carriers in combat, began with a mental outline and then resorted to a written outline somewhat like Pett's when his plan didn't work. He explains:

I was essentially one of two general-assignment reporters for Europe. The [story was a] piece that I did while I was a correspondent in Paris. I'm a military history buff. I've long been fascinated by the idea of aircraft carriers. The paper does not routinely allow people to go out and fulfill their fantasies, however. You have to have a reason for doing it. Aircraft carriers were in the news during this period.

[The Navy] eagerly agreed to help me do the piece. My goal in going out on the carrier was simply to provide some color for what I thought would be, frankly, a rather dry piece about military policy, military strategy. I knew that issue to the average reader would be pretty boring if you discussed it in the abstract. Aircraft carriers. How much do they cost? What do we use them for? Are they the right [kind of] ships? I needed some color around which to build the story.

When I got there and spent three days, I was enthralled by what I [saw], and realized that I had to tell people this in detail—what it's like to work on one of these ships. And that realization made the story much harder to write because there was no inherent connection between the beauty of watching an F–14 be catapulted off a carrier and whether aircraft carriers are wise investments as military strategy. There's obviously a connection, but not an easy one to make. [So] while I was on the ship, I came up with what I thought was a brilliant solution. I would pick about half a dozen individuals aboard the ship who were performing tasks that I thought were amazing. The men who were hooking the aircraft to the catapult. The men who were helping them land. The Air Boss in the control tower.

I didn't sit down to start writing the story until more than three weeks after I had been on the carrier. When I sat down to actually write the story, I realized that this was unworkable. It made no sense. I couldn't bounce back and forth between interesting individuals and their jobs versus big policy discussions. What was the linkage? There was none. I realized that my brilliantly conceived plan of execution wasn't going to work. I went through days of, "Why am I in this business? Whose idea was this? I'll shoot him." I really foundered, probably as badly as I have ever, in 14 years in the business.

I finally hit upon a solution, the one that ended up in the paper. It seemed to me that there were certain things that had occurred on the ship that led naturally into the bigger policy issues. The fact that the carrier had, in fact, been used in the raid on Libya showed you its operational capability. The fact that all those ships that follow the carrier—little task force ships that are called "small boys"—led naturally into a discussion of the Navy's efforts to defend the ship. The sheer statistics of size led into a discussion of size: Is this the best way to go? I did start to find linkages between being on the ship and the big policy discussions.

And [I] ended up writing an outline—which I rarely do—in which the story would move through an introductory section, followed by the big cosmic section of "These ships are beautiful, but there are a lot of questions about whether they mean anything, whether we should have ships this big." Which led into a discussion of "Just how big is the *America?*" Which led into a discussion of "It's big, and what can big ships do?" Which led into the Libya raid and then, "What is the threat to those big ships?" Which led into a discussion of the Soviet Navy and "What is the Navy's system for dealing with that threat?" Which led to "What are the things that can overcome the Navy's defenses against that threat. Then [the story ended] with the landing at night on the carrier, which in effect brought the story and the plane back home.

[Writing the story took about] three weeks, one week of which was spent in additional reporting by telephone—back to military experts, getting the big picture stuff. [But] a great deal of that time was also spent smashing my head against every available wall and telling myself that I didn't know how to organize my story.

Camp, of the *St. Paul Pioneer Press,* mentally outlined his farm stories while driving back from interviews. "I would go down to the farm two or three times without writing anything, then I would internalize all that," he says. "Each drive down and each drive back is four hours. When you're out there driving and there's nothing to look at in the prairie, there's a lot of time to think about what you're doing. So I'd be sitting in the car thinking about all that and when I came back I'd be really primed to write. I'd just sit down and boom, it all came out. It had been thought out and mulled over."

STORY STRUCTURE

Let's assume your reporting and rough outline are completed. Your task now is to figure out how to tell a story from the information you've gathered. The most effective feature storytelling methods are *chronological, least-to-most-important, problem and solution, catalog* and *repetitive* structures. In addition, these structures can be *combined* (just like story, appeal, and, as you'll soon see, lead categories).

Now let's look at these structures in detail.

The *chronological* structure is easiest to understand. The writer simply tells a story from beginning to end, much like Blais of *The Miami Herald* does in "Zepp's Last Stand." Carpenter, in "Death of a Playmate," also uses chronological structure, as does Camp in his farm series. Banaszynski's diagnosis-to-death story of a Minnesota AIDS sufferer, published in the *St. Paul Pioneer Press,* and the story of two seriously burned Colorado children by Curtin of the *Colorado Springs Gazette Telegraph,* which is examined in Chapter 7, also use chronological structure. In addition, Zucchino's *Philadelphia Inquirer* features about being black in South Africa use this structure, as do the Pulitzer Prize–winning feature stories for 1992 and 1993 by Raines of *The New York Times* and Lardner of *The Washington Post.* More recent Pulitzer Prize winners such as *The Wall Street Journal*'s Suskind (who wrote about Cedric Jennings's university goals), Pollak of the Baltimore *Sun* ("The Umpire's Sons"), French of the *St. Petersburg Times* (who wrote "Angels and Demons") and Henderson of *The Wall Street Journal* (who wrote about a pharmacist who killed an armed robber) also use chronological structure. Sonia Nazario's Prize-winning story of "Enrique's Journey" is structurally chronological as well. Nazario of *The Los Angeles Times* explains: "The story is fairly straight-forward. The mother leaves. He leaves. There's the train trip" and Enrique finds his mother.

It's important to note that a movement back in time, called a flashback, and forward in time, called a flash-forward, is acceptable and common when using chronological structure. At the minimum, most skilled feature writers use some flashbacks with chronological structure. For example, Lardner introduces "The Killing of Kristin" by telling readers how he learned about his daughter's death, then begins a long flashback to retrace the events leading to Kristin's brutal murder and her killer's suicide. Raines uses flashbacks far more extensively in "Grady's Gift," a coming-of-age story about his boyhood introduction to civil rights by a maid his parents employed. Raines sets the scene for a reunion with the former maid, then repeatedly digresses to incidents from their lives in the segregated South. French, the 1998 winner, describes the grisly 1989 murders of an Ohio woman and her two daughters while on a Florida Disney vacation, then travels back in time to the beginning of the trip, carries the reader forward past the murders and the trial of the killer and finally ends the story in the present. Henderson uses flashbacks much more sparingly than Lardner, Raines and French in his 1999 Pulitzer winner. He takes readers to Detroit's Redford Pharmacy for a 1990 robbery, moves forward in time to a description of a man who robbed the same pharmacy in 1997, briefly returns readers to the early days of the pharmacy, and then moves forward again to the 1997 robbery and fatal shooting and aftermath.

The *least-to-most-important* structure is the opposite of the news story's inverted pyramid, which—after a lead—presents the most important information first.

The least-to-most-important structure is much like a teacher's lesson. For example, primary school instructors teach students the alphabet before they ask them to read short stories. And *The Seattle Times*'s Rinearson, in his feature series about the making of a Boeing 757 jetliner (portions of which you'll read later in this chapter), begins with an airline placing the initial order and then proceeds to more complicated matters such as construction and testing of the airframe. The headlines on Rinearson's series even suggest progression from relative simplicity to complexity (as well as chronological progression): "The Big Gamble," "Making the Decision," "Designing the 757," "Pulling It Together," "Will It Really Fly?," "An Act of Faith" and "The Delivery."

In addition, as you've read, *The Philadelphia Inquirer*'s Twomey uses this approach to explore with ever-increasing complexity the value of aircraft carriers.

In summary, the least-to-most-important structure always moves the subject from the simple to the complex. It may or may not present the information chronologically, however.

The *problem and solution* structure is quite common. Pett's story is an example. How did the bureaucracy get so big? he asks, citing the problem. He then subdivides the issues, provides answers and moves on to the big answer. Bragg of *The New York Times* uses a variety of structures for his five Pulitzer features, but his story about Oseola McCarty's $150,000 gift to her local university (which you'll read later in this chapter) uses the problem and solution structure to answer the story's most compelling question: Why? Often this structure begins with one or more anecdotes or examples of problems, then moves to solutions to those problems.

The *catalog* structure is essentially a list, in which people, places or events are classified and then explained. If you're writing a travel feature about the sights to see and avoid in Lincoln, Nebraska, a catalog structure may be your best bet.

The *repetitive* structure introduces a concept and continues to hammer away at it until the point is made. This structure is used in Steinbach's "A Boy of Unusual Vision," which you'll read later in this chapter. Steinbach, of the Baltimore *Sun,* introduces readers to a blind boy, and quickly explains that he'll make his way in the world. And throughout the story, she reinforces that concept with quotations and anecdotes. Wilkerson, *The New York Times* reporter who wrote about a poor boy growing up much too quickly on Chicago's tough South Side, also uses a repetitive structure. You'll read her story in Chapter 7. And Moehringer of *The Los Angeles Times* returns again and again to the symbolism of how a proposed ferry linking the Alabama River communities of Gee's Bend and Camden might change everything and everyone in "Crossing Over." The 2000 Pulitzer Prize–winning feature uses the ferry—which was promised but never delivered—and the Alabama River to symbolize change, fear, fate, death and salvation.

The final structure is the *combination* approach. In a sense, most features use a combination structure because writers seldom assemble a story the way a child builds a model airplane. Rather, writing is a creative process that draws inspiration from many sources and escapes blueprint-like precision.

For example, Franklin, of the Baltimore *Evening Sun,* uses problem and solution as well as chronological structure for "Mrs. Kelly's Monster." The problem is Edna Kelly's "monster"; the solution is surgery. And the surgery is described in a chronological order. This combination structure also is used in Robertson's *New York Times* first-person story of her encounter with toxic shock syndrome. Robertson's problem is her illness and the recovery is the solution. At the same time, the recovery is described chronologically. James of the *St. Petersburg Times* also uses this combination in her story about the abandonment of a baby in Florida. The mother's motivation for leaving her baby in a cardboard box is the problem. The mother's explanation—unacceptable though it may be—is the solution. And like Franklin and Robertson, James guides the reader to the end of the story by using chronological structure: James's story begins with the discovery of the abandoned baby, follows the investigation and arrest of the mother and concludes with her trial and an explanation from her. Hallman of *The Oregonian* uses it as well to tell the story of a 14-year-old Portland boy's quest to look like other high school students, despite a disfiguring birth defect and the life-threatening surgery needed to correct it. Hallman's 2001 four-part Prize winner, called "The Boy Behind the Mask," relates Sam Lightner's struggle chronologically as he and his family search for a solution to his medical problem.

Siegel of *The Los Angeles Times* uses an unusual combination of chronological and repetitive structure in "A Father's Pain, a Judge's Duty, and a Justice Beyond Their Reach." The story, the lead of which you'll read in a few pages, profiles Utah judge Robert Hilder and distraught father, Paul Wayment, whom the judge sentenced to jail for negligence in the wilderness death of his little boy, and Wayment's suicide. Told largely chronologically, Siegel also infuses the story with the judge's view of justice. Of Hilder, Siegel writes: "For Paul Wayment, he decided, there's got to be a consequence. Wayment was not a monster; Wayment was no more or less than any man. All the same, he'd exposed Gage to significant risk. He'd caused Gage to wander through the forest, terrified and suffering."

It's also possible, though not always desirable, to apply dramatic unity to the structure you've selected. As you'll recall from "Mrs. Kelly's Monster" in Chapter 1, that unity begins by introducing a character and following that character through rising action or increasing complications, a climax or crisis, falling action and then a catastrophe or a solution. Obviously, this approach works best with very dramatic stories, and seems to fit especially well with chronological, problem and solution, repetitive and combination structures.

In short, the feature with dramatic material should open with an intriguing lead, build slowly to a climax, then wind down to a foreshadowed conclusion—whatever the structure.

WRITING THE LEAD

As you've read, the feature has a distinct beginning, body and end. The lead, of course, is the beginning. It has several tasks: It must intrigue the reader, set the tone for the story, and move the reader to the body of the story in a logical manner. Carpenter explains: "The lead signals to the reader what type of story this is to be—it sets up the pacing for the entire story. That lead telegraphs a lot of information."

Because of those requirements, Curtin, of the *Colorado Springs Gazette Telegraph*, decided to significantly change the lead of his story about Adam and Megan Walter, who were severely burned in a house fire. The 1990 Pulitzer Prize–winning story of the recovery of the Walter children originally concluded with a description of the family decorating their Christmas tree and listening to a cassette tape that the children had made for their father. That description ultimately became the lead, Curtin explains. "My editor suggested that we move that to the top [of the story] because it was topical [because of a January publication date] and [because] it was somewhat happy, to tell the readers that this was not going to be a story of doom and gloom. It was going to be a story that you could find inspiring in your own life."

Sheeler of the *Rocky Mountain News* also moved material from deep in an early draft of his 2006 Pulitzer Prize–winning story to the lead of the final draft, although the movement only traded one horrifying scene for another. Sheeler begins "Final Salute" with a description of the arrival of 24-year-old Marine Second Lieutenant Jim Cathey's body at the Reno, Nevada airport, as his widow, Katherine, waits with Marine casualty assistance personnel. The original lead of the 12,000-word story featured a Marine knocking on the door of a fallen Marine's family. You'll read the lead of "Final Salute" in Chapter 7.

Unlike the news lead, the feature lead may be a single sentence fragment or hundreds of words in many paragraphs, such as Carpenter's lead in "Death of a Playmate" and Curtin's lead in "Adam & Megan."

For example, here's a four-paragraph lead by Tamara Jones, a national writer for the Associated Press. Jones's story about America's female Vietnam veterans, headlined "Vietnam's Most Ignored Veterans," won an honorable mention in an AP competition.

> The nightmare always begins with Lin McClenahan in civilian clothes, boarding a public bus in San Francisco.
>
> She gets off in fatigues, back in Vietnam and under heavy enemy fire.
>
> Broken bodies lie all around her. Suddenly she is hit and crumples to the ground. A helicopter appears and evacuates the casualties. All but Lin. She cries out as the chopper flies off, "Don't leave me. I hurt, too."
>
> In a sense, the United States did forget Lin McClenahan and thousands of other women it sent to Vietnam as nurses, non-combat soldiers and civilian volunteers. No one even knows for sure how many were there.

The first three paragraphs intrigue the reader while the fourth prepares the reader for the story of a number of women trying to forget the carnage that was Vietnam. All four paragraphs suggest the story will be terse, grim and revealing.

A Dozen Lead Categories

Newspaper feature stories can be categorized, you recall. Leads can, too. Like a story category, each lead type is known by a variety of names, and each category can be combined with another to form a new kind of lead. However fluid, the lead names and categories are useful because they serve as models for beginning writers.

Delayed Lead. The delayed lead withholds identification of the person, group, place or event that is central to the story. Identification is usually delayed for only a few paragraphs, but in some circumstances identification may be suspended until the end of the story. Here is the lead of a feature about the birthplace of much of America's computer hardware and software. The author is Sid Moody, an Associated Press Newsfeatures writer. Moody's story is called "Silicon Valley: The Log Cabin Game."

> PALO ALTO, Calif. (Ap)—Like most newborns, this electronic wonderchild is into everything. Chews it. Grabs something else. Astounds its elders.
>
> It does not totally resemble any forebearer, yet it carries the promise of a maturity beyond imagining.

Silicon Valley is where new companies, called startups, multiply like Medflies.

Where Daddy moves Little Sister into Big Sister's room so he can use the space to invent video games and make millions.

Where the sun always shines and clouds are as rare as American cars.

Where the divorce rate exceeds the marriage rate.

Where new technology is outmoded in 18 months; where most companies lack pension plans because everybody will have made his millions by then; where three-bedroom homes list for "only" $374,000; where management is so laid back one executive goes barefoot except in the halls, and where money is good but the "game," innovating more than the next guy, is better.

It's also the place where America may yet prove it's No. 1 because for all the electronic witchcraft, for all the sport-shirted bosses (a salesman counted one tie among his 200 customers), Silicon Valley is a throwback to something that made this country No. 1 in the first place.

The first two paragraphs delay identification of the subject, while teasing the reader. Paragraphs three through seven support the first two paragraphs and prepare the reader for the eighth paragraph, which ties into the body of the story.

Here's another delayed lead, this one by Associated Press writer Henry Gottlieb, who wrote about recruiting for the all-volunteer armed forces.

TOWANDA, Pa. (AP)—In the hills above the Susquehanna River, the hunting season never ends for Dick Wilson, even in summer and even in the pockets of population along the dusty roads that wind past the hamlets and dairy farms.

Once in a while, an unwary woodchuck pops up its head as Wilson passes in his government-issue sedan, or a deer feeding at night on the edge of Route 6 stands transfixed by the headlights.

But Wilson is searching for more elusive game. In the words of the competition, he's "looking for a few good men and women," and it isn't easy.

A more subtle variation of the delayed lead is used by French of the *St. Petersburg Times* for "Angels and Demons," his 1998 Pulitzer Prize–winning story about the murder of three women and the hunt for their killer.

One year had gone by since the murders, and then another, and now the investigators were deep into a third. They were working day and night, working weekends, putting off vacations, losing weight, gaining weight, growing pale and pasty and haggard, waking at 3 A.M. with a jolt and scratching notes on pads beside their beds. Their sergeant did not know if they would ever find the answer. As far as he was concerned, the case was not even in their hands.

Ultimately, he believed, it was up to God whether they made an arrest.

A born-again Christian, the sergeant carried a Bible in his briefcase. He had no doubt that both heaven and hell were real. He saw good and evil not as theoretical or philosophical concepts, but as absolute realities walking upright through the world. He believed in the forces of light and darkness. He believed in demonic possession. He took it as a matter of fact that Satan and his cohorts currently reigned over the Earth.

"I believe there are demons all around us," he would say, "just as I believe there are angels all around us."

And when he looked at the evidence from the case before them now, studied the photos of the bodies and the ropes and the concrete blocks, the sergeant had no doubt that he and the other investigators were pursuing someone driven by Satanic forces.

Of course demons were real. They were hunting one now.

The final paragraph of French's six-paragraph lead links the lead to a flashback describing the Florida vacation of Jo Rogers and her two daughters, which in turn leads to their murders in the murky waters of Tampa Bay and then to the successful search by Florida investigators for their killer.

Descriptive Lead.　This lead simply paints a word portrait of a person, group, place or event. Steinbach's Pulitzer Prize feature about a blind 10-year-old uses a descriptive lead. Here is the first paragraph of Steinbach's six-paragraph descriptive lead.

First, the eyes: They are large and blue, a light, opaque blue, the color of a robin's egg. And if, on a sunny spring day, you look straight into these eyes—eyes that cannot look back at you— the sharp, April light turns them pale, like the thin blue of a high, cloudless sky.

The descriptive lead is sometimes called a situation lead if a scene is set or an atmosphere is created.

The situation lead in Twomey's aircraft carrier story both creates an atmosphere and sets a scene. While the lead is very long—29 paragraphs—it's in proportion to Twomey's long, long story.

Air Boss looked aft. Through the haze of a June morning off Sicily, an F–14A Tomcat fighter was already banking in low over *America*'s wake, a couple of miles out and coming home to the Bird Farm. Air Boss looked down. Damn. Still no place to put the thing.

On the flight deck below, opposite Air Boss's perch in the control tower, an A-7E Corsair II bomber sat astride the No. 4 steam catapult amidships. By now, the A-7 should have been flying with the rest of the day's second mission. Nobody would be landing while it straddled *America*'s only available runway.

"What's taking 'em so long down there?" Air Boss growled. He had left his leather armchair in his glass booth in *America*'s superstructure. He was standing up for a better look, which he always does when the flight deck crunch is on.

The ship's 79,724 tons suddenly shuddered. Steam billowed from No. 4. The A-7 had vanished, rudely flung out over the Mediterranean by the "cat stroke," like a rock from a slingshot. Finally.

"Launch complete, sir!" said Mini Boss, his assistant.

"Clear decks!" Air Boss boomed into the radio to his launch crews. It would be close, maybe too close. "Secure the waist cat! Prepare to recover aircraft! Hubba, hubba!"

The F–14 was closing at 150 miles per hour. A mile out now. On the deck, crews were frantically stowing launch gear. They had to seal the long slit down which the catapult arm—the "shuttle"—races as it yanks a plane along the deck and flips it heavenward. They had to shut hatches and make them flush with the deck. *America* had to become seamless for its bird.

"Commmme on, commmme on," said Air Boss. His eyes flitted from the looming F–14 to his crews working below. The plane's variable wings were swept wide for landing, 64 feet tip to tip. Its wheels were down, its twin tail jets were spewing heat waves. It was a ptero-dactyl about to prey on the carrier.

"We're not going to make it!" said Air Boss.

"We'll make it!" said Mini Boss.

Unless they made it, the F–14 would have to be waved off, sent around for another approach. In peacetime, that is not fatal. It costs fuel—266 gallons a minute for an F–14, $1,100 an hour—but no more. In war, a carrier's ability to cycle its jets in seconds—to launch them, land them, rearm them, refuel them, launch them again—could mean victory or defeat. *America* is not at war now. But *America* trains as if it is.

"We're not going to make it!" Air Boss said again.

"We'll make it!" said Mini.

Catapult crews had almost finished. The F–14 was just off the stern and plunging, a long hook dangling from its belly that would, it was hoped, catch one of four cables laid across the rear flight deck to stop the plane cold. It was time to decide: Wave it off or land it. The last of the crew was scampering out of the landing area.

"They made it!" said Mini.

Over the stern, down, down.

Bam.

Fifty-six thousand pounds of F–14 slammed home. Simultaneously, the pilot pushed to full throttle. Heat blasted down the aft flight deck. If the hook missed all the cables, the pilot would simply keep going, over the now-dormant site of the No. 4 catapult, flying off and coming around again. But he was no "bolter." He snagged a wire for a clean trap. Time from the last launch to the first landing: 45 seconds.

Air Boss grinned.

Mini Boss grinned.

Hubba, hubba.

It is hard not to love the dance of the carrier deck—the skill, beauty and sheer guts of men launching and landing warplanes on a 1,000-foot slab on the sea.

Seventy-five times on an average day, up to 400 times during crises such as Libya, *America*'s crew members dodge sucking jet intakes and whirring props to hitch aircraft to the catapults and send them flying. That many times, they help them home and snare them and park them. They can launch planes a minute apart. They can launch and land at the same time. They can do it in the dark or in the rain. Their average age is $19\frac{1}{2}$.

Engines whine, then race—and a plane disappears from the deck in 2.5 seconds. Its exhaust heat bathes launch crews. The air reeks of jet fuel. Steam seeps from the catapult track. The next plane is already moving forward to take the "cat stroke," and there's another behind it. Noise overwhelms the deck. All the while, the carrier slices through the blue.

"There's no way to describe it," said an A-7 pilot aboard *America*. "There's no way to see it in a movie. You've got to come out here and smell it and see it. It's too dynamic. The whole thing's like a ballet."

In all, the United States' carriers number 14; no other nation has more than four. They are the largest engines of war; no one else's are half as big. They bear the names of battles won, Coral Sea, Midway and Saratoga; of leaders gone, Eisenhower, Forrestal, Kennedy, Nimitz and Vinson; and of Revolutionary War vessels, Constellation, Enterprise, Independence and Ranger. One evokes the place where man first flew, Kitty Hawk. And one is called *America*.

With their pride of escorts, the 14 carriers and 878 carrier-based fighters and bombers are the most tangible sign of U.S. power that most people around the world ever see. They are the heart of the nation's maritime defense, its glamour boys. They are the costliest items in the military budget, the price of one carrier and its escorts equaling the bill for 250 MX ballistic missiles.

Yet, for all their impressiveness and for all the importance the Pentagon attaches to the vessels, many congressmen and defense analysts argue that the supercarriers' day is history. The critics fear they are now unnecessary, too expensive and, worse, easy marks. Some of the doubters are even Navy men: Stansfield Turner, a retired admiral and the former director of the Central Intelligence Agency; Elmo Zumwalt, the retired Chief of Naval Operations; and Eugene J. Carroll Jr., a retired admiral who once commanded *Nimitz.*

"Like the battleship the carrier replaced, its magnificence cannot nullify basic changes in the nature of war at sea," Sen. Gary Hart, the Colorado Democrat, writes in his new book on U.S. defense, *America Can Win.* "The day of the large aircraft carrier . . . has passed."

Here is a somewhat shorter situation lead from James's "A Gift Abandoned," a four-part *St. Petersburg Times* series about a helpless newborn child stuffed in a cardboard box and left on the ground near a trash bin. Finding a discarded baby had become common in west central Florida in the early 1990s. In the Tampa Bay area alone, six infants had been abandoned by their mothers over the preceding 10-month period. Some, like the infant featured in this 1991 Pulitzer Prize–winning feature series, survived. Others were found dead.

To set the mood, James starts each of the four parts in her series with a descriptive lead. Each segment begins with a different person's point of view, then is developed chronologically from material James gleaned through exhaustive interviews, court files, transcripts and police records. Note that the link to the rest of the story is rather weak. The more satisfying linking paragraph appears rather late—in the middle of the first installment of the series.

TEMPLE TERRACE, Fla.—That day, Ryan Nawrocki was just an ordinary sixth-grader living an ordinary life. He was 11 years old, with blond hair that hung straight and heavy over his forehead. He was a stocky kid, and it was easy to imagine him carrying a baseball mitt or playing video games after dinner.

That day, Thursday, April 27, Ryan strode across the street from his house in Wildwood Acres, a complex of shoe-box-shaped duplexes on streets that curl into other streets lined with more shoe boxes. He headed toward a small courtyard where his 16-year-old sister, Melissa, was doing laundry in a small community building. Walking along a worn foot path, he passed the dumpster and a large oak tree.

He heard something. A kitten?

His eyes followed the sound to a videocassette recorder box lying on the ground beneath the oak tree about 10 feet from the dumpster. The flaps of the box were closed but unsecured. Ryan walked over to the box. He opened the flaps.

It was a painful, jolting sight: a newborn baby marked with dried blood and a cheesy substance, lying on a bloody towel. The baby gnawed on its fist and cried again.

Ryan tore over to the laundry room.

"There's a baby in a box over there!" he told his sister.

"You're lyin'," she replied.

"No, I'm not!"

His sister peered at Ryan, unsure. Then she stopped stuffing clothes into the washer. "If you're lyin', I'm gonna kill you," she announced, walking out the door.

Moments later, she reached the box. *"Oh, my God."*

Melissa rushed across the street to her apartment. Inside, her mother, Lisa Nawrocki, was watching *Night Court* on television. She looked up as her daughter ran in. The girl was almost hysterical. Melissa told her mother what they had found.

Call 911, Lisa Nawrocki said. She told Ryan to bring the box over, but Ryan said, "I can't look at it! I can't look at it!"

His mother walked across the street, brought the box back and laid it on her living room floor. A licensed practical nurse, she checked the baby's vital signs. Melissa was too upset to speak plainly on the phone. Her mother took the receiver.

The baby was a boy, she told the 911 operator. His color was good, and he didn't seem to have any respiratory problems. His mother, whoever she was, must have cut his umbilical cord and tied the end off with blue thread or fishing line.

An ambulance was on the way, and Melissa ran next door to borrow a diaper from their neighbor, who had 1-year-old twins. Lisa carefully wrapped the child in it; the diaper nearly swallowed him, reaching from his kneecaps to his chest. It made him look even more pitiful, Lisa thought, as she picked him up and wrapped him in a plaid blanket.

She rocked and talked softly to the baby. The ambulance arrived within minutes—too soon for Lisa. She felt as if she could have held the baby forever.

The emergency services technicians, a man and a woman, came in. They checked the baby and fired off questions: Who delivered the baby? Did you name him? They seemed a little cold, Lisa thought. She placed the baby on the stretcher. He was sucking his thumb. The technicians put the stretcher into the ambulance and then drove off to Tampa General Hospital.

By then, things were hectic. Police lights flashed outside. Officers came in to interview the Nawrockis. Reporters and television cameras swarmed around with lights, microphones and notebooks. Neighbors streamed in. Everybody was asking questions. The same questions:

Who was the mother? The University of South Florida was nearby; was she a student, afraid to tell her parents, deserted by her boyfriend? How could any mother do such a thing? She oughta be strung up, someone said.

God only knows what was going on in her mind, Lisa Nawrocki thought. I hope she gets help because she needs it. I'm going to wonder about this baby for the rest of my life. I hope whoever adopts him never tells him he was found by a dumpster. That's a heck of a way to start life: Your mother threw you away.

This slightly shorter situation lead, which begins the first part of Banaszynski's sad Pulitzer Prize–winning series about the life and death of a Minnesota farmer and political activist, features multiple images that contrast a healthy man with an AIDS-ravaged man.

The tiny snapshot is fuzzy and stained with ink. Two men in white T-shirts and corduroys stand at the edge of a barnyard, their muscled arms around each other's shoulders, a puzzled bull watching them from a field. The picture is overexposed, but the effect is pleasing, as if that summer day in 1982 was washed with a bit too much sun.

A summer later, the same men—one bearded and one not, one tall and one short—pose on the farmhouse porch in a mock American Gothic. Their pitchforks are mean looking and caked with manure. But their attempted severity fails; dimples betray their humor.

They are pictured together often through the years, draped with ribbons and buttons at political rallies, playing with their golden retriever, Nels, and, most frequently, working in their lavish vegetable garden.

The pictures drop off abruptly after 1985. One of the few shows the taller man, picking petunias from his mother's grave. He is startlingly thin by now; as a friend said, "like Gandhi after a long fast." His sun-bleached hair has turned dark, his bronze skin pallid. His body seems slack, as if it's caving in on itself.

The stark evidence of Dick Hanson's deterioration mars the otherwise rich memories captured in the photo album. But Hanson said only this:

"When you lose your body, you become so much closer to your spirit. It gives you more emphasis of what the spirit is, that we are more important than withering skin and bone."

Hanson sat with his partner, Bert Henningson, in the small room at Minneapolis' Red Door Clinic in April 8, 1986, waiting for the results of Hanson's AIDS screening test.

He wouldn't think about how tired he had been lately. He had spent his life hefting hay bales with ease, but now was having trouble hauling potato sacks at the Glenwood factory where he worked part time. He had lost 10 pounds, had chronic diarrhea and slept all afternoon. The dishes stayed dirty in the sink, the dinner uncooked, until Henningson got home from teaching at the University of Minnesota-Morris.

It must be the stress. His parents had been forced off the farm and now he and his brothers faced foreclosure. Two favorite uncles were ill. He and Henningson were bickering a lot, about the housework and farm chores and Hanson's dark mood.

He had put off having the AIDS test for months, and Henningson hadn't pushed too hard. Neither was eager to know.

Now, as the nurse entered the room with his test results, Hanson convinced himself the news would be good. It had been four years since he had indulged in casual weekend sex at the gay bathhouse in Minneapolis, since he and Henningson committed to each other. Sex outside their relationship had been limited and "safe," with no exchange of semen or blood. He had taken care of himself, eating homegrown food and working outdoors, and his farmer's body always had responded with energy and strength. Until now.

"I put my positive thinking mind on and thought I'd be negative," Hanson said. "Until I saw that red circle."

The reality hit him like a physical punch. As he slumped forward in shock, Henningson—typically pragmatic—asked the nurse to prepare another needle. He, too, must be tested.

Then Henningson gathered Hanson in his arms and said, "I will never leave you, Dick."

Linda Wilson of *The Daily News* in Longview, Washington, also uses a situation lead for her feature sidebar about two of the more than five dozen deaths caused by the 1980 volcanic eruption of Mount St. Helens. Wilson's story was included in a package that won the 1981 Pulitzer Prize for local news reporting. You'll read her entire story in Chapter 7.

Gail Varner stood alone, with his head bowed, and stared at his daughter's closed casket for the last time.

A tall, proud man, he did not cry.

When he finally glanced up, two men in work clothes, which were covered with a fine, grey volcanic ash, were waiting to take the casket to its grave.

Varner turned and walked away.

The men carefully lifted the steel-blue box and rolled it outside into the blowing ash. Each step kicked up a small cloud of dust in Longview Memorial Park, still adorned with Memorial Day flowers.

They lowered the casket into the ground and returned for the second coffin—that of Terry Crall.

What had begun 12 days earlier as a weekend camping trip for Karen Varner, Terry Crall and four friends was finally over.

At 8:32 A.M. Sunday, May 18, Mount St. Helens had ended it for them. The mountain heaved and exploded and killed.

The four friends survived, but Terry and Karen's bodies weren't dug out from under the fallen trees until five days later. Of the 18 identified victims of the mountain, Terry and Karen, both 21, are so far the only ones from Longview. Emmanuel Lutheran Church on the banks of Lake Sacajawea was packed for their joint funeral Wednesday.

And here's an even shorter situation lead by Zucchino of *The Philadelphia Inquirer.* Zucchino's 1989 Pulitzer Prize–winning nine-part series, titled "Being Black in South Africa," describes life for many citizens in the Republic of South Africa as it was in 1988. Examine the four-paragraph descriptive lead, including the fourth-paragraph link to the body of the story. In particular, note how the lean language of the lead sets the tone for this grim little story of an auto worker who lives in Kwanobuhle township.

> UITENHAGE, South Africa—Every morning for nine months, Patrick Stalli was there at the gate. He would walk the four miles from home in the dark and join the thousands of other job-less black men pressing against the fortified gates of the towering Volkswagen plant.
>
> Every day for nine months, he walked back home without a job. One morning, the white foreman said he needed 20 men. Thousands surged for the gate. Stalli pushed and clawed. Somehow his body popped through the tiny opening. He had a job.
>
> "I was so desperate, I would do anything for a job. A little fighting and pushing was nothing to me," Stalli said recently, riding a bus at dawn to his 4.98-rand-an-hour ($2.08) job as a press operator who cuts out upholstery for car seats.
>
> For millions of black Africans, the concerns that eat away at their daily lives have little to do with the struggle for political rights or the faltering, bloody war of black revolution. Protest and confrontation are remote concepts. Life boils down to the basics—a decent house and a job, any job.

Direct Address Lead.   The direct address lead, which usually uses or implies the second person, "you," is designed to involve the reader in the story without introducing the writer. Associated Press special correspondent Jules Loh uses the technique to lead "Success Story of a Born-Again Town."

> EUREKA SPRINGS, Ark. (AP)—Driving here, you're not sure whether you're entering hill-billy heaven or just plain heaven.
>
> But you know you're in the Ozarks.

Obviously, "you" involves the reader more than "I." For example, here's how the lead would read if Loh had used the first person. Notice the change in tone.

> EUREKA SPRINGS, Ark.—Driving here, I'm not sure whether I'm entering hillbilly heaven or just plain heaven.
>
> But I know I'm in the Ozarks.

This second version would be acceptable for some magazines. Most newspaper and magazine editors, however, discourage journalists from writing about their adventures. In fact, many editors would require that a lead such as Loh's be changed to the third person, perhaps something such as this:

> EUREKA SPRINGS, Ark.—Driving here is like entering hillbilly heaven—or perhaps just plain heaven.
>
> Eureka Springs, nestled in the Ozarks . . .

Expression Lead.   An expression lead has many variations. One variation is the adage, a traditional, familiar expression of wisdom such as "Don't count your chickens until they're hatched." Other variations include the maxim (a traditional, practical rule), the motto (a traditional moral code of conduct, such as "In God We Trust"), the epigram (a terse, witty, well-phrased expression often of known authorship, such as Franklin's "A penny saved is a penny earned"), the proverb and the somewhat similar aphorism (which are traditional, well-known illustrations of basic truths). This type of lead incorporates an expression with one or more sentences that agree with or dispute the saying. Here's an example from a story about a coin collector.

> Benjamin Franklin said a penny saved is a penny earned. But for Jim Penney, collector of rare 1 cent pieces, that saved coin may mean thousands of dollars earned.

The expression lead may also mimic words from literature, film, television, theater or even a person in the news in an amusing but critical way. Such imitation is called a parody, travesty, satire or lampoon.

First-Person Lead.   As you've read, the first person is sometimes acceptable to magazine editors and rarely acceptable to newspaper editors. But newspaper editors often relent when the writer experiences something personal and extraordinary—such as recovery from a deadly disease.

First, here's the lead from Robertson's 1983 Pulitzer Prize–winning feature, written after her near-fatal encounter with toxic shock syndrome.

> I went dancing the night before in a black velvet Paris gown, on one of those evenings that was the glamour of New York epitomized. I was blissfully asleep at 3 A.M.
>
> Twenty-four hours later, I lay dying, my fingers and legs darkening with gangrene. I was in shock, had no pulse and my blood pressure was lethally low. The doctors in the Rockford, Ill., emergency room where I had been taken did not know what was wrong with me. They thought at first that I might have consumed some poison that had formed in my food. My sister and brother-in-law, whom I had been visiting, could see them through the open emergency-room door: "They were scurrying around and telephoning, calling for help, because they knew they had something they couldn't handle, that they weren't familiar with," was the instinctive reaction of my brother-in-law, Warren Paetz.

Here's a lead by Tad Bartimus, an Associated Press special correspondent. Her Father's Day story, which was a finalist for the 1991 Pulitzer Prize in feature writing and which won an award for the best AP feature in 1990, uses a long first-person lead.

> March 19, Monday:
>
> My father is dying.
>
> It is my worst childhood dread, the terror in the night come true. I sit by his bed and hold his hand, trying to ward off my fears. I am failing in my duty. I cannot save him.
>
> There is a scene in the film "Terms of Endearment" where the mother stands at the nurses station and screams for another pain shot for her terminally ill daughter. Now I, too, stand at a nurses station and say quietly, politely: "I think it is time for my dad's shot."

They look up at me, these kids, many of them young enough to be my own daughters, and say, "OK, we'll get it in a minute," and then go back to talking about last night's date, a friend's birthday party.

I feel my face contort. I have become Frankenstein. I stand there and fidget, my hands balling into fists, my eyes welling with tears. My eyelids are already so swollen I can hardly bear to touch them. I say again, between clenched teeth: "I'm sorry to trouble you, but it is time NOW for my dad's shot. NOW. NOW. NOW!"

My breath gets shorter. My voice rises to a screech. I turn into a monster in that antiseptic hallway. I hate myself for being this way, but I seem to have no control over my rude behavior. It seems my only way to fight back against a medical system that has my whole family in its strangling grip of tubes, wires, needles, thumping noises, offending smells and cadre of strangers invading at their convenience our tiny cubicle of pain and grief.

Cancer has transformed me, molded me into a 42-year-old daughter whose only aim in life is to help her father die as comfortably, and with as much dignity, as I can provide.

And here's a lead from a feature that accompanied early news reports from Mexico City after several powerful 1985 earthquakes killed more than 7,000 persons. The story is by Associated Press writer Eloy O. Aguilar.

MEXICO CITY (AP)—Minor earthquakes are common in Mexico, and it wasn't surprising to feel the building slowly swaying as I sipped my first cup of coffee Thursday morning. A few seconds and it should stop.

It didn't.

A variation of the first-person lead is the diary lead, which uses first person but in a telegraphic style. An example of Aguilar's lead in diary style might read something like this:

MEXICO CITY—Earthquake today as I drank coffee. Took minute for shaking to stop.

Freak Lead.   Freak leads are relatively rare. Examples include definition, fragment, onomatopoeia, poetry, pun and script leads.

The definition lead often begins with a dictionary-like description, followed by one or more paragraphs bonding the definition to the body of the story.

A fragment, of course, can be a single word. But more often, the fragment lead uses three or four sentence fragments to capture the sight, sound and smell of a person, group, place or event. For example, if you're covering a tornado that destroys a small Illinois town main street and kills eight people, such as Julia Keller did for the *Chicago Tribune* when she won the 2005 feature writing Pulitzer, you might write a lead like this:

December 5, 2004

Ten seconds. Count it: One. Two. Three. Four. Five. Six. Seven. Eight. Nine. Ten. Ten seconds was roughly how long it lasted. Nobody had a stopwatch, nothing can be proven definitively, but that's the consensus. The tornado that swooped through Utica at 6:09 P.M. April 20 took some 10 seconds to do what it did. Ten seconds is barely a flicker. It's a long, deep breath. It's no time at all. It's an eternity.

If the sky could hold a grudge, it would look the way the sky looked over northern Illinois that day. Low, gray clouds stretched to the edges in a thin veneer of menace. Rain came and went, came and went, came and went.

The technical name for what gathered up there was stratiform cloud cover, but Albert Pietrycha had a better way to describe it: "murk." It was a Gothic-sounding word for a Gothic-looking sky. A sky that, in its own oblique way, was sending a message.

Pietrycha is a meteorologist in the Chicago forecast office of the National Weather Service, a tidy, buttoned-down building in Romeoville, about 25 miles southwest of Chicago. It's a setting that seems a bit too ordinary for its role, too bland for the place where the first act of a tragedy already was being recorded. Where the sky's bad intentions were just becoming visible, simmering in the low-slung clouds.

Where a short distance away, disparate elements—air, water and old sandstone blocks—soon would slam into each other like cars in a freeway pileup, ending eight lives and changing other lives forever.

The survivors would henceforth be haunted by the oldest, most vexing question of all: whether there is a destiny that shapes our fates or whether it is simply a matter of chance, of luck, of the way the wind blows.

Here's another one, from the second part of Camp's Pulitzer farm series.

Making hay.

A scorching sun, south wind, the sweet smell of fresh-cut alfalfa mixed with gravel dust thrown up by passing cars and the scent of diesel fuel; down on the farm, south of Worthington, staring dry-mouth and aching through the shimmering heat waves toward the gleaming white grain elevators of the town—the town with its beckoning bar, the cold beers and the air conditioning—that stands a mile farther south on the Iowa line.

Wherever farm people get together, the farm crisis dominates serious talk. But talk is not the real material of the spring and early summer on a farm. Talk may dominate a prairie winter, when the planting loans are in doubt. With the crops in the ground, the spring and summer are for work.

Now read how that lead was written: "Most of it was dictated to a tape recorder in the field," Camp says. "If you run through your senses—ask what does it taste like, smell like, what do you see, what do you hear, what do you feel, is it hot, cold?—you'll come up with great stuff. You almost can't help it."

The onomatopoeia lead utilizes a word that emulates a sound, such as "pop, pop, pop" or "bzzzzt." Franklin used those "words" in "Mrs. Kelly's Monster" to simulate the sound of a heart monitor and an electrical device for sealing brain arteries. While the words weren't part of Franklin's lead, they could have been if they were central to the theme of the feature.

The poetry lead uses verse to tease the reader and, of course, is followed by a tying paragraph.

The pun lead uses wordplay. Here's a pun about food. The lead is from an Associated Press story by Anthony Collings.

BONN (AP)—For Germans trying to lose weight, the wurst is yet to come.

Doctors and health experts plead with them, but Germans find themselves unable to cool their ardor for their favorite food—the sausage.

The script lead simulates dialogue and stage directions from a stage or screen script.

The freak lead category frankly opens the door for whatever works. As writer Jacobi puts it: "Whatever piques the reader is a good lead—as long as it's honest—and whatever doesn't isn't a good lead."

Prediction Lead.   This lead ties a startling forecast to a reputable source. If you're writing a story about the United States' most potentially devastating earthquake zone—the New Madrid Fault, which zigzags across Arkansas, Tennessee, Missouri and Illinois—you might lead with a prediction of what experts say a major quake would do to a city near the epicenter. Here's a long prediction lead:

> The first people to feel the wrath of the giant are driving south from Blytheville, Arkansas, on Interstate 55.
>
> Near the Burdette, Arkansas, interchange, about seven miles south of the city, the highway pavement begins to shake and roll. Drivers, already straining to see in the twilight of an early December afternoon, struggle to keep their cars on the heaving, buckling road.
>
> At Mississippi County Community College, south of Blytheville's main business district, students walking to class lose their balance and fall to the ground while glass shatters around them.
>
> In the Blytheville business district, the shaking lasts for a full two minutes.
>
> When the earth finally stops moving, downtown is burning rubble. The giant has turned multistory buildings into piles of masonry and wood. The giant has also wrenched and partially collapsed single-story buildings. Live wires dance across the torn, buckled pavement of Highway 61 south of downtown.
>
> Throughout the city, fires fed by broken gas mains send flames 40 feet into the air. Water from smashed mains spurts skyward, then cascades down the sides of broken buildings and across the city's cracked streets.
>
> In residential areas, the giant has torn many homes from foundations. Walls are cracked, ceiling fans are pitched to the floor, and bookcases and furniture are overturned.
>
> In some parts of town, structures sink into the now-jellied earth, and the ground, in turn, forces some objects, including septic tanks, to the surface.
>
> The giant, of course, is an earthquake, long awaited and long dreaded by area residents, and long predicted by geologists. The quake is of an intensity geologists would call "moderate," measuring 6.5 on the Richter scale.

Elements of the description lead are obvious here, but the lead is unique because it is fiction based on an accurate description of what might happen—according to experts. The experts would be identified in subsequent paragraphs.

Question Lead.   Imagine you're writing a feature about brain surgery, like Franklin does. Imagine that you've tried several kinds of leads, but are still unsatisfied. Finally, you write a lead that reads:

> How is brain surgery performed?

Your lead is terrible. Why? Because the lead lacks intrigue and prepares the reader at best for a boring, pedagogical essay on cortical surgery. Unfortunately, question leads rarely rise above this level because they are too easy to write. Question leads are the court of last resort, and should be avoided. When they cannot be avoided, skilled feature writers at least ask several intriguing questions one after another—coupled to a transition to the body of the story, which, in turn, will provide answers.

Quotation Lead.   This lead—with direct, indirect or partial quotation—is usually tied to some sort of description of the person speaking or the setting in which the quotation occurs. For example, Al Martinez of *The Los Angeles Times* uses this technique to open a story about the manager of an L.A. outlet for three house demolitionists.

> LOS ANGELES—Gloria the Junkyard Queen is proud of her old toilets. "Why buy a new one?" she demands, walking down a row of 80 used commodes piled four high. "A toilet is a toilet." She raps one with her knuckles. "I'll make you a good deal."

Relationship Lead.   The relationship lead, which has several variations, is perhaps the most common feature opening.

The most familiar relationship lead is one that describes cause and effect, which explains how one event triggers another. Blais's opening in "Zepp's Last Stand" is an example. Zepp is going to Washington because of an event that took place decades earlier.

Tad Bartimus, about whom you've already read, won an award for best Associated Press feature writing in 1988 with a stunning story of the death of three Missouri brothers. Her story, which was a Pulitzer finalist in 1989, uses a relationship lead describing cause and effect.

> BUCKNER, Mo. (AP)—There is so little left.
>
> A red cardboard valentine with torn paper lace, which proclaims, "I love you Mom." A carefully penned Thanksgiving essay in which the writer says he's grateful for his family "to have someone to love me." A child's "Life Story" book with extra pages left blank for future adventures.
>
> Chad Eugene Gragg, 12, Aaron Wayne Gragg, 11, and Stephen Douglas Gragg, 8, died together at dusk on the cold afternoon of Feb. 4.
>
> It was Aaron's 11th birthday. Despite admonishments from a teacher and a chum who rode home with him on the bus, he chose to celebrate it by sliding on the frozen surface of a farmer's pond.
>
> The ice broke. Aaron fell into the frigid water. His big brother Chad, doing what his parents taught him to do, attempted to save him. He, too, fell in. Stevie, strong for his age, also tried to be his brother's keeper. His body plunged through the thin crust.
>
> A horrified neighbor boy ran for help. Frantic firemen pulled the brothers from the pond within 30 minutes. They weren't breathing and had no pulse. Two helicopters and an ambulance rushed them to three separate hospitals.
>
> Thus began the agonizing pilgrimage of Charles and Mary Gragg, two ordinary people who now stagger in the footsteps of Job.

Yet another example of a cause-and-effect lead is the one used by Dave Hogerty for a feature he wrote while a student at the University of Florida. Hogerty's story, "Convenience Is in the Eye of the Beholder," won first place in feature writing in the William

Randolph Hearst Foundation journalism awards program in the 1980s. The story focuses on the recovery of a student wounded in a holdup.

> As the characteristic rattle and squeak of the convenience store door broke the early-morning silence, Dan Eifert looked up from behind the counter to see two men entering the store. Moments later, Eifert would be lying on the floor with blood oozing from a bullet wound in his chest. His nighttime job at the neighborhood Majik Market would be over.

A variation of the relationship lead occurs when people, groups, places, events or concepts—which may or may not be alike—are compared. If two or more essentially unlike things are compared using "like" or "as," you're using a figure of speech called a simile. If you compare unlike things without using "like" or "as," you're using a metaphor.

This lead is from an installment of Rinearson's "Making It Fly" series about the birth of the Boeing 757 jetliner. The story, "Buying a Jetliner—An Act of Faith," explains how aircraft manufacturers court customers. A simile is used in the first paragraph.

> Selling jetliners is a bit like peddling religion. Buying one requires an act of faith.
>
> The salesman demands part of the payment up front, but the airline has to wait—sometimes for years—for the payoff. Meanwhile, there may be doubts: Will the airplane be ready on time? Will it do what the manufacturer says? And will the maker be there, indefinitely, continuing to tend to the buyer's needs?

In "Mrs. Kelly's Monster," Franklin compares the activities of the two principals—Dr. Ducker and Mrs. Kelly—who are separated by geography but not by destiny. Here's the lead:

> In the cold hours of a winter morning, Dr. Thomas Barbee Ducker, University Hospital's senior brain surgeon, rises before dawn. His wife serves him waffles but no coffee. Coffee makes his hands shake.
>
> Downtown, on the 12th floor of the hospital, Edna Kelly's husband tells her goodbye.
>
> For 57 years Mrs. Kelly shared her skull with the monster. No more. Today she is frightened but determined.
>
> It is 6:30 A.M.
>
> "I'm not afraid to die," she says as this day approached. ". . . I wouldn't want to live like this much longer."

Surprise Lead.   The surprise lead, also known as the astonisher, punch or cartridge lead, initially shocks the reader. Only when the reader reaches the transition to the body of the story does the meaning of the lead become clear. For example, Rinearson uses a surprise lead, which also has elements of a summary lead, a prediction lead and a relationship lead, to open his "Making It Fly" series in a segment called "The Big Gamble."

> Boeing loses millions of dollars on every new 757 it sells.
>
> But someday—if fate cooperates, if the wager pays off, if enough of the twin-engined jetliners are sold—the 757 will become hugely profitable. Or at least that's Boeing's hope.

Then there's this surprise lead about a youthful businessman, from Ann Hencken of the Associated Press.

> NEW YORK (AP)—John Scher has been designing women's clothes for more than half his life. He is now 10.

A word of caution is in order here. The surprise lead should not misinform the reader. Like any good lead, it should tease, but also promise and deliver.

Summary Lead.   The summary feature lead is a cousin to the summary news lead. The summary feature lead sums up in a few sentences—or, at most, a few paragraphs—the essence of the feature.

In 2002, Siegel of *The Los Angeles Times* won a feature Pulitzer for a story called "A Father's Pain, a Judge's Duty, and a Justice Beyond Their Reach." Siegel, in his six-paragraph lead, sums up the story of a Utah judge who made an agonizing decision, with deadly consequences.

> SILVER SUMMIT, Utah—He sat in his chambers, unprepared for this. "Just giving you a heads up," his court administrator was saying. "Paul Wayment hasn't reported in yet. They can't find him." Judge Robert Hilder felt uneasy. Wayment was supposed to start his jail sentence this morning.
>
> The 52-year-old judge walked slowly to his Summit County district courtroom. The trial underway passed as a blur. More than once, clerks pulled him off the bench to give him updates on Wayment. Each time, in his chambers, he stared out windows at the jail, hoping to see Paul drive up. At the lunch break, he went into Park City to eat, alone with his thoughts.
>
> He'd sentenced Wayment to jail even though the prosecutor didn't want this distraught father to serve time. Hilder felt he had to. Wayment's negligence caused his young son's death. There must be consequences, the judge ruled.
>
> Now there were—more than he intended.
>
> On his way back from lunch, Hilder punched off the car radio, wanting to avoid the news. As always, his 6-year-old son's drawings and broken Lego toys covered the floor of his Ford Taurus. At the courthouse, he walked down a hallway that took him past the administrator's glass-walled office. She rose and waved him in. Concern, he saw, strained her face. He approached the door, bracing himself.
>
> Had he driven Wayment to suicide? Hilder believed it possible. Just as he believed it possible that he'd caused his own father's suicide, 20 years before.

Wayment was, in fact, dead. At this point, Siegel returns the reader to the events that led to the suicide. Siegel explains how little Gage Wayment wandered off from his father's truck in the Utah mountains, details Hilder's background, and then returns to the search for Gage. After the toddler is found dead, Siegel explains the prosecutor's position, then carries readers through legal maneuvering and to the sentencing decision. Finally, Siegel returns to the moment the judge learns of the suicide.

Two final notes about leads. Most feature writers—such as Carpenter—write the lead before they write the rest of the story. "Once I have that lead, I'm off," Carpenter explains. Other writers, such as Blais of *The Miami Herald,* take an opposite approach. Blais says: "I write the ending first. If you know where the story is going, if you can write the ending, you know where you're going." Camp offers a third perspective: "Sometimes I sit down and write the third paragraph and pretend the lead is there. In the course of writing the rest of the story, the lead appears and then I just go back and put it on top."

The other note is this: For almost all newspaper feature writers, crafting the lead is a challenge. For example, Wilkerson of *The New York Times* had to reconstruct her lead because she was not present to witness the event described by it, despite a month of close observation. Here is the lead, as it was written in "First Born, Fast Grown: The Manful Life of Nicholas, 10," which won the feature Pulitzer in 1994 and which you'll read in its entirety in Chapter 7.

> CHICAGO, April 3—A fourth-grade classroom on a forbidding stretch of the South Side was in the middle of multiplication tables when a voice over the intercom ordered Nicholas Whitiker to the principal's office. Cory and Darnesha and Roy and Delron and the rest of the class fell silent and stared at Nicholas, sitting sober-faced in the back.
>
> "What did I do?" Nicholas thought as he gathered himself to leave.
>
> He raced up the hall and down the steps to find his little sister, Ishtar, stranded in the office, nearly swallowed by her purple coat and hat, and principal's aides wanting to know why no one had picked her up from kindergarten.
>
> It was yet another time that the adult world called on Nicholas, a gentle, brooding 10-year-old, to be a man, to answer for the complicated universe he calls family.

Because Wilkerson did not witness the situation described in the lead, she had to reconstruct the events. Here's how.

> I was not there for the lead. I went every day for a month and I had to break away to begin the writing. Other [reporters] had already submitted their stories. . . . I didn't want to be the one holding up the process. . . . It was on one of those days that I called [the children] to see how they were doing and Nicholas told me, "They called me to the principal's office." I said, "They what?" I go [to school] every day for a month and nothing happens and the first week I'm away they call him to the principal's office. Then I began interviewing him like a detective. What did they do? Why did they do this? When did this happen? What were you all doing at the time? I had to begin this investigation of a moment. It was a single moment and the whole thing may have lasted 10 minutes and I needed to get everything.
>
> At the moment, I realized then that that was the lead. I did not have a lead at that point. My lead at that point was a broad description of him and where he lived. I wasn't pleased with what I had, but I knew that I needed to start somewhere. I had a lot of examples to bolster my case. I had a lot of moments of him doing something, but they were not to me strong enough to grab the reader's attention and say, "This is what this child is forced to do." When I heard it was because his mother's boyfriend had not picked up . . . his sister, and they had called upon him to explain this—pulled him out of school, I mean, he's 9 years old—(I thought) what could he possibly say? What could he do? I knew that that was the lead, but then there was the problem of trying to reconstruct what had happened in order to tell that. I spent days just reconstructing these few moments.

Of course, if Wilkerson had been with Nicholas on the day he was called to the office, she says school officials would have asked *her* for information, and the material for the lead would not have occurred.

WRITING THE BODY OF THE STORY

Once an appropriate story structure is selected and the lead written, writers tackle the body of the story.

As they write, many feature writers try to picture a typical reader. Says Rinearson: "You're writing for the general reader. Sometimes it helps to visualize the reader. Think of a school teacher in the suburbs. A ninth-grade student. Pick a mythical person who doesn't have an inherent knowledge or interest. They never thought they were interested in [what you're writing about]. You think about this person and write for [the] person."

Although journalists differ in their approaches to writing, many feature writers say they try to sit down at a terminal and write one complete draft without stopping to check anything—including sentence sense, paragraph order, transitions or grammar. Then they rewrite the story. On the other hand, some writers create the first draft very carefully, editing as they go along. Then they write additional drafts if necessary. Whatever the approach, the goal is the same: to write as effectively and as quickly as possible.

For example, Camp wrote each seasonal installment of his farm series in less than five hours—and at one sitting. "Mrs. Kelly's Monster" was also written quickly, Franklin notes. "I did a couple of hours' worth of interviews with Mrs. Kelly and Ducker, showed up and watched the surgery, went back to the office and pounded it out. The next day I tinkered with it and turned the story over to the editor," Franklin explains. However, the fast assembly of "Mrs. Kelly's Monster" was preceded by more than a year of experimentation with the problem and resolution story structure, Franklin points out. "In other words, 'Mrs. Kelly' was quick and easy, but it was quick and easy only because of the grueling work I'd put into the four previous experimental stories," he says.

Raines's emotional and personal Pulitzer Prize–winning *New York Times* story of segregation in Alabama took longer to write—about two weeks—partly because he drafted it in pieces and partly because he was working on other projects at the same time. Raines explains:

> The way I worked on it was . . . to get up in the morning and try to write about 500 words and not try to feel like I had to sit down and do it in one big block. I found that [technique] works very well . . . where you're writing out of memory. . . . It kind of gives your subconscious time to recharge over night. . . . I wrote it pretty much straight through. I made a few false starts because I couldn't get the beginning just right. But then it flowed pretty much along the narrative line that you see now.
>
> One of the things that I [learned when] I did a previous piece about white sharecroppers in Alabama who had been visited by James Agee and Walker Evans for Let Us Now Praise Famous Men [was] that in dealing with emotional material, writing very simply works very well for me. It's a little like the old newspaper dictum that the bigger the story, the simpler the lead. You know, "Hell froze over today." So I wrote ["Grady's Gift" with] a very clean timeline and a stripped down style.

Other recent Pulitzer Prize–winning feature stories have required far more time to complete. For example, Banaszynski's three-part AIDS story took about three weeks of writing time spread over more than a month of work time because of other *Pioneer Press* projects. Lardner's *Washington Post* story about the murder of his daughter also took more than a month to write because he was busy with other projects. And James's four-part series about a Florida mother who abandoned her baby required six grueling weeks of writing. Sheeler's gripping *Rocky Mountain News* "Final Salute" story about Marine casualty officers assisting the families of the Iraq war dead also took six weeks to write, but the writing phase was preceded by nine months of heart-breaking reporting.

As you have read, a feature writer looks for ways to improve the story as he or she works toward a final draft. Such improvement is called editing or revising or polishing or, more simply, rewriting. Chapter 9 explains that process in detail, but here's an overview.

The amount of rewriting depends on the quality of the first draft, the dedication and skill of the writer, and the deadline for the story. Accuracy and sentence clarity are the highest priorities in that rewriting process, but "flow" also has a high priority.

Flow is determined by the successful use of transitions. Transitions are used to link the body to the lead and paragraphs to one another. They are like the nails that hold a house together.

There are three common kinds of transitions: words that connect, words that bridge and sentences that bridge.

Common words that connect include: also, and, another, besides, but, consequently, finally, first, for example, for instance, however, in addition, in fact, in other words, later, meanwhile, nevertheless, next, now, of course, on the other hand, still, then and therefore.

Here's how Franklin uses "now" in "Mrs. Kelly's Monster."

> Mrs. Kelly, at the time of her first intracranial bleed, was carrying her second child. Despite the pain, she raised her children and cared for her husband. The malformation continued to grow.
>
> > She began calling it "the monster."
>
> *Now,* at 7:15 A.M. in Operating Room 11, a technician checks the brain surgery microscope and the circulating nurse lays out bandages and instruments. Mrs. Kelly lies still on a stainless steel table.

"Now" obviously takes the reader from a previous time to the present. Without that word, the transition would have been too abrupt.

Bridge words are identical or synonymous words used in proximity to link sentences or paragraphs. Here's an example, also from "Mrs. Kelly's Monster."

> Mrs. Kelly was born with a *tangled knot of abnormal blood vessels* in the back of her brain. The *malformation* began small, but in time the vessels ballooned inside the confines of the skull, crowding the healthy brain tissue.

"Tangled knot of abnormal blood vessels" and "malformation" are synonymous in this case. If the word "it" has been used instead of "malformation," the sentence would have been less clear and less fluid.

Finally, sentence order can provide a transition in that the idea at the end of the sentence links it to the next sentence. Look at this example from the same story.

> Still, he studies them again, eyes focused on the two fragile aneurisms that swell above major arteries. Either may burst on contact.

See what might happen if the order of the first sentence were reversed, such as this:

The two fragile aneurisms that swell above the major arteries are the focus of Dr. Ducker's eyes. Either may burst on contact.

See the difference, the lack of clarity and flow?
As journalists write or rewrite, they're also alert to dozens of other gremlins, such as:

■ *Long paragraphs.* No newspaper feature paragraph should exceed three or four sentences. And paragraph length should be alternated because short paragraphs that follow long ones have additional power.

■ *Weak verbs.* For example, in "Zepp's Last Stand," Blais tells the reader that Zepp's "fingers . . . attacked several documents." "Attacked" is a strong verb; "touched" would be weak.

■ *Telling rather than showing.* Remember Franklin's description of the brain:

The grey convolutions of the brain, wet with secretions, sparkle beneath the powerful operating theater spotlights.

■ *Wordiness.* The rewriting ideally should shorten the story while improving clarity. For example, in 1978 Franklin wrote a series of featurized interpretive articles about brain chemistry. "Mrs. Kelly's Monster" was part of that series. Franklin updated the series in 1985 with "The Mind Fixers." Both series included sections explaining how human activities result from interactions of molecules. Franklin says the 1978 article explaining the same concept required thousands of words, whereas the 1985 version needed fewer words. He explains that the difference was because of his use of the phrase "tinkertoy-like molecules." Here is part of that explanation from the 1985 series:

Molecular psychiatry, like the new genetics, is based on a chemical interpretation of events in and around the living cell. Human perception, feelings and behavior are seen to result from submicroscopic interactions—the complex interplay of tinkertoy-like molecules that make up natural substances resembling heroin, Valium and alcohol.

Franklin notes: "Very much of what a . . . writer does is to come up with concepts like a tinkertoy molecule. That idea probably saved me 15,000 words. With that, I don't have to explain what a molecule is."

Nazario's story of the 17-year-old Honduran seeking his mother in the United States is an example of extraordinarily rigorous editing. The first draft, originally conceived as a seven-part series and later published as a six-part series on six days over two weeks, was nearly 70,000 words or about 160 single-space pages. The 12th and final draft was half that length: 30,000 words in print and 34,000 words on the Web. Even Nazario's footnotes required five drafts, she notes.

■ *Lack of anecdotes.* Anecdotes are examples, stories. Abstract or important statements should be supported by anecdotes using direct, indirect or partial quotations.

- *Jargon.* Recall Rinearson's advice. You're writing for someone who's barely interested in your subject and who doesn't want to learn a new vocabulary to read the article.

- *Clichés.* Words such as "cool as a cucumber" have no place in your work.

WRITING THE END OF THE STORY

Like the lead, the ending needn't be a single paragraph, although it certainly may be.

Some journalists, as you've read, write the end of a feature first. Most don't. However and whenever the ending is written, it's usually one of three types.

The first, and perhaps most popular, finish is the *circle technique* ending. The circle technique, which requires the story to begin and end with approximately the same idea, phrase, question, statement, or description, gives the feature unity. "Mrs. Kelly's Monster" uses a circle technique because the story begins and ends with food, which Franklin points out is a symbol of life. Here are the first and final paragraphs of that story.

First paragraph
In the cold hours of a winter morning, Dr. Thomas Barbee Ducker, University Hospital's senior brain surgeon, rises before dawn. His wife serves him waffles but no coffee. Coffee makes his hands shake.

Last two paragraphs
Dr. Ducker bites, grimly, into the sandwich.
　　The monster won.

Banaszynski, the *St. Paul Pioneer Press* writer who won a Pulitzer for a series about a Minnesota AIDS sufferer, often uses the circle technique ending. Here's how Banaszynski crafts her endings:

If I'm working on anything over 25 to 30 inches, I work real hard to come up with a lead that is six to eight to 10 inches long that will set things up, set a sense of place or a mood or perhaps describe a person, something that will tease at what's coming. Then I tend to write in sections—break things up so they're paced a little bit more easily for the reader. And then I always try to have an ending that brings things full circle. Either I bring it back to the beginning, or I refer to some image that I started with, or I allude to something that will happen in the future. I like my endings to be as strong as my beginnings. I save some of my best quotes for the ending, for the kicker. That's the biggest struggle for me because by the time I get there I'm often pretty tired and it's real hard to hold something together, especially if you're working with a longer piece. My goal is to bring the reader back so that the ending is as satisfying as the beginning was.

The *surprise* ending is the second kind of conclusion. It's used almost inevitably with a chronological story such as "Zepp's Last Stand." Zepp's honorable discharge and subsequent anger is a surprise.

Henderson of *The Wall Street Journal* uses a surprise ending in his 1999 Pulitzer Prize–winning profile of a Detroit druggist, Dennis Grehl, who confronted and killed an armed robber. Henderson draws a portrait first of the pharmacist and then of the robber. Henderson then takes readers to the drugstore on the day of the robbery and killing, which was later ruled justifiable homicide. Henderson ends the feature with an examination of the aftermath of the shooting for both the white druggist and the black armed robber's family. The ending:

> Mr. Grehl tries to be philosophical. "I can't say I'm glad I did it—kill somebody," he says. "But I'm glad it didn't turn out the way it could have."
>
> But will it ever end?
>
> Not long ago, a teenager Mr. Grehl didn't know entered the pharmacy alone. She asked: "Is this the place where the shooting was?"
>
> Mr. Grehl replied: "Yes."
>
> The girl said: "I just wanted to see who killed my baby's daddy."
>
> She was out of the store before her words could sink in.

A postscript: Henderson learned about the woman's visit early in the interviewing. Grehl did not want it used in the story, Henderson says. At the conclusion of the interviewing, Henderson made the request again and Grehl agreed to its use. Interviewing "is negotiation," Henderson notes.

The third approach to concluding a feature is the *summary* ending. Here, the ending is a natural progression of what has gone before. "The Bureaucracy: How Did It Get So Big?" by Pett uses a summary ending.

So does "Death of a Playmate." Carpenter's story, which is structured chronologically after a long lead, concludes with a summary of the reactions of the principals. Here are the final two paragraphs of the story:

> Hype, of course, often passes for prophecy. Whether or not Dorothy Stratten would have fulfilled her extravagant promise can't be known. Her legacy will not be examined critically because it is really of no consequence. In the end Dorothy Stratten was less memorable for herself than for the yearnings she evoked: in Snider a lust for the score; in Hefner a longing for a star; in Bogdanovich a desire for the eternal ingenue. She was a catalyst for a cycle of ambitions which revealed its players less wicked, perhaps, than pathetic.
>
> As for Paul Snider, his body was returned to Vancouver in permanent exile from Hollywood. It was all too big for him. In that Elysium of dreams and deals, he had reached the limits of his class. His sin, his unforgivable sin, was being small-time.

Steinbach's Pulitzer-winning feature, which you are about to read, also uses a summary ending to sum up the essence of the story. Look for it as you read the story.

Needless to say, as with story categories, appeals, structures, and leads, a combination of endings is also possible. The most logical combination is the circle technique and the summary ending.

ANALYZING TWO FEATURE STORIES

Steinbach of the Baltimore *Sun* won the 1985 Pulitzer for feature writing with an "enterprise" (or unassigned) story called "A Boy of Unusual Vision."

Steinbach rarely wrote for her newspaper's magazine, where the article appeared. More typically, she wrote somewhat shorter profiles for the *Sun*'s Sunday "People" section, and even shorter features for the daily paper. The 3,500-word profiles typically required two days for research and perhaps five days for interviewing and writing, she says. "A Boy of Unusual Vision"—at nearly 6,000 words—is both longer and more complicated than a Sunday profile, Steinbach notes. She explains: "From the time I first talked to the family about the possibility of doing this until I turned my story in to the editor, maybe somewhere between six and eight weeks" passed. "A month is average" for a magazine article, she says.

"A Boy of Unusual Vision" is a profile story. The article is Pulitzer quality because of Steinbach's reporting—her research, interviewing and observational skills—and her fine writing.

PULITZER PRIZE WINNER

ALICE STEINBACH

A BOY OF UNUSUAL VISION

First, the eyes: They are large and blue, a light, opaque blue, the color of a robin's egg. And if, on a sunny spring day, you look straight into these eyes—eyes that cannot look back at you—the sharp, April light turns them pale, like the thin blue of a high, cloudless sky.

Ten-year-old Calvin Stanley, the owner of these eyes and a boy who has been blind since birth, likes this description and asks to hear it twice. He listens as only he can listen, then: "Orange used to be my favorite color but now it's blue," he announces. Pause. The eyes flutter between the short, thick lashes. "I know there's light blue and there's dark blue, but what does sky-blue look like?" he wants to know. And if you watch his face as he listens to your description, you get a sense of a picture being clicked firmly into place behind the pale eyes.

He is a boy who has a lot of pictures stored in his head, retrievable images which have been fashioned for him by the people who love him—by family and friends and teachers who have painstakingly and patiently gone about creating a special world for Calvin's inner eye to inhabit.

Picture of a rainbow: "It's a lot of beautiful colors, one next to the other. Shaped like a bow. In the sky. Right across."

Picture of lightning, which frightens Calvin: "My mother says lightning looks like a Christmas tree—the way it blinks on and off across the sky," he says, offering a comforting description that would make a poet proud.

"Child," his mother once told him, "one day I won't be here and I won't be around to pick you up when you fall—nobody will be around all the time to pick you up—so you have to try to do something on your own. You have to learn how to deal with this. And to do that, you have to learn how to think."

There was never a moment when Ethel Stanley said to herself, "My son is blind and this is how I'm going to handle it."

Calvin's mother:

"When Calvin was little, he was so inquisitive. He wanted to see everything, he wanted to touch everything. I had to show him every little thing there is. A spoon, a fork. I let him play with them. The pots, the pans. *Everything.* I showed him the sharp edges of the table. 'You cannot touch this; it will hurt you.' And I showed him what would hurt. He still bumped into it anyway, but he knew what he wasn't supposed to do and what he could do. And he knew that nothing in his room—*nothing*—could hurt him.

"And when he started walking and we went out together—I guess he was about 2—I never said anything to him about what to do. When we got to the curbs, Calvin knew that when I stopped, he should step down and when I stopped again, he should step up. I never said anything, that's just the way we did it. And it became a pattern."

(continued)

PULITZER PRIZE WINNER   CONTINUED

Calvin remembers when he began to realize that something about him was "different": "I just figured it out myself. I think I was about 4. I would pick things up and I couldn't see them. Other people would say they could see things and I couldn't."

And his mother remembers the day her son asked her why he was blind and other people weren't.

"He must have been about 4 or 5. I explained to him what happened, that he was born that way and that it was nobody's fault and he didn't have to blame himself. He asked, 'Why me?' And I said, 'I don't know why, Calvin. Maybe there's a special plan for you in your life and there's a reason for this. But this is the way you're going to be and you can deal with it.' "

Then she sat her son down and told him this: "You're *seeing,* Calvin. You're just using your hands instead of your eyes. But you're seeing. And, remember, there is *nothing* you can't do."

It's spring vacation and Calvin is out in the alley behind his house riding his bike, a serious looking, black and silver two-wheeler. "Stay behind me," he shouts to his friend Kellie Bass, who's furiously pedaling her bike down the one-block stretch of alley where Calvin is allowed to bicycle.

Now: Try to imagine riding a bike without being able to see where you're going. Without even knowing what an "alley" looks like. Try to imagine how you navigate a space that has no visual boundaries, that exists only in your head. And then try to imagine what Calvin is feeling as he pedals his bike in that space, whooping for joy as the air rushes past him on either side.

And although Calvin can't see the signs of spring sprouting all around him in the neighboring backyards—the porch furniture and barbecue equipment being brought out of storage, the grass growing emerald green from the April rain, the forsythia exploding yellow over the fences—still, there are signs of another sort which guide him along his route:

Past the German shepherd who always barks at him, telling Calvin that he's three houses away from his home; then past the purple hyacinths, five gardens away, throwing out their fragrance (later it will be the scent of the lilacs which guide him); past the large diagonal crack which lifts the front wheel of his bike up and then down, telling him he's reached his boundary and should turn back—past all these familiar signs Calvin rides his bike on a warm spring day.

Ethel Stanley: "At 6, one of his cousins got a new bike and Calvin said 'I want to learn how to ride a two-wheeler bike.' So we got him one. His father let him help put it together. You know, whatever Calvin gets he's going to go all over it with those hands and he knows every part of that bike and what it's called. He learned to ride it the first day, but I couldn't watch. His father stayed outside with him."

Calvin: "I just got mad. I got tired of riding a little bike. At first I used to zig-zag, go all over. My cousin would hold on to the bike and then let me go. I fell a lot in the beginning. But a lot of people fall when they first start."

There's a baseball game about to start in Calvin's backyard and Mrs. Stanley is pitching to her son. Nine-year-old Kellie, on first base, has taken off her fake fur coat so she can get a little more steam into her game and the other team member, Monet Clark, 6, is catching. It is also Monet's job to alert Calvin, who's at bat, when to swing. "Hit it, Calvin," she yells. "Swing!"

He does and the sound of the ball making solid contact with the bat sends Calvin running off to first base, his hands groping in front of his body. His mother walks over to stand next to him at first base and unconsciously her hands go to his head, stroking his hair in a soft, protective movement.

"Remember," the mother had said to her son six years earlier, "there's *nothing* you can't do."

Calvin's father, 37-year-old Calvin Stanley, Jr., a Baltimore city policeman, has taught his son how to ride a bike and how to shift gears in the family's Volkswagen and how to put toys together. They go to the movies together and they tell each other they're handsome.

The father: "You know, there's nothing much I've missed with him. Because he does everything. Except see. He goes swimming out in the pool in the backyard. Some of the other kids are afraid of the water but he jumps right in, puts his head under. If it were me I wouldn't be as brave as he is. I probably wouldn't go anywhere. If it were me I'd probably stay in this house most of the time. But he's always ready to go, always on the telephone, ready to do something.

"But he gets sad, too: You can just look at him sometimes and tell he's real sad."

The son: "You know what makes me sad? 'Charlotte's Web.' It's my favorite story. I listen to the record at night. I like Charlotte, the spider. The way she talks. And, you know, she really loved Wilbur, the pig. He was her best friend." Calvin's voice is full of warmth and wonder as he talks about E. B. White's tale of the spider who befriended a pig and later sacrificed herself for him.

"It's a story about friendship. It's telling us how good friends are supposed to be. Like Charlotte and Wilbur," he says, turning away from you suddenly to wipe his eyes. "And when Charlotte dies, it makes me real sad. I always feel like I've lost a friend. That's why I try not to listen to that part. I just move the needle forward."

Something else makes Calvin sad: "I'd like to see what my mother looks like," he says, looking up quickly and swallowing hard. "What does she look like? People tell me she's pretty."

The mother: "One day Calvin wanted me to tell him how I looked. He was about 6. They were doing something in school for Mother's Day and the kids were drawing pictures of their mothers. He wanted to know what I looked like and that upset me because I didn't know how to tell him. I thought, 'How am I going to explain this to him so he will really know what I look like?' So I tried to explain to him about facial features, noses and I just used touch. I took his hand and I tried to explain about skin, let him touch his, and then mine.

"And I think that was the moment when Calvin really *knew* he was blind, because he said, 'I won't ever be able to see your face . . . or Daddy's face,'" she says softly, covering her eyes with her hands, but not in time to stop the tears. "That's the only time I've ever let it bother me that much."

But Mrs. Stanley knew what to tell her only child: "I said, 'Calvin, you can *see* my face. You can see it with your hand and by listening to my voice and you can tell more about me that way than somebody who can use his eyes.'"

Provident Hospital, November 15, 1973: That's where Calvin Stanley III was born, and his father remembers it this way: "I saw him in the hospital before my wife did, and I knew immediately that something was wrong with his eyes. But I didn't know what."

The mother remembers it this way: "When I woke up after the caesarian, I had a temperature and couldn't see Calvin except through the window of the nursery. The next day a doctor came around to see me and said that he had cataracts and asked me if I had a pediatrician. From what I knew, cataracts could be removed so I thought, 'Well, he'll be fine.' I wasn't too worried. Then when his pediatrician came and examined him he told me he thought it was congenital glaucoma."

Only once did Mrs. Stanley give in to despair. "When they knew for certain it was glaucoma and told me that the cure rate was very poor because they so seldom have infants born with glaucoma, I felt awful. I blamed myself. I knew I must have done something wrong when I was pregnant. Then I blamed my husband," she says, looking up from her hands which are folded in her lap, "but I never told him that." Pause. "And he probably blamed me."

(continued)

PULITZER PRIZE WINNER   CONTINUED

No, says her husband. "I never really blamed her. I blamed myself. I felt it was payback. That if you do something wrong to somebody else in some way you get paid back for it. I figured maybe I did something wrong, but I couldn't figure out what I did that was that bad and why Calvin had to pay for it."

Mrs. Stanley remembers that the doctors explained to them that the glaucoma was not because of anything either of them had done before or during the pregnancy and "that 'congenital' simply means 'at birth.' "

They took Calvin to a New York surgeon who specialized in congenital glaucoma. There were seven operations and the doctors held out some hope for some vision, but by age 3 there was no improvement and the Stanleys were told that everything that could be done for Calvin had been done.

"You know, in the back of my mind, I think I always knew he would never see," Mrs. Stanley says, "and that I had to reach out to him in different ways. The toys I bought him were always toys that made a noise, had sound, something that Calvin could enjoy. But it didn't dawn on me until after he was in school that I had been doing that—buying him toys that would stimulate him."

Thirty-three year old Ethel Stanley, a handsome, strong-looking woman with a radiant smile, is the oldest of seven children and grew up looking after her younger brothers and sisters while her mother worked. "She was a wonderful mother," Mrs. Stanley recalls. "Yes, she had to work, but when she was there, she was with you every minute and those minutes were worth a whole day. She always had time to listen to you."

Somewhere—perhaps from her own childhood experiences—Mrs. Stanley, who has not worked since Calvin was born, acquired the ability to nurture and teach and poured her mothering love into Calvin. And it shows. He moves in the sighted world with trust and faith and the unshakable confidence of a child whose mother has always been there for him. "If you don't understand something, ask," she tells Calvin again and again, in her open, forthright way. "Just ask."

When it was time to explain to Calvin the sexual differences between boys and girls, this is what Mrs. Stanley said: "When he was about 7 I told him that when you're conceived you have both sexes. It's not decided right away whether you're going to be a boy or a girl. And he couldn't believe it. He said, 'Golly, suppose somebody gets stuck?' I thought, 'Please, just let me get this out of the way first.' "

"And I tried to explain to him what a woman's sexual organs look like. I tried to trace it on the table with his fingers. I said, well you know what yours look like, don't you? And I told him what they're called, the medical names. 'Don't use names if you don't know what they mean. Ask. Ask.' "

"When he was little he wanted to be Stevie Wonder," says Calvin's father, laughing. "He started playing the piano and he got pretty good at it. Now he wants to be a computer programmer and design programs for the blind."

Calvin's neatly ordered bedroom is outfitted with all the comforts you would find in the room of many 10-year-old, middle-class boys: a television set (black and white, he tells you), an Atari game with a box of cartridges (his favorite is "Phoenix"), a braille Monopoly set, records, tapes and programmed talking robots. "I watch wrestling on TV every Saturday," he says. "I wrestle with my friends. It's fun."

He moves around his room confidently and easily. "I know this house like a book." Still, some things are hard for him to remember since, in his case, much of what he remembers has to be imagined visually first. Like the size and color of his room. "I think it's kind of big," he says of the small room. "And it's green," he says of the deep rose-colored walls.

And while Calvin doesn't need to turn the light on his room he does like to have some kind of sound going constantly. *Loud* sound.

"It's 3 o'clock," he says, as the theme music from a TV show blares out into his room.

"Turn that TV down," says his mother, evenly. "You're not *deaf,* you know."

From the beginning, Ethel and Calvin Stanley were determined their blind son would go to public school. "We were living in Baltimore county when it was time for Calvin to start school and they told me I would have to pay a tuition for him to go to public school, and that really upset me," Mrs. Stanley says. "I had words with some of the big honchos out there. I knew they had programs in schools for children with vision problems and I thought public education should be free.

"We decided we would move to Baltimore city if we had to, and I got hold of a woman in the mayor's office. And that woman was the one who opened all the doors for us. She was getting ready to retire but she said she wasn't going to retire until she got this straight for Calvin. I don't know how she did it. But she did."

Now in the fourth grade, Calvin has been attending the Cross Country Elementary School since kindergarten. He is one of six blind students in Baltimore city who are fully main-streamed which, in this context, means they attend public school with sighted students in a regular classroom. Four of these students are at Cross Country Elementary School. If Calvin stays in public school through the 12th grade, he will be the first blind student to be completely educated within the regular public school system.

Two P.M., Vivian Jackson's class, Room 207.

What Calvin can't see: He can't see the small, pretty girl sitting opposite him, the one who is wearing little rows of red, yellow and blue barrettes shaped like airplanes in her braided hair. He can't see the line of small, green plants growing in yellow pots all along the sunny windowsill. And he can't see Mrs. Jackson in her rose-pink suit and pink enameled earrings shaped like little swans.

("Were they really shaped like little swans?" he will ask later.)

But Calvin can feel the warm spring breeze—invisible to *everyone's* eyes, not just his—blowing in through the window and he can hear the tapping of a young oak tree's branches against the window. He can hear Mrs. Jackson's pleasant, musical voice and, later, if you ask him what she looks like, he will say, "She's nice."

But best of all, Calvin can read and spell and do fractions and follow the classroom work in his specially prepared braille books. He is smart and he can do everything the rest of his class can do. Except see.

"What's the next word, Calvin?" Mrs. Jackson asks.

"Eleven," he says, reading from his braille textbook.

"Now tell us how to spell it—without looking back at the book!" she says quickly, causing Calvin's fingers to fly away from the forbidden word.

"E-l-e-v-e-n," he spells out easily.

It all seems so simple, the ease with which Calvin follows along, the manner in which his blindness has been accommodated. But it's deceptively simple. The amount of work that has gone into getting Calvin to this point—the number of teachers, vision specialists and mobility instructors, and the array of special equipment is staggering.

Patience and empathy from his teachers have played a large role, too.

For instance, there's Dorothy Lloyd, the specialist who is teaching Calvin the slow and very difficult method of using an Optacon, a device which allows a blind person to read a printed page by touch by converting printed letters into a tactile representation.

(continued)

PULITZER PRIZE WINNER   CONTINUED

And there's Charleye Dyer, who's teaching Calvin things like "mobility" and "independent travel skills," which includes such tasks as using a cane and getting on and off buses. Of course, what Miss Dyer is really teaching Calvin is freedom; the ability to move about independently and without fear in the larger world.

There's also Lois Sivits who, among other things, teaches Calvin braille and is his favorite teacher. And, to add to a list which is endless, there's the music teacher who comes in 30 minutes early each Tuesday to give him a piano lesson, and his homeroom teacher, Mrs. Jackson, who is as finely tuned to Calvin's cues as a player in a musical duet would be to her partner.

An important part of Calvin's school experience has been his contact with sighted children.

"When he first started school," his mother recalls, "some of the kids would tease him about his eyes. 'Oh, they're so big and you can't see.' But I just told him, 'Not any time in your life will everybody around you like you—whether you can see or not. They're just children and they don't know they're being cruel. And I'm sure it's not the last time someone will be cruel to you. But it's all up to you because you have to go to school and you'll have to deal with it.' "

Calvin's teachers say he's well liked, and watching him on the playground and in class you get the impression that the only thing that singles him out from the other kids is that someone in his class is always there to take his hand if he needs help.

"I'd say he's really well accepted," says his mobility teacher, Miss Dyer, "and that he's got a couple of very special friends."

Eight-year-old Brian Butler is one of these special friends. "My *best* friend," says Calvin proudly, introducing you to a studious-looking boy whose eyes are alert and serious behind his glasses. The two boys are not in the same class, but they ride home together on the bus every day.

Here's Brian explaining why he likes Calvin so much: "He's funny and he makes me laugh. And I like him because he always makes me feel better when I don't feel good." And, he says, his friendship with Calvin is no different from any other good friendship. Except for one thing: "If Calvin's going to bump into a wall or something, I tell him, 'Look out,' " says Brian, sounding as though it were the most natural thing in the world to do when walking with a friend.

"Charlotte would have done it for Wilbur," is the way Calvin sizes up Brian's help, evoking once more that story about "how friendship ought to be."

A certain moment:

Calvin is working one-on-one with Lois Sivits, a teacher who is responsible for the braille skills which the four blind children at Cross Country must have in order to do all the work necessary in their regular classes. He is very relaxed with Miss Sivits, who is gentle, patient, smart and, like Calvin, blind. Unlike Calvin, she was not able to go to public school but was sent away at age 6, after many operations on her eyes, to a residential school—the Western Pennsylvania School for the Blind.

And although it was 48 years ago that Lois Sivits was sent away from her family to attend the school for the blind, she remembers—as though it were 48 minutes ago—how that blind 6-year-old girl felt about the experience: "Oh, I was so *very* homesick. I had a very hard time being separated from my family. It took me three years before I began getting used to it. But I knew I had to stay there. I would have given anything to be able to stay at home and go to a public school like Calvin," says the small, kind-looking woman with very still hands.

Now, the moment: Calvin is standing in front of the window, the light pouring in from behind him. He is listening to a talking clock which tells him, "It's 11:52 A.M." Miss Sivits stands about 3 feet away from him, also in front of the window holding a huge braille dictionary in her hands, fingers flying across the page as she silently reads from it. And for a few moments, there they are as if frozen in a tableau, the two of them standing in darkness against the light, each lost for a moment in a private world that is composed only of sound and touch.

There was another moment, years ago, when Calvin's mother and father knew that the operation had not helped, that their son was probably never going to see. "Well," said the father, trying to comfort the mother, "we'll do what we have to do and Calvin will be fine."
He is. And so are they.

Source: © 1984. The Baltimore *Sun*. Reprinted by permission.

First things first. What do you think the story is about?
Steinbach offers her view:

To some extent, what a reader gets out of a story is what the story is about. But, if you're asking me what I think the story is about, I can only say that the more I wrote this story and the more I read it I realized that in some ways it's more a story about Calvin's mother. It's about his father, too, about his teacher, about the school, about him, but I felt that this story was written because of Ethel Stanley. If it had not been for her, there would be no story.

To me, it is a story not about a blind boy, not about "mainstreaming" [blind children into regular classes], not about how you can help a kid overcome difficulties. It's a story that's much more universal than that; it's a story about the endurance that can be built into a person who has a really loving mother, or a figure in their life who will be there for them. It's really about the nature of the child/mother bond and how it can overcome anything. This story is about what a loving, mothering relationship can do, what it can overcome.

Steinbach's 78-paragraph story, which uses a repetitive structure, is divided into four parts. The first part—comprising the first six paragraphs—asks the question, "Who is Calvin?" Physical description and quotations partially answer the question and tease readers into continuing to follow the story.

The story's second part tells readers why Calvin Stanley is being singled out for coverage. Paragraphs 7 to 31 show that Calvin is exceptional because, as Ethel Stanley says, "there is nothing" he can't do. Through Steinbach, readers see Calvin riding a bike, playing baseball, swimming, learning.

The third part of the story—paragraphs 32 to 38—explains in a flashback why Calvin is blind and that he will remain sightless.

The last part of the article deals poignantly with the central issue of Calvin's story—that, with the help of his family, Calvin "will be fine," as the next-to-last paragraph notes.

This complex structure is not a haphazard afterthought. "I work very hard on the lead and I work very hard on figuring out the structure," Steinbach explains. "The structure is the hardest part for me. The writing is the easiest part. Once you've got the [structure], you sort of apply the various layers until you've got a finished product.

"I wanted to get people immediately emotionally connected to this boy and his family and to get them into his life and the fact of blindness. Then I realized that once they have become connected, we had to say, 'Why this boy? There are lots of blind boys.' So we then need to see this boy riding his bike and doing things that are very unusual. [Then] people will want to know why he is blind, and how long, and could [doctors] have done anything about it. You want to get all of these things out of the way, but I didn't want to go into that until I got the reader sufficiently interested in the boy, in his family, in what they had accomplished. The reader needed to understand why the story is being told and then get the facts."

Let's look at Steinbach's story in more detail. As you've probably noted, the story's lead also is part one. In these six paragraphs, Steinbach intrigues the reader, sets the tone for the story and then ties the lead—with paragraph six—to the body of the article.

The ending, about 70 paragraphs later, is a summary of what has gone before and, as *Miami Herald* writer Blais says, sums up the writer's feeling about the people in the story.

Between the lead and the ending, Steinbach effectively uses many weapons in the feature writer's arsenal, including

- anecdotes

  The mother: "One day Calvin wanted me to tell him how I looked. He was about 6. They were doing something in school for Mother's Day and the kids were drawing pictures of their mothers. He wanted to know what I looked like and that upset me because I didn't know how to tell him. I thought, 'How am I going to explain this to him so he will really know what I look like?' So I tried to explain to him about facial features, noses and I just used touch. I took his hand and I tried to explain about skin, let him touch his, and then mine.

  "And I think that was the moment when Calvin really *knew* he was blind, because he said, 'I won't ever be able to see your face . . . or Daddy's face,' " she says softly, covering her eyes with her hands, but not in time to stop the tears. "That's the only time I've ever let it bother me that much."

  But Mrs. Stanley knew what to tell her only child: "I said, 'Calvin, you *can* see my face. You can see it with your hand and by listening to my voice and you can tell more about me that way than somebody who can use his eyes.' "

- repetition for effect

  Then she sat her son down and told him this: "You're *seeing,* Calvin. You're just using your hands instead of your eyes. But you're seeing. And, remember, there is nothing you can't do."

  "Remember," the mother had said to her son six years earlier, "there's *nothing* you can't do."

- humor

  "Turn that TV down," says his mother, evenly. "You're not *deaf,* you know."

- and strong direct, partial and indirect quotations throughout.

In addition, Steinbach has imbued the story with an overall gentleness. For example, read paragraph 45 again:

> He moves around his room confidently and easily. "I know this house like a book." Still, some things are hard for him to remember since, in his case, much of what he remembers has to be imagined visually first. Like the size and color of his room. "I think it's kind of big," he says of the small room. "And it's green," he says of the deep rose-colored walls.

Notice how the tone of this paragraph would have change to a mocking one if the third sentence were removed:

> He moves around his room confidently and easily. "I know this house like a book." Like the size and color of his room. "I think it's kind of big," he says of the small room. "And it's green," he says of the deep rose-colored walls.

The third sentence is important because it explains why Calvin doesn't know what his room looks like and, more important, that he has much to learn about his world.

You've probably also noticed that Steinbach's punctuation is unusual. On occasion, scenes are set with a sentence fragment, followed by a colon. The story's first paragraph is an example.

> First, the eyes: They are large and blue, a light, opaque blue, the color of a robin's egg. And if, on a sunny spring day, you look straight into these eyes—eyes that cannot look back at you— the sharp, April light turns them pale, like the thin blue of a high, cloudless sky.

More frequently, Steinbach introduces a source, then uses a colon to separate the source's quotation, such as in this example.

> Calvin: "I just got mad. I got tired of riding a little bike. At first I used to zig-zag, go all over. My cousin would hold on to the bike and then let me go. I fell a lot in the beginning. But a lot of people fall when they first start."

Steinbach explains that she uses colons to pace the story. "That's the way I write. To me, there's a rhythm to everything. And I can hear it. And I will work and work on it until I get that rhythm. It has nothing to do with rules. It has to do with the way I feel. [It's] . . . a musical kind of thing. I'm trying to slow the reader down, speed him up, stop him in his tracks."

Certainly writing is important, but without a good idea supported by first-rate reporting—research, interviewing and observation—Steinbach's story would not have acquired national recognition.

A less talented feature writer might have been content to interview the Stanleys superficially and then write the story. Steinbach, on the other hand, researched the issues raised in the story, interviewed and re-interviewed the participants and participated in various aspects of Calvin's life. When Calvin rode his bike, Steinbach was there, reporting. And when Calvin batted a ball, played in his room and went to school, Steinbach was there also, reporting.

Only when a feature writer blends all of these elements—a strong idea, thorough research and interviewing, keen observation and fine writing within a useful structure—do you have a story such as "A Boy of Unusual Vision."

Now let's compare "A Boy of Unusual Vision" with a profile from a 1996 Pulitzer Prize–winning story by Rick Bragg called "All She Has, $150,000, Is Going to a University." Steinbach's story about Calvin Stanley appeared in the pages of the Baltimore *Sun*'s expansive magazine, while Bragg's story of Oseola McCarty was published on the front page of *The New York Times*. As a consequence, Steinbach's timeless story was expected to be, and is, rich and delicious in structure and language, whereas Bragg's very timely piece was expected to be, and is, by necessity, simpler in structure and more economical in language.

Bragg was a veteran journalist when he joined the *Times* in 1994. By 1995 Bragg was based in Atlanta, writing both news and feature stories about the South. His five Pulitzer Prize–winning feature stories, unlike Steinbach's long article, were reported and written quickly—typically in one or two days. The McCarty story, in fact, was written on the day the interview took place. Bragg explains how the McCarty story came about:

> The story was out there, and the local paper had done it and had done a good job on it. The one question that hadn't come out of any of the stories was exactly who this woman was. And why it wouldn't bother her to turn loose of $150,000, which is something that would bother a lot of people. They kind of glossed over the fact that the reason she did this was because she knew she was going to die soon. Not next week or next month or next year, but she knew—in her late eighties—that her time was coming to an end. Which made it even more poignant. All I wanted to do instead of *telling* people why she was different was to *show* them why she was different.

Bragg located McCarty and made arrangements to fly from Georgia to Mississippi to interview her.

> I didn't even know where to begin. But I figured that the smart thing to do would be to call the university and ask them what the drill was. I'd love to say that I hunted her down walking down the street, but the fact is that I knew that any time that you do anything that has to do with the university or any other kind of school, there's a bureaucracy involved in it. The bureaucracy in this case at Southern Mississippi was a friendly one. They were proud of what she had done and they were proud of her. And there wasn't any posturing. They were just really touched, I think. Everybody there was really touched by what had happened.

Examine the four-paragraph descriptive lead in the following story, including the linking or why-am-I-reading-this? or "nut" fourth paragraph. In particular, note how the lead sets the tone for this poignant story of an unlikely elderly Mississippi philanthropist. Also look for the overall problem and solution structure and the summary ending.

PULITZER PRIZE WINNER

RICK BRAGG

ALL SHE HAS, $150,000, IS GOING TO A UNIVERSITY

HATTIESBURG, Miss., Aug. 10—Oseola McCarty spent a lifetime making other people look nice. Day after day, for most of her 87 years, she took in bundles of dirty clothes and made them clean and neat for parties she never attended, weddings to which she was never invited, graduations she never saw.

She had quit school in the sixth grade to go to work, never married, never had children and never learned to drive because there was never any place in particular she wanted to go. All she ever had was the work, which she saw as a blessing. Too many other black people in rural Mississippi did not have even that.

She spent almost nothing, living in her old family home, cutting the toes out of shoes if they did not fit right and binding her ragged Bible with Scotch tape to keep Corinthians from falling out. Over the decades, her pay—mostly dollar bills and change—grew to more than $150,000.

"More than I could ever use," Miss McCarty said the other day without a trace of self-pity. So she is giving her money away, to finance scholarships for black students at the University of Southern Mississippi here in her hometown, where tuition is $2,400 a year.

"I wanted to share my wealth with the children," said Miss McCarty, whose only real regret is that she never went back to school. "I never minded work, but I was always so busy, busy. Maybe I can make it so the children don't have to work like I did."

People in Hattiesburg call her donation the Gift. She made it, in part, in anticipation of her death.

As she sat in her warm, dark living room, she talked of that death matter-of-factly, the same way she talked about the possibility of an afternoon thundershower. To her, the Gift was a preparation, like closing the bedroom windows to keep the rain from blowing in on the bedspread.

"I know it won't be too many years before I pass on," she said, "and I just figured the money would do them a lot more good than it would me."

Her donation has piqued interest around the nation. In a few short days, Oseola McCarty, the washerwoman, has risen from obscurity to a notice she does not understand. She sits in her little frame house, just blocks from the university, and patiently greets the reporters, business leaders and others who line up outside her door.

"I live where I want to live, and I live the way I want to live," she said. "I couldn't drive a car if I had one. I'm too old to go to college. So I planned to do this. I planned it myself."

It has been only three decades since the university integrated. "My race used to not get to go to that college," she said. "But now they can."

When asked why she had picked this university instead of a predominantly black institution, she said, "Because it's here; it's close."

(continued)

PULITZER PRIZE WINNER   CONTINUED

While Miss McCarty does not want a building named for her or a statue in her honor, she would like one thing in return: to attend the graduation of a student who made it through college because of her gift. "I'd like to see it," she said.

Business leaders in Hattiesburg, 110 miles northeast of New Orleans, plan to match her $150,000, said Bill Pace, the executive director of the University of Southern Mississippi Foundation, which administers donations to the school.

"I've been in the business 24 years now, in private fund raising," Mr. Pace said. "And this is the first time I've experienced anything like this from an individual who simply was not affluent, did not have the resources and yet gave substantially. In fact, she gave almost everything she has.

"No one approached her from the university; she approached us. She's seen the poverty, the young people who have struggled, who need an education. She is the most unselfish individual I have ever met."

Although some details are still being worked out, the $300,000—Miss McCarty's money and the matching sum—will finance scholarships into the indefinite future. The only stipulation is that the beneficiaries be black and live in southern Mississippi.

The college has already awarded a $1,000 scholarship in Miss McCarty's name to an 18-year-old honors student from Hattiesburg, Stephanie Bullock.

Miss Bullock's grandmother, Ledrester Hayes, sat in Miss McCarty's tiny living room the other day and thanked her. Later, when Miss McCarty left the room, Mrs. Hayes shook her head in wonder.

"I thought she would be some little old rich lady with a fine car and a fine house and clothes," she said. "I was a seamstress myself, worked two jobs. I know what it's like to work like she did, and she gave it away."

The Oseola McCarty Scholarship Fund bears the name of a woman who bought her first air-conditioner just three years ago and even now turns it on only when company comes. Miss McCarty also does not mind that her tiny black-and-white television set gets only one channel, because she never watches anyway. She complains that her electricity bill is too high and says she never subscribed to a newspaper because it cost too much.

The pace of Miss McCarty's walks about the neighborhood is slowed now, and she misses more Sundays than she would like at Friendship Baptist Church. Arthritis has left her hands stiff and numb. For the first time in almost 80 years, her independence is threatened.

"Since I was a child, I've been working," washing the clothes of doctors, lawyers, teachers, police officers, she said. "But I can't do it no more. I can't work like I used to."

She is 5 feet tall and would weigh 100 pounds with rocks in her pockets. Her voice is so soft that it disappears in the squeak of the screen door and the hum of the air-conditioner.

She comes from a wide place in the road called Shubuta, Miss., a farming town outside Meridian, not far from the Alabama line. She quit school, she said, when the grandmother who reared her became ill and needed care.

"I would have gone back," she said, "but the people in my class had done gone on, and I was too big. I wanted to be with my class."

So she worked, and almost every dollar went into the bank. In time, all her immediate family died. "And I didn't have nobody," she said. "But I stayed busy."

She took a short vacation once, as a young woman, to Niagara Falls. The roar of the water scared her. "Seemed like the world was coming to an end," she said.

She stayed home, mostly, after that. She has lived alone since 1967.

Earlier this year her banker asked what she wanted done with her money when she passed on. She told him that she wanted to give it to the university, now rather than later; she set aside just enough to live on.

She says she does not want to depend on anyone after all these years, but she may have little choice. She has been informally adopted by the first young person whose life was changed by her gift.

As a young woman, Stephanie Bullock's mother wanted to go to the University of Southern Mississippi. But that was during the height of the integration battles, and if she had tried her father might have lost his job with the city.

It looked as if Stephanie's own dream of going to the university would also be snuffed out, for lack of money. Although she was president of her senior class in high school and had grades that were among the best there, she fell just short of getting an academic scholarship. Miss Bullock said her family earned too much money to qualify for most Federal grants but not enough to send her to the university.

Then, last week, she learned that the university was giving her $1,000, in Miss McCarty's name. "It was a total miracle," she said, "and an honor."

She visited Miss McCarty to thank her personally and told her that she planned to "adopt" her. Now she visits regularly, offering to drive Miss McCarty around and filling a space in the tiny woman's home that has been empty for decades.

She feels a little pressure, she concedes, not to fail the woman who helped her. "I was thinking how amazing it was that she made all that money doing laundry," said Miss Bullock, who plans to major in business.

She counts on Miss McCarty's being there four years from now, when she graduates.

Source: © 1995. *The New York Times.* Reprinted by permission.

As you have read, Bragg's 37-paragraph story of McCarty uses a simple problem and solution structure. After the four-paragraph lead, two paragraphs explain why McCarty gave away $150,000. The explanation is followed by paragraphs 7 to 12, which tell readers more about the reasons for the gift. Paragraphs 13 to 17 give background about the gift, while 18 through 20 are an introduction to the first recipient of the gift. Bragg provides more details about how McCarty saved for the gift in paragraphs 21, 22 and 23 and then provides the reader with an abbreviated biography of McCarty through paragraph 30. The remainder of the story reintroduces the first scholarship winner and explains her relationship to McCarty. Paragraph 37 links the recipient with McCarty and the reason for the gift in an effective summary ending, although one with a hint of a circle back to the reason for the gift.

Bragg says he is least happy with the ending of the story.

The story probably took at the most a day to report. It was a day job. I wrote it in New Orleans (because) I was doing some other stories in New Orleans. I sat at a table in the old Pontchartrain Hotel and wrote it in one sitting. I was sitting there writing late at night and the only regret I have about the story is that as I was sitting there writing I was real sleepy and I don't think that the story has a particularly good ending on it. It's an appropriate ending, but it doesn't sing. I basically stopped writing and looked at the end of the story and went to sleep.

Although Bragg's description is minimal and almost always dispassionate, he does use physical description, description of McCarty by other people, description of McCarty by the style of language she uses and description of McCarty's surroundings, and her response to various situations. The overall effect is that Oseola McCarty's world is one of dignity and tranquillity. That is no accident, Bragg says, because that is what he witnessed. "She was very polite," he explains. "The first thing she did was turn the air conditioner on. She didn't talk a lot. She would answer your questions politely. Every now and then there would just be a gem, like when she said the only trip she'd ever made out of Mississippi was to Niagara Falls and she said, 'It scared me.' She was very nice, but she was still very much taken aback by everything that was happening to her: She was still puzzled at why anyone was interested."

By the way, the University of Southern Mississippi awarded an honorary doctorate to McCarty in 1998. It was the first time in the institution's nearly 100-year history that it made such an award.

The story of Oseola McCarty—a profile—is a good introduction to Chapter 7, which explains the specialized world of sidebars, profiles and feature series. Read on.

CHAPTER SEVEN

WRITING THE SPECIALIZED FEATURE STORY

It's 12 noon, and the deadline for the first edition of your afternoon newspaper is 12:45 P.M. You don't have much on your mind except lunch when the city editor beckons you over. He's talking on the phone, but he puts his hand over the mouthpiece and tells you, "Allen says that kid who got bitten by the rabid skunk just died. Give me a piece on the rabies epidemic we had five or six years ago, will you?"

The city editor means that another reporter is writing the straight-news story of the child's death and that you are to write a backgrounder on a previous rabies outbreak as an accompanying story. He means now. He means in time for the next edition.

You know enough to trot to the newspaper library or computer archives and look under R for rabies. With copies of old news clips in hand, the lazy writer—and there are many such—would be content to rehash old facts and hand the city editor a short review of the earlier news event.

But you're enterprising. While the clock ticks, you put in a call for a rabies expert in the state health department whose name you've spotted in the old coverage. He's out, so you leave a call-back and phone the city communicable disease officer. You next phone the head of animal pathology at a nearby university. Then you phone this year's president of your county's veterinarian association.

Now you have fresh quotes and new facts to go with the old ones. The state health department expert doesn't get back to you, but you're able to hit your computer and put together a fast feature about a worried citizenry that has quadrupled its calls to animal control officers about strays since the news first broke that a rabid animal had bitten a boy. You include potential danger signs in the behavior of both wild and pet animals. And certainly you include facts about the previous rabies outbreak that hit the city.

Instead of a simple backgrounder, you've written a sidebar.

Sidebars, profiles and series are three great staples of the newspaper and magazine writer. Like any feature article, they can be thought up and proposed by individual writers, but they are among the features most commonly assigned by editors. Sidebars, meaning any story that accompanies a main story, might be little more than statistics, such as listings of polling places to be run with a story on an upcoming election, but like profiles they often tend to be "color" stories, whether they accompany a newspaper story or a magazine article. Series can be colorful, too, but they can also be anything at all that interests you, your editors, and your readers. They are often fact-filled and cover highly important topics.

THE DEADLINE FEATURE SIDEBAR

Sidebars for a magazine, like any other magazine piece, are seldom written against extreme deadline pressures. But newspaper sidebars don't always have that advantage. Because they often accompany breaking news, they are frequently written against a ticking clock.

The subject matter of deadline feature sidebars is as varied as a day's news. They do, however, have certain characteristics:

The sidebar can be straight fact, but it's often a feature story, strong on human interest.

The sidebar, as mentioned, is usually assigned by the editor.

The straight-news story that the sidebar is written to accompany is usually breaking news.

The sidebar may run on the same page as a straight-news story, or it may run on the jump page or another page altogether.

The sidebar must be able to stand independently. That is, it must contain a tie-back to the main story or enough brief mention of the salient facts to enable readers to understand it even if they skipped the straight-news story.

The sidebar often must be written with as much haste as the straight-news story it accompanies, but it can be and often is written very well.

As with any color story, the sidebar can be bright if the main news event is a happy one, or it can be gray if the event is tragic. The details you select to tell your tale will be dictated by the news event.

A deadline feature sidebar written by Linda Wilson of *The Daily News* in Longview, Washington, was part of a massive Pulitzer entry in 1981. It is also a common type of feature written in exceptional circumstances.

Wilson was assigned to cover a funeral.

Every reporter covers a funeral sooner or later. An assistant city editor hands you a scrappy pile of your day's assignments, or the city editor simply yells at you, and you're off to attend the last rites of some noted person, either famous or infamous, or some anonymous citizen unfortunate enough to have died during a major news event.

The latter was the case for Wilson. Two young people were dead, victims of the May 1980 eruption of Mount St. Helens.

The staff of *The Daily News* in Longview stayed on top of the story for days, writing some 500 stories in coverage of the disaster. Wilson's sidebar was one of the many, and the package was so good it took the 1981 staff Pulitzer for general local reporting.

Standing alone, the one sidebar still gleams with Pulitzer quality. And it wasn't an easy story to cover. As in any funeral coverage, Wilson had to interview grieving family members and friends. Not many mourners welcome reporters at such times. To complicate the picture, the two dead 21-year-olds lived together but weren't married, a common enough situation for the times but one for which suitable terminology and even attitudes still hadn't been developed.

Terry Crall and Karen Varner went camping together on an unlucky day, and they died together. Wilson had a joint funeral to cover. She did so delicately, skillfully and with impact.

Watch Wilson's structure as she starts with a situation lead as solemn as a tolling bell. In the eighth paragraph ("graf" 8, in writer's jargon), she provides the customary tie to the body, then in the next paragraph (graf 9) continues the tie and moves smoothly forward to her starting point, the funeral. The space break between grafs 14 and 15 then establishes the structure she will utilize throughout the story.

Essentially, Wilson's 2,000-word deadline feature sidebar is written in five parts: lead, Karen Varner's brief biography, Terry Crall's brief biography, their lives together and their deaths together, all moving relentlessly in a full circle back to their joint funeral.

Wilson wasn't content merely to observe the funeral. As with profile writing, she interviewed family and friends to present a rounded story of the pair's lives, as well as their deaths. In the second section, treating Karen Varner, also watch how skillfully Wilson handles "missing" material. Varner's grieving mother is not quoted at all; the grieving father is quoted only a couple of times, and then briefly. By first presenting Karen Varner's biographic material, Wilson does not set up reader expectation, and she is then able to quote Terry Crall's mother extensively in the third section without the lack of Varner quotes jarring, however slightly, the reader's eye.

Why bother, in the first place, to give minor biographical facts about the dead pair? It could be argued that it is completely extraneous to the intent of Wilson's story for the reader to be informed that Karen Varner broke her school's record for the hurdles when she was 17 or that Terry Crall once got into a school kid's fistfight. But the bits and pieces of their everyday lives slowly form a poignant mosaic, and the poignancy is nowhere more powerful than at the moment of their deaths.

PULITZER PRIZE WINNER

LINDA WILSON

ASHES TO DUST

Gail Varner stood alone, with his head bowed, and stared at his daughter's closed casket for the last time.

A tall, proud man, he did not cry.

When he finally glanced up, two men in work clothes, which were covered with a fine, gray volcanic ash, were waiting to take the casket to its grave.

Varner turned and walked away.

The men carefully lifted the steel-blue box and rolled it outside into the blowing ash. Each step kicked up a small cloud of dust in Longview Memorial Park, still adorned with Memorial Day flowers.

They lowered the casket into the ground and returned for the second coffin—that of Terry Crall.

What had begun 12 days earlier as a weekend camping trip for Karen Varner, Terry Crall and four friends was finally over.

At 8:32 A.M. Sunday, May 18, Mount St. Helens had ended it for them. The mountain heaved and exploded and killed.

The four friends survived, but Terry and Karen's bodies weren't dug out from under the fallen trees until five days later. Of the 18 identified victims of the mountain, Terry and Karen, both 21, are so far the only ones from Longview. Emmanuel Lutheran Church on the banks of Lake Sacajawea was packed for their joint funeral Wednesday.

The families filed into the sanctuary and took their places on the front pews. Terry's mother, dressed in pants "because that's the way Terry would have wanted it," clung to her husband, her hand resting on his knee.

A song floated down from the choir loft: "The Lord wants me to sing you a love song. The song about the good times and the bad."

Terry's brother sat with his head down. Madelin Varner looked straight ahead.

Many cried.

"We must somehow pull it together," the Rev. Daniel Dowling comforted the bereaved, many of them in jeans and T-shirts. "We will never understand. We will never understand the disaster, the hurt. All we can do is ache."

Terry and Karen had been inseparable for almost three years.

Both were tall and lithe with sandy blond hair. Friends say they looked so much alike they were often mistaken for twins.

"Say something about Terry and you say something about Karen," said Sue Ruff, one of the four campers who survived.

Their trademark was identical T-shirts—usually picked up at a rock concert—and they were known for being the first couple out on the dance floor.

They were small-town kids who didn't ask for much, content to live in the town where they grew up.

Karen Marie Varner was born Dec. 19, 1958, in Ellensburg where her parents, Gail and Madelin Varner, lived in a married students housing complex while her father finished college.

In 1961, the Varner family moved to Los Angeles, but managed to spend every summer camping on the Toutle River. In 1971, the family, which included Steve, Mike and Sheryl, moved to Longview and Karen attended Cascade Junior High and Mark Morris High School—where her dad coaches girls' basketball and teaches the metals' class.

Her parents said Karen was a "serious child" and always on the honor roll in junior high and high school.

"With her own age group she was pretty outgoing; around home she was quite a bit more reserved," her father said. She was hurt when her parents got divorced a trifle over a year ago.

Karen picked strawberries every summer since she was 12 and when she turned 16 she worked at Sambo's to support her new Datsun.

What she really wanted was to be a nurse. She had completed a year at Lower Columbia College and was working as a receptionist for Dr. Jasper Vink. She was thinking about returning to LCC this fall.

Karen's scrapbook is like every other kid's. A sentimental girl, she saved everything: school report cards, restaurant matchbooks, valentines, cards—"for a dear daughter on her birthday"—and soap wrappers from vacation hotel rooms.

In 1965, she won $2 in a school art show for a picture of a tree and her photograph made the local paper. She made the paper again when she ran the hurdles in 12.6 seconds and broke a school record Aug. 23, 1975.

Karen made scrapbook notes to herself in blue ink. "Tom, Sandra, Stacy, Curt, Lori, Sue and I ate dinner here," is jotted next to a pizza order number from Me-n-Ed's Pizza.

"Sweet 16. Sue, me, mom and dad. Best present ever!" is neatly written next to a card from Henri's Restaurant.

Karen's photo album is full of pictures of Terry. There are pictures of Karen and Terry hamming it up on the beach during their eight-day trip to Hawaii, of Karen and Terry skiing and of Karen and Terry hiking and swimming.

The last pictures entered in the album are a series of aerial photographs of Mount St. Helens erupting in March. The rest of the album is empty.

Terry Crall was born Aug. 10, 1958, and raised in Longview. His mother and stepfather, Fred and Sallie Nichols, both work for Weyerhaeuser and so did Terry—although he dreamed of getting a job as a game warden.

"Terry was the type of kid you had to forgive for everything," his mother said. "He was kind of outgoing and kind of nervous and high-strung like me."

Terry's parents were divorced 11 years ago and his mother raised him on her own until she remarried three years ago. Terry was close to his family, which includes Cyndi, 18, and Tony, 15, and he always introduced his stepfather as Dad.

He was always an outdoor boy and his mother encouraged it.

He played Little League, went fishing with his mom and learned to camp and hunt.

"Me and him used to go out on the river and fish near Willow Grove when he was 9 and 10," his mother said with tears in her eyes. "He used to love that."

Terry graduated from Broadway Elementary, Monticello Junior School and B.A. Long High School. He was an average student.

(continued)

PULITZER PRIZE WINNER   CONTINUED

"I remember one time in ninth grade he came home and said he was flunking and I rushed down and signed him up for summer school," his mother said. "Later I found out he wasn't flunking, but I made him take it anyway because I had already paid for it. He kind of liked it."

When he was about 15, Terry got into his one and only fight. His mother said Terry and a neighbor boy had it out one day over "some dumb thing" and Terry came home afterward and told her he would never do it again. He kept his word.

When he was a sophomore in high school, Terry spent every free weekend visiting his grandparents—Papa and Granny—at Silver Lake.

"He was devoted to his grandfather and didn't miss more than one or two weekends in five or six months," his mother said.

"It wasn't until after my dad died that kids started showing up around the house," she said. "Terry had lots of friends—every place he went he met people—but he was kind of a homebody. His friends always came over to our house because we had a pool table in the basement."

Terry didn't have girlfriends until he was in high school, but when he started dating he always picked quiet girls.

Karen and Terry met at a party. Karen walked up and asked Terry to dance. They were together from then on.

They lived in an old house on Hillcrest Avenue in Longview, which they called their "grandpa and grandma house" because it looked so old from the outside.

They talked about getting married—and even mentioned August—but they wanted to wait until they were financially secure. Terry was laid off from his job on the green chain in the Weyerhaeuser paper mill about a month ago.

"They were always looking at rings in the Jafco catalog," Terry's mother said. "They had all sorts of plans."

Karen and Terry spent most of their time either outdoors or hanging around with a Portland-based rock band called Alost.

"There is not one gig in the last two and a half years that they haven't been to," said Mike Leak, the band's lead guitar. "We'd go play a prom and they'd be there."

Terry and Karen heard the band for the first time more than two years ago. "They were the kind of people who came right up and introduced themselves," said drummer Chris Carter.

Eventually Terry joined the group as the light technician and Karen would take tickets at the door. The band only had seven lights but Terry could really make them jump.

"Instead of doing switches, he'd sit there and pull the plugs in and out," Mike said. "He'd always be sitting down there smiling with Karen sitting right next to him. He knew every word to every song. If I forgot the words, I just looked down at him."

Terry and Karen's favorite songs were *The Cretin Hop* and *Rockaway Beach* by the Ramones.

"They were always yelling for one more song, one more song, when it was over," Mike said.

Because they liked the outdoors so much, Terry and Karen introduced most of the band to camping. They had wanted the band to come up from Portland and go camping with them that fateful Sunday but the band couldn't make it.

Instead Terry, Karen and two Kelson friends, Sue Ruff, 21, and Bruce Nelson, 22, hiked in at night with a lantern to the 2500 Road on Green River below Miners Creek Friday, May 16. They were well outside the Mount St. Helens restricted area.

The next morning Dan Balch, 20, and Bryan Thomas, 22, both of Longview, joined the group, but camped some distance away. The six spent the day hiking. The guys teased the girls about being lost in a mine shaft after their lantern went out while they were exploring an old mine.

"That night we cooked ourselves an outrageous dinner," Bruce said. "We had elk roast which we packed in, corn on the cob, baked potatoes and potato salad."

On Sunday morning, Bruce and Sue were the first out of bed and were making Irish coffee for the others when Terry came dragging out of his tent.

Bruce said: "Sue and I were standing in front of his tent and Terry looked up and said, 'Wow! Look at the sky.'

"We all knew what it was right at the same time.

"The last thing I remember was Terry calling Karen's name and flying into the tent," Bruce said. "I grabbed Sue and it was over in a snap of a finger."

Bruce and Sue were buried alive in eight feet of fallen timber and ash so hot they could barely touch it. They dug themselves out and screamed for their friends. But Terry and Karen's tent was buried by logs.

Breathing through their sweatshirts, Bruce and Sue started hiking out while the mountain continued to rumble and pelt them with rocks and chunks of ice.

Finally they heard noises and found Bryan and Dan and Sue's dog. Bryan had a broken hip and Dan was badly burned. "From the tip of his fingers to his elbows there was no skin," Sue said.

Together they tried to carry Bryan out. But it proved to be too much for them and they had to leave him in a makeshift lean-to.

"The whole time we were building the lean-to, he screamed and cried, 'Don't leave me here,'" Bruce said. "It was a hard thing to do."

Bruce, Sue and Dan, who was without shoes, hiked on. They sloshed through knee-deep hot ash on the road.

"Dan ran through it barefoot letting out a scream you wouldn't believe," Sue said.

Eventually Dan was also left behind to wait.

Bruce and Sue hiked on. They joined a 60-year-old man whose car had been disabled as he was trying to outrun the ash. But it wasn't until almost dusk that they were able to signal rescue helicopters by beating their clothes in the dust. The helicopter flew back to pick up Bryan and learned that Dan had already been flown to a hospital.

But the ordeal was not over.

The Varners and the Nichols had to wait until last Thursday before an NBC television crew convinced the National Guard and the Army Reserves to go in and look for Terry and Karen. Bruce flew in with them and dug Terry and Karen out with a chainsaw.

They were found in each other's arms.

And at a little after noon on a warm and dusty May 28 Karen and Terry's bodies, in matching gold and blue caskets, were lowered into the ground.

They were buried the way they would have wanted it—side by side.

Source: © 1980. *The Daily News,* Longview, Washington. Reprinted by permission.

As you will see in the next section, "The Profile," it's best to interview both subjects and the subjects' acquaintances to get a fully rounded picture. But as you have also seen, a good profile can be written without ever talking to the subject. In effect, Wilson's poignant sidebar is also a profile study of this dead couple.

Several interesting writing techniques give extra punch to Wilson's story. Her short paragraph style probably caught your eye as you went through it. A half-dozen words per sentence, one sentence per paragraph. Wilson is by no means boringly uniform in her use of the one-sentence paragraph; she frequently uses longer paragraphs, and she concentrates the one-per-graf technique in the beginning and end of the story, where she most needs dramatic effect, first to interest the reader enough to start the story and then to bring the feature sidebar to a strong conclusion. Although magazine writers rarely use this short-paragraph technique, you'll find it useful from time to time in writing newspaper features. One journalist even created a successful career as a columnist by developing a particular style that rarely varied from the one-sentence paragraph, but it suited his material well. As with most writing techniques, however, overuse is rarely a good idea.

Overall, Wilson uses extreme simplicity of presentation in this Pulitzer feature, choosing to refer to the principals as Terry and Karen instead of Crall and Varner. The choice fits. She doesn't fuss with the situation of their living together and simply states that, after they met, "they were together from then on." The apparent simplicity by no means prevented Wilson from skillful use of solid literary techniques, such as the foreshadowing of the couple's standard matching T-shirts, mentioned high in the feature, and their matching coffins, mentioned in the penultimate paragraph. She saddens the reader by beginning with the grieving father, lulls you by telling you about Varner's scrapbook and Crall's granddad, but doesn't let you forget that the story is a tragedy. With each mention of the couple's love of hiking and camping, the funeral bell tolls distantly, reminding you why you're reading the piece. Tension builds as the couple and their friends depart on their camping trip. Wilson's details mount. Precise wheres and whens are reported. Still simply, with telling details, you learn what the campers ate for dinner, learn that they were making Irish coffee for breakfast. Then volcano and the tragedy erupt, and Wilson carries you with the same simplicity to the strong ending. She does editorialize mildly in the end, a practice to be avoided for most features, but the tilt of the entire story is to teach the reader to know and understand this pair of "small-town kids." Wilson succeeds in her aim, and you readily accept as fact the statement that they would have wanted to be buried as they died, side by side.

All this, while writing on deadline. Good writers with well-polished writing tools know they can rely on their skills.

THE PROFILE

Profiles, like sidebars, are major contenders for both newspaper and magazine space, though the term itself may not always mean the same thing to editors and writers. For a daily newspaper, the line blurs between the profile, the personality piece and the interview. In fact, profiles are often referred to as personality pieces or personality sketches, the major difference being that of length, whereas interviews may have a typical profile lead then move on to basic interview material. For a magazine, profiles tend to retain the characteristics given to them by *The New Yorker*, which coined the term and set a high standard by which profiles can still be judged. Profiles are in-depth studies of miscellaneous people of whom nothing is required except that they be interesting. Magazine profiles usually run much longer than newspaper profiles, but the major ingredient is *depth*. A true profile, whether short or long, must enable readers to see and get to know the subject, and you can't accomplish that just by throwing in a couple of adjectives.

Most profiles are staff-written, because most newspapers and magazines have well-qualified writers on their staffs who can handle any good profile idea. The freelance writer who doesn't yet have a big name stands little chance of an exclusive interview or series of interviews with a Hillary Rodham Clinton or a Michael Jackson to peddle to a *New York Times* or a *TV Guide*. But lesser folk can be of great interest to lesser markets, particularly trade markets. The trades rarely have staffers or travel budgets to fly up to Anchorage to profile a trainer of search-and-rescue sled dogs for a health and recreation magazine, or to pop down to Tucson to profile a new bar for a bar-management magazine. The freelancer on the spot gets the opportunity.

Whatever your field of action, the profile is a staple of the writer's diet. Ways of writing them are as varied as the people about whom they are written. Present tense is commonly used but is by no means mandatory. Attaining the necessary depth is the trick, and this is accomplished by research, observation and skillful interviewing.

You've already read four prize-winning profiles about individuals: Katie McCabe's "Like Something the Lord Made," Teresa Carpenter's "Death of a Playmate," Alice Steinbach's "A Boy of Unusual Vision" and Rick Bragg's "All She Has, $150,000, Is Going to a University." Now consider a Pulitzer Prize profile of a family, written by reporter Dave Curtin for the *Colorado Springs Gazette Telegraph*.

If a feature story has a news peg, the writer always is smart to make good use of it, and Curtin's story had a strong, straight-news element from the beginning. That came at about 5:30 P.M. on a June day in 1988, and Curtin, the "day cop reporter," was about to sign out when a call came over the scanner: Two children and their father had been critically burned in a gas explosion at their home on a cattle ranch east of Colorado Springs. Another reporter was sent to the home, and Curtin took off for a local hospital to which the children were being transported by helicopter and the father by ambulance.

"When I saw them, I thought I would be reporting on a triple fatality," Curtin recalls. Instead, after days, then months of follow-up news stories, Curtin wrote a profile of courage that was sparked by a remark made by the children's aunt, Candy Entingh, when they had first turned the corner and were slowly beginning to recover at the Shriners Burn Institute in Galveston, Texas.

"Do you know how they're going to feel when they get home?" Entingh had said. "Like misfits. They're going to feel ugly, different, like they don't fit in. We want people to see them and say, 'Hi, Adam! Hi, Megan!'"

Curtin explains:

At that point, I thought, "Wonder what a story would be like to kind of track that?" How they were reintegrated into the community, church, into school. How people looked at them or what they said to them on the street, in the shopping malls and grocery stores. What is it like for them, to be brought back into the community? They're not different on the inside but they certainly are on the outside, and so her comment set the ball into motion.

The children's parents, Bill and Cindy Walter, had already been warned at the burn center that the kids would have to wear special masks and pressure-garment suits that could make them look like "monsters" or "mummies" to other kids. They wanted to do everything they could to help Adam and Megan overcome being ostracized, and they agreed to let Curtin and photographer Tom Kimmell be their shadows for six months.

Curtin says he never did figure out how much time he spent reporting the story "because it was piecemeal. Sometimes it was whenever I could find time. I'd just pick up the phone and give them a call and say, 'Can I come out for a while?' And they'd say yes." At other times, Curtin would arrange to spend the night with the family or fly with them to the burn center for medical checkups, compiling notes all the while for the eventual feature article, "Adam & Megan: A Story of One Family's Courage."

In reading it, remember again the difficult process of selection that writers face when they have plenty of material for a book-length manuscript but have only limited space in which to tell their stories. Curtin and his editor, deputy city editor Carl Skiff, decided to shoot for 200 to 250 inches of copy, no more, yet Curtin managed to work in the telling details. Notice "June," the section in which the children are first burned, and Megan, who'd just gotten a new hairdo, had only one tuft of hair left after the accident. When her mother strokes it as the little girl is rolled into surgery, the tuft falls out. In the same section, when the children are at the burn center, notice the careful medical reportage that avoids too much technicality but still graphically portrays what the kids are going through.

Notice especially how Curtin consistently portrays the kids as kids. For example, in the section "September," they're back in Colorado Springs in the hospital therapy gym, dancing. And they don't just dance, they bop their way out of the elevator and into the parking lot like any lively children. They may have endured agony, but throughout the story Curtin allows them to be what they had succeeded in remaining—typical six- and four-year-old kids.

Here's the story.

PULITZER PRIZE WINNER

DAVE CURTIN

ADAM & MEGAN: A STORY OF ONE FAMILY'S COURAGE

Megan Walter carefully arranges brightly colored ornaments three and four deep on the Christmas tree branches within her reach. Consequently, all the branches at the 3-foot height bend toward the floor from the weight.

"Megan, we need to spread out the ornaments a little more," her mother, Cindy, says gently, rearranging the bulbs.

Members of the Walter family had hoped to be back in their ranch home for Christmas, but construction is not completed. They are trimming their tree in an Ellicott rental home on a crisp, clear night, as they listen to a church-service program over the radio.

In the room illuminated only by the blinking of the multicolored lights on the tree, Cindy turns on a cassette tape. It is one the children had made to their father, Bill, five months earlier when they were in hospitals 1,100 miles apart.

In the background on the tape is the humming and beeping of hospital monitors. The children's voices quiver, their breathing is labored. Their words are more like gasps.

In the explosion, all suffered third-degree burns: Megan over 75 percent of her body, Adam over 58 percent and Bill over 38 percent of his body.

Third-degree burns—the most severe—destroy all skin layers. Bill, Adam and Megan were in critical condition for several weeks.

The blast killed the family's black Labrador retriever, Max.

"Dad, I think you're the specialest dad in the world," Adam begins on the tape. "And you're the only one I have. I'm glad we're still one family. I'm glad I don't have a stepdad or a stepmom. I'm so glad you guys don't fight and that we can be together. And that we can see each other, and that we can pray for each other, and that we can try to get better."

Then Megan's voice comes onto the tape. She is whispering, "Mom, can Dad talk back to me?"

"No," Cindy is heard to explain in the background. "Dad will have to talk back to you later on another tape."

Then, Megan begins: "Dad, you know what? Max is dead, Dad. And do you know why he's dead? Because he was standing right behind Adam and the wind blew him. The wind blew him so hard that it blew him right out the door and he broke his back. And now he's dead, Daddy. I'm really sad about that. I bet Adam's sad, too. When Mom talked about it to me, I got really scared. I thought Max got his fur burned. Mom told me his fur didn't get burned, he just got killed. Don't be sad, Dad, because when we get home, we're gonna get another puppy. Do you know that Dad? When you come see me, I'm going to start walking and you're going to see me walk."

Bill, sitting by the twinkling Christmas tree, quietly weeps as he listens to the tapes.

"What's wrong with Dad?" Adam asks.

"This tape is very special to Dad," Cindy says. "He has special feelings when he listens to it."

(continued)

PULITZER PRIZE WINNER   CONTINUED

JUNE

It is another summer evening on the plains 16 miles east of Colorado Springs. Ominous, black clouds roll in as a weary Bill Walter comes in from the fields of the 1,120-acre cattle ranch he manages. Bill, 36, the son of an Illinois dairy farmer, is a big man with a hearty laugh.

His 34-year-old wife, Cindy, arrives home with groceries in one arm and 7-week-old Abby in the other. Adam, 6, and Megan, 4, scramble into the house ahead of her. Cindy and the children have been in Colorado Springs shopping and getting Megan a new hairdo.

Cindy and Bill, married for 14 years, met at Grand Rapids (Mich.) School of Bible and Music. They sing in their church choir, and she is a director of the youth ministry.

The family likes living on the Ellicott ranch, their home of three years since moving from Savanna, Ill. In the mornings, sunlight decorates the sprawling fields. In the evenings, thunderclouds rattle the windows like a temperamental neighbor.

But most importantly, the children are happy here. Adam loves horses, riding his bicycle and helping his dad feed the cattle. When he grows up, he wants to be a policeman, "so I can go fast and not get a ticket."

Megan can't wait for Abby—"my baby"—to grow up so she'll have a girl to play with. Megan loves to play hide-and-seek and, like her mother, she is meticulous. She follows her mother around the grocery store straightening the cans on the shelves. And Megan loves to hug, especially Abby and the family dog, Max.

Now, Adam and Megan are sitting on the floor of the mud room at the top of the basement stairs to change their shoes before going out to play. Max is wagging his tail, waiting for them. Adam is hoping his mother will make his favorite dinner, macaroni and cheese. Megan wonders what will be for dessert. Even after breakfast, she had asked, "What's for dessert?"

Cindy removes Abby from the blanketed infant seat in front of the kitchen window and places her in her crib in the children's bedroom. As Cindy prepares dinner at 5 P.M., she realizes that there is no hot water. Bill, still wiping the sweat from his sun-drenched brow, heads down to the basement to light the pilot light on the hot-water heater. He doesn't know that propane has leaked into the basement. He lights a match.

Suddenly a fiery explosion rocks the house.

"There was a boom and I saw a fireball," Cindy says later. "I don't know what happened. I thought the house was hit by lightning."

"Call the hospital!" Bill shouts breathlessly. Trying to run, he staggers up the basement stairs. Only the collar of his shirt is left dangling from his neck.

The children are swept up in the sudden tunnel of fire. Most of their clothes are plastered to the walls of the mud room. The rest are melted onto their bloody bodies.

Six windows and a door are blown out into the yard. The blanket that had covered Abby moments earlier shoots through a shattered window and lands about 100 feet from the house.

Megan, her eyes stinging, wonders why Mommy is talking on the phone *now*. She thinks her mother is calling a friend.

The children and their father blindly stumble to the shower. They stand under a stream of cold well water to douse their burns.

"Daddy, my knees are weak. I'm falling," Megan cries.

"Hold on to me, Meggy," Bill says. "Hold on to me for support."

"I'm cold!" cries Adam. He has little skin to keep him warm.

Paramedics wrap the screaming children in wet sheets and carry them to the ambulance. Megan is crying out that her eyes hurt. Her corneas are burned and doctors at first fear she will be blind. But that fear will disappear after further examination.

In the ambulance, paramedics work desperately to keep the three conscious.

When Cindy sees her children at the Penrose Hospital emergency room in Colorado Springs, they are burned beyond recognition. She can't tell Adam from Megan.

"They didn't look anything like them," Cindy later recalls. "But their eyes, their eyes were the same and I knew it was Adam and Megan inside."

Megan is calm. "Look Mommy, my foot's burned," she says, not knowing that her entire body is burned.

Adam is calm until he sees how badly burned Megan is. Then he becomes hysterical. He is struggling against the doctors, battling the oxygen, fighting the intravenous tubes. "His eyes, they were crazy," Cindy remembers.

"Adam, it's Mommy," Cindy calls to her son. But she can't make contact with him.

Not far from his children, Bill is hallucinating from the morphine anesthetic and shivering so violently that he is bouncing on the gurney.

Cindy walks alongside Megan into the operating room. Just one tuft of hair is left from the girl's new hairdo. When Cindy tenderly strokes it, it falls out.

"They're very critical," Dr. John Marta, an anesthesiologist, tells Cindy. "They might not make it. They're your kids out here. But they're mine in there," Marta says, pointing to the operating room. "I'll do everything I can. But I can't make any guarantees."

Cindy to this point has had unfaltering strength in living out this horror story. But now, she feels her strength pouring out as if through a sieve.

She buries her head in her hands.

"I prayed," she says later. "I prayed that my children would die.

"I didn't want them to have to go through it. I knew they had accepted the Lord as their savior. I knew they were going to heaven, that they would be with him. I didn't want them to go through all the pain and disfigurement. I didn't pray for Bill to die. He wasn't going to leave me all alone."

"I have to change my thinking," Cindy thinks the next morning when her children are still alive. "The Lord has not taken them to be with him. We can work through this."

Later, Bill is put in a wheelchair and pushed in to see his children. Megan doesn't recognize her father.

"Megan, it's Daddy," Cindy says.

The girl seems unconvinced. Then Bill speaks.

"Megan, honey, I love you," Bill says.

Megan's eyes keep circling her father's face, trying to piece it back together as she remembered it. Finally, she speaks.

"Daddy, you stepped on me!" she moans, remembering the frantic moments on the basement stairs after the explosion.

Since Megan did not immediately recognize her father, Cindy decides to prepare Adam for Bill's visit.

"Adam, your Daddy's coming to see you," she tells him. "He'll look different. Just look at his eyes."

Six days after the explosion, Megan and Adam are transferred to the Shriners Burn Institute in Galveston, Texas, which is 1,100 miles away. But doctors warn they may not survive the flight.

Bill sees his children moments before they are boarded onto the specially equipped medical jet. "I knew it might be the last time," he says.

"Am I going to die?" Adam asks daily from his Galveston hospital bed. "I'm not going to see Dad again, am I? Either I'm going to die or Dad is."

(continued)

PULITZER PRIZE WINNER   CONTINUED

Nanny—the children's grandmother, Audra Shoemaker—and Cindy cannot truthfully tell Adam that he is not going to die. Instead, they work to calm his fear by changing the subject—"The *Lone* Ranger" is on television. This seems to brighten the boy.

"How come he's called the Lone Ranger when he always has a friend with him?" Adam wants to know.

Adam and Megan will spend seven weeks in the burn institute. Both are suffering from pulmonary edema, an excessive buildup of fluid in the lungs. Megan has a partially collapsed lung, and Adam had a cardiac arrest earlier.

Doctors work around the clock to prevent a collapse of circulation, a shutdown of the stomach and bowel system, upper lung and wound infections, kidney failure, pneumonia and prolonged shock.

The children are covered with cadaver skin as a temporary covering, and they undergo several blood transfusions and skin-graft operations. Back in Colorado Springs on one July day, 104 people from the Walter family's church, Mesa Hills Bible Church, respond to a call for blood.

The children are suffering from relentless nausea, burning fever and excessive chills. An automatic cooling blanket and fans control Megan's 104 fever.

The children relive the explosion in nightmares that might recur for months or even years.

Adam says the hospital isn't the solution—it's the problem. "Get me out of this hospital," he demands of Nanny.

During the final weeks of their first stay at the Galveston hospital, Adam and Megan are taught to sit up, to feed themselves and eventually to walk.

One day, Megan sees her reflection for the first time in a bedside cart and exclaims, "I think my hair's growing faster than Adam's."

On a bright day, Megan announces her wedding plans. She will marry "Dr. Bill"—surgeon Bill Baumgartl. Cindy and Nanny tell her she can't marry Dr. Bill, but she can have him for a boyfriend for now. Megan considers this for a moment and then declares, "I'll be a kid nurse!" Surely, that would be next best to marrying Dr. Bill.

Each child is given 3,200 calories of milk a day as part of a special diet rich in calcium, protein and potassium. Megan and Adam are fed a pint of milk an hour, 24 hours a day, for six weeks through a gastric-nasal tube.

Burn victims use calories at two times the normal metabolic rate. Not only is their rate of protein breakdown increased, but they lose protein through their wounds, says Shriners dietitian Megan Duke.

Doctors have learned how to replenish the tremendous amount of fluids lost through burn wounds. Before that, some severely burned people starved to death because they couldn't be fed fast enough, Duke says.

Adam is horrified when he sees the silicone-rubber face mask he and his sister will wear. "Take it away," he demands. "It scares me."

The masks, made from plaster molds of the children's faces, put pressure on the skin to control scarring.

The children will wear the $800 masks 23 hours a day for 1½ to three years, until the scars are mature and can no longer be changed.

"It's hot, it's itchy, it burns, it makes people afraid. There's a lot of reasons not to wear it," says Roland Morales, the medical sculptor who made the masks.

"It comes down to the parents. Kids start telling their parents, 'I hate you,' and the parents let it go and say, 'A plastic surgeon will correct it later.' A lot of people think a plastic surgeon can correct anything. That's not true."

The children also will wear pressure garments called Jobskins. Invented 20 years ago by an engineer, Conrad Jobst, the $1,000 elastic suits are custom-made to tightly fit their bodies like second skins to control scarring.

When skin is severely burned down to the third underlayer, it loses the benefit of the tight skin pressure that once was on top. The underlayer literally grows wild as it heals and forms a scar. If no pressure is applied when a scar is forming, skin will grow into irregular knots and swirls.

Without the mask and Jobskins, ugly, disfiguring and constrictive scars will develop.

The Jobskin must be worn for 12 to 18 months. Before pressure garments were used, burn victims were forever unable to function and grotesquely scarred.

Megan and Adam will wear a mouth spreader, a taut rubber-band contraption that keeps the mouth opening from growing shut. "You won't be able to eat a Big Mac unless you wear it," Morales tells the children.

They also will wear pads underneath their arms to prevent their armpits from growing shut.

Meanwhile in Colorado Springs, Bill is able to feed himself applesauce for the first time since the explosion five weeks ago. He now can shake hands, brush his teeth and blow his nose.

On Aug. 11, Adam, Megan, Cindy and Nanny return from Galveston.

But before they had left the burn institute, Cindy and Nanny were reminded that the children are returning to a world that may not be ready for them—a world that values physical beauty. They were told that severely burned children are stared at and often avoided. Other children may ask them why they look like a Martian, or a mummy or a monster.

Cindy and Nanny learned that some children live through their burns only to die a slow, social death.

"Do you know how they're going to feel when they get home?" asks the children's aunt, Candy Entingh. "Like misfits. They're going to feel ugly, different, like they don't fit in. We want people to see them and say, 'Hi Adam! Hi Megan!' "

AUGUST

"Hey!" Danny Spanagel shouts to Adam. "You lost two teeth, too!"

They are at children's church at Mesa Hills Bible Church on West Uintah Street. Adam and Megan are being reunited with their friends for the first time since the explosion, eight weeks earlier.

Danny doesn't seem to notice Adam's face, blotched red with open wounds. Or his shaved head. Or his awkward two-legged hop forced by constrictive scarring of the joints.

Danny sees only that Adam has lost his two front teeth.

Adam smiles and pats his best friend on the shoulder as only 6-year-old pals can do.

There are three dozen children ages 4 to 8 sitting in tiny chairs in the crowded room.

When Megan walks in, she sees little girls with long, flowing hair. Their skins are silky, their complexions radiant. They are in their Sunday dresses.

Megan's head is shaved. Her scalp has been used for donor skin for most of her five skin grafts. Her hands are gnarled and knobby, her fingers webbed together. Her face is scarred. Her body is bandaged from neck to toe.

The children stare. A tear rides unevenly down Megan's pockmarked cheek.

"Hi Megan," comes the squeaky call of a young, hesitant voice from across the room. This starts a flurry of greetings, and Megan quietly acknowledges them.

On the bulletin board is a poster of the Walter family with the words, "Can You Help?" In the portrait, the family is smiling, unburned, unscarred.

The children in the class look at the poster, then at Adam and Megan.

(continued)

PULITZER PRIZE WINNER   CONTINUED

"Kids are curious by nature," teacher Sybil Butler says after class. "They've heard Adam and Megan have been burned. Now here they are in front of them and they're trying to figure it out. I told them that Adam and Megan will look different. But they're still Adam and Megan."

After church, family members go to their temporary home—the house of "Auntie" Candy and Uncle David Entingh.

There, Adam and Megan are shuffling around in rigid, robotlike motions with their cousins. Adam can't push his Hot Wheels cars along the floor as he used to. So he cradles them in his bent arms, drops them on the floor and pushes them with his feet.

"Eight weeks ago, we didn't know if they were going to live," Bills says. "Now they're running around. It's a miracle."

Then Bills turns solemn. "You don't wake up everyday and say I might die today. People are too preoccupied with what they're doing—where they're going—to think like that. What happened to us took 30 seconds and changed our lives forever. Things will never be the same for us," he says.

"We don't want to just be alive," Cindy says. "We want to be normal."

SEPTEMBER

"How come your face is the same?" Adam asks his father during a two-hour therapy session at Penrose Hospital. "How come you don't have to wear the Jobst thing?"

"Because I'm not burned as bad as you are," Bill tells him.

Later, as Bill waits for his therapists, he tries to explain Adam's questions.

"What he's getting at," says Bill, "is 'How come you weren't burned as bad? Weren't you in the same explosion? You lit the match.'"

Adam denies he is burned, his father explains, and becomes angry when he is reminded. Sometimes Adam goes into uncharacteristic rages when he is forced to wear the mask or when he must go through another painful daily bath, Bill says.

"Sometimes . . . he'll yell and scream. I'll pick him up and Adam won't be inside."

One day, when Bill paddles him, Adam screams, "I hate being burned!"

"Then this look comes over his face like 'Oh-oh, I admitted it,'" Bill says.

Another day, Bill asks his son, "How come you never say 'Thank you' anymore?"

"Why should I say 'thank you' for something I don't want?" Adam fires back.

"It's like he's saying, 'I didn't ask for this,'" Bill says. "He doesn't want this anymore. He just wants to be a kid."

While Adam is at times overcome with denial and anger, Megan struggles with feelings of shame, Bill and Cindy say.

Earlier in the week, when the children were going to a monthly checkup in Galveston, Megan was following her Auntie Candy through the Colorado Springs airport. But Auntie wasn't aware that Megan, in her mechanical straight-legged gallop, was trying desperately to keep up with her. Finally, Megan stumbled, falling breathlessly to the cold tile floor. She was unable to pick herself up.

On the plane, a disheartened Megan muttered for an hour, "I want to be burned. I'm glad I was burned. Take my ears off."

In an effort to relieve such feelings, the family is seeing a psychologist. "The kids have feelings that they don't know why they have," Bill says. "Sometimes I think if the Lord took them, they wouldn't have to go through this. They're tired. Tired of the pain."

"They don't know this is going to last a long time," Cindy says. "They think it's just for now."

Across the Penrose Hospital therapy gym, therapist Cathy McDermott asks Megan to make a fist. The girl strains with all the fury a 4-year-old can muster and succeeds in cupping her hand. "That's very good!" Cathy says.

Recognizing her own progress, Megan wiggles the knuckles on her right hand as if to wave and exclaims, "Look!"

The children's burns cause severe pain when they try to move their arms, legs and fingers. Thick scarring of the joints keeps them from moving normally. Therapists will work to mold the scar tissue while it is still active. When the scars mature, they will turn white and cannot be changed.

Cathy asks Megan what she is going to do on her birthday. Megan shrugs and says, "I'll eat cake."

Megan also hopes she will get earrings for her birthday. "Before I was burned, I used to have lipstick," she says in her best ladylike manner.

Later, another therapist, Janese London, places Megan on a large mat and removes her bandages. She encourages Megan to lie on the mat and point her toes "like a ballerina."

"I don't want to be a ballerina," Megan says.

"Why?" Janese asks.

"Because," Megan giggles, "they wear purple shoes and a pink dress!"

Megan tells Janese that she bathed herself today. "But I couldn't put the shampoo on," she laments. Which reminds her, "I have more hair than my baby does," she says of her sister Abby. "I'm gonna have long hair. Before I was burned, I had it all the way past my back."

As the therapy session comes to an end, Adam and Megan eagerly ask if they get to dance. Their father asks also, because he knows how much dancing means to them: During these minutes, Adam and Megan can forget they are scarred and burned. They can forget the painful struggles of eating, brushing their teeth, bathing. They can escape.

Adam and Megan put on oversized sunglasses that dwarf their shaved heads, and therapist Patti Stafford leads them in energetic, gyrating moves to the thumping sound of "Walk Like An Egyptian."

The children's excited laughs fill the gym. Without realizing it, their sudden exuberance equates to therapeutic exercises that it is hoped will one day allow them to do the things others take for granted—walking normally, dressing without pain, grasping a fork and a spoon.

As the session ends, Patti waves goodbye and the music fades.

Adam and Megan silently continue their high-stepping, arm-flinging liveliness. Into the elevator, they're still dancing. Down three floors, they're still shaking their heads rhythmically to the imagined beat. Then they bop out of the elevator and into the parking lot of the hospital—the same hospital where 10 weeks ago, 80 friends had gathered to hold hands and pray for the two critically burned children. Praying that Adam and Megan would again smile and laugh. And dance.

Adam arrives at his seventh birthday party wearing the hated mask. Ten other first-graders are with him at The Boardwalk, an amusement center. Adam at first had demanded, "No girls." But his mother had explained that girls *will* be there and that he *will* be nice to them.

The party is the first time he has seen all but one of his school friends since the explosion.

Sharing the party is Adam's friend Roy Webb, also turning 7. Cindy didn't want Adam to think he was being showered with gifts because he had been burned. The joint party should help dispel such a notion.

"I don't want him to be ugly and I don't want him to be spoiled. I just want him to be normal," Cindy says.

"Mom, take my mask off so I can go play," Adam says. His mother relents. After all, it is his birthday.

(continued)

PULITZER PRIZE WINNER   CONTINUED

"Adam wants to get this over with by forgetting about the mask," Bill says. "With Adam, it's 'bring on the scars. I'm going to play. This isn't going to last.'

"The first impression you get of someone is by the expression on their face," Bill says. "But if you can't see the face, Adam thinks the mask scares people."

The maskless Adam has made his way to a bumper car. His gloved hands clutch the levers. At first, the other children are afraid to bump into his car, afraid that perhaps his frail body will break. But Adam quickly sets them straight. He bumps their cars with reckless abandon and sports a large smile that everyone can see.

In contrast to her brother, "Megan wants to get it over with by wearing her mask," Bill says. "She is very conscious of being pretty. She wants everyone to know that she's a girl. She saw what the Jobst gloves did for my hands."

Megan has been hiding behind her mask, Bill says. The masks must be removed to eat, and when it's time for meals, she says she's not hungry.

Megan arrives at the party fashionably late, with her mask on. She's wearing a party dress over her Jobskin and a ribbon—not in her hair, but atop her Jobst hood. Her fingernails are painted red, and her earrings sparkle.

Auntie had fashioned the ribbon, following an incident two nights earlier. A pizza delivery man, upon leaving the Entingh home, waved goodbye to Megan and said, "See ya later, fella!"

"I hate it when someone calls me fella," Megan says, rolling her eyes.

Her eyes tell it all. You can tell whether she is smiling or frowning underneath her mask by the glint or sorrow in those sky-blue eyes. At the moment, she is frowning.

Some of the children at the party shy away from the masked girl. But not Justin Herl, one of Adam's classmates. Without a word, Justin grabs Megan's gloved hand and, gently but deliberately, marches her to a video game. He has become her protector.

"Kids are so compassionate," says Jan Henderson, Adam's kindergarten teacher who is at the party. "How come we can't carry that compassion with us all our lives?"

In Galveston the night before she and Adam go through their monthly clinic at the Shriners Burn Institute, Megan stares at her dinner. She quietly describes the other children she has seen at the institute.

"I see little children with no feet and no hands." She pauses. "Children with their ears and noses burned off."

The family is eating at Western Sizzlin'. Megan sticks a piece of steak with her fork and struggles to lift it to her mouth. Others in the restaurant watch curiously. Although it is a battle for Megan to feed herself, Bill and Cindy believe their children must learn to do everyday tasks for themselves.

During dessert, a chocolate chip takes a long plunge from atop Megan's sundae to the table. It takes her 30 seconds to pick it up in gloved fingers and hoist it to her mouth. "I got it!" she boasts.

At the daylong clinic, Megan and Adam go through the painful, comprehensive examination. They will undergo the checkups indefinitely. The Shriners will pay for their care at the burn institute until they are 18 years old.

The possibility for reconstructive surgery won't be known for at least two years, when the scars mature, says Dr. Bill Baumgartl. But the surgeons are optimistic.

"They were burned very severely, and they were here initially for only two months," Baumgartl says. "People with half the burns have stayed six months. Their progress has been remarkable."

Therapist Stephanie Bakker, who three months ago had taught the children to walk again, today will lead them in exercises to increase their range of motion, strength and endurance.

"The family as a unit must be very involved with the burned victims," Stephanie says. "Cindy was a rock through the whole thing. She's a great source of strength. She was determined they were going to make it. . . . She's been a real inspiration for the other parents, and she's been admired by all the staff. Because we're so impressed with Cindy and Bill, that tells you about the rareness of their strength," Stephanie says.

"These kids are really a pleasure to work with—their smile, their big hug. That's the reward for working here—seeing them go from critically ill to being independent children again."

When the children go to therapy, they think it's a place to play. But therapists with psychology backgrounds are trained to learn what the kids are thinking by how they play. "If a 4-year-old is playing with dolls, and the doll who's supposed to be mommy is nagging the doll representing the child saying, 'That's what happens when you don't mind Mommy,' we know that's something we have to work on," says Sara Bolieu, a hospital spokeswoman.

"Children think that everything bad that happens to them is a punishment," says Andrea Royka, head of the child-life development department. "We had one boy who dressed up for Halloween as Freddy Krueger, the burned character in 'Nightmare on Elm Street.' Then he was burned two months later. He thought God was punishing him for dressing up as Freddy Krueger.

"The kids will ask, 'When I'm 21, will my scars go away?' Then it's time for reality therapy."

Across the room, music therapist Rocio Vega hands Adam bongo drums and instructs, "Beat it like you're really mad."

The exercise serves as a release for anger and tension, she explains.

"Music therapy is actually psychology," she says. "The kids will handle stress through music, and often are encouraged to write their own songs. Maybe they're real angry and have no other way to express it. It's OK to be mad or sad, and Adam and Megan know that."

Therapists have made a "re-entry" video that will reintroduce Adam and Megan to their classmates at home.

"You can prepare a child only so much for going back to school," Andrea says. "But when you don't prepare everyone else . . . everything we've done with Adam and Megan is shot. It's scary to the other children because their friends look different."

In Adam's re-entry video, the therapist tells Adam's first-grade classmates that he is "scared about going back to school. He wants people to know he is the same inside although he looks different on the outside. Adam is still the same Adam, and Megan is still the same Megan."

At the end of the film, Adam, dressed in hospital pajamas, tells his classmates, "I hope I can see you soon. Maybe the first day, I won't come."

Adam and Megan usually do not display an abundance of affection for each other. But on this day, after having gone through so much together, they are being separated for the first time. Adam is going home. Megan is staying in Galveston 10 more days. She will have skin grafts tomorrow on her chest, elbows, knee and thigh. She is devastated by the unexpected turn of events and she is crying uncontrollably. Adam is trying not to cry.

Adam limps toward the van parked near the hospital entrance. Megan waddles after him the best she can. Because of contractures in the elbow joints, she can't straighten her arms and he can't bend his.

Megan stops at the curb. Adam, bawling, turns to his sister. As he works desperately to curl his frail arms around her, Megan tries just as hard to unfold her bent arms to receive him. Finally, they hug.

(continued)

PULITZER PRIZE WINNER   CONTINUED

As the van rolls way, Adam tells his father through gasping sobs, "I didn't think it would be so hard."

OCTOBER

Five days before Halloween, the family goes to see "Bambi" at the Super Saver Eight theater at Citadel Crossing.

The cashier looks down at the two masked children. "Oh, great masks," he says. "I've never seen one of those before. Those are funny. Hey, those are great."

As the family walks in, Cindy corrects him. "Those aren't Halloween masks. My children have been burned."

A pallor stretches across the cashier's face, and he is speechless. After the movie, he approaches Bill. "I'm sorry. I didn't know. I really didn't know."

After the movie, the family goes shopping for tricycles. Therapists at Penrose Hospital have recommended the tricycles for the children to exercise their knee joints and improve their ability to grip by grasping the handlebars.

For Adam, the decision to accept a tricycle is tough. He was adept at riding his bicycle "very fast." He already had picked out a new bicycle for Christmas. It was the bike of his dreams.

"It's *very* fast," he had said. "And it has *very* good brakes. . . . It's an adult bike."

Bill explains to Adam that he's not yet strong enough to balance a bicycle and that he wouldn't be able to grip the handlebars.

After much consternation, Adam decides he'll accept a trike. But not until Bill tells him he can pick out any horn he wants.

While they are shopping, a small boy spots the children. "Look, Mom, they're wearing masks," he says.

"They have to wear the masks," his mother explains, "because they have 'owies.'" The boy appears to accept the explanation.

Moments later, a little girl sees Megan and says, "Look Mommy, she has a pig nose."

Megan's feeling are hurt, and she runs to Cindy. "Mommy, I don't have a pig nose."

"No," Cindy assures. "You don't have a pig nose. She just doesn't know about your mask."

On a moonless night, the family returns to the Ellicott ranch for the first time since the explosion four months earlier. Megan naps during the 16-mile ride. When she awakens, she's home—at last.

But she's troubled because it doesn't look like home.

The mud room—at the top of the stairs where Megan and Adam were nearly killed by the fireball—is dark, vacant and hollow. It echoes. The doors and windows, blown out by the blast, are boarded.

The washer, dryer and freezer have been moved into the kitchen.

Megan walks into the kitchen. Cindy opens a cupboard, and scorched, wilted rose petals come fluttering out. She had kept a basket of the petals on top of the refrigerator. "What a mess!" Megan says. She limps quickly across the kitchen and into the children's old bedroom. She is comforted when she sees her bedroom is undisturbed.

Adam, meanwhile, has romped straight to the big wooden toy box made by his father and is digging feverishly for his cars and trucks. Megan soon arrives at her toy box. Side by side, they are absorbed in their long-lost toys.

This is Bill's second visit to the house. He had been here a couple of weeks ago. He had spotted melted pieces of clothing and skin, plastered to walls from the force of the explosion, and removed what he could.

Now he hesitates before going into the basement. "How will this make me feel?" he asks himself. "Can I handle this?" But he continues down, each of the 11 steps taking him closer to the source of the tragedy that so drastically had changed their lives. A cardboard box next to where Adam had been seated on the stairs is unscathed. The blast also hadn't disturbed a plastic bag, tennis rackets and baseball mitts in the basement.

"Sometimes I think the kids would have been better off if they were standing right behind me," Bill says. "But I can't change it."

For Cindy, this is the fourth trip to the home since the explosion. She had gone to the house the day after to get some clothes, and at other times to clean up the rooms. "It doesn't bother me anymore," she says. "I didn't like to go at first because of the smell. It was the smell of burned flesh. It was a people smell. It was the same smell as in the burn unit."

The family walks out the door of the mud room and stands at the evergreen bush where Max had gone to seek his final refuge. Max, with broken back and scorched lungs, had crawled under the evergreen to die.

NOVEMBER

Adam and Megan are wearing new winter coats and mittens on a cold, windy day in Ellicott. Their old coats were destroyed in the explosion. They each carry a sack lunch, and Adam carries a book bag for both on his back. Today is their first day of school.

Cindy and Bill escort them to their classrooms at Ellicott Elementary School.

Adam and Megan are not wearing their masks so their new classmates can see that they have features and hair.

Without hesitation, Cindy introduces Megan to the hushed kindergarten class. Then she holds up Megan's mask and carefully explains that her daughter must wear it. "If she doesn't, the bumps on her face will get real big and ugly," Cindy says.

The 20 kids watch Cindy put the mask on Megan. "Megan knows that when she wears her mask, you can't see her smile," Cindy says. "If you don't know how she's feeling, ask her. Ask her if she's feeling sad or happy."

Teacher Jan Henderson asks the boys and girls whether they are glad to see Megan. They respond with a resounding "yes!"

"Megan, are you happy to be here?" Mrs. Henderson asks. Megan nods, but unconvincingly.

The teacher tries again. "Megan, are you happy or sad?"

"Happy," Megan says, softly.

Her classmates, still silent, continue to look at the masked girl for several minutes.

Down the hall, Cindy repeats the introduction in Adam's class, where he is a celebrity, at least for today, among the 18 first-graders who are competing for his attention.

"Adam's face is red because his blood is working hard to heal it," Cindy tells them. "Underneath his suit, his skin is OK. It's just real red. After a year, Adam can take the suit off. You can touch Adam's skin if you want. Adam will let you.

"If he needs help, he will ask, 'Will you please help me?' but don't rush up to do things for him because we make him do a lot of things for himself," Cindy says.

After Cindy and Bill leave, the first-graders are asked by teacher Lynda Grove what they learned.

"He can do most things we can do," says one student.

"You can touch his skin and it won't hurt," another says.

"He can do things by himself," another says.

When first-grade teacher Jolynn Olden brings her students into the room to meet Adam, she asks the children if they have questions for him.

(continued)

PULITZER PRIZE WINNER   CONTINUED

"Can you go across the monkey bars?" asks one.

"Not yet," Adam replies.

"Can you go down the slides?" asks another.

Adam nods.

"Can you run?" another wants to know.

"Yes," Adam says.

Now the true measure of worth for a first-grader becomes evident. "Fast" to a 7-year-old is everything important.

"Can you run as fast as in kindergarten?" a youngster carefully queries. "Faster," Adam says unflinchingly.

"Can you ride a bike?"

"No," Adam answers reluctantly. "We're still working on balance."

Miss Olden turns Adam's answer into a lesson. "Class, what's balance?" she asks. The answer is universal. "It's staying up on two wheels," the pupils chime.

"Were you scared to come to school today?" a classmate asks.

"A little at first," Adam says. "But I got over it."

The questions continue to pour in. "Do you have fingernails? (Yes). What do you do at home? (Homework). Does your neck get tired of holding your mask up? (No).

"Can we touch you?" one boys asks. Adam nods.

The children scramble to their feet and rush to circle Adam. All at once, they begin touching him. They are convinced that he's just like them.

A cutback in their daily therapy allows the children to attend school three days a week. Cindy and Bill want to get their children back into the mainstream as quickly as possible.

Though Adam and Megan are starting school $2^{1}/_{2}$ months late, they have been working math problems and reading books at home in rare moments when not consumed by therapy and treatment.

Adam needs no practice at art. In art class today, the students are drawing what they will eat for Thanksgiving. Adam uses crayons to draw a dinosaur and what he describes as "worm pie."

Meanwhile, Megan is learning to write V's in her class. But gripping the pencil hurts her right hand. "Megan will learn by watching," says Luann Dobler, a student teacher.

In the cafeteria at lunch time, all the kids are eager to sit next to Adam. Roy Webb and Jason Harding are the winners. They and Adam recall the old days. "Do you remember when the girls attacked?" Adam asks. The two nod furtively and smile. Undoubtedly, it was a memorable event.

Two tables away, Megan wrestles with her sandwich Baggie over possession of a peanut butter and jelly sandwich. A third-grade boy who enters the lunchroom fails to notice Megan's effort to look pretty; she's wearing her ribbons, earrings and her best dress. Having not heard Cindy's earlier lesson, he asks no one in particular, "What's wrong with Megan? She doesn't look too good. Her face is all red."

The harsh words fail to distract the little girl. Minutes later in math class, Megan is called to the blackboard to draw two of anything. On this blustery, gray day of this devastating year, Megan shuffles up to the board and draws two smiling suns.

EPILOGUE

"You always hear the cliché, 'life isn't fair,'" says Bill Walter. "I guess I've learned that. Even though it isn't fair, it doesn't mean your world has to go to pieces. This has helped me gain a better appreciation of life, what's serious and what's not.

"For my children, for myself, for my family, it doesn't seem fair. But being a Christian, I feel there's a reason for things to happen. The lives you touch and those that touch you—I wonder what the purpose is behind it all?

"More than anything, it was such a shock to me. I never really felt it was my fault. Just a freak accident. When you read of people who are hurt or see it on TV, you feel bad about it, but only for a little while. Then you go on. You never think of something like this happening to you.

"I was the one who lit the match. It seemed so unfair to the children. I've woken up many times at night with a real great sorrow. If I could, I'd like to back up to June 21 and go on from there. But in reality, you can't change that. The Lord has given us the strength to pick up the pieces and go on. Bitterness isn't going to help anyone—me being bitter or Cindy and I being bitter toward each other. Why destroy the kids with bitterness?"

"It's good to be alive. More and more, the kids see that. They realize life will come back to a point of being normal. At first, they doubted if anything was ever going to be good again. Now they see that it will be.

"One thing that's really neat is to know that our community—El Paso County, Colorado Springs, Calhan, Ellicott—was pulling for us. That's hard to express. I thank everyone so much. 'Thank you' seems awful small for what we feel at a time like this."

Source: © 1989. *Colorado Springs Gazette Telegraph.* Reprinted by permission.

When "Adam & Megan" was announced as a 1990 Pulitzer Prize winner, one of the judges, Gene Roberts, executive editor and president of *The Philadelphia Inquirer,* said, "The board was very impressed [with Curtin's story]; it was very well written and very sensitively handled throughout. It isn't very often that stories about tragedies make their way to the finals. Very often, the board is turned off by these kinds of stories. But this was so sensitive. It was just a fine example of how these stories should be written." Bob Christopher, administrator of the Pulitzer Prizes, added, "A lot of the time, these are written like tearjerkers. This was not overdone, and that's where it got a lot of its power."

Curtin's editor, Carl Skiff, regarded these words as "a tribute to Curtin." Curtin tends to share the praise, recalling, "When it came time to write the story, Skiff warned me to resist the temptation to overwrite. 'Let the story tell itself,' he said."

In all, the story that took six months to research took Curtin only two weeks to write, working from the solid foundation of diary-form notes. Then he and Skiff sat down for another two weeks of editing. Curtin had written the final draft in present tense. Together, at the start of the editing process, they tried changing it to past tense, then decided they liked it better in the present tense.

There weren't many more changes. Praising the reporter again, Skiff says:

It was beautifully written from the start. It was simple, clean. No fancy stuff, just plain perfection. No tearjerker, it tugged at your heart nonetheless. You wanted to keep reading. Aside from eliminating one sidebar, there was just one major alteration. The Christmas scene, with the Walter family decorating their tree, was moved from the end to the story's lead for two reasons: The scene was topical, the freshest, the most recent; and it was an uplifting, happy scene. Our readers needed to know right from the start that this story rising from a terrible tragedy was a positive one about courage, faith, hope, the best of human qualities.

The reporter, the deputy city editor, the photographer, two copy editors, the design director, photo editors, the city editor, the managing editor, the *Gazette Telegraph* management—all, according to Curtin and Skiff, worked together as a team to shepherd the project to completion.

Maybe that's why Curtin says, remembering how the realization finally set in that "Adam & Megan" had been singled out from all other feature entries, "*We* had won a Pulitzer Prize."

THE FEATURE SERIES

The series is a showcase of the daily newspaper, just as it is a standard for many top magazines. Writing a series requires great chunks of time from both writers and editors. Running a series requires great chunks of space. Although a feature series, like any other feature, can be written about any interesting subject, the time and space commitment usually mandates that the feature series be focused on important subjects and issues. What effect will budget and tax cuts have on state aid to the poor? Is our water supply running out? Is the religious right unduly influencing the selection of a state's public school textbooks? Any topic of profound or far-ranging influence on a newspaper's or magazine's readership can be and has been considered a suitable topic for a series. And a good series is often impressive to contest judges. Take the Pulitzer awards, for example. A finely crafted multipart series can win in almost any category—public service, investigative reporting, explanatory journalism, national reporting, international reporting. And, of course, the feature category.

Not every series can win a Pulitzer, of course. Series often treat subjects of lesser importance. For example, when cities or states approach major anniversaries, a replay of history is usually seen in series form. Beats, such as medical beats, can turn up a feature series on new treatments or threatening diseases in a region. Spring wildflowers can be a series topic in season, and wire services can and do generate series on both serious and frivolous topics.

When a series is specifically a feature series, it, like general features, is usually told in terms of people, rather than numbers and statistics. No series of any type can be written successfully using a straight-news, inverted pyramid form. The series demands that each new installment be read as a one-shot story by the casual reader: It must have an attention-getting lead; it must have enough of a tie-back to preceding installments to make the general topic comprehensible; and it should have a solid, preferably suspenseful ending to hook the reader into coming back for more the next day.

The ability to be divided into satisfying segments, whether three parts or seven, distinguishes the newspaper feature series from a single magazine article on the same subject. Apart from this, the feature series and the article both require strong feature techniques and excellent research and writing. The prose style of a series can be deliberately simple and understated. It can be richly textured and bristling with apt quotes and facts. Or it can be some other style altogether, suitable to the subject matter and well honed by the individual writer. But the prose must be excellent, for you're writing a showcase piece.

When Isabel Wilkerson wrote "First Born, Fast Grown: The Manful Life of Nicholas, 10," a gripping portrait of a poor boy on Chicago's South Side, it was only one installment in an extensive 10-part series planned for *The New York Times*. Determined to alert their readers to the plight of children growing up in today's inner cities, editors assigned themes to 10 reporters and sent them out to find young people through whom they could demonstrate their themes. A story a day, for 10 days. All to run on the front page. The 10 topics covered a wide range of inner-city problems—drugs, schools, crime, gangs. Wilkerson, bureau chief for the *Times* in Chicago, drew a difficult one. Family.

It was a long-term project. Each of the reporters had regular writing assignments to maintain and it took almost eight months to search out the perfect people, gather information and write the stories. Wilkerson says, "All of the reporters—10 of us—were somewhat bonded in the pressure to find the perfect child to represent our topic. So we checked in with each other. . . . Many of them found their people much earlier than I did. I had to live with the constant reminder that I was getting behind in my search."

Some of the reporters found older children, but Wilkerson wanted someone very young. She says,

> I wanted an average child in a tough situation. I wanted a child who was between 9 and 12 because I wanted someone who was old enough to verbalize his feelings but young enough to still view the world with a child's eye. . . . The obvious place to go would be to a public school, but I never went to the public school. I felt there would be too much bureaucracy. I [also] was afraid they—the school—would choose a child for me. . . . The other obvious place to go would have been the welfare office because these families were on the edge. I didn't go there because I did not want to fall completely into the stereotype.

She also wanted a parent who was trying to climb out of a bad situation. So she used sign-up lists, posted at night school, adult education classes, typing classes and data-processing classes, asking parents with children in the right age group to add their names to the list. She says,

> I needed a cooperative parent. I needed a magnetic child who also understood or was willing to talk. You needed the siblings who would also be cooperative and play off one another. You needed all these things to come together. Inevitably, in the search process, it was one thing or the other. Stage mothers who were eager to get their child in the paper. Children who would be non-verbal. Then I would hear about children who seemed ideal, but the parents weren't cooperative. It was always something.

One of her sign-up lists was in a nursing class at Kennedy-King College on the South Side. Wilkerson went by in December and told the class what she was looking for. One woman came in late and missed what Wilkerson had said, but the list was being passed around the room and when it came to her, another student told her she was supposed to sign it if she had children between 9 and 12. The woman signed the list automatically. She was Angela Whitiker, Nicholas's mother.

Wilkerson called her on the phone. "From the very first interview on the telephone, it was magic. She told me several stories about how difficult it was for her, and what she tells her children. And how she had prepped (Nicholas) for a hard life by saying that we don't always know that there would be a man in our life to protect us and that's the reason you have to be the man in the family. I knew instantly that the parent at least was ideal."

Then she met the children in January. Five in all. Wilkerson says, "It was wonderful. They were very open. They were very comfortable with the idea of a stranger coming in and very friendly. It was all I could have ever hoped for. And it just grew from there."

Nicholas, when she found him, was 9. He was the leader, the father figure for the children. By the time the story ran, he was 10, but he was still the youngest person in the series. And in some ways, perhaps the oldest.

Wilkerson didn't want to write as an outsider. She knew she had to establish rapport with the children in order to blend in. She took them on outings to McDonalds, on drives around Chicago. The mother gave her access to the house, but she also had to convince school officials, a difficult task, since, as she says, "Schools have had an adversarial relationship with the press—especially in Chicago—and are very sensitive to any outsiders being there." But she managed to convince the principal that she wasn't planning an exposé of the school. She was there to tell a young man's story.

She was in the classroom every day during the reporting process. She went with Nicholas and his siblings to the cafeteria for lunch, on field trips, sometimes spending a full day just to get a single phrase. She kept it up for a month, then started the writing process. It took her a week and a half to write the story, but her editors said it was too long and asked her to cut 1,000 words. It took another week to edit it down.

Nicholas's story kicked off the series with a bang when it ran on the front page of *The New York Times* on April 4, 1993. As you read it, you'll see that there are no statistics. Nor does she quote experts. Only Nicholas and his immediate family are quoted. The entire story is told from their point of view. Strong reporting? You bet. In its final form, the story runs about 2,800 words. And every one of them will affect you.

PULITZER PRIZE WINNER

ISABEL WILKERSON

FIRST BORN, FAST GROWN: THE MANFUL LIFE OF NICHOLAS, 10

CHICAGO, April 3—A fourth-grade classroom on a forbidding stretch of the South Side was in the middle of multiplication tables when a voice over the intercom ordered Nicholas Whitiker to the principal's office. Cory and Darnesha and Roy and Delron and the rest of the class fell silent and stared at Nicholas, sitting sober-faced in the back.

"What did I do?" Nicholas thought as he gathered himself to leave.

He raced up the hall and down the steps to find his little sister, Ishtar, stranded in the office, nearly swallowed by her purple coat and hat, and principal's aides wanting to know why no one had picked her up from kindergarten.

'I DON'T KNOW'

It was yet another time that the adult world called on Nicholas, a gentle, brooding 10-year-old, to be a man, to answer for the complicated universe he calls family.

How could he begin to explain his reality—that his mother, a welfare recipient rearing five young children, was in college trying to become a nurse and so was not home during the day, that Ishtar's father was separated from his mother and in a drug-and-alcohol haze most of the time, that the grandmother he used to live with was at work, and that, besides, he could not possibly account for the man who was supposed to take his sister home—his mother's companion, the father of her youngest child?

"My stepfather was supposed to pick her up," he said for simplicity's sake. "I don't know why he's not here."

Nicholas gave the school administrators the name and telephone numbers of his grandmother and an aunt, looked back at Ishtar with a big brother's reassuring half-smile and rushed back to class still worried about whether his sister would make it home O.K.

Of all the men in his family's life, Nicholas is perhaps the most dutiful. When the television picture goes out again, when the 3-year-old scratches the 4-year-old, when their mother, Angela, needs ground beef from the store or the bathroom cleaned or can't find her switch to whip him or the other children, it is Nicholas's name that rings out to fix whatever is wrong.

He is nanny, referee, housekeeper, handyman. Some nights he is up past midnight, mopping the floors, putting the children to bed and washing their school clothes in the bathtub. It is a nightly chore: the children have few clothes and wear the same thing every day.

CURBSIDE SERVICE

He pays a price. He stays up late and goes to school tired. He brings home mostly mediocre grades. But if the report card is bad, he gets a beating. He is all boy—squirming in line, sliding

(continued)

PULITZER PRIZE WINNER   CONTINUED

down banisters, shirt-tail out, shoes untied, dreaming of becoming a fireman so he can save people—but his walk is the stiff slog of a worried father behind on the rent.

He lives with his four younger half-siblings, his mother and her companion, John Mason, on the second floor of a weathered three-family walkup in the perilous and virtually all black Englewood section of Chicago.

It is a forlorn landscape of burned-out tenements and long-shuttered storefronts where drunk men hang out on the corner, where gang members command more respect than police officers and where every child can tell you where the crack houses are.

The neighborhood is a thriving drug mart. Dealers provide curbside service and residents figure that any white visitor must be a patron or a distributor. Gunshots are as common as rainfall. Eighty people were murdered in the neighborhood last year, more than in Omaha and Pittsburgh combined.

Living with fear is second nature to the children. Asked why he liked McDonald's, Nicholas's brother Willie described the restaurant playground with violence as his yardstick. "There's a giant hamburger, and you can go inside of it," Willie said. "And it's made out of steel, so no bullets can't get through."

THE FAMILY

MANY EYES, MANY HANDS
It is in the middle of all this that Angela Whitiker is rearing her children and knitting together a new life from a world of fast men and cruel drugs. She is a strong-willed, 26-year-old onetime waitress who has seen more than most 70-year-olds ever will. A 10th-grade dropout, she was pregnant at 15, bore Nicholas at 16, had her second son at 17, was married at 20, separated at 21 and was on crack at 22.

In the depths of her addiction, she was a regular at nearby crack houses, doing drugs with gang members, businessmen and, she said, police detectives, sleeping on the floors some nights. In a case of mistaken identity, she once had a gun put to her head. Now she feels she was spared for a reason.

She has worked most of her life, picking okra and butterbeans and cleaning white people's houses as a teen-ager in Louisiana, bringing home big tips from businessmen when she waited tables at a restaurant in downtown Chicago, selling Polish sausages from a food truck by the Dan Ryan Expressway and snow cones at street fairs.

She is a survivor who has gone from desperation to redemption, from absent mother to nurturing one, and who now sees economic salvation in nursing. Nicholas sees brand-name gym shoes and maybe toys and a second pair of school pants once she gets a job.

STUDYING FOR MIDTERMS
She went through treatment and has stayed away from drugs for two years. Paperback manuals from Alcoholics and Narcotics Anonymous sit without apology on the family bookshelf. A black velvet headdress from church is on the windowsill and the Bible is turned to Nehemiah—emblems of her new life as a regular at Faith Temple, a Coptic Christian church on a corner nearby.

For the last year, she has been studying a lot, talking about novels and polynomials and shutting herself in her cramped bedroom to study for something called midterms.

That often makes Nicholas the de facto parent for the rest of the children. There is Willie, the 8-year-old with the full-moon face and wide grin who likes it when adults mistake him for Nicholas. There is Ishtar, the dainty 5-year-old. There is Emmanuel, 4, who worships Nicholas and runs crying to him whenever he gets hurt. And there is Johnathan, 3, who is as bad as he is cute and whom everyone calls John-John.

That is just the beginning of the family. There are four fathers in all: Nicholas's father, a disabled laborer who comes around at his own rhythm to check on Nicholas, give him clothes and whip him when he gets bad grades. There is Willie's father, a construction worker whom the children like because he lets them ride in his truck.

There is the man their mother married and left, a waiter at a soul food place. He is the father of Ishtar and Emmanuel and is remembered mostly for his beatings and drug abuse.

The man they live with now is Mr. Mason, a truck driver on the night shift, who met their mother at a crack house and bears on his neck the thick scars of a stabbing, a reminder of his former life on the streets. He gets Nicholas up at 3 A.M. to sweep the floor or take out the garbage and makes him hold on to a bench to be whipped when he disobeys.

Unemployment and drugs and violence mean that men may come and go, their mother tells them. "You have a father, true enough, but nothing is guaranteed," she says. "I tell them that no man is promised to be in our life forever."

There is an extended family of aunts, an uncle, cousins and their maternal grandmother, Deloris Whitiker, the family lifeboat, whom the children moved in with when drugs took their mother away.

To the children, life is not the neat, suburban script of sitcom mythology with father, mother, two kids and golden retriever. But somehow what has to get done gets done.

When Nicholas brings home poor grades, sometimes three people will show up to talk to the teacher—his mother, his father and his mother's companion. When Nicholas practices his times table, it might be his mother, his grandmother or Mr. Mason asking him what 9 times 8 is.

But there is a downside. The family does not believe in sparing the rod and when Nicholas disobeys, half a dozen people figure they are within their rights to whip or chastise him, and do. But he tries to focus on the positive. "It's a good family," he says. "They care for you. If my mama needs a ride to church, they pick her up. If she needs them to baby-sit, they baby-sit."

THE RULES

READY TO RUN, QUICK TO PRAY

It is a gray winter's morning, zero degrees outside, and school starts for everybody in less than half an hour. The children line up, all scarves and coats and legs. The boys bow their heads so their mother, late for class herself, can brush their hair one last time. There is a mad scramble for a lost mitten.

Then she sprays them. She shakes an aerosol can and sprays their coats, their heads, their tiny outstretched hands. She sprays them back and front to protect them as they go off to school, facing bullets and gang recruiters and a crazy, dangerous world. It is a special religious oil that smells like drugstore perfume, and the children shut their eyes tight as she sprays them long and furious so they will come back to her, alive and safe, at day's end.

These are the rules for Angela Whitiker's children, recounted at the Formica-top dining-room table:

"Don't stop off playing," Willie said.

(continued)

PULITZER PRIZE WINNER   CONTINUED

"When you hear shooting, don't stand around—run," Nicholas said.

"Why do I say run?" their mother asked.

"Because a bullet don't have no eyes," the two boys shouted.

"She pray for us every day," Willie said.

THE WALK TO SCHOOL

Each morning Nicholas and his mother go in separate directions. His mother takes the two little ones to day care on the bus and then heads to class at Kennedy-King College nearby, while Nicholas takes Willie and Ishtar to Banneker Elementary School.

The children pass worn apartment buildings and denuded lots with junked cars to get to Banneker. Near an alley, unemployed men warm themselves by a trash-barrel fire under a plastic tent. There is a crack house across the street from the school.

To Nicholas it is not enough to get Ishtar and Willie to school. He feels he must make sure they're in their seats. "Willie's teacher tells me, 'You don't have to come by here,'" Nicholas said. "I say, 'I'm just checking.'"

Mornings are so hectic that the children sometimes go to school hungry or arrive too late for the free school breakfast that Nicholas says isn't worth rushing for anyway.

One bitter cold morning when they made it to breakfast, Nicholas played the daddy as usual, opening a milk carton for Ishtar, pouring it over her cereal, handing her the spoon and saying sternly, "Now eat your breakfast."

He began picking over his own cardboard bowl of Corn Pops sitting in vaguely sour milk and remembered the time Willie found a cockroach in his cereal. It's been kind of hard to eat the school breakfast ever since.

THE CHILDREN

WHEN BROTHERS ARE FRIENDS

Nicholas and Willie on brotherhood:

"He act like he stuck to me," Nicholas said of Willie. "Every time I move somewhere, he want to go. I can't even breathe."

"Well, what are brothers for?" Willie asked.

"To let them breathe and live a long life," Nicholas said. "Everytime I get something, they want it. I give them what they want after they give me a sad face."

"He saves me all the time," Willie said. "When I'm getting a whooping, he says he did it."

"Then I get in trouble," Nicholas said.

"Then I say I did it, too, and we both get a whooping," Willie said. "I save you, too, don't I, Nicholas?"

"Willie's my friend," Nicholas said.

"I'm more than your friend," Willie shot back, a little hurt.

Once Willie almost got shot on the way home from school. He was trailing Nicholas as he usually does when some sixth-grade boys pulled out a gun and started shooting.

"They were right behind Willie," Nicholas said. "I kept calling him to get across the street. Then he heard the shots and ran."

Nicholas shook his head. "I be pulling on his hood but he be so slow," he said.

"Old slowpoke," Ishtar said, chiming in.

NO FRIENDS, ONE TOY

In this neighborhood, few parents let their children outside to play or visit a friend's house. It is too dangerous. "You don't have any friends," Nicholas's mother tells him. "You don't have no homey. I'm your homey."

So Nicholas and his siblings usually head straight home. They live in a large, barren apartment with chipped tile floors and hand-me-down furniture, a space their mother tries to spruce up with her children's artwork.

The children spend their free time with the only toy they have—a Nintendo game that their mother saved up for and got them for Christmas. The television isn't working right, though, leaving a picture so dark the children have to turn out all the lights and sit inches from the set to see the cartoon Nintendo figure flicker over walls to save the princess.

Dinner is what their mother has time to make between algebra and Faith Temple. Late for church one night, she pounded on the stove to make the burners fire up, set out five plastic blue plates and apportioned the canned spaghetti and pan-fried bologna.

"Come and get your dinner before the roaches beat you to it," she yelled with her own urban gallows humor.

RHINESTONES IN CHURCH

Faith Temple is a tiny storefront church in what used to be a laundry. It is made up mostly of two or three clans, including Nicholas's, and practices a homegrown version of Ethiopian-derived Christianity.

At the front of the spartan room with white walls and metal folding chairs, sits a phalanx of regal, black-robed women with foot-high, rhinestone-studded headdresses. They are called empresses, supreme empresses and imperial empresses. They include Nicholas's mother, aunt and grandmother, and they sing and testify and help calm flushed parishioners, who sometimes stomp and wail with the holy spirit.

The pastor is Prophet Titus. During the week he is Albert Lee, a Chicago bus driver, but on Sundays he dispenses stern advice and $35 blessings to his congregation of mostly single mothers and their children. "Just bringing children to the face of the earth is not enough," Prophet Titus intones. "You owe them more."

Nicholas's job during church is to keep the younger children quiet, sometimes with a brother asleep on one thigh and a cousin on the other. Their mother keeps watch from her perch up front where she sings. When the little ones get too loud, their mother shoots them a threatening look from behind the microphone that says, "You know better."

GRANDMOTHER, EMPRESS

On this weeknight, Nicholas and Willie are with cousins and other children listening to their grandmother's Bible lesson.

She is a proud woman who worked for 22 years as a meat wrapper at a supermarket, reared five children of her own, has stepped in to help raise some of her grandchildren and packs a .38 in her purse in case some stranger tries to rob her again. On Sundays and during Bible class, she is not merely Nicholas's grandmother, but Imperial Empress Magdala in her velvet-collared cape.

The children recite Bible verses ("I am black but beautiful," from Solomon or "My skin is black" from Job), and then Mrs. Whitiker breaks into a free-form lecture that seems a mix of black pride and Dianetics.

"Be dignified," she told the children. "Walk like a prince or princess. We're about obeying our parents and staying away from people who don't mean us any good."

(continued)

PULITZER PRIZE WINNER   CONTINUED

The boys got home late that night, but their day was not done. "Your clothes are in the tub," their mother said, pointing to the bathroom, "and the kitchen awaits you."

"I know my baby's running out of hands," she said under her breath.

This is not the life Nicholas envisions for himself when he grows up. He has thought about this, and says he doesn't want any kids. Well, maybe a boy, one boy he can play ball with and show how to be a man. Definitely not a girl. "I don't want no girl who'll have four or five babies," he said. "I don't want no big family with 14, 20 people, all those people to take care of. When you broke they still ask you for money, and you have got to say, 'I'm broke. I don't have no money.'"

A SISTER SAFE

Ishtar made it home safely the afternoon Nicholas was called to the principal's office. Mr. Mason was a couple of hours late picking her up, but he came through in the end.

Nicholas worries anyway, the way big brothers do. He worried the morning his mother had an early test and he had to take the little ones to day care before going to school himself.

John-John began to cry as Nicholas walked away. Nicholas bent down and hugged him and kissed him. Everything, Nicholas assured him, was going to be O.K.

Source: © 1993. *The New York Times.* Reprinted by permission.

Wilkerson begins her story with a four-paragraph lead that concludes with a linking paragraph, showing the reader that Nicholas is being called upon to be a man. Using a repetitive structure, Wilkerson reinforces this concept throughout the story. Her ending—a tie-back to the lead—further reinforces the theme.

Wilkerson's story is so powerful, her reporting so true to life, that she knew she had to be careful to keep herself out of it. No pontificating asides, no dramatic or literary curlicues. Just straight, simple writing. Well, perhaps "simple" is the wrong word. It takes an excellent reporter to write as plainly, as powerfully as Wilkerson. She set out to see the world through the eyes of a fourth-grade Chicago boy and succeeded remarkably well. Her ear for speech, her keen observation of details, her fluid, seemingly effortless writing made the story of Nicholas so powerful that, along with two other Wilkerson feature submissions, it won the 1994 Pulitzer Prize for distinguished feature writing.

The plight of Nicholas and his family also caught some pretty high-powered attention. The President of the United States wrote to her. Business executives across the country got in touch to tell her that her portrait of this one young boy and his family had done more to demonstrate to them the devastating bleakness of poverty than all of the statistic-strewn stories that preceded it. She got letters of thanks from schoolchildren, from college students and, of course, from other journalists. Especially from other journalists. After all, who better than her peers would recognize the hard, hard work that went into making a story seem so effortless?

THE SPECIALIZED FEATURE STORY AND
MULTIMEDIA JOURNALISM

Specialized features are another example in which the Internet comes into play. Newspapers continue to run them in day-to-day print coverage, but they often repeat the features on the newspapers' Web sites, where they may well become part of the papers' electronic archives, available for reading long after printed articles vanish in the bottom of a birdcage. Magazines do the same thing with reviews and features, as do broadcast facilities. This is especially true for network broadcast materials. Networks have so little air time for feature news that they are often forced to consign more detailed coverage to the network Web site. That's why you may hear a national network news anchor, after a brief one-minute report, say, "If you want to learn more about the rising cost of pharmaceuticals, check our Web site at www.msnbc.com."

Although many newspapers and magazines offer readers multimedia coverage on Web sites, some news organizations also offer exclusive reporting on their Internet sites, publishing material on the first or best platform available. The three stories reprinted in this chapter were published before many newspapers offered extensive Internet sites and coverage with television partners. However, here's how the three stories in this chapter might have been presented on the Internet if they had been published in this new, converged environment.

"Ashes to Dust," for example, could be offered on the newspaper's Web site with many powerful enhancements, including a video segment showing details of the two young victims' joint funeral and brief biographical sidebars about each person. Informational graphics could include an interactive map showing the victims' campsite location on Mount St. Helens. The newspaper also might offer a first-person story by the writer, describing the difficulties of covering a funeral. In the case of "Adam & Megan," the newspaper could offer extensive still photographs and numerous video packages about important milestones in the recovery of the children, as well as a visual timeline showing the recovery. Given the amount of time spent reporting the story, the reporter, photographer and editors also might create a "how-we-covered-the-story" video package. There might be audio interviews with the children and links to their personal e-mail accounts. In addition, there might be links to the hospitals and schools that served them and detailed interactive sidebars about the medical technology used to treat severe burns. "First Born, Fast Grown" could use all of the multimedia suggested in the "Ashes to Dust" and "Adam & Megan" coverage as well as sidebars about the financial challenges faced by a single parent. The newspaper could provide reader opinion polls about aspects of the story as well. In each case, writers could be asked to participate in online chat rooms.

"Final Salute," which won the 2006 feature Pulitzer Prize, is an example of a story that used many multimedia journalism forms. As you'll recall, the 12,000-word *Rocky Mountain News* Veteran's Day story follows a Colorado-based Marine major named Steve Beck and his casualty team as they notify and care for families whose loved ones were killed in the Iraq War. Here is Jim Sheeler's lead to give you a feeling for the story's somber, respectful tone.

> Inside a limousine parked on the airport tarmac, Katherine Cathey looked out at the clear
> night sky and felt a kick.

"He's moving," she said. "Come feel him. He's moving."

Her two best friends leaned forward on the soft leather seats and put their hands on her stomach.

"I felt it," one of them said. "I felt it."

Outside, the whine of jet engines swelled.

"Oh, sweetie," her friend said. "I think this is his plane."

As the three young women peered through the tinted windows, Katherine squeezed a set of dog tags stamped with the same name as her unborn son:

James J. Cathey.

"He wasn't supposed to come home this way," she said, tightening her grip on the tags, which were linked by a necklace to her husband's wedding ring.

The women looked through the back window. Then the 23-year-old placed her hand on her pregnant belly.

"Everything that made me happy is on that plane," she said.

They watched as airport workers rolled a conveyor belt to the rear of the plane, followed by six solemn Marines.

Katherine turned from the window and closed her eyes.

"I don't want it to be dark right now. I wish it was daytime," she said. "I wish it was daytime for the rest of my life. The night is just too hard."

Suddenly, the car door opened. A white-gloved hand reached into the limousine from outside—the same hand that had knocked on Katherine's door in Brighton (Colorado) five days earlier.

The man in the deep blue uniform knelt down to meet her eyes, speaking in a soft, steady voice.

"Katherine," said Maj. Steve Beck, "it's time."

Closer than brothers.

The American Airlines 757 couldn't have landed much farther from the war.

The plane arrived in Reno on a Friday evening, the beginning of the 2005 "Hot August Nights" festival—one of the city's biggest—filled with flashing lights, fireworks, carefree music and plenty of gambling.

When a young Marine in dress uniform had boarded the plane to Reno, the passengers smiled and nodded politely. None knew he had just come from the plane's cargo hold, after watching his best friend's casket loaded onboard.

At 24 years old, Sgt. Gavin Conley was only seven days younger than the man in the coffin. The two had met as 17-year-olds on another plane—the one to boot camp in California. They had slept in adjoining top bunks, the two youngest recruits in the barracks.

All Marines call each other brother. Conley and Jim Cathey could have been. They finished each other's sentences, had matching infantry tattoos etched on their shoulders, and cracked on each other as if they had grown up together—which, in some ways, they had.

When the airline crew found out about Conley's mission, they bumped him to first-class. He had never flown there before. Neither had Jim Cathey.

On the flight, the woman sitting next to him nodded toward his uniform and asked if he was coming or going. To the war, she meant.

He fell back on the words the military had told him to say: "I'm escorting a fallen Marine home to his family from the situation in Iraq."

The woman quietly said she was sorry, Conley said.

Then she began to cry.

When the plane landed in Nevada, the pilot asked the passengers to remain seated while Conley disembarked alone. Then the pilot told them why.

The passengers pressed their faces against the windows. Outside, a procession walked toward the plane. Passengers in window seats leaned back to give others a better view. One held a child up to watch.

From their seats in the plane, they saw a hearse and a Marine extending a white-gloved hand into a limousine, helping a pregnant woman out of the car.

On the tarmac, Katherine Cathey wrapped her arm around the major's, steadying herself. Then her eyes locked on the cargo hold and the flag-draped casket.

Inside the plane, they couldn't hear the screams.

Source: "Final Salute," by Jim Sheeler, *Rocky Mountain News* (November 11, 2005). Copyright 2005, *Rocky Mountain News*. Reprinted by permission.

Although the story was printed on Friday, November 11, it was published on the *News'* Web site on November 9, and included a variety of multimedia journalism features. For example, the site featured eight narrated slide shows of photographs used to illustrate the printed story, as well as photographs never published in the newspaper. The shows were narrated by Beck and by Jim Cathey's widow, Katherine, who provided extraordinary access and who also was in the *News* newsroom when the Pulitzer was announced five months after publication. In addition, the "Final Salute" site was linked to a video segment, a reader's forum and readers' letters-to-the-editor. The site also featured direct e-mail links to Sheeler and photojournalist Todd Heisler, who also won the Pulitzer Prize for his work.

The *News* could have used far more multimedia journalism tools but elected not to do so perhaps because of the sensitivity of the subject and a desire for somber simplicity. For example, the *News* could have provided blogs—written or video—by Sheeler and Heisler, graphics such as maps of Iraq where casualties occurred or perhaps timelines contrasting progress of the war with casualties by gender, race and ethnicity, notes by Sheeler and Heisler showing how the reporting was accomplished, podcast versions of the story or the slide shows, video illustrating the use of improved explosive devices that killed and maimed many service members, and links to external Internet sites such as those showing the complete list of Colorado war dead. Multimedia is limited only by the imagination of the journalists and designers.

There are at least three implications for writers in this new multimedia environment. First, newspaper and magazine deadlines will become more like broadcast deadlines: When a story is ready for publication, it will be published immediately, even if the platform is the Internet or a channel belonging to a television partner. Second, publication platforms will become more numerous. Today a story might be printed, posted on the Internet or broadcast. Tomorrow the publishing platforms might include personal digital appliances yet undiscovered. Third, writers must become familiar with the story-telling tools of the future: among them, various writing formats, digital still and video cameras and audio recording technologies.

CHAPTER EIGHT

MARKETING AND WRITING THE MAGAZINE ARTICLE

Why does the title of this chapter place marketing first and writing second? Because the smart freelancer always works in that order.

For the freelancer, coming up with a suitable idea is only the first step in a long process. The idea must be matched to a specific market. Theme and focus must be determined. A query letter must be crafted carefully to show off both the idea and the freelancer's ability to deliver on it. Once an editor responds with an expression of interest, there is more research ahead, interviews to conduct, facts to be gathered. If the research is thorough, there is a substantial amount of material to be organized. All the while you'll be pondering a writing approach, something that will be compatible with the material that usually appears in your chosen magazine market. Only then can you settle down and begin to construct your article in the proper language.

CASE HISTORY

Perhaps the best way to study this ticklish process is to take a successful idea and follow it through its various stages, from inception to the printed page. The following case history is based on an article that ran in one of the top consumer magazines, but we're going to treat it as if it were happening now, and ask you to take over the writing and marketing process. Ready? See if you can find a home for your idea and, at the same time, collect a fat check.

The Idea

Suppose you are using the file folder system of generating ideas. You have, among your many folders, one marked "Smuggling." In it, a pile of newspaper clips has begun to accumulate, so you take the clips out and look them over. You discover that the clips are more or less evenly divided. About half of them deal with professional smuggling—sinister stories filled with intrigue and danger. Most of them are about drug smugglers, heroin busts, shootings, inflated "street values." A few are about arms smuggling and the threat of terrorism. And there are a couple about people-smuggling—airtight vans that bump through the night, carrying frightened illegal aliens across the border, often with disastrous results.

Is there a magazine article here? Sure. Several of them. But you aren't very enthusiastic. Drug stories have been written to death. Unless you can come up with a fresh angle, something other writers have missed, you're out of luck. You're not too fond of the arms-smuggling and people-smuggling stories, either. They're both pretty grim. And you aren't in a grim mood.

So you turn to the remaining clips. They are lighter in nature, a collection of brief stories that have caught the fancy of wire service and newspaper reporters in some of the bigger ports of entry. They deal with average people and some of the odd items they try to sneak past customs officials. There's a clip about a man who tried to slip a live orangutan through customs in his steamer trunk. And another about a woman who hid packets of once-banned Krugerrands in peach cans. Here's a man who was caught in the Belkens smuggling 6,000 marbles. Marbles? And another in New York who tried to smuggle a big shipment of vitamin B-12.

You consider. What about a magazine piece on amateur smugglers, the tricks and foibles of the average, everyday traveler, people just like you? It could be funny. Filled with amusing anecdotes. There are bound to be lots of bizarre smuggling stories out there, if you can find them. Not only wacky items being smuggled, but some pretty strange hiding places for getting them through customs. You could hit the library for more newspaper material. You could pick up some U.S. Customs literature, the handouts prepared for all travelers. You can drop in at the nearest customs office and talk to a few veteran customs officials. Any city with an international airport will have a few. You can talk to friends, too, for personal anecdotes. Everyone has chums who pop off to Europe or Mexico on vacation. So the material should be available, right?

Okay, now you have the germ of an idea. You've even given it a rough focus, narrowing it to amateur smuggling. You won't be able to focus it more finely until you decide on a market.

The Market

Remember the four steps to marketing a magazine article? You read about them in Chapter 3. The first step was to check out the markets that might be interested in your idea. So you whip out your trusty *Writer's Market*. The most logical type of magazine for the amateur smuggling story would be one directed to travelers. They're the people who go through customs themselves and who have surely been tempted at one time or another to try to sneak some item through without declaring it. And there are plenty of magazines available to you. Some devoted exclusively to travel. Another long list of airline magazines. Still other magazines for affluent credit-card holders and members of auto clubs. Riches. If your library trip produces enough material, you could rewrite this story and place it several times.

But you still have to test the idea. You run down the list of travel magazines, because they pay the highest rates, and you pick one towards the top of the line, a magazine that offers from $750 to $3,000 per article. There are two schools of thought, of course, about picking markets. If you have confidence in your ideas and your writing ability, and if you're patient enough and thick-skinned enough to take rejections, begin at the top and work down. On the other hand, if you're a beginner and rejections curdle your soul, it might be smarter to start small and work up. Competition is less extreme at the bottom, and your chances of beefing up your portfolio are better. Rejection can come at either end, so eventually you must train yourself to expect and accept those letters that say, "Thanks, but no thanks." Only when your idea has been rejected six, eight or 12 times do you want to stand back and take another look at the basic idea to see whether it might not be as good as you thought it was.

Now you've got an idea and a tentative market. The next step is to check copies of the magazine and run a library search to see whether they've recently run anything similar. So you drive down to the public library and drop into the reference room for a check of *Reader's Guide*. You get your first jolt. Apparently the idea is not new. Similar articles have appeared in a number of magazines over the years. Does this mean a good idea is down the drain?

You decide to check more closely. Many of the listings are quite old. Six years ago. Eight years. Eleven. Maybe it would help to read the old stories and see just how close to yours they were. (Frankly, a lot of writers would be tempted to give up at this point, but you're stubborn. You're already at the library, and you are foolishly convinced you can give a fresh twist to anything if you work at it. Right?)

Fortunately, you go the next step, wandering up into the stacks to pull out bound volumes of the magazines that published the most likely *Reader's Guide* listings. You don't bother to read them now. You're too dispirited. So you hit the copy machine and feed coins until you have copies of all the similar stories.

You drive home, muttering to yourself, then settle down to read the bad news, expecting the worst. The first article mixes smuggling stories of all stripes, professional and nonprofessional, as a prelude to a detailed history of smuggling. Aha! Maybe the news isn't so bad, after all. You read on. More of the same. A couple of pieces are a mishmash of smuggling anecdotes, strung together like jokes, with no particular focus or theme. All of the articles are heavy on anecdotes, and a couple are well written, but they don't really focus on the minor wars and skirmishes being fought between customs officials and your own white-collar criminals. Maybe there's a chance. You'll write a query letter and test the idea on an editor. What can you lose? A bit of time. A sheet of paper. A postage stamp.

The Query Letter

The query letter is often the most crucial step in marketing a magazine article. You can't just sit down and write a good query letter off the top of your head. The quickest way to get an idea rejected is to send an editor a vague, wishy-washy query, so before you approach your computer, be sure you have your story idea clearly established in your mind.

First you sift through your clips and try to firm up your approach, narrowing, focusing. Another trip to the library is in order. You could have done this on the earlier trip if you hadn't come away from the literature search with such jangled nerves. But there's time. And your confidence is growing. You still think you can turn this into a winning article.

The query letter has several functions. In addition to forcing you to consider your story idea and to bring it into sharp focus, it gives you a chance to poke at the edges and probe for weaknesses before you ever pass it on to the editor. You pick a tentative theme. You might even tinker with the organization a bit, in order to organize your letter. This will help you greatly when it's time to write the finished article.

The query also helps the editor. It's a sales pitch. It has to be written clearly, persuasively, and with a faint flavor of your personal writing style. An editor can scan the letter easily and decide whether the idea will be of any interest to the magazine's readers. But the idea isn't everything. A good editor will also learn a lot about you from the letter. Remember, a query is designed not only to sell your idea, but also to sell yourself as the writer. If you write a sloppy letter, filled with grammatical errors and misspellings, an editor will assume that it represents your usual writing style.

The query saves time and energy. A query will get you a quick yes or no from an editor without the back-breaking fuss and bother of writing the whole article. And it gives you a chance to run down a list of editors, one at a time, to see if your idea can spur interest somewhere along the line. If they all say no, then perhaps the idea isn't strong enough.

The point is, you don't write the article until you get an expression of interest. If no one is interested, you've saved a lot of time and work.

For an experienced writer with a good track record, the query letter may bring a firm assignment. The editor will tell you what he or she wants, how much you'll be paid and possibly even offer you a "kill fee." That means you'll get a certain amount of money even if the magazine decides later not to run the article, as well as the right to sell the story to another publication. The beginning writer isn't so lucky. If your list of credits is short, most editors will consider you still unproven. The most they're apt to offer you is a promise to look at the finished piece "on speculation." Don't be dismayed. At least the editor has given you a strong indication of interest. If you can deliver an article that is as good as the query, you'll get your sale.

There is no set format for a query letter, but editors generally agree that the best queries are short, 300 to 500 words, and typed on a single page. Perhaps the most popular form is one that comes in three stages. You open with a brief paragraph that summarizes the general theme of your article. Then, still briefly but with more detail, you give some specifics (this is a good chance to show the kind of material that will appear in anecdotal form). After the fuller middle section, you revert to a brief paragraph that tells why you should be the one to write it. Again, for the experienced writer, this is easy. A partial listing of better credits will quickly prove to the editor that the writer is dependable and can deliver. The beginner with no credits uses other ammunition. Perhaps you have access to persons or facts not generally available. Or maybe you have personal experiences or a background that has prepared you to write the story. If you have nothing at all to offer here, then detail the writing approach you will take on the story and hope your query is crafted smoothly enough to convince the editor that you can write.

Let's look at a couple of examples. First, you'll write a query letter to pitch your smuggling story. Assume you've done some extra research now, and also assume you are tackling the story as a beginner, with no writing credits worth boasting about. Remember, you start with a general statement of theme, follow it with a few specific examples, then wrap up with your suggested method of treatment. A one-page query might look something like this:

Mr. Caskie Stinnett, Editor

Dear Mr. Stinnett:

Would you be interested in a capsule guide to white-collar smuggling? Amateur smugglers have become wildly ingenious in their attempts to beat customs officials, and the items they choose to smuggle are frequently as unlikely as the methods they use.

Professional smugglers and amateurs alike are attracted by the profits of such stable items as gold, silver, watches, jewelry, liquor and narcotics. But odd import laws around the globe have placed the profit incentive on other such unpredictable items as tropical fish, steak sauce, nylon underwear, lottery tickets, cloves and Korean seaweed. It has reached the point that officials not only don't know where to look, they aren't sure what they'll find when they look there. For example:

> Two husky Texas men were led to an airport search room in New York and forced to undress. Each of the burly Texans was found to be wearing a lace pantie girdle, stuffed with contraband watch movements.

> A woman bringing six cans of peaches home from South Africa ran into trouble when customs officials X-rayed the cans and found a stack of Krugerrands in each, sloshing in the peach juice. The coins had been inserted through holes cut in the sides, rewelded, then covered with new labels.

> A smuggler was caught in Serbia with 6,000 marbles. Serbien importing agencies have cut back on imports. The marbles would have brought the man a profit of $400.

> Other odd items have been found embedded in chocolate bars, tucked in diapers, in false-bottomed chamber pots, in the gas tanks of cars, even sewn inside a teddy bear.

Humorous smuggling methods, oddball contraband items, the penalties and embarrassments that befall the unsuccessful amateur, all will be covered in the proposed article, as well as some tongue-in-cheek suggestions for beating the game. Suggested length: 2,000 to 3,000 words. Suggested treatment: light, simple, factual, some anecdote.

Does the idea interest you?

Most sincerely,

Now you'll put it in the mail and wait, and while you're waiting, let's talk about some alternative query forms. You may be wondering why no mention has been made of e-mail queries. And some freelance writers prefer to place their queries by telephone or in person. E-mails and face-to-face meetings may be fine once you get to know an editor and do some work for a magazine. But it's too easy to ignore unsolicited e-mails and strange voices on the telephone. Besides, a more formal snail-mail letter forces you to marshal your thoughts and present your ideas in the most advantageous light. Many writers aren't that good on an oral level anyway. They may be a whiz behind the computer, stringing words together with éclat and élan, but when they have to talk on the telephone, they freeze up, punctuating pedestrian language with "uhs" and "you knows."

As for talking to editors face to face, that's an excellent plan—if you happen to live in New York or Chicago or Los Angeles where most editors seem to congregate. However, most freelancers live in smaller communities of the American heartland and are lucky if they have five or six small publications within driving distance. Once you get to know your editors, e-mails and the telephone will probably become your best friends. Not only will you be able to query by e-mail, but receive assignments by e-mail. Magazine style sheets are furnished by e-mail, as well as review templates to show you exactly how to put the reviews together. You send all finished copy, as well as illustrations, to your editor as an e-mail attachment. Scanned art or screen shots can be attached to e-mail as jpeg files (quick and easy), or as tiff files (slower to send, but minus some of the "artifacts" that creep into jpegs). If you need screenshots, a couple of the better capture devices are Snapz Pro for Mac, and HyperSnap for Windows.

In the meantime, let's stick with a formal written query to break our editorial ice. Our first example is not your only choice. There are alternative written query forms as well. You'll want to look them over to find the one that works best for you. Some writers sidestep the three-stage query and opt for a shorter version that is intended only to tickle the imagination of the editor. Here is a simple query that could just as easily have been the lead for a pleasant, lightweight feature article. It was addressed to one of the in-flight magazines, published by an airline that does a lot of business with international flights.

> Dear Mr. Huddleston:
>
> If you find out your spouse is being unfaithful, you can bite off his nose. If your luck has turned from poor to worse, you can visit your local evil-eye lady who will remove the evil spirits and restore your happiness. If your daughter's fiancé runs out at the last minute, your sons and husband can kill him.
>
> That is, if you happen to be Cretan.
>
> To the average tourist, Crete is the largest and one of the most fascinating of the Greek isles. It boasts miles and miles of secluded beaches. The people are warm and hospitable, from the typical ruddy-faced Cretan, chewing moussaka while he plays with his worry beads, to the vibrant tavernas where dark men dance and laugh between crowded tables.
>
> But there is another side to the Cretan way of life. Cretan culture, folkways, and superstitions make the Cretan character one of the most puzzling of all the Mediterranean people.
>
> In an article of about 2,000 words, I plan to spin out some of the little-known aspects of Cretan life: the mystery of the "Evil Eye," how marriages are prearranged and how some unlucky men get tricked into it, what makes a Cretan violent, and many other offbeat cultural facts. I have spent the past five summers living with a Cretan family and have a slew of anecdotes, stories, and myths to offer.
>
> Would you be interested in seeing the article on speculation?
>
> Yours very truly,

This particular query was written by a young woman just getting into the freelance business. Although it's shorter, it still tells enough about the proposed article to interest an editor. And it's smoothly written, which gives the editor confidence in her ability to pull it off. Notice the way she personalized it at the end. With no credits to offer, she offers instead a rich personal involvement, pointing out her five summers of invested time gathering anecdotes, stories and myths. And, knowing her limitations in writing experience, she offers the article on speculation. The editor gave her a quick yes.

For the experienced writer, a simpler approach is available. The next sample query was written by John Simpson, a freelance writer who began writing only after he retired from military life. Simpson always writes to magazines first, requesting copies and writer's guidelines. Then, when he's had a chance to study the market, he whips up an idea proposal and sends it off. He doesn't bother with catchy phrasemaking and provocative leads. He presents his idea simply, adds a quote or two, then offers proof of his ability by referring to his writing background and enclosing representative samples of his work.

This query was written to *Candy Industry,* a journal for the candy-making trade, after Simpson saw a story in his local newspaper about the opening of a new candy plant. He didn't even have to do preliminary research. The newspaper story provided adequate query materials. All he had to do was wait for a positive response, then set up an appointment to gather his story information.

Dear Ms. Magee:

Thank you for the writer's guidelines you recently sent me.

Dinstuhl's was founded in 1902 in a small downtown store in this community, and the family-owned candy company is still growing. The owners recently opened a new 11,000-square-feet, free-standing plant to supply four retail stores and the candy departments they operate in six Goldsmith's (Federated Stores) department stores.

"We don't try to compete on price with the big candy makers because we use only double-x cream, real butter, and pure dark chocolate in our candies," says Gene Dinstuhl, who at age 15 started learning candy making from his father. His grandfather started the original store. Gene's wife, Grace, manages the sales end while Gene and son Gary mix and stir the chocolate and fillings for 200 kinds of candies.

I would like to do a feature for you on Dinstuhl's operations, covering all aspects of the business in accordance with your guidelines. I can provide pics in black-and-white or color, using a 35-mm camera. Interested?

I do a weekly column for a local business journal and I am a correspondent for the money section of *USA Today*. I also write for several trade journals. Representative samples of my work are enclosed.

Most sincerely,

The Waiting Game

Once the query is in the mail, how long do you wait for an answer? That's a tough question and one that freelance writers have to face over and over. Most editors are very good about responding in two to four weeks. Some take longer. A few, unfortunately, never seem to answer at all. Editors are human. As in all professions, there are good ones and bad ones. A few just can't get organized. Your letter might sit with a pile of other unanswered letters for months before the editor gets around to writing back. If at all.

Should you wait? A reasonable time, yes. Patience is a necessity, not a virtue, for freelance writers. But if you have several ideas floating among the markets, the time will come when you've waited at least six weeks to hear editorial response to a favorite idea without a glimmer of an answer. What do you do? Most market listings give you an approximate response time—"Reports within four weeks." If your topic is timely, give them that long and no longer. If time isn't a problem, give them an extra two weeks as a courtesy. Then write a follow-up letter. Keep it polite. You're not out to antagonize editors. You just want to make sure they received your query. You might send a photocopy of the original query letter along with your cover note (always keep copies of everything— queries, articles, correspondence). If you still get no satisfaction, you might try a phone call. Or you might just cross the magazine off your list and route the query to a new editor.

It isn't considered cricket to submit the same idea to more than one editor at a time. And it's dangerous. If you get two yes responses, then you'll have to write one editor and confess that you've sold the idea to another. That will put you on a "drop dead" list at that magazine. But once an editor has exceeded the stated response time, especially if you've given the editor a couple of "grace" weeks on top of the usual response time, then you are no longer committed to that editor. You may go ahead and submit your proposal elsewhere without violating your own personal set of ethics.

There's another school of thought about simultaneous submissions. Some highly respected freelancers point out that it's tough enough to make a living as a freelance writer without giving editors the definite advantage of one-at-a-time queries. They say go ahead and query as many magazines as may be viable markets for a story, and do it simultaneously. Even if two editors want the article (this doesn't happen often, admittedly), just send it to the first editor who asks for it and offer to write a different version for the second editor. These same freelancers suggest that instead of ending up on a "drop dead" list, you may well impress the editors with the popularity of your story ideas and whet their appetites for future ideas. And next time they may not drag their feet so long before saying yes.

Whichever school of thought you follow, you'll probably find that you have the best chance of success if you design your query precisely for one specific market, the best, and send it only to that market. The reason is simple. One needs to focus each query just as carefully as one focuses the written article. If you decide to query more than one market at the same time, at least make sure you tailor each query to fit each specific market. Sending photocopied letters with a different address at the top of each is the least likely way to make a sale.

You'll have to decide which position, individual queries or simultaneous queries, you prefer to follow. Personal ethics, as you'll see in Chapter 10, can't be imposed. You have to weigh the evidence and make up your own mind. But the once-strong insistence on presenting your ideas to one market at a time is beginning to loosen.

It's time to get back to your smuggling proposal. You've been lucky. Your response has taken only 10 days. That makes you nervous. A quick response can mean either that they liked your proposal and hurried to pin it down, or that they considered it so bad they didn't have to think very long before rejecting it. You tear the envelope open. The news is good. The letter says:

Hello there—

We like your smuggling proposal very much. We're prepared to offer $3,000 for first North American rights, and in the unlikely event that your ms. is refused, we will return it plus a 20% guarantee of the original fee.

Stick to your proposal, concentrating on the temptations and shenanigans of the average American traveler, how he or she is unmasked by customs, and what attitude customs people have toward this sort of thing. Are they bored, amused, exasperated, what? What sort of article is the average traveler most likely to smuggle? What are the trite concealments that each, no doubt, believes to be a unique contrivance? Do amateur smugglers give themselves away with telltale attitudes? *Und so weiter.*

I needn't remind you that anecdotes, anecdotes, anecdotes make the piece. Use the best for your opening, and save the second-best for your tag. Oh, and lay off professional smuggling unless it can provide a good story or illustrate some specific point you want to make. We're interested in focusing on the amateurs.

Good luck. Write hard. Write well.

Best wishes,

Excellent. Not only do you have a go-ahead, but the editor has given you some definite pointers on how to handle it. The editor has even refined your focus slightly. You're going to deal primarily with American travelers, and you want to know something about the official attitudes of customs inspectors.

Gathering the Information

Now it's time to go to work. You'll have to finish your library research and set up interviews. Obviously you'll want to talk to customs officials early in your interview schedule. If there's a border town handy, you'll drive to it. Or you'll settle for an office in a federal building, or the nearest international airport. But you'll need a list of questions. What should you ask? You pull your thoughts together and come up with the following:

Tentative Questions for Customs Officials

1. How many U.S. customs inspectors are there?
2. How are you trained? School? On the job?
3. Question thoroughly on the behavior of smugglers:
    a. How do you unmask potential smugglers?
    b. How do they give themselves away?
    c. What behavior patterns are typical of smugglers?
    d. What is the attitude of customs? (bored? amused? exasperated?)
4. Why do people try to smuggle? What motivates them?
5. Who smuggles most often? Men? Women?
6. What about kids? Do children smuggle? What items?
7. What kinds of things are most likely to be smuggled?
8. What are some of the unusual items that are smuggled?
9. What are the trite hiding places that each potential smuggler thinks is unique?
10. What are some of the unusual hiding places?
11. What is the rate for informers? Still 25 percent?
12. Do people often smuggle animals? Examples?
13. Do people ever use animals to divert suspicion?

14. How does border inspection differ from other points of entry, like airports and seaports?
15. How many cars, for example, cross the border daily from Mexico? From Canada? Can you give an estimate?
16. What leads to a thorough car search? Tips? Behavior? Spot checks?
17. Does the list of duty-exempt (and dutiable) items change periodically?
18. Are people ever foolish enough to offer bribes?
19. What's the punishment when a person is caught?
20. Can you estimate how many people get away with it?

The list grows longer, but you try to keep it manageable. And, of course, you'll be prepared to drop questions and follow any digression that sounds potentially useful. You'll also ask customs personnel to show you where they store confiscated items. Just walking among the shelves and asking questions about what you see may give you some new leads.

The fact-gathering process is mandatory. You'd far rather do too much research than do too little. So you set out. You strain your eyes looking at microfilm and microfiche and the results of electronic searches. You spend a couple of days interviewing customs officials and asking your questions. You make telephone calls to friends for personal anecdotes. You gather and scour and question and scribble notes. And finally you heap all of your notes and pieces of scrap paper and index cards and pamphlets and photocopies into a swelling mound several inches high. You groan. Out of this chaos of notes and quotes and loose bits of information, you must now create order.

Organizing the Story

A magazine article is constructed like a building, piece by piece and all interlocking. There has to be a solid foundation. Then you need a strong framework to support the rest of the structure. Only at the end can you deal with niceties such as carpeting and wood paneling and tinted windows. Like the builder, the article writer needs a blueprint. The way you build your story becomes a public demonstration of your logic, your thinking processes, your ability to link materials together coherently. You'll sit down and choose your foundation, your structural framework, your ultimate design. All before you start to write. Once you've decided the purpose of your article—to instruct, to inform, to entertain or whatever—you choose your materials carefully, making sure that each fits in its logical place, contributing to the final design. If your organizational blueprint shows weaknesses, you correct them. If some of your research materials don't fit or fail to contribute in a meaningful way to your central structure, you discard them. If you find your inventory of facts lacking in some respects, you go back to the research stockpile for more. It's far easier to make corrections and to supplement your research during the planning stages than it is once you start writing.

How do you prepare a blueprint? Generally, there are three basic methods for organizing material. Some writers use file cards. Others use the outline method. Some even turn to an approach called "cut-and-slash," or the "paper doll" process. There are other approaches as well, but they are usually variations of one of the three. The important thing is to use the one that works best for you. You'll probably try all three on one story or another before you make your final choice. Some writers never settle for a single method. They continue to use all three, skipping back and forth from method to method as the spirit moves them. Again, if it works for you, then it's right, no matter how illogical it may sound.

The most orderly method is the index-card approach. It's perfect for people with tidy minds and mountains of material to put in order. But it's also time consuming. It calls for transcription of every anecdote, every solid quote, every usable fact on a separate index card. The advantage is that the cards can be shuffled endlessly until you have them in some kind of logical, acceptable order. Then you can just lay the cards by your computer and begin to write, turning the cards one by one as you put the story together.

A faster method is the outline procedure. You still have to go through all your notes and become thoroughly reacquainted with them before you can put a good outline together, but then your final structure can be put to paper and pinned to a bulletin board above your word processor for easy reference. The finished outline can take many forms. It may be a single sheet that lists only your broader topics in the order that you intend to present them, or it may be an exhaustive outline, several pages long, giving you clues to each of your research and interview notes and how you plan to incorporate them.

The cut-and-slash method is the sloppiest, but it's also the easiest. All it takes is a pair of scissors, your regular notes in their original form, and a large space where you can shuffle and organize your material. You go through your notes with scissors in hand, cutting individual ideas and thoughts apart. If you have a sheet with six entries on it, for example, you cut the sheet into six separate strips and lay them out like paper dolls on a table or on the floor or on whatever large, clear surface will allow you to see all of your entries at once. If the source of your individual entries or facts or quotes is important (and sources nearly always are), be sure to make a note on each strip. Once you cut them apart, it's sometimes hard to remember just which set of notes a free-floating strip came from. You'll end up with all kinds of shapes—fat stubs of paper, thin strips, odd squares, dog-leg shapes. Then you pick through them and organize them as you would with more orderly index cards, but without having to retype any of them. (Warning: If you use the cut-and-slash method, make sure you live alone or with someone who is patient and understanding. You may end up covering an entire living-room floor, and the floor may stay littered for two or three days before you finally come up with an order that pleases you.)

What you're looking for is some logical formula that will make the writing process easier. This is where analysis of successful articles comes into play. You may have noticed that your target magazine uses variations of some simple formula, such as:

1. opening anecdote
2. statement of theme or subject
3. anecdote
4. factual background material interspersed with anecdotes
5. interview
6. concluding anecdote

If so, you may then sort through your materials and prepare your own version of the same formula. Or perhaps your target magazine uses a tabulated form, in which you follow your lead with a statement of theme, then present your material in separate sections in which you first define your topic, then give examples, then follow with factual background material before moving to the next topic. Once you have analyzed what your magazine prefers to use, it makes your own organizational chores easier.

Your organizational formula for the smuggling story is somewhat simplified by the letter from your editor. You've already been told to start with an anecdote and end with an anecdote, and you know that each of your subtopics should also be laced with anecdotes. You decide to use an invisible version of the formula listed above. You're going to use a tabulated approach, but without concrete sections. You want a smooth flow that makes each subject seem to lead logically to the next, and that calls for transitions, not subheads. So you separate your notes, quotes and facts into distinct piles, trying to find some common ground for each of several groupings. You come up with the following:

1. ingenious methods for smuggling
2. predictable methods for smuggling
3. kinds of people who smuggle
4. items most likely to be smuggled
5. unlikely items that are smuggled
6. how smugglers are caught
7. attitudes of customs officials
8. checking customs regulations

You know you'll have to shuffle some of the categories around, rather than just present them as big blocks, but at least you have an orderly progression in mind. You may well intersperse methods with types of people who smuggle, and you may want to use some of the unlikely items in describing methods. But with your materials in discretely organized piles, individual facts and anecdotes will be easier to find.

Sitting Down to Write

At last, you're ready to write the article. You have a structural plan you can live with, and you have a solid idea of how to treat the lead. It should be an easy romp from here. But you need one more thing. You need your original query within easy reach. Remember, the query sold the idea, so it's up to you to deliver what you've promised (this is why you must always keep a copy of your query). You know a number of your gathered notes will fall by the wayside during the writing process. Some things simply won't fit. Others, by the time you get to them, will seem extraneous. But if something was mentioned in the query, you need to make a special effort to get it in. Unless, of course, the game plan has changed. For example, your query mentioned a man caught in Serbie with 6,000 marbles. Your editor has indicated a preference for the foibles of American travelers. The Serb can be dropped. But you must try to deliver on the rest of the query. You might even use one of your query entries as the lead.

In addition to the lead and the outline, you've added another contrivance to help you put this article together. You've written yourself a brief note, defining the purpose of the article, and you've posted it in a prominent place above your desk. The purpose of this note is twofold: It will remind you constantly of the direction you intend to take and keep you from drifting into blind alleys, and it will also be useful when you write your state-ment of theme and incorporate it into the article following the lead. Some magazine writ-ers like to add a fourth prewriting contrivance. They toy with titles until they come up with a tentative working title that they can live with. The title, like the note defining the aim of the article, keeps them from straying.

Crutches. That's all these prewriting devices are. They help you write easily and smoothly. But like any good crutch, sometimes they have to be adjusted to fit the stride. Leads can change. And there are times when you will have to deviate from even the most carefully prepared outline. Titles will almost certainly be changed, if not by you then by the editor. The least likely crutch to be adjusted is the definition of purpose, since the pur-pose of your article is usually what sold the idea in the first place. But there are situations in which even this device must be sacrificed.

Now you're ready to sit at your word processor and go to work. In essence, there are two basic approaches to writing: the rough-draft approach and the fine-draft approach. Each has advantages and disadvantages. You must choose the one that works best for you.

The rough-draft writer works fast, and sometimes incautiously. The idea is to get ideas and words down on paper, as quickly and painlessly as possible. After organizing carefully, the rough-drafter writes through the entire article, from beginning to end, taking the first word choice that comes to mind. Then rough-drafters may work through three or four more drafts, polishing and refining more and more with each succeeding draft. Even so, a rough-draft writer has to be careful not to allow sloppy grammar or poor spelling to slip into a first draft. If you aren't sure how to spell *silhouette,* and you just slop it in any-old-which-way on your first draft, it's apt to look okay to you on your second draft and you'll forget to look up the correct spelling. The same holds true for direct quotes. If you use your own words on the first draft, without checking the precise words used by your source, you may forget in later drafts that you've paraphrased, and never get around to correcting the quote. A good rule of thumb, if you opt for the rapid-rough-draft technique, is to enter a parenthetical question mark (?) after any spelling, grammatical usage, quote or piece of information that you aren't sure of. The question mark will remind you later to check up on it.

Fine-draft writers, on the other hand, work at a slower pace, polishing phrases as they go along. These writers are trying for a finished product on the first draft. They check spellings and grammatical constructions as they come to them. They check quotes and sources for absolute accuracy. They reach frequently for a thesaurus in an attempt to select the exact, precise word. They stare at the keyboard, reaching inwardly for some colorful turn of phrase. They work hard at balancing sentence length so there will be a refreshing mix of long and short sentences. They work very carefully throughout the first draft, pol-ishing away until everything pleases them.

The fine-draft writer, as a result, usually does less rewriting than the rough-draft writer. But even a good fine-draft writer will have to do some rewriting. After the copy goes cold, a writer will nearly always find paragraphs that don't link together as neatly as they should or passages that sag and don't hold interest. To be successful, a writer must be prepared to correct any faults in the copy, no matter how hard he or she worked the first time around.

Both methods take about the same length of time. A rough-draft writer can hash through three drafts in about the same length of time that it takes the fine-draft writer to tune and retune a single draft. Both methods work. Both are valid. Pick the one that best fits your temperament and personality.

The Lead.   You learned a lot in Chapter 6 about leads and the many types available to you. The list works well for both newspapers and magazines, though magazine leads are usually longer, and are often called "lead blocks" because of the many paragraphs involved. But there is another type of lead you should meet now. In addition, there is a kind of lead you met in Chapter 6 that you should meet again in its expanded form. The new lead is called the *anecdotal lead*. The lead you met previously is called the *situation lead*. Anecdotal leads can be quite long when fully developed, but they're probably the most popular lead types of all for magazines. An anecdotal lead tells a small story, with a beginning, a middle and an end. The situation lead, as you read in Chapter 6, sets a scene or creates an atmosphere. Actually, the two leads are close cousins. An anecdotal lead nearly always uses the scene-setting or atmospheric elements of a situation lead. But a situation lead doesn't have to tell a story. You'll see examples of both lead types in the next chapter, when you study devices that can be used to improve your writing. You'll also be treated to some hints on how to unearth anecdotes.

But you're ready now to write the lead for your smuggling story. Following your editor's suggestion, you're going to use the anecdotal lead approach. But you've decided to improve on the suggestion. For starters, you're going to use a lead block with three distinct anecdotes to set the tone of your story. You'll use three modes of travel (plane, ship and car) and three different entry points (New York, San Francisco and a Mexican/American border town) in order to convey the point that amateur smuggling happens all the time and in lots of different places. You'll also combine the anecdotal approach with the direct address lead mentioned in the earlier lead list, in order to involve your reader. You'll put your reader in all three episodes, suggesting that he or she is also a world traveler (it never hurts to stroke the reader's ego). Finally, you'll deliberately contrast your burly Texans with the feminine undergarments they're both using to smuggle watch parts, in an attempt to set the stage for a few snickers and smiles. You want your readers to know they're going to enjoy themselves.

This is what you come up with:

> Maybe you were there when they climbed off the plane at New York's Kennedy International, the two tall Texans who held to the rear of the customs line, politely giving room to those of your fellow passengers who pressed forward impatiently. They were big men, square-shouldered and tan. You might have given them a second look, but the Customs men gave them a third, noting that they were both a shade paunchy and that both walked stiffly, with short mincing steps. Thirty minutes later, in the airport search room, the two Texans were red-faced and mortified, and Customs inspectors were suppressing smiles. Each of the burly men wore a frilly lace pantie girdle. One girdle contained close to one hundred expensive Swiss watch movements. The other, more tightly packed, held nearly two hundred.
>
> Or perhaps you were in San Francisco not long thereafter, on the passenger liner, maybe coming down the gangplank behind the well-dressed elderly woman wearing a new mink stole who rushed excitedly to embrace her sister. When the pair parted, the stole was on the sister. Two minutes later both fur and traveler were taken in tow by Customs inspectors, and the lady was making the inevitable protests and explanations of "I didn't know it was wrong," and "It was just too hot to wear it through the inspection."

Or maybe it was Nogales, Arizona, and you were parked in the inspection shed waiting for the Customs man while he listened to similar protestations from a pleasant young couple returning from a two-week auto trip to Mexico. They had willingly relinquished an extra bottle of Kahlúa after the inspector had explained that no liquor allowance could be made for their three-year-old son. Their cooperative smiles vanished, though, when the inspector took the top off the big water jug on the floorboards. Four liters of contraband Herradura tequila were sloshing gently inside.

Now you've set the stage. Your lead block is complete and you're ready to follow the three anecdotal paragraphs with your statement of theme, the flag that tells readers succinctly what they will be reading about. Not every magazine article carries a statement of theme, of course, but most of them would be improved if they did. It's an excellent device for summing up the material that is to follow, and both editors and readers appreciate it. Your statement of theme, based on the statement of purpose that you pinned on the bulletin board, comes in two paragraphs. The first short paragraph is purely transitional, to lead from the three anecdotes to the statement itself. The statement of theme goes like this:

Chances are, even if you were there, you didn't linger over the imbroglios of your fellow travelers. Because chances are you were running contraband yourself.

By land, by sea, by air they come, America's growing band of amateur smugglers, each convinced his hoary dodge is a brand-new wrinkle on how to beat the Customs inspectors. Trying to slip contraband past Customs is almost as popular as flimflamming the Internal Revenue Service. Practically everyone has tried it at one time or another. The game might be something as simple as bootlegging an extra bottle of trade-marked perfume or fudging a few dollars on the declaration forms, or it might be something extravagant, like hiding a pearl necklace in a hollowed-out cheese or contending that the $2,000 Swedish camera hanging around your neck was bought in the U.S. before you left.

Now you have a lead and a statement of theme and you're ready to tackle the body of the story.

The Body.   Writing the body of the article should be easy now, if your outline works. You'll start with a couple of quotes, to give your article the aura of authority, then move from topic to topic with a blend of general statements and specific anecdotes. At this point, rather than interrupt the flow for author interpolations, try another exercise. Watch for shifts in subject matter and search out the transitional devices. For example, at the end of the next paragraph, which deals with motivation for smuggling, a Customs inspector refers to amateur smugglers as "white-collar cheats." The following paragraph introduces the subject of hiding places. To link the two paragraphs, the article resorts to repetition of a phrase. "Because they are amateurs, many of the white-collar cheats are . . ." This use of brief repetition as a connective creates overlapping paragraphs, even though the topics may be quite different. It is a standard device, and you will see it used often in the copy to come. A quote ends, "And we miss it everyplace." The next paragraph carries over by saying, "But the would-be smuggler can't rely on their missing much." Repetition, when used intentionally and carefully, can be effective. Conversely, accidental repetition, using the same word too often or adding nothing to improve the flow or to propel the story, can be irritating to the reader. So use it with care.

A number of other connective and technical devices are used in this article to keep the reader involved. See how many of them you can recognize. You'll delve more deeply into writing and technical devices in the next chapter, but several of them are demonstrated in the body of this smuggling story.

Here then, uninterrupted, is the remainder of the article.

Why do amateurs try to smuggle? "Profit," one veteran U.S. Customs Bureau official says. "Or, say, 90 percent profit; 2 percent for the thrill of it. And up to 8 percent are just born crooked." An inspector in the field comments, "You'd be surprised at the number of so-called respectable people who smuggle. The more affluent, the better educated a man or a woman is, the more likely they are to try to sneak in items without paying duty. We call them 'white-collar cheats.'"

Because they are amateurs, many of the white-collar cheats are predictable, constantly re-inventing trite old dodges. But amateur smuggling techniques can be wildly ingenious, and the items smuggled are frequently as unlikely as the methods used. It has reached the point where harried Customs agents not only don't know where to look, they're not sure what they'll find when they look there. "They hide stuff everyplace," an officer says. "We find it everyplace. And we miss it everyplace."

But the would-be smuggler can't rely on their missing much. While lengthening lines of travelers have inspired large international airports such as Kennedy to adopt the spotcheck system after checking hand luggage, smaller airports and land ports of entry still have a 100 percent baggage check policy. Grit and luck are needed to be a successful smuggler under such circumstances. It would also help if the Customs Bureau's employees would lose all files and develop amnesia, for their sagacity in spotting smugglers is as deep as the Mariana Trench, and their memories of past subterfuges are limitless.

"Sometimes they hide a thing so well it almost has to reach out and bite us before we spot it," one East Coast agent says. He describes the brief smuggling career of a mild animal-loving grandmother with blue-gray hair who kept crooning to a sleeping cat in a basket on her arm while the inspector went through her luggage. When she saw him looking at the cat, she promptly produced a properly documented health certificate and said, "I had to give her a tranquilizer. Poor kitty, she's so nervous about this sort of thing." The inspector, an animal lover himself, reached out to stroke poor kitty, and the woman jerked back in horror, but too late. Kitty was unusually stiff and hard. Upon closer investigation, he found she was stuffed, with an Italian gold necklace and matching earrings hidden in the stuffing.

Little old ladies can be hell. Smuggling appeals to their instinct for stretching the shopping dollar, well-developed after years of exposure to bargain basements, discount houses and August white sales. But women of all ages, men, children and even live animals (as accomplices) are consistently tagged. Kitty is only one of a whole zoo of teddy bear tummies, terrycloth ducks, stuffed armadillos, stuffed Oriental fish and, for the less imaginative, plain old pillows and chocolate bars. The Customs catalogue of sneaky-hiding-places-we-have-nabbed covers a gamut of oddball devices from a fake hunchback hump and a hollow glass eye to rewelded cans of tomato paste or peaches with gold Krugerrands inside, and hollowed-out picture frames, golf clubs, billiard cues and crutches.

Clever concealment isn't the only dodge. Some amateur smugglers pin their hopes more on unsettling Customs men than they do on fooling them. Like the wise-guy Texas motorist who carefully trained his pet bulldog to snap at Customs men. When courageous officials collared both dog and man, they found twenty-four liters of assorted Mexican booze, a popular border item, under the upholstery of the car seat. A less violent method for turning off Customs men worked three times in a row for the wife of a museum curator—before she got caught. On return trips from Europe, she always placed her contraband in a small overnight case and covered it with a neat layer of sanitary napkins. Young Customs officials closed the bag immediately or searched cursorily, too uneasy to do a good job. But she met her downfall on the fourth trip, when she drew a grizzled inspector who turned the bag inside out, exposing four bottles of undeclared perfume. "He'd been married for twenty-two years, had three daughters and was beyond embarrassment," she relates. "Oh well, at least it worked for a while."

Some gambits don't ever work. Neophytes should ponder two choice cases of amateurs who didn't do their homework. One man was caught with a diamond ring inside an apple, and the other was found with smuggled watches hidden inside a hollowed-out book. Both might have succeeded, except that apples—potential carriers of the fruit fly—are never admitted, and the book the other guy chose was a copy of *Fanny Hill,* at that time on the prohibited list. While *Fanny Hill* is no longer excluded from the country (Supreme Court pornography rulings some years ago drastically shortened Customs' list of banned reading matter), the apple still gets stopped. One fruit fly can cost a million dollars in damaged crops and illegal fruit and plants are seized on an average of one lot every three minutes of the year.

To be a successful smuggler, one should be wary of the creaking, overused gimmicks which still hold up the Customs counters almost daily. Most popular (and most obvious to the inspectors) is the ubiquitous girdle and its bulging variations—canvas belts strapped to the body, special pockets sewn into a dress, long winter underwear, "pregnant" women without a suitable quantity of maternity clothes in their luggage, and the old chestnut that every beginner thinks is new, the baby's diaper.

An amazing number of travelers also try the Edgar Allan Poe *Purloined Letter* procedure, attempting to hide things out in the open. They drape new coats over their arms, slide watches on their wrists and rings on their fingers, don the new Gucci moccasins, convinced that Customs officials will never notice. They do. Customs agents also have a specialist's eye for the switched clothing label. Women are all too often convinced they can bamboozle inspectors by replacing the foreign label on a new frock or fur with a Bonwit Teller or Neiman-Marcus label brought from home. But they have been known to make the mistake of tossing exotic foreign labels they can't bear to part with back into the trunks. Label-switching won't work anyway. Customs agents can usually recognize hand-sewing immediately.

Routine smuggling techniques are used to smuggle routine items. "It depends on where people have been," one Customs agent says. "Whatever is the best buy in the countries they've visited, that's what they usually try to sneak through." In the large international airports and seaports on the East Coast, inspectors automatically watch for cameras, jewelry and clothing from Europe, while on the West Coast such items as jade and silk turn up. Canadian border favorites include furs and whiskeys. Inspectors along the Mexican border expect and get amateur traffic in marijuana, liquor, leather goods and fruit.

There are 20,000 items on the dutiable list, however, and some pretty far-out things have been grabbed by customs: an orangutan at Dulles International; pure vitamin B-12 valued at $96,000 in New York; cows on the Canadian border—wearing galoshes to avoid leaving a trail of hoofprints in the snow and chewing soap (they liked it) to muffle their moos; parrots from Mexico, chloroformed or with their beaks taped to keep them from squawking. "Any time people see where they can make a few dollars—or a lot of dollars—you'll find people who will try to figure out some way to beat the government out of the money," an official explains.

Some profit-hungry beginners can lose their amateur standing. The sixteen-year-old boy who pedaled his bicycle daily between Ciudad Juarez and El Paso lost his when inspectors who had watched him daily began to wonder why all the exercise didn't peel off his premature paunch. A closer examination uncovered fifteen pounds of raw steak strapped around his waist. In eleven months he had biked three-and-one-half tons of cheap Mexican steak across the border providing meals for fourteen thousand customers of an El Paso restaurant. Inspectors reported the youngster griped, "Now you'll have to find me a new job."

Teenagers tend to be cool smugglers. "Hurry up, Dad, I've got to go," they badger as they hustle through inspection. Little kids (yes, there really are mini-smugglers as well; their specialty is fireworks) are also comparatively unawed by officialdom, but they are basically honest, a tough attitude for a successful smuggler. When asked specifically if they're toting contraband, they will usually admit it. Adults, however, are generally the easiest to bag, even though they try to brazen it out. They nearly always give themselves away.

The knack of the Customs agent is knowing consistently just who should be subjected to a closer look. The legitimate traveler suffers Customs with the attitude of a person going through a necessary delay in his or her travels who wants to get it over with as quickly and painlessly as possible. "But they act a little differently when they're trying to get away with something," an airport inspector says.

Mostly, snagging amateur smugglers is a matter of watching for a variation in the pattern. The Customs agent, through training and years of experience ("It takes seven years to make an inspector"), instantly recognizes deviations. You're a candidate for closer examination if, for instance, you: talk too loud, laugh too much, seem too sleepy or bored by it all, kid the inspector too much, drop too many important names, quote the Customs regulations too closely, freeze up, or are a shade over-cooperative and over-polite. Some inspectors judge a traveler just by the way his or her bags are packed. They're also alert for people who won't let their coats or handbags be casually brushed. They interpret declaration lists. If a woman declares a new pair of shoes, they look for a matching dress or handbag. If she declares a skirt, they look for a harmonizing blouse or sweater.

But inconsistent behavior is the big item. The deviation may be very small, as with the well-dressed, quiet-spoken woman who took a large wad of chewing gum out of her mouth and stuck it to the edge of the inspection counter while the officer went through her bags. She didn't seem the gum-chewing type, but that wasn't enough of a pattern variation to spook the inspector. It was only when the Customs routine was completed and she popped the gum back in her mouth that the inspector called her back. Inside the wad of gum was an undeclared ruby.

All inspectors are alerted by the overly nervous traveler, for beginning smugglers often find it a nerve-wracking affair. But a mild case of nerves won't necessarily get you hauled off to the search-and-seizure room. Customs agents recognize that many people are automatically nervous in the presence of a uniform or any kind of authority. Nevertheless, there's a threshold of fidgets the traveler shouldn't pass over or he may find himself learning more than he wants to about the thoroughness of search procedures.

Some travelers are in for a rough time, no matter how steady their nerves or innocent their behavior. These are the would-be smugglers who are informed upon long before they return to the United States, sometimes by tattletales interested in Uncle Sam's reward of up to 25 percent of the smuggled item's value, and sometimes by good citizens who just disapprove of smuggling. Personal resentment can also motivate informers. A classic case is the art history professor returning from conducting a student tour of Europe who got it all three ways. He planned on augmenting his professor's pay by bringing in six diamond-encrusted precision Swiss watches, but was informed upon by (1) the profit-motivated clerk in the store where he bought them, who registered the information on the hunch that the professor might try to smuggle; (2) the conscientious Englishman to whom he had prematurely bragged on the boat coming back; and (3) one of the students, affronted because the professor had refused to let the group drink wine at restaurant stops.

The Customs attitude toward the caught contrabandist is, like its attitude toward inspections, quite businesslike. The questions are polite, the seizures are calm, and the levy of penalties (for the first offender with a routine item the penalty is usually seizure of the item plus a penalty equal to its full U.S. value) is dispassionate. One of the few smuggled items which shakes the Bureau's studied composure is narcotics. Beginners today are smuggling more and more of them. "Usually, making a seizure is just routine," an inspector says. "There's no big deal about a piece of fruit or a few firecrackers. But narcotics—it's just sad for everybody when you catch them carrying stuff like that."

In the war against narcotics smuggling, Customs officials enlist every possible weapon, from informers to professional marijuana sniffers.

Narcotics head a long list of prohibited items, things which can't be brought into the United States with or without payment of duty. Federal law restricts among others, the importation of wild bird feathers and eggs, absinthe, potatoes and yams, liqueur chocolates, avocados unless they've been deseeded, and curios made by convict labor.

For the timid traveler, too chicken to smuggle, too parsimonious to pay duty, but still determined to spend more than his $400 allowance, Uncle Sam has provided a list of duty-free items that he can import to his heart's content. The range is from asafetida (as long as it hasn't been shredded, chipped, crushed or ground) to zaffer, with stops in between for such souvenirs as skeletons, dried blood, wormgut, ivory tusks in their natural state and ylang-ylang oil. The list changes occasionally, however, so before snapping up that cute little skeleton from the Madrid flea market for Aunt Sue in Dubuque, you would be well-advised to have checked with Customs before leaving home.

For that matter, querying Customs in advance will provide a variety of useful booklets or polite answers to specific questions. "If you're in doubt about an item, ask before you go," an official advises. "It can save you a lot of trouble."

It certainly can. Consider the poor woman, a green-thumb expert, determined to beat the agricultural restrictions by smuggling in Mexican plants for her garden. She endured summer after summer of raw nerves and that choked-up feeling of "They're going to catch me this time" as she smuggled papaya seeds in the air vents of her car, poinsettia cuttings under the dashboard, tiny cacti in the dark corners of the trunk compartment, only to discover a few years later that the precious items were all perfectly legal through a simple, one-time import permit. "I almost wish I'd never found out," she sighs now. "I sort of enjoyed thinking of myself as a big-time smuggler."

You roll the last sheet off the printer and set it aside. It's taken you about three days to write it, working off and on, making an occasional phone call to recheck a fact or a quote. You let it sit for another day, to grow cool, then you read it carefully to make sure it works, tinker with some phrases and bland wording, double-check some spellings and generally assure yourself that it all hangs together. Then you make a hard copy of the final draft and mail it.

The article heads toward New York in September. It will be accepted, edited and checked for accuracy, and some correspondence will float back and forth when the editor asks for clarification on a couple of minor points. You are cooperative, because you want this article to be as strong as possible, and you also want the editors of this magazine to remember you. You'd like to work with them again. Because of the long lead time (most magazines work four to six months ahead), your piece won't appear until the April issue— approximately seven months later. The timing is good: April is the beginning of the spring travel season. But it's also a long time off. You will have worked on several more articles by the time it comes out.

The Aftermath

The smuggling piece enjoys a modest success. It is reprinted three times after its initial appearance, once in an in-flight magazine, again in a magazine for credit-card holders and finally in a commercial airline trade magazine. Each reprint brings another check. It also prompts a book offer from a packager in New York who has seen it and thinks it could be expanded. In addition, it creates an area of specialization that leads to quick publication of a number of spin-off articles, including one on the theft and smuggling of antiquities, another on the traffic in alien workers and one on art forgeries.

The point here is that a well-crafted consumer magazine piece is worth the effort. The rewards are numerous. The payment is important, of course, but the intangibles can be just as meaningful. If the job is done properly, you've made valuable contact with a set of editors who will be eager to see future articles. To some extent, you'll also gain quick recognition from a variety of other editors, as well as your writing peers. You will have taken a valuable step forward in your freelance career.

But writing for a major consumer magazine is also a lot of work. You've had a small taste of it in this case study. From idea to final copy, you've spent an extraordinary amount of time in preparation. You've written a persuasive query letter. You've haunted the library, conducted interviews and gathered facts and anecdotes. You've labored over a structural outline. You've tinkered with lead ideas and honed your statement of purpose. And that's before you even got to the tough job of writing.

And that leads you to an axiom: *If you want to be successful, you must recognize the enormous amount of preparation and hard work necessary to write a good consumer magazine article.* Remember that and accept it. When you step up to the better-paying markets, you open yourself to a concentrated expenditure of physical and mental energy. Your ideas must be sharper. Your research must be more thorough. Your writing must be first-class. If you get sloppy or careless, there are a thousand other hard-working writers out there who will do their best to beat you by doing a better job.

If writing for major consumer magazines is such an "iffy" proposition, where do you serve an apprenticeship? How do you hone your skills? To which markets can you turn to learn the proper methods of research, preparation and writing, and still hope to get paid for it? Remember Simpson's query letter to a candy-making trade market? A smart beginning freelancer like Simpson usually dips a toe into the more receptive lower markets. Editors there are just as hungry for material. Hungrier, since there are so many more of them. The competition is less stiff. The editorial needs and expectations, while still high, are not so extreme. You can even get away with occasional spots of uninspired writing, though it's best not to. Standard advice is always to do the very best job that you can. You'll place more articles that way, and you'll constantly improve. As your skills rise, so can your aim.

As a matter of fact, lower levels can be so lucrative that some writers never leave them. Not because they can't. Many good writers make a home for themselves in the secondary markets simply because there are so many markets, all eager for material and all willing to pay for a good job. Good trade-market writers can spin out eight to 12 pieces in the time it takes to put one consumer piece together. And the articles they write can be just as smooth and interesting to read as anything you'll find in the top markets.

SEND IN THE CLONES

Okay, so now you know how important it is to study your potential markets, query them until you get an expression of interest and then adjust your writing voice to match the style and sound of any market that responds positively.

But what happens if you can't follow the rules? Let's face it, not all writing projects will settle comfortably into a recognizable mold. And no amount of squishing the content or manipulating your writing style can get them to fit. Let's take a look at a prize-winning magazine essay that flies in the face of the rules. Superbly.

The essay, of course, is a rogue writing form that we haven't talked about much as yet. And with cause. Most essays are either very personal or they expound on some weighty topic that has popular appeal. Most beginning writers either have very little of universal appeal to say about their own personal lives, or they aren't well known enough for readers to care what they think on weighty issues. So essays are not a very promising learning ground for new writers. Usually.

The next article is a truly vivid exception. It's an examination of the Human Genome Project, a scientific DNA study launched in 1990 to map the three billion nucleotides contained in the gene sequence and identify an estimated 30,000 genes in the human genome, all things we need to know and understand if cloning is ever to become an ethical scientific reality. To achieve these goals, scientists not only studied human gene composition, but also the DNA of several nonhuman organisms, like bacteria, fruit flies and lab mice. The mapping took a long, long time. Preliminary results were released 10 years later, in the year 2000, but it wasn't until 2003 that project scientists nervously suggested the process of mapping might be essentially complete.

Phew. A 13-year scientific study, crammed with chromosomes, billions of chemical base pairs and bewildering genetic jargon. Who could understand it, much less write cogently about it? Enter Priscilla Long, a Seattle-based poet, historian and essayist. Long was fascinated by the study for a very personal reason. She is an identical twin. One of nature's clones.

Her interest in the genetic study began in earnest when she visited an art gallery at the University of Washington and saw some rather splendid paintings in an exhibit called "Gene(sis): Contemporary Art Explores the Human Genome." She says, "I saw the exhibit several times and began obsessing on the Human Genome Project. All of the arts and especially the visual arts stimulate my work greatly."

Long has written poetry and essays for numerous literary magazines, and she decided to write an essay about the Genome Project. Because she is a poet, she thought in poetic terms and decided to write the essay as a ghazal, an ancient Persian form of verse containing a collection of couplets, one for each of the 23 chromosomes uncovered by the project. She built the DNA essay around her own personal history, piecing her genetic past together in what might be called 23 mini-essays.

It sounds an easy structure, doesn't it, 23 small sub-sections, no transitions required and very little research? Sure, one could knock that off in no time at all, right? Don't be fooled. Long may make it look easy, but she says it took her almost three years from idea to finished copy, and much of that time was spent in the library. Remember, Long is a poet and historian, not a scientist and she says she had to read and digest a huge number of books and articles to make sure she could get her facts straight.

As a successful writer, Long also knows the importance of marketing. But she didn't bother for this one. She knew what she wanted her essay to say and she assumed she could find a home for it. She didn't even query it. "I'm used to publishing in literary magazines," she says, "and in that mode you don't usually query. Rather, you send in the completed work with a short letter telling who you are and thanking them for considering it for publication. My only question was where to send it." She was confident it would find a home, especially since one of the better literary magazines was putting together a special theme issue on the Human Genome Project. She says flatly, "I felt that 'Genome Tome' was a shoo-in and that I would need to spend no further time marketing it."

So over a long period of time, she wrote it. And tinkered and polished it. And finally sent it. And not long after that she opened her mail to find a standard printed rejection slip. Ouch! Whether you're a veteran or a beginner, rejection hurts. But what occurred next should provide encouragement for any writer who labors hard and long on a written masterpiece only to get back a rejection notice. Editors can be wrong. And this one was. Long was convinced the essay was good and would find a proper home. She says, "I decided to send my brilliant if unappreciated piece to the absolute top drawer."

She considered trying *The New Yorker* next, but didn't think the magazine's three-column format would work for her poetically structured Genome essay, so she chose instead to send it to *The American Scholar,* Phi Beta Kappa's flagship publication. "It's probably the only journal I actually read from cover to cover," she admits. She wrote her usual cover letter and sent it off. "The editorship was in transition," she says, "and I actually addressed my cover letter to the wrong person, but new editor Robert Wilson and his team had their wits about them. They loved it and it was wonderful working with them."

And in 2006 Long's *American Scholar* essay, "The Genome Tome," won the National Magazine Award for Feature Writing, based on stylishness, flair and originality. Judges said they were specifically impressed by "her inventive, deeply informed and memorable meditation" on the recent breakthroughs in genetics.

Good news for her? You bet. "It was thrilling," she says, after attending the 1,000-person black tie award ceremony at the Lincoln Center for Jazz. "The other nominees were so good. To be announced the winner was a moment of feeling recognized, of feeling *read,* that I will never forget."

She's not the only one who'll never forget. How about the original journal editor who rejected her essay? How do you suppose he feels now? Ha! Serves him right.

NATIONAL MAGAZINE AWARD WINNER

PRISCILLA LONG

GENOME TOME

TWENTY-THREE WAYS OF LOOKING AT OUR ANCESTORS

> *Suddenly all my ancestors are behind me.*
> *Be still, they say. Watch and listen.*
> *You are the result of the love of thousands.*
> —Linda Hogan, "Walking"
> from *Dwellings: A Spiritual History of the Living Word*

The scientific revolution known as the Human Genome Project began in 1990 as an international effort to map the human genome. With jubilation, scientists announced in June 2000 that they had completed a rough draft. By 2003, they had discovered most of the estimated 20,000 to 25,000 human genes found on our double-strand of 23 chromosomes. This essay is a montage with 23 chapters, one for each chromosome. It was inspired by a 2002 art exhibition titled "Gene(sis): Contemporary Art Explores the Human Genome" mounted here in Seattle at the University of Washington's Henry Art Gallery. The exhibition sent our town into a flurry of lectures mutating into poetry readings mutating into PowerPoint presentations on elementary genomics. But the deep origin of my obsession has to do with my own genome. I am an identical twin—one of nature's clones . . .

1. GRANDMOTHER
Six million years before we were born (before any of us were born) there lived in Africa a great ape, which our species has named *Pan prior*. Out of *Pan prior* both the chimpanzees and our own line evolved. This grandmother ape, how shall we think of her? Shall we despise her as if she were a massive piece of crud in our shiny kitchen? Shall we deny that we have inherited her genes? Shall we strut about as if we ourselves were made of computer wire and light?

2. CORPS OF DISCOVERY
The Human Genome Project is the Lewis and Clark Expedition of the 21st century. In 1804 Meriwether Lewis and William Clark and 31 other souls (the Corps of Volunteers for Northwest Discovery) traveled into a country that was to them entirely unknown. They traversed rivers, mountains, prairies, swamps, rapids, cataracts. They took specimens and made notes and drew maps. To map the human genome, from 20,000 to 25,000 genes strung along 23 pairs of chromosomes, is also to journey into the unknown. Lewis and Clark meant to befriend the Indians, but in the end, they cleared the way for the destruction of indigenous ways of life thousands of years old. As human genomes are mapped, as the genomes of mice and flowers and fleas are recorded, much will be revealed—the secrets of life itself. And make no mistake about it: much will also be destroyed.

(continued)

NATIONAL MAGAZINE AWARD WINNER   CONTINUED

3. ALBA

Take the gene that produces florescence in the Northwest jellyfish. Inject the green gene into the fertilized egg of an albino rabbit. Get Alba. Alba, the green-glowing bunny. Alba, designed by an artist in Chicago, created by a lab in France. Alba, a work of art, a work of science. Alba, the white bunny with one strange gene. Alba's jellyfish gene makes Alba glow green. Oh Alba. Oh funny bunny. Oh unique creature, foundling, sentient being without fellow being. Oh freak without circus, star without sky, noise without sound. Alba the ur-orphan among the creatures of the earth, for what mother rabbit would accept into her litter a newborn that glowed like a green light bulb?

4. RECOMBINANT RECIPE: MILK-SILK

The spider web is the strongest natural fiber in existence. But for centuries attempts to raise spiders in the manner of raising silkworms have failed, due to the spiderly taste for other spiders. Spiders eat spiders eating spiders. The genomic solution: introduce a spider gene into the goat genome. Spider-goats in their spider-goat barns are renewing the economy of rural Quebec. Spider-goats look like goats—curious eyes, heads cocked to one side, perky ears. Their milk, strained like cheese, spun like silk, produces a filmy fabric, lightweight, stronger than steel, softer than silk. So strong is milk-silk that a bullet fired at point-blank range bounces off, unable to penetrate. And beautiful it is. Milk-silk is a natural fabric. It is as natural as daffodils or baby crows or maggots creeping in a cow pie. It is as natural as a spring breeze or a drop of spring rain. And, too, milk-silk is an unnatural fabric. It is as unnatural as a robot or a tack or an airplane taking off for Peru. Milk-silk is both natural and unnatural. Still, it is more natural than Nylon.

5. NEXT OF KIN

Chimps have long arms for climbing and for swinging in trees, and they have opposable thumbs and opposable big toes. They knuckle walk—walk on all fours with their hands folded into fists. They are born with pale faces that gradually turn brown or black.

Chimps live in large sociable communities that have an alpha male, and several (less dominant) alpha females. They express affection by grooming each other with obvious pleasure and elaborate precision (they can remove a speck from the eye or a splinter from a toe). They can be quite aggressive; communities have been known to go to war. Chimps are territorial, and when they happen upon an isolated foreign individual on their border, they kill. Like humans, they are capable of cannibalism, of infanticide. But chimps also laugh and kiss and hug. They dine on a diet that varies from plants to ants, using stick-utensils to work the ants out of the ant cupboard. During the day they spread out in small groups to forage for food. While they are thus scattered, the males drum, stamp, and hoot: the chimpanzee Global Positioning System. At night they gather and make nests high in the trees.

When a chimp is born, the other chimps come around offering to groom the mother for a chance to inspect her baby. Mother chimps are fiercely attached to their infants. Baby chimps suckle for three to five years. Adolescents stick with the family and help to baby-sit the little squirt. The baby requires a long time, five to seven years, to learn all the ways of chimpanzees from chimp talk (so to speak) to tickling to hunting food to building the nightly nest. A chimpanzee becomes an adult between 11 and 13 years of age, and can live to age 60.

In December 2003, a chimpanzee genome was read for the first time. Chimps are so genetically similar to humans that some scientists want to reclassify them to the *Homo* (hominid) genus. Others disagree, arguing that language and culture may have a minuscule genetic basis, but major species consequences.

6. LAMENT FOR HAM AND ENOS

In the late 1950s, the United States Air Force acquired 65 juvenile chimpanzees. Among them were Ham and Enos. No doubt Ham and Enos and the others had witnessed the slaughter of their mothers.

Let the new life begin. The Air Force used the chimps to gauge the effects of space travel on humans. The small chimps were spun in giant centrifuges. They were placed in decompression chambers to see how long it took them to lose consciousness. They were exposed to powerful G forces—forces due to acceleration felt by pilots or by riders on roller coasters.

Three-year-old Ham was the first chimpanzee to be rocketed into space. This occurred on January 31, 1961. NASA archives record "a series of harrowing mischances," but Ham returned alive. The results pleased astronauts and capsule engineers, and three months later Alan Shepard became the first American to be shot into space.

Enos, age five, was launched on November 29, 1961. Enos had undergone a meticulous year of training to perform certain operations upon receiving certain prompts. Upon launch, however, the capsule malfunctioned, and Enos received an electric shock each time he acted correctly. Nevertheless, he continued to make the moves he knew to be right, shock after shock after shock. He orbited earth two times and returned alive.

The following year John Glenn orbited earth three times. On March 1, 1962, in lower Manhattan, four million people greeted Glenn and two fellow astronauts with a huge ticker-tape parade, confetti falling like snow at Christmas.

Ham and Enos were transferred to "hazardous environments" duty. To test the new technology of seatbelts, they were strapped into sleds, whizzed along at 30, 50, 100 mph, slammed into walls.

By the 1970s the Air Force, done with the chimps, leased them out for biomedical research. These highly sociable primates, now adults in their 20s, were stored in cement-block cells with bars in front, but with no windows between cells to provide contact with fellow chimps.

After such a life, Ham died. After such a life, Enos died.

7. LUCY IN THE SKY WITH DIAMONDS

The fossilized skeleton of Lucy, discovered in 1974 in Hadar, Ethiopia, was the oldest hominid remains then known. Lucy died 3.2 million years ago. While her discoverers, Donald Johanson and his team, were looking at her bones in amazement, a Beatles tape played in the background. They named Lucy after the Beatles song "Lucy in the Sky with Diamonds." Lucy was short, about four feet high, with long arms for climbing. She stood upright. That's the important thing. Her proper species name is *Australopithecus afarensis*. From her group, several species of hominids evolved. *Homo erectus* evolved. We evolved. That's the old story. It's a nice story. It has a nice beginning, middle, and end.

But it's probably not true. Bones speak, but they do not enunciate. Skulls and femurs and molars are measured and compared and recompared, and theories replace theories. Thighbones and skulls "from the same species" placed side by side look different, and fossilized bones, alas, do not produce DNA.

In 2000 the creation story got a new beginning. About six million years ago, our human ancestor split off from *Pan prior*. This missing link, this halfape, half-hominid has been the longed-for find, the physical anthropologist's Holy Grail. In Kenya, in 2000, scientists Martin Pickford and Brigette Senut discovered a very few very old bones. *Orrorin tugenensis* lived six million years ago, the time our oldest human ancestor split off from *Pan prior*. These scientists claim that Lucy was not our direct ancestor but an offshoot that died out. That *Orrorin tugenensis* were our true ancestor hominids. This being stood upright, but also displayed the attributes of knuckle-walking, treeclimbing apes. Donald Johanson thinks they might be right.

(continued)

After that (if that really was that), perhaps 15 different species of humans evolved. From one million to three million years ago (before *Homo sapiens*), perhaps 10 different human species lived simultaneously. There were side branches and extinctions. *Homo neanderthalensis* was one of the side branches, and these beings shared the earth with *Homo sapiens,* our people, who evolved, in Africa, not so very long ago, 150,000 years ago.

8. MOTHER

Our ancient mother, the mother of us all, lived in Africa some 150,000 years ago. She was one individual in a world population of *Homo sapiens*—recently evolved out of *Homo erectus*—amounting to 2,000 individuals at most. There were other females of course, but their lines died out long before historical times. Everyone alive today descends from this one woman, from one of her two daughters. This is the astonishing news revealed by the book of the human genome, the book whose pages we are just beginning to turn.

9. HISTORY AND GEOGRAPHY

We are apes evolved into *Homo erectus*. We are Africans, *Homo sapiens* evolved from a group of *Homo erectus* who lived in Africa 150,000 years ago. Not so very long ago. Twelve thousand generations ago.

We are *Homo sapiens,* alone knowing. We know and we don't know. We wonder. We wonder where we came from. We wonder who we are. We wonder where we are going. We pose questions.

10. QUESTIONS

1. Are we, then, the greatest of the great apes?
2. Is human kindness more human than inhuman cruelty?
3. What makes a cell divide? Am I dividing against myself?
4. If we were once single-celled creatures, was I once a single-celled creature?
5. Identical twins: aren't we the pioneer clones?
6. How does Earth's age, 4.5 billion years, relate to our age?
7. If grammar is innate, is iambic pentameter innate?
8. If you could read the book of your genes, would anything there surprise you?
9. Would it surprise you to learn that you were mixed race?
10. Can humans and chimpanzees mate?
11. What will life look like after 500 years of genetic experiments?
12. Is human selection less natural than natural selection?
13. Where did we come from? Where are we going?
14. If a twin is not the same person, why would a clone be the same person?
15. Should art include the creation of life?
16. Is there a gene for creativity, and if so what protein does it express?
17. If a scientist creates a new species, is the scientist the parent? Who gets custody?
18. Do I belong to myself, in the cellular sense?
19. Who wrote the book of life?
20. Is my cell line mine? Is my genome mine?
21. Considering that more genetic variation exists within racial groups than between racial groups, what is race?
22. Was our first mother happy?
23. How can you say that?

11. THE GRAMMAR GENE

Linguist Noam Chomsky argues that grammar is not learned, that it somehow comes with our DNA. People in any language recognize grammatical structures, apart from the sounds or meanings of words. Grammar is innate, whereas diction and meanings are cultural and, over the slow centuries, in flux. Others argue that what is inherited isn't grammar, it's a propensity to search for patterns in speech. We move from "Mama!" to "Mama get ball!" to "I think Johnny went to the store to get milk, at least that's what he said he was going to do before he found out he won the lottery"—a construction that will forever elude the most brilliant chimps taught to "speak."

Did language evolve out of primate vocalizations? Or did it evolve out of an entirely different part of the brain, the part that can practice throwing to improve one's aim, the part that can plan to marry off one's unborn daughter to the as-yet unconceived son of the future king.

Our first mother had no words to speak. Our earliest *Homo sapiens* ancestors were anatomically identical to ourselves, but had no cognition. They had no symbols. They had our vocal chords, but no language. They were osteologically modern but neurologically archaic. They had our bones, but not our wits. About 50,000 years ago something changed. After that, there were bone flutes and symbolic marks and cave paintings. The *Homo sapiens* who painted on cave walls with charcoal and red ochre had metaphor, symbol, language. The change had to do with the brain growing, not larger, but more complex.

There is something about language that we inherit. Perhaps our mother taught us to speak, but she could never teach a chimp to speak, except in the most rudimentary way after years of work. We are born with something structural about language in our DNA.

The structure of language lurks below the meaning of words. Chomsky wrote, "Colorless green ideas sleep furiously." This grammatical sentence illustrates that grammar and meaning have about as much relationship to one another as strangers on a blind date. Grammar is the towny. This dude, this thug, knows the ins and outs of the place by heart. He runs the show, and he practically owns the territory. His date just blew into town. She's all fluttery in this gaudy multipart outfit she copped at various exotic bazaars and flea markets. Half the time she's got no idea what she's saying, but she's easy, in actual fact a slut willing to go along with just about anything.

Oh my.

12. GRAMMAR GENE MUTATION

Courtly cows dispense with diphthongs. Chocolate-covered theories crouch in corners. Corners rot uproariously. Refrigerators frig the worms. Catastrophe kisses the count of five. A statement digests its over-rehearsed rhinoceros. Bookworms excrete monogamous bunnies. Blue crud excites red ecstasy. All this during the furious sleeping of colorless green ideas.

13. THE GHAZAL GENE

The ghazal is an old poetic form, very old, very stringent, very strange. It is older than the sonnet. Or so writes the poet Agha Shahid Ali. According to Ali, *ghazal* is pronounced to rhyme with *muzzle* and the initial *gh* sound comes from deep in the throat like a French rolled *r*. Like a smoker quietly clearing his throat.

The ghazal goes back to seventh-century Arabia, perhaps earlier, in contrast to the sonnet, which goes back to 13th-century Italy. If grammar is genomic, could the ghazal be genomic?

A ghazal performs itself in couplets, five or more. The couplets have nothing to do with one another, except for a formal unity derived from a strict rhyme and repetition pattern. In the last couplet it is customary for the poet to mention him or herself by name, by pseudonym, or as "I." In all other couplets this is strictly illegal.

The ghazal is the form of choice for the incorrigible narcissist because it always returns to the subject of the poet, rather like a bore at a cocktail party.

(continued)

NATIONAL MAGAZINE AWARD WINNER   CONTINUED

The ghazal has been tortured and butchered in English, which pained Agha Shahid Ali and moved him to write a rant. This humorous but headstrong harangue precedes an anthology of good ghazals in English, *Ravishing DisUnities.*

Or maybe they're not so good. Some are exquisite. Others stand in complete violation of Ali's ground rules. What does it matter?

If you construct a ghazal on a subject, so that each couplet chews on the theme announced in the title like a meat chopper, or if you violate the form by using slant rhyme—say, *white/what* instead of *white/fight*—or if you violate the rule of no enjambment between couplets, the form disintegrates. The eerie magic of the ghazal, its ravishing disunity, its weird indirection, falls to pieces. The thing becomes awkward, stiff, forced like a too-fancy, out-of-date party dress purchased at a thrift shop, which, besides missing a button, is too tight and unsightly.

I have committed God-awful ghazals. At first, I missed the point about autonomy of the couplets. Then one day I was visited by the muse, Keeper of Classical Forms. Perhaps she was sent by Agha Shahid Ali, who died of a brain tumor on December 8, 2001. He was 52 years old.

I gutted my ghazals and began again.

14. GENOME GHAZAL

One earth, one ur-gene, in the beginning.
Mountain air. No green, in the beginning.

Black towers. Steel and glass. Blue dawn
downtown. Pristine in the beginning.

Old friend, did you slip into not-being,
or was death like a dream, in the beginning?

Dirt-obliterated bones, bits of bowls,
stone tools—unseen in the beginning.

Sibilant hiss, susurrus sigh—Priscilla—
What did it mean, in the beginning?

15. IN THE BEGINNING

When I was 12, I took up bird watching. On the first day of my new hobby, I set out down the dirt road of our dairy farm noting in my tablet any bird I saw. Crow. Red-winged blackbird. Sparrow—I had no idea what kind. Turkey buzzards spiraling down. A cardinal flashing red in a black locust tree. That evening over supper, I read my list to my brother and sisters, and to my rather worn-down parents.

The next day my sister Pammy took up bird watching. She returned with a list twice as long. Besides my birds, she had recorded a wood thrush, a blackcapped chickadee, and a yellow finch. Our mother put an immediate stop to Pammy's bird-watching hobby. She forbade Pammy to watch for birds or to put down the names of birds. Pammy was not even to speak of birds. Bird watching was my hobby, not Pammy's hobby.

Pamela is my identical twin. We each, like everybody else, have three trillion cells, give or take a few. Most of these cells have at their center a copy of our genome. My genome is identical to Pamela's genome. Therefore, Pamela and I feel we have something to interject into the debate on cloning. But here I speak for myself.

I speak for myself because I am looking out of my own eyes. I live in the Puget Sound region—a land of clouds, salmon, Orca whales, congested traffic, and double-leaved bascule bridges. Like many Seattleites, I grumble at the excessive sunshine in mid-July. I like foghorns and ducks and snowcapped mountains. Rainy Seattle with its cafés and bookstores is a perfect reading-and-writing city, and I am happy here, happy as a coot bobbing on Green Lake. My place, the Pacific Northwest, affects who I am.

Genes don't even determine all physical characteristics. I have curly hair; Pamela has straight hair. That could be because of the weather, or maybe I have more kinky thoughts.

Once an old friend of mine, long out of contact, saw Pamela in Washington, D.C., jogging in Rock Creek Park.

"Priscilla!" she screamed.

"I'm not Priscilla!" Pamela called back. She waved, but did not bother to stop.

Years later I reunited with my friend, and she informed me of my mental lapse, my rudeness, my inexplicable behavior. I reminded her that I have a twin sister who may or may not have identical fingerprints. In any case, I'm not responsible—for anything.

In my memory, our childhood is fused. For years I told the story of how our mother taught us to read at the age of three. Once I told the story in the presence of my mother, who informed me that Pamela had learned to read at the age of three. I had exhibited zero interest in reading until I was six or seven. I must have thought, as Pammy was learning to read: Oh! Look! We can read!

Twins share the same genome, but they do not share the same environment. One twin dominates; the other carves a niche out of whatever space the dominant twin—in our case Pamela—leaves available. One may be more conservative, the other more deviant.

Our desires send us out on our various paths; they color the persons we become. Pamela grew up wanting to be a scientist, and at eight or nine this moved her to collect white mice and to experiment with questionable liquid mixtures in her chemistry laboratory. When she was 16 (in the bad old days of 1959), she wrote to medical schools asking how she should prepare herself to be admitted. Each and every school wrote back: Girls need not apply. We are formed by our generation, our era, as much as by our genes.

But times changed. After Pamela graduated from college and worked for a decade as a social worker, she came to her senses and got a Ph.D. She is now a brilliant historian of Renaissance science and technology.

I wanted to be a poet, and that sent me down a different road.

If a twin is not the same person, why would a clone be the same person?

How could you replace one twin with another? Each looks at the world through his or her own eyes. Place, choice, chance—all affect who a person is. Who could imagine that one person—that ineffable, multivarious, complicated, constantly changing complexity that is a single human being—could be the same as another?

Today Pamela and I are the best of friends, a mutual-aid society, career consultants, fashion consultants. I live by myself; she lives with her husband and receives visits from her college-age daughter. We both write books—utterly different sorts of books.

I'm not a bird watcher, but I like watching widgeons paddling about on Green Lake squeaking like a flock of bathtub toys. They look identical to me, probably because I do not take the time to distinguish their particulars. Pamela would do better. I think she has a Life List, and I think widgeons are on it.

16. DOLLY

Dolly, cloned from an udder cell of a six-year-old sheep, was born on July 5, 1996. She looked very lamblike, with her white wool and curious eyes. Dolly the newborn had six-year-old cells.

(continued)

She soon went stiff with arthritis. She soon came down with lung disease. Sheep live for 11 or 12 years and in old age typically suffer arthritis and lung disease. Dolly's caretakers, considering her progressive lung disease, put her to sleep in February 2003. She was not yet seven years old.

Dolly illustrates the difficulties of reproductive cloning. She was just a lamb, like any other lamb, soft and woolly and frisky. But she was one cloning success out of hundreds of failed tries, and even then, she had complications and died young, if you count her age from the time she was born. Since Dolly, other large mammals have been cloned. One calf's hind end is fused into one back leg. Extreme abnormalities in cloned animals are routine. Life is not easy to create in the lab.

The idea of using reproductive cloning to clone human babies is fought, and it's fraught with the nightmare of grotesque "successes"—infants with severe abnormalities. Any cloned infant will enter a life of many problems and early death. The most heartwarming argument used in favor of reproductive cloning is that human cloning could provide the grief-stricken parents of terminally ill babies a copy of their lost child. It could give them their baby back.

I am here to speak as one of nature's clones. A genetically identical being is not the same being. A cloned baby would not return a dying baby to its parents. It would not erase the grief of losing a child. A cloned baby is a different baby. It is an identical twin, not the same little boy, not the same little girl. A cloned baby would start life in the wake of grief and death—already a vitally different life beginning. It would delete neither the death nor the grief over the death of the child that lived for only a short while. Imagining that a cloned baby could replace a lost child is as insensitive as the idiot persons who say to grieving parents, "You can always have another child!"

17. STEM-CELL RESEARCH

But stem-cell research is a different thing. Stem cells are fetal cells; no born child is involved. Stem cells are the body's ur-cells, the first to grow after the sperm and egg join. Stem cells are poised to become any body tissue, from liver to brain to skin. Stem-cell research holds the promise of curing paralysis, Alzheimer's, multiple sclerosis, Parkinson's . . .

To my way of thinking, stem cells are not a human being but a potential human being. I do not disrespect the right-to-lifers, but I've always wondered why they don't go on a campaign to save the world's 18 million infants and toddlers who die every year, mostly from diarrhea—preventable deaths of born children.

18. THE ANCIENT ONE

Looking into this petri dish, into this dish of our own cells, we can see, after a fashion, our ancestors. We can unravel their journeys. It is as if DNA were a telescope with multiple lenses pointed at the deep past, each lens revealing a different scene. The Human Genome Project, added to the archeological breakthrough of carbon dating, added to new archeological digs, added to the study of languages living and dead, added to the study of blood types, added to sonar sweeps of ocean floors that were once dry land, will rewrite the story of who we are and who our ancestors were.

We know now that *Homo sapiens* spread out from Africa. That is a long story. We know the species spread to Asia and to Europe. Another long story. Then some of them came to America.

The old story is that peoples out of some sort of Asian gene pool walked to the North American continent over the Bering land bridge, when the Bering Strait was iced over, some 12,000 to 13,000 years ago. These people, these ancient ones, evolved into American Indians, into South American Indians, into Cherokee and Crow and Sioux and Mayan. That's the old story. A newer old story is that they came earlier, in waves, and that some may have come by boat.

Kennewick Man threatened to rewrite the old story. Teenagers found a man's bones half-buried in a bank of the Columbia River, in eastern Washington on July 28, 1996, during

Kennewick's annual unlimited hydroplane races. The bones were determined to be 8,400 years old, one of the oldest complete skeletons ever found in the Americas. Controversy flared when an archeologist working for the Benton County coroner's office declared that they were Caucasoid bones (a white man's bones). The skeleton had a narrow, elongated skull, like Europeans, unlike Native Americans. This would suggest that the ancestors of Europeans arrived in the Americas before the ancestors of Native Americans did.

However, genetic research has uncovered that Native Americans have a common ancestor with native peoples who now occupy south-central Asia. Several of these peoples have narrow, elongated skulls. The scientist who breezily declared in the first week of the find that the Kennewick Man's bones were white man's bones spoke in haste.

In the case between Native Americans who want to bury the Ancient One's old bones and certain scientists who want to examine them, the courts have ruled that Kennewick Man's bones may be studied. Although DNA has yet to be extracted (it's difficult and sometimes impossible to extract DNA from old bones), it is now considered quite far-fetched to think of Kennewick Man as European.

19. MY ANCIENT ONES

My ancestors are European. They came out of Africa, just as all of our ancestors did. They lived for many generations in the cold steppes of Russia and in the cold steppes of eastern Europe. During these many generations, groups that would become Asian were moving east, probably along the seacoast. Eventually some arrived in North America. At the same time, groups that would become Caucasian were moving into what were then the steppes of Germany. The earth was becoming colder. *Homo sapiens* were hunting with more social cooperation than before. Neanderthal bones show that the Neanderthals were having a hard time. They were starving. This was about 20,000 years ago. The last ice age lasted a long time. Then it got warm again. Germany grew trees. Germany grew the Black Forest. Children played in the woods, got lost in the woods. The woodcutter's children, Hansel and Gretel, found their witch . . .

20. THE COURAGE OF THE ANCESTORS

Back in the forested hills and hollows of Old Germany, the Brothers Grimm went about collecting fairy tales, legends, riddles, ridiculous superstitions. This was in the early 1800s, but the stories they collected were of course much older, handed down from previous generations. Grimm's fairy tales are known the world over and can be compared to analogous fairy tales from just about every culture.

Their legends are less well known. One of them, Number 328 in the Brothers Grimm published collection, is titled "The Dead from the Graves Repel the Enemy." According to this legend, the town Wehrstadt got its name—related to the verb *wehren,* to repel—after this happened: The town suffered an attack by "foreign heathens" of vastly superior force. At the moment of defeat, the dead rose from their graves "and courageously repulsed the enemy, thus saving their descendants."

21. GRANDMA HENRY'S LOVE STORY

My mother's father, whom I called Granddaddy, was hard working and rather taciturn. He spoke little, except when he was laughing and talking in Pennsylvania Dutch with his insurance customers. My mother's mother, whom I called Grandma, talked in a constant stream in English, considering herself to be emancipated from Pennsylvania Dutch. My grandparents did not speak overly much to each other.

One day Grandma told me the following story. Decades after their wedding day, their three children grown, grandchildren already born, Granddaddy told Grandma, "You were the most beautiful girl in the whole town!" At this point, Grandma paused in her telling of the story. Then she said, "Why didn't he ever tell me that before? I never knew I was beautiful!" *(continued)*

NATIONAL MAGAZINE AWARD WINNER   CONTINUED

22. MOTHER'S LOVE STORY

My mother once told me, "I was the adored first child."

My mother wrote to her mother, my Grandma Henry, every single week from the time she went away to Bucknell College to the time (that same year) she married my father and they had their first three children before they turned 20. She continued writing to her mother every week, regular as clockwork, for decades, until her mother, my Grandma Henry, died on August 29, 1987.

My mother's own dying was long and painful, involving diabetes and strokes. During the years of her extreme disablement, my father was her caretaker. Dr. Barbara Henry Long died on May 29, 2003, at 11:45 at night.

A couple of weeks after she died, in the midst of all the turmoil and arrangements, my father took out a framed photograph of my mother, taken when she was 18. "She gave me this picture after our first date," he told us. In the photograph, Barbara Jane Henry is young with a long and thinner face. Her brown hair curls softly around her face, and her eyes are shining with happiness.

23. NAMING NAMES

The crime of Christoph Tanger, a German innkeeper, was stealing horses. He was tempted by the devil to associate with thieves. These are the facts reported in the printed account of his hanging, which took place on March 13, 1749, in Gemersheim, a town on the Rhine River in what is now southern Germany. The "leading out" of Christoph Tanger occupied four hours. The procession cheering him on to his execution sang "more than 20 of the finest Evangelical Lutheran hymns." Upon "entering the circle" it was intoned, "Now we are praying to the Holy Spirit." Christoph Tanger himself thanked the Lord and, according to his pastor, "repeatedly recommended to me his wife and children, that the latter should be raised in his religion, which is so much a consolation to him. Whereupon under constant cheering up he died without much pain!"

Two years later Christoph's widow, Anna, and their children arrived in Pennsylvania. Their German became Pennsylvania German, their Dutch became Pennsylvania Dutch. I am here because of the broken love between Christoph and Anna. I am here because of their son Andreas, witness at age six to his father's broken neck. I am here because of the love between Andreas Tanger and Catherine Lottman, married in 1768. I am here because of their children and their children's children, ending with my mother. They are the vessel from which my genes were poured. They are the ancestors who gave me this world. They are the lovers who put me into this blue dawn, watching and listening . . .

Source: © 2005. by Priscilla Long. Reprinted from *The American Scholar,* Vol. 74 No. 3 (Summer 2005)By permission of publisher.

Quite moving, isn't it? Gives one some idea what it must be like to grow up an identical twin. And it doesn't necessarily sound like an easy life of churning out those "double your pleasure" gum commercials.

Ready to put together your own magazine article and send it out into the cold to see what will happen? Then read on to the next chapter for hints about some of the techniques and devices available to feature and article writers. You'll also study some of the pitfalls and perils, smoothing the way for more successful submissions.

CHAPTER NINE

WRITING AND
REWRITING LIKE A PRO

In preceding chapters, you've encountered feature examples by writers from metropolitan newspapers, small-town newspapers, Sunday supplements, wire services, consumer magazines, city magazines and literary magazines. Now it's time for you to meet James Lake, a tough, hard-boiled, macho-mouthed writer for men's magazines.

Actually, James Lake is a pseudonym for two mild-mannered people—a successful husband-and-wife writing team who came up through the ranks writing for newspapers, then switched to freelance writing. Each has an array of sophisticated writing credits in good consumer magazines, as well as novels and nonfiction books. Four of their books have been selected by book clubs, and a couple have even been modest best-sellers.

They became James Lake almost by accident. When they first turned to freelance writing, they tested miscellaneous magazine markets at all levels. Their idea was that as newcomers to the business of freelancing they could learn more quickly if they were willing to write for any available market. Because they were experienced writers and their ideas were trendy, they got positive responses from editors across the magazine spectrum. One of the many magazine markets they tried was the lucrative field of men's adventure magazines.

Until they sent their first query to a magazine designed primarily for men, suggesting an article about mercenary soldiers and mercenary wars, they had written under their real names, either together or separately. But shortly after receiving a go-ahead from an action/adventure editor, they concluded from a careful analysis of the market that they didn't necessarily want it to haunt their future writing credits. It was a good magazine in its field, full of tough reporting and solid research, but it called for a different writing voice. The male readers of this particular magazine expected their articles to sneer and growl and do a lot of masculine chest pounding. So the writing pair decided to do the best job they could, and sign the piece with a pseudonym. They became, for the space of one article, James Lake.

Or so they thought. They did so well at growing hair on their vocabularies that the editor asked for another. And another. They continued writing more prestigious articles under their own names, but they ended up writing almost an article a month as James Lake. They kept it up for several years. Some articles they wrote together. Some were written by the husband and others by the wife, working alone, writing in whatever voice was required by the market. They did it so successfully that their articles could be used interchangeably under the James Lake byline without the readers ever becoming aware that some were written by a man and others by a woman. The editor knew, of course. It was he who made most of the assignments, and he was always told which of the husband-and-wife writing duo was currently free of writing projects. But he also knew that the finished product would be what his readers were accustomed to seeing in the pages of his magazine, and he had confidence in both writers.

WRITERS MUST BE VERSATILE

Writers, if they are to be successful, must learn not only to write in different voices, but also to cover a wide variety of topics, depending on the market and the target audience. And they must deliver the topics in a manner expected by readers, whether it be the dry, newsy approach of a business trade magazine or the breathless melodrama of an adventure magazine. Let's look at a pair of typical James Lake anecdotal lead blocks, one written by the husband and the other by the wife, and make some comparisons. The first is from an article called "The Hunt for the Peking Man." The assignment came when the editor called the writers and told them to look at a front-page story that had run that day in *The New York Times*. The story was about a man who was searching for the long-lost archaeological remains of Peking Man. The story had everything—mystery, suspense, money, looting, a sunken ship, American Marines captured by the Japanese in World War II. "It's a good piece," the editor told them. "I thought about calling the *Times* and buying it, lock, stock and barrel. But I think there's a hell of a story to be written which would improve even on the *Times* piece. Can you develop it?" One of the two writers was busy on another project, but the other said yes. The editor suggested arranging an interview with the man who thought he had a lead on the missing skeletal remains. "Hurry with this one," the editor said. "Remember, this was on page one of the *Times*. A lot of magazine editors are pretty myopic, but our competitors can't miss this one."

So one of the two writers, acting as James Lake, read the *Times* story, did a quick sweep of the library to pick up background and history on the missing archaeological find, did phone interviews and dashed off 5,000 words in the next six days. Because the readers of the target magazine expect action-packed anecdotal leads, filled with dialogue and melodrama, this is what they got—a 17-paragraph lead block, followed by a two-paragraph statement of theme:

> The high-speed elevator whooshed upward, more than a quarter-mile into the muggy atmosphere above the heart of Manhattan. Christopher G. Janus, 62-year-old Chicago investment banker, felt tense, but it wasn't just the fear of heights that people so often felt at the top of the Empire State Building.
>
> Would she be there? She swore she would come, but he couldn't be sure. When she telephoned, Janus suggested that she meet him for lunch, but the whispery voice on the other end of the line said no, she was afraid to be seen with him. It took some hard talking to get her to agree even to this anonymous meeting at the Empire State observatory.
>
> Tourists were everywhere, and the gray-haired, well-built Janus tried conscientiously to look like just another sightseer finding out for the first time how hot it can get in New York

in late June. The vast sweep of the city unwound before his eyes. There, to the northeast, stood the United Nations tower. Spotting it was appropriate. Their missions, in a curious way, were so much the same: improving the relations between nations. If only—.

"Mr. Janus?" the voice said uncertainly at his elbow. He turned. She was nervous, that was for sure. Even his slight movement made her jump. Janus smiled reassuringly. His eyes rapidly assessed the middle-aged woman before him. The widow of a Marine who died seven years ago, she had told him guardedly on the phone. And then the electrifying words, *"He left me a wooden chest. It contains the bones. It is my legacy."*

Janus tried his best to calm the woman, to give her confidence. He had to have evidence, he explained. He had to have proof. Finally she nodded and drew a photograph from her purse.

There, in a sturdy box, was the dome of a skull. Fragments of other bones that could be parts of a skull, others that might be a shoulder blade, parts of leg bones, lay in a grisly jumble. A fever flared in Janus' blood as he stared at the photograph. The bones looked human.

"Where are the bones now?" he asked excitedly. "When can I examine them?"

"I must be extremely careful," the woman said. She took the picture back. "My husband warned me to be extremely careful with the bones."

"Of course," Janus said, "but—."

"He told me they are priceless," the woman said. "But they were ill-gotten. They were smuggled out of China at great personal risk."

Another group of sightseers poured from the direction of the elevators. Janus and the woman moved a few feet closer to the edge of the observation deck where they could be alone.

Janus said, "As to the legal liability, we can't know—."

But suddenly the woman whirled, and her face went white.

"What is it?" Janus said. He looked around quickly, but he saw only the tourists surging toward them, jostling for position at the rail. Then he saw a man in a light green-plaid jacket, pointing a Kodak Signet 35 vaguely in their direction, trying to focus in on the sprawling cityscape.

"It's a trap!" the woman gasped. She glared at Janus for half a heartbeat, then rammed the photograph back in her purse and ran for the elevator, shielding her face from the bewildered amateur photographer as she hurried past him.

More tourists flooded from the constantly shuttling elevators. The woman ducked around them, but Janus was cut off. He tried to make his way through. But, oh God, she was into an elevator. The door was closing. Janus' heart sank with the elevator. She was gone. And he didn't know her name, her address, not even what town she lived in. New York? That would mean he had only eight million people to sift through.

Such a little quirk of fate, a man choosing that split second to raise a camera. And in that one split second, chance had snatched out of his hands the opportunity to solve one of anthropology's greatest mysteries: Where is Peking Man?

New facts have now been added to the baffling case of the Peking Man, an invaluable relic of human existence whose 500,000-year-old remains were first unearthed near Peking in 1926, then mysteriously disappeared in the turmoil that followed Pearl Harbor on December 7, 1941.

Accusations, bitter feelings, international politics, rumors, violence, conflicting stories—all have dogged the ghostly footsteps of this prehistoric forerunner of modern man, whose remains are beyond price to frustrated scientists and are revered as a national treasure by the unhappy People's Republic of China.

Source: © 1973. *Man's Magazine.* Reprinted by permission of the author.

The story goes on to detail Janus's one-man diplomatic mission, and to trace the disappearances of the bones at the outset of World War II when the Japanese overran a Marine base in China and the many failed attempts to relocate the bones. But that's enough to give you the flavor.

For the record, let's make a point. Men's magazines, for all that they speak with a different voice and to a specific audience, can be just as strict on accuracy checks as any other magazine publication. Editors want to review sources, check for errors, make sure there are no libelous statements being made, just like any other sensible magazine editor. In the Peking Man story, as well as the one that follows, the James Lake writing team had to be careful about facts and quotes and events. The only real latitude came in description and story-telling devices. Since readers expect drama and action, some leeway exists when the writer re-creates a scene. But even here you have to stay as close as possible to the existing facts. It calls for additional research and probing interviews, always with an eye on the visual and the dramatic.

Here's the next example, this one written by the opposite member of the team. It is about POW Americans, but with a special twist that merited a top-of-the-cover "exclusive" blurb on the magazine. This sample lead, like the first, is anecdotal in form and contains elements of melodrama. The main difference is that the mental state of the prisoner is important, so the writer chose to combine anecdote with the direct address approach and put the reader in the detainee's place, to let the reader feel the fear and tension.

It begins like this:

They shove you into a line with the other new POWs and you stand there at attention, exhausted, nervous, scared. Three enemy guards huddle in front of you and start to whisper, pausing every once in a while to stare ominously in your direction.

They let you stand there, sweating, worrying, the sun beating down on you. It's summer and the heat burns through your skin and the sharp tang of pine resin drifts past your nose and birds are chittering cheerfully somewhere in the tall trees that flank the camp. But the birds are the only thing around here with anything to whistle about. Not you. Definitely not you. Because this is a prisoner-of-war camp, and you've just become one of its newest inmates.

Another enemy guard, this one with red shoulder boards on his fatigues, strides out to face the line. "Good morning, prisoners," he says. "Welcome to your new home." He gestures at the sprawling grounds and the tents and the eight-foot fences with the barbed wire on top.

Your eyes stray to the watchtower that looms over the compound. Two more guards in fatigues are up there, cradling submachine guns, watching impassively as the showboat in the red shoulder boards strolls back and forth, preening himself and talking about the security in the camp.

The place sure looks secure. How the hell can you break out of this joint? There seem to be guards everywhere. You let your head move to the side, carefully, sweeping the area with your eyes, probing for weak spots.

"You are looking for something, prisoner?" Oh-oh, he's standing right in front of you. Cursing mentally, you yank your head back. But too late. It's almost as though he reads your mind. He reaches up and squeezes your cheeks with his hand, holding you there, barking at you from a distance of about four inches, his spittle spraying your face as he shouts, "You will pay attention when I speak. Do you hear me, war criminal? You will face me and you will listen. You will erase from your mind any thoughts of escape."

He turns you loose, giving your face a shove as he does, and steps back. Automatically you suck in your gut, tuck in your chin. He glares at you coldly, but you stand your ground, returning stare for stare. You're not going to give him an inch. Let him play his games. They might wring confessions of war crimes out of the others, but they aren't going to break you.

The indoctrinator weighs your insolence for a moment, then breaks into a slow smile. "Perhaps it is difficult for you to pay attention," he says. "So many distractions. We can take care of that." He gestures at two of the guards and they fetch a pile of cloth bags, about the size of laundry bags, from a tent and bring them back to the assembled prisoners.

The indoctrinator nods calmly. "Take a good look around, prisoners. It is the last thing you will see for a long time." He jabs his hand curtly in a signal and the two guards start at the end of the line, jerking the bags roughly over the heads of the prisoners, one by one, working their way down the row toward you.

Then they're in front of you. You take one last look at the spruces looming green and cool around the compound. Your eyes fall on the black isolation boxes with numbers painted on them beyond the tents. The bag comes over your head. Darkness. The guards elbow past you.

Then everything gets quiet. And stays quiet. The minutes stretch out. Your breath collects in front of your face in the darkness of the bag and begins to smell foul. You continue to stand quietly, feeling disoriented. More time passes. Are they still there?

Suddenly you know they are. Someone is standing only inches in front of you, laughing softly. You raise your hand involuntarily, and he slaps it down. "Now, prisoner," he says, "do thoughts of escape still preoccupy you? And how do you propose to escape, when you can't even see?"

"I'll manage," you breathe into the bag.

"Take them to the group indoctrination tent," the voice snaps.

Somebody shoves you. You go down, off balance, and feel a sharp pain in the right knee. You quickly regain your feet. Someone pushes you again, hard, deliberately. Pushed, pushing, you stumble and grope against milling bodies. They walk you for a while, then finally call a halt. You slyly feel around until you encounter canvas. You're in one of the tents.

A voice barks orders: "All prisoners will assume a squatting position. Space yourselves out. You there, move to your left. Your left, you fool!"

Flesh slaps flesh, a flat, smacking sound, and you jump despite yourself. Clumsily, you hunker down on your heels, wondering who got hit.

They leave you waiting again. That seems to be one of their favorite tricks. Only this time it brings more than blind disorientation. The minutes stretch out and your feet begin to go numb. And that knee you skinned when they shoved you down in the dirt starts aching. Maybe you sprained it. But soon the other knee is aching, too. No, not just the knee. More like the whole leg. And next your back. You squirm. But don't sit down. Don't give the guards an excuse, or they'll be right over yelling at you again.

You can take it. And you do. Literally for hours. The guy next to you grunts and slumps against you. "Straighten up," you whisper hoarsely. But it's no good, they've seen him, and feet move in your direction.

"Prisoner, did you go to sleep?" a guard's voice demands.

"No, sir," the guy mumbles defensively.

"I say you did," the guard snaps. "I say you are lying. Shall we show you what we do to prisoners who lie?"

The guy next to you groans involuntarily as they yank him to his feet. You can follow his progress by the mumbles of the POWs he stumbles against, and then his tormentor sneers, "All right, prisoner. Here is what we do to miserable lice who lie to guards."

You hear feet shuffling and the pop of a fist and someone moans. There are sounds of scuffling as they drag the poor guy out of the tent, struggling. They are no more than 40 or 50 feet away from you when you hear a voice start screaming with pain. Damn, what are they doing to him? What's happening? If only you could see.

It is a rough and frightening experience, spending your first hours in a prisoner-of-war camp, not knowing what to expect, how to react, what to do. They say the tough POW guards in North Vietnam had ways of breaking a man. Ways to wear him down, make him admit to anything.

But this isn't happening in North Vietnam. It's happening in the mountains of Colorado. And the enemy guards aren't North Vietnamese troops. They are upper-classmen at the United States Air Force Academy.

And if you could see, you would discover that it isn't the prisoner who is screaming his head off. The guards have their hands clapped over the prisoner's mouth, and it's one of the upperclassmen screaming so authentically while he slaps his fist into his own palm. But that doesn't help you. You've heard the stories of terror and brutality at the camp (some true, some exaggerated), and you're ready to believe anything.

Because this is the CCTF (Code of Conduct Training Facility) site, a mock POW compound hidden away in a secret area on the academy's 18,000-acre mountain reservation in the Rampart Range near Colorado Springs.

Every summer for the past five years, Air Force cadets have been shuffled through POW training inside the steel chainlink fence surrounding the CCTF site. Until June of this year, the area was "classified." Cadets were instructed not to discuss the compound with outsiders. There were rumors, but newsmen and photographers were barred from the area and nothing could be proved.

Source: © 1979. *Man's Magazine.* Reprinted by permission of the author.

The article goes on to explain Air Force rationale for setting up the camp, and offers a blend of comments from angry congressmen who were offended by the secret existence of the mock POW camps, as well as reports of brutality and an examination of the federal funds used to set up the camp.

Ask either member of the James Lake writing team about magazine articles they've written, and it's extremely unlikely they would mention "James Lake." Neither of them is especially proud of having written for men's adventure magazines. It was a writing job, and they did it.

If you guessed that the wife wrote the first piece and the husband wrote the second, you're right. But the point is that both were experienced professionals, and they knew enough to sublimate their own writing styles to the needs of a specific market. They both knew the basics. A successful article must have an attention-getting beginning, a good middle and a solid ending. It must be written clearly, and the reporting must be thorough and accurate. These basics hold for all feature writing, whether for newspapers or magazines. But if you want to increase your writing versatility, you have to go beyond the basics. And to do that, there are certain lessons, techniques and pitfalls that you must meet and absorb in order to grow.

REVISING YOUR COPY

One of the hardest lessons to learn is how to revise one's copy. Most writers, no matter how experienced, find it difficult to put words to paper with exactly the right order, tone and quality on the first try. So they continue to refine and polish what they have written.

The refining process doesn't come easily. Too many writers fall in love with their own language. Once they commit it to paper, they can't bring themselves to throw away this beautifully turned phrase, or that five-syllable word, or those scintillating, unnecessary adjectives, no matter how injurious the wording might be to the finished product.

As writers, you must train yourself to treat words as tools, not as tiny mirrors to your own brilliance and wit. You must force yourselves to stand back from your own copy and study it on its own merits. In effect, each writer is his or her own worst enemy. As any good professional can tell you, you'll begin to improve as a writer only when you learn to spot your mistakes and weed them out. If you think everything you write is great, you may as well pack up and go home.

Some state governments require a cooling-off period after anyone signs a contract or buys a house or gets involved in any complex financial arrangement, just so both parties have a chance to reflect on their decisions and make sure they really want to go on with it. Maybe it would be a good idea if writers were required by law to do the same thing. Time creates distance. It allows personal enthusiasm to wane. It sharpens judgment. Unfortunately, newspaper feature writers are often denied the luxury of time. Unless they're working on a longer, complex feature, they're expected to gather material, write the piece and hand it in. And the features often suffer because of it.

If you aren't pressed for time, take advantage of it. Give yourself a mandatory cooling-off period. Stack your copy and lay it aside for a couple of days. When you come back to it, divorce your ego from it. Try to read it as though it came from someone else's computer. Examine it from several perspectives. Check the structure to see if it works. Test each paragraph for flow and linkage to its neighbors. Get even closer. Study each sentence for weaknesses. Check your dubious points of grammar. Make sure you have no spelling or punctuation problems. Then pick up your magnifying glass and focus in on the smallest unit—the individual words. Is each one the precise word you need? Are some too flabby? Too esoteric? Unnecessary? Cherish nothing. Be ruthless with your editing pencil. But make sure each correction improves the copy. Editing purely for the sake of editing accomplishes nothing.

Useful Writing Devices

Let's look at some standard writing devices that can strengthen your material in the process of revision. You've come across several of these devices in earlier chapters, and you've seen them at work in a number of the writing examples, but it's time to group a few of them for easy study. Once you add these simple techniques to your personal writing kit and learn to incorporate them automatically into the first draft of anything you write, a lot of the pain will go out of the revising process.

Be Specific. Every writer will give you this advice, and it will invariably be toward the top of the list. It's an important rule. Whenever possible, skip generalizations and be concrete. "Mary Jones was attacked by an animal" isn't nearly as effective as "Mary Jones was bitten on the knee by a 110-pound male Rottweiler." Focus on things that can be seen or heard or measured. Give the reader specific people, places, sounds, colors, smells, scenes and sensations.

Remember Ed Weathers, the city magazine editor who wrote the Cybill Shepherd interview piece that appears in Chapter 5? In addition to writing and editing, Weathers also acts as a talent scout for his magazine, seeking out good new writers and working with them to improve their skills. And he knows that the first lesson each must learn is to stop relying on generalities. To show you vividly the difference between generalities and specifics, Weathers has prepared an alternate lead for the Cybill Shepherd article. Contrast this next paragraph, which speaks in vague abstractions, to the three paragraphs that follow, narrowing each abstraction to its precise meaning:

> When Cybill Shepherd comes out to the deck of her downtown living quarters, she's wearing a skimpy bathing suit and the accoutrements of a typical Yuppie. "Hi!" she says, shaking hands and proceeding to comment on the view and the weather. She orders refreshments and then settles down for the interview. She seems to be trying to get a tan in her hometown before having to get back to her career.

It's an adequate lead—good, but nothing special. The language is clean, the information is there, but you can't see it. The writer hasn't placed you in the scene. Everything is fuzzy, as if seen through smoked glass. Now read this version:

> When Cybill Shepherd materializes on the deck of her apartment overlooking the Mississippi this late spring day, she is wearing a "Memphis Country Club Member-Guest 1982" visor, aviator sunglasses, and a black bikini that would be right at home on the Côte d'Azur.
>
> "Hi!" she says, with barely a trace of Southern accent. She offers her visitor a surprisingly firm handshake, comments on the terrific view of the river and Mud Island, measures the height of the midday sun, and, after arranging for ice water all around, stretches out on a lounge chair to bask in the rays of her hometown.
>
> Memphis sunshine, it seems, suits Cybill Shepherd, and on this day she is trying to get as much of it as possible before she has to return to Los Angeles to film a TV movie for CBS—before she has to go back to her career.

Generalities are too abstract. They mean different things to different people. If you want all your readers to see the same thing, be precise in your selection of words and images.

Use Active Verbs. It's better to make the subject of your sentence do something, rather than let something be done to it. "The owl hooted" is stronger than "An owl's hoot was heard." The first is active, the second passive. But there's more to putting action in your verbs than merely avoiding the passive voice. Just as with the first device, the advice here is to be precise. English is a rich, living language, one of the ripest writing tools in the entire world. Take advantage of it. Never settle for the first verb that pops into your mind if there's a better one available. Look for verbs that are closer to your meaning. Don't use "shout" if what you really mean is "bawl" or "bellow" or "roar" or "shriek." Check your thesaurus for synonyms. Thumb your dictionary for precise meanings.

Remember, verbs can be abstract, too. "The wind blew through the trees" tells the reader something, but not enough. Was it a soft breeze? Try imagery. "The wind whispered through the trees." Perhaps it was a heavy wind. "The wind thrashed the trees." Either verb gives the reader a better clue than the first to the strength of the wind. But if you use imagery, be selective. Many writers have a tendency to get cute. Be careful. Imagery should be used to illuminate, not to show off.

Brighten Your Article with Quotes.   Your readers like to hear people talk. If you're writing a profile about a specific person, as Katie McCabe did on Vivien Thomas and Ed Weathers did on Cybill Shepherd, by all means let the reader listen in on what the profile subject has to say. But quotes will enliven your copy even if you aren't writing a profile. For example, if you're writing about a thing or an event or an idea, and you refer to some authority to buttress your presentation, open the authority's mouth and let him or her say something. Use quotes freely. But again, be selective. Don't give the reader simple pleasantries or small talk, unless the quotes say something important about the person. Make sure your quotes are meaningful.

At the same time, no matter how valuable the quotes might be, you'll seldom want to put together an article that is all quotes. Too many quotes can be just as boring to a reader as too few quotes. If you have a piece that calls for many, many quotes, paraphrase a number of them. Otherwise your pace and flow will suffer.

Use Characterization.   Not only do your readers want to hear a person talk, they want to see the person. Give them a glimpse, such as this example from a newspaper feature written by Tom Tiede for one of the feature syndicates:

> François Sommer is a short, rumpled little man who wears a blue beret and his collar turned up. He has a fat nose and big ears and he looks a bit like one of the gargoyles on the Cathedral Notre Dame.

Or give them a long, close look, such as this example from a profile written by Carlos Vidal Grath for the *Austin American-Statesman:*

> You don't want to fool with Joaquin Jackson. His face, as worn and weatherbeaten as the scabbard of his Winchester rifle ("If I can see you, I can hit you with it"), is sometimes about as friendly as a "Don't Mess With Texas" sign. A fine Swiss-made cheroot or a Lucky Strike often projects horizontally from his lips. The forbidding visage surmounting a 5-foot-5, 200-pound body adds up to one intimidating character.

One sees both men clearly. And, of course, there's more to characterization than description. A writer can also give readers insight into a person's character by showing the person in action, or by demonstrating the person's attitudes and personality, or by presenting significant biographical details or even through the reactions and comments of other people.

If you intend to delve into a subject's character, you should get to know the subject well. So be observant when you go in for an interview. Watch for mannerisms. Make notes of things that impress you visually, as well as taking down the subject's words.

Lard Your Copy with Anecdotes.   You've already learned about anecdotes, but let's add another word or two here. Anecdotes are important. Not only do they keep a story moving and keep a reader's interest at high peak, but they also help to illustrate character traits. The essence of any good article is the anecdote, a small story that shows your people in action. Newspaper features use them. Magazines go in for them heavily.

How do you rake up good anecdotes? You talk to people. You can ask leading questions, depending on the subject of your story. "What's the strangest thing that ever happened to you on the job?" Or "What city is the most expensive you've ever visited?" Or even "Who is the strongest woman you ever wrestled?" The answers may often hold the seeds of an anecdote. But you don't have to ask leading questions. Most anecdotes are gathered by listening closely to the people you interview. Get them talking. Keep them talking by asking the occasional quiet question. If they say something funny, laugh a bit. People love to play to a good audience. And make thorough notes. Don't be afraid to ask oddball questions. (To a nuclear physicist, "What did you want to be when you were a little kid?" Or to a Nobel prize–winning author, "Did you ever have any spelling hangups?") If you get snubbed, drop it and change topics. But oddball questions often lead to oddball answers, and that's where many anecdotes are lurking.

If you're writing about one person, talk to the subject's friends and enemies. Look through your subject's press clippings. If you have time, follow your subject around on the job and watch carefully. Observation leads to many good anecdotes. And a key anecdote is worth the effort. It offers telling details to help your readers see, hear, feel and enjoy what you have written.

Show, Don't Tell.   This device is related to both the anecdote and the first rule, to be specific. Don't be judgmental. If you tell the reader a person is friendly, or nervous, or angry, or despondent, the reader may get some idea what you mean, but judgmental words represent different things to different people. So show the reader. Show the shy smile, or the shaking hands, or the gritted teeth or the long, low sigh. Don't write, "The professor acted strange." Instead, write, "The professor drooled on his tie, staggered against the blackboard and slid to the floor, moaning." Now the reader knows what you mean by "strange."

Describe Scenes.   While on the subject of visuals that put your reader in the middle of the action, here's another. Vivid, brief description of scene and setting can help immensely in holding readers' attention and propelling them through a story. Of course you can't avoid using descriptive passages when you're presenting anecdotes. They're part of the package. But description can also create atmosphere or mood without telling a story. Here's an example from an *Arizona Republic* Sunday supplement about a cowboy bar:

> The jukebox is almost hidden under the stuffed head of a buffalo. Someone has dropped in a quarter and punched that old western favorite "Lara's Theme," by Roger Williams. Diners are

sipping screwdrivers and martinis and whittling on two-pound T-bones. Every so often there is a "choink" as somebody pops a beer top.

A quick description like this not only allows a reader to visualize the place, it also tells the reader something about the patrons. "Lara's Theme"? Screwdrivers and martinis? These are not your average cowboys.

Use Vivid Figures of Speech.   This device is a dandy, but it can be dangerous. Some figures of speech sparkle and are entirely appropriate. Like H. Allen Smith's famous weather forecast: "Snow, followed by small boys on sleds." Remember Saul Pett's piece on government spending? Pett was a master of the turn of phrase. His article is filled with them. He called the bureaucracy "an immoveable yeast." He told us Uncle Sam yearly lets "billions slip through his fingers and disappear into the sinkholes of waste, mismanagement and fraud." He described that same Uncle Sam as a "10-ton marshmallow, lumbering along an uncertain road of good intentions."

If you can bring off a fresh, original approach to some colorful saying or simile or outright cliché, you can brighten your copy immeasurably. The danger is that they often fall flat. And a coy, cutesy or overcontrived figure of speech is worse than none at all.

Use Analogies.   Like figures of speech, bad analogies can get you in trouble, but good analogies are effective. An analogy is a comparison of similarities. Here's a nice one from the *St. Petersburg Times* after a local youngster won a spelling bee:

> Thirteen-year-old Lane Boyd is to spelling what Billy the Kid was to gunfighting: icy-nerved and unflinchingly accurate.

Often, with technical information, the use of analogies can help explain complex ideas. In "Mrs. Kelly's Monster," for example, you will remember that one of the doctors compared an aneurism on an artery to a bump on a tire that is about to blow out. The image comes to mind instantly, helping to clear away confusion. Here's another quick medical example:

> Each of the millions of cells that make up the human body has a life of its own. The individual cell must work to preserve that life, but it also has a duty to the body as a whole. In a way, cells are like the members of a well-organized community. Each person, no matter what his work or trade, works not only for himself, but also for the good of the community.

Use Humor.   Readers welcome the light touch. Even if your subject is serious, slide a bit of humor into it if you can. Anecdotes can be funny. So can quotes. Or simple narrative. Brock Yates, writing about the speedboat industry for *Esquire,* describes one macho craft as "a rakish, shark-bowed thunder boat with enough power to rupture your spleen and with roughly the same usefulness as a Pomeranian guard dog." Humor can spruce up your copy and keep it moving. But humor is surprisingly difficult to write. Don't press for it. It will come naturally, or not at all. And keep it brief. No joke works well if you spin it out too long.

Use Direct Address.   A standard device for involving your audience, as James Lake did with the POW story, is to address the reader directly. Watch how Seymour Britchky does it when rating Manhattan's Third Avenue bars for *New York* magazine. Britchky writes:

> If you start at 72nd Street, walk north on Third Avenue, and have a glass of beer in every restaurant/bar along the way, you will die of alcohol poisoning at around the 79th Street bus stop.

Direct address reaches out to readers and pulls them into the story, making them active participants rather than passive observers. No matter how well you write, if you don't weave your facts around your readers and force them to participate, your mass of information may be too remote to keep them interested. The appeal may be direct, as in the Britchky example, or it may be merely implied. But if you decide to use the open, direct, "you" approach, make sure it shows up quickly in the article, preferably in the lead, or even in the first sentence, to signal readers that it's coming.

Use the Question-Asking Device.   Another technique that helps to involve readers is to ask them a question. Theoretically, readers will try to come up with an answer, reacting to your question. But don't bank on it. Once you've introduced the question, go on quickly to answer it, either briefly or at length. Unless you're purposely striving for suspense, leaving a question unanswered may seriously irritate your readers and send them away from the article, muttering.

Equally important, the question-asking device often serves as a useful transitional instrument. It can get you from one completed topic to the next with very little effort. Consider this example from a *Newsweek* cover story on the popularity of mystery and detective thrillers. The article works its way through several brief profiles of top-selling mystery authors, then wants to get back to a more general discussion of thrillers. It begins a new paragraph with a question, "Just what accounts, in the end, for the thriller's amazing staying power?" Then it promptly answers its own question, moving to new material with scarcely a ripple.

Use Carry-Over Transitional Devices.   Often, when you're writing, you find yourself in the same predicament as the *Newsweek* writer above, ending a thought with one paragraph, then needing to begin an entirely new train of thought with the next. This is a dangerous moment. If you blithely skip on to the next thought without any bridge or link between the two, the effect can be jarring. Jar your readers often enough and you may lose them. It's better to keep your copy flowing smoothly by providing some kind of transition or hook to pull the reader along. One method is to forge a link between the first sentence of your new paragraph and the last sentence of the preceding paragraph. Examples might include:

> His books depart from tradition in another way . . .
>
> Perhaps so, but DEA officials say . . .
>
> The Russians have other cards to play as well . . .
>
> But that's only half the answer . . .

Still not satisfied? Then try . . .

But most circus fans were asking a different question . . .

Meanwhile, a search for solutions continues . . .

Use Overlapping Words or Ideas.   This is another good transitional device. You were introduced to it briefly in Chapter 8. It calls for fashioning your link between divergent paragraphs by repeating words or ideas, even though the new paragraph will tackle a totally new concept. An example from a James Lake article on fraternity initiations and hazing practices reads like this:

> It was only a harmless prank.
>   But even a good-natured prank can go hideously wrong. Ask the freshman who suffered a brain concussion last November when . . .

Stick to "Said" for Attributions.   Some beginning writers go to extraordinary lengths to find synonyms for the most common of all speech attributions. They follow their direct quotes with such constructions as: he expostulated, she averred, he remarked, she stated, he added, she recounted, he responded, and on and on and on. The best advice is: Don't. "Said" is one of the most useful tools in the writer's kit. It becomes like punctuation—a comma or a period, unnoticed by the reader except to identify the speaker. If someone "shouts" or "snarls" or "hisses," fine. Say so. But if your speaker is talking at a normal conversational level, stick to "said" or "says."

Furthermore, if a direct quote is long or complex, don't wait to the end of it to identify your speaker. Play fair with your reader. Put the attribution high, after the first spoken sentence or even at the beginning of the paragraph.

> "I've read his book," says director Steven Spielberg. "It's got everything—mystery, nostalgia, intrigue. The action scenes come fast and furious. It's going to make a great movie. It could be the *JAWS* of World War II."

If Spielberg had not been identified as the speaker until the end of his five-sentence speech, the reader would have been forced either to wallow in confusion or to sneak a look ahead to see who was talking.

Above All, Write Clearly.   Your reading audience can't read your mind. They have only your words to help them follow the logic of what you're saying. If you commit something to paper that you think may be confusing, back up and start over. Clarity is vital. If your writing language is clear, you can use all sorts of writing tricks and techniques with good effect. If not, forget it. Your readers will already have flipped the page and gone on to another article.

These writing devices are a sampling of the professional tricks available to help you turn good prose into better prose. There are many others. But these 16 are all basic. You'll learn more as you extend your writing experience, and you'll invent a few for yourself.

AVOIDING COMMON MISTAKES

Basic errors in spelling and grammar can slip into anyone's copy and weaken the writing. Most writers have blind spots when they're first getting started, and it takes a kindly, sympathetic editor to point them out. Unfortunately, most editors don't have the time to be kind. If you're freelancing to magazines and you submit copy with many mistakes, editors will assume you're sloppy or a clod and will return your manuscript. You'll lose sales. If you're working for a newspaper, it can be worse. You could end up losing a job. It works this way: You're in too much of a hurry to check a dictionary or a grammatical rule. Why not let the copy desk earn its pay? After all, that's why copy editors are hired—to correct spelling errors and style errors and punctuation errors. But copy editors are busy, too. If they see you make the same mistakes over and over, they'll assume you're too lazy to learn. They'll grouse. Word will get back to your editor. Your editor will begin to lose confidence in you. Sooner or later, you could find yourself assigned to the most boring, unimportant stories available. They won't trust you with the good stories. And eventually, if you keep making the errors, someone will call you over and suggest maybe you'd be happier selling shoes or making big money as a plumber.

A good writer learns constantly. Not only must you spend time sharpening your language and improving your writing technique, you must also teach yourself to eliminate those nagging problems that do injury to your copy. The first rule in selling yourself as a writer is to assume a professional attitude. But if your copy is littered with spotty grammar, misuse of the language or any of the dozens of other common mistakes, it will mark you clearly as an amateur.

Don't fall into that trap. Remember, the English language is, to a writer, only a working tool. It's a piece of equipment, like a power saw. You can use it properly and build beautiful sentences, or you can use it carelessly and get your hands chopped off.

Generally speaking, our English-language power saw has three blades: formal English, general English and informal English. The highest and sharpest level is formal English, usually found in scholarly treatises, professional journals and formal situations, limited primarily to an intellectual audience. The most widely used form is general English. It has a good versatile cutting edge, and you'll find it in newspapers, books, magazines, on television and in the speaking patterns of educated people. This middle range is less limited than its two cousins, and can drift past the boundaries of either to make a point. At the bottom is informal English, a rough cutting tool, and it is usually reserved for use among people you know and like. It includes slang and street talk and the kind of social chitchat that shows up in diaries and notes you write for your own amusement. Some language experts add a fourth category, called nonstandard English, to cover regional and local variants. Unless you are writing for some special purpose or special audience, you will probably always use the middle ground—general English—for your newspaper features and magazine articles.

Common Writing Problems

Let's look at some of the most common errors that creep into general English. Earlier, with the positive writing devices, the advice was to study the techniques, understand them and use them. Here the advice is similar. Study the following common errors, understand them and AVOID them.

Eliminate Unnecessary Words.   Most writers agree that it's easier and quicker to write long than it is to write short. But tight copy consumes fewer column inches, and it's punchier and more interesting to read. So stop before you write. Ask yourself what your article is about. Ask yourself what you want to say. When the answer to these two questions are firmly in mind, it's easier to stay on track.

Eliminate Clichés.   Most people often think and talk in clichés and stereotypes. Clichés are a kind of mental and oral shorthand, allowing you to create quick images without having to work at it. But don't let the clichés go from thought to paper. Needle in a haystack. Busy as a bee. Straight as an arrow. Throw caution to the winds. If it sounds too familiar to you, strike it from your copy.

Don't Overuse Adjectives and Adverbs.   As juicy as they might be, adjectives and adverbs slow the pace of reading. And if you've chosen your noun or verb precisely, an adjective or adverb may weaken the impact. Look at every sentence you write. Check the adjectives. Are they necessary? What about the adverbs? Can you get along without them? If they seem important to the sense of the sentence, leave them. If they seem superfluous, strike them.

Don't Use Too Many Big Words.   Every writer likes to show off. If you know words like "propinquitous" or "sesquipedalian," you're tempted to drop them into the copy to demonstrate how erudite you are. Don't. If the word is too big or too unusual, it will stop readers in their tracks. And if the reader has to go the dictionary just to see what you mean, you've defeated your purpose—to keep the reader moving smoothly through the copy.

Don't Misuse Words.   On the other hand, you, as the writer, should stop and use a dictionary. Use it often. Misuse of words is one of the more common writing errors. You think words mean one thing, but the dictionary will tell you clearly that they mean something else. The most flagrant misuses occur with similar-sounding constructions such as lie/lay, sit/set, affect/effect, compose/comprise and imply/infer. You would be wise to brush up on the proper meanings of all five of these potential disasters. For example, "imply" means to insinuate. "Are you implying that I'm a linguistic dolt?" "Infer," often used incorrectly as a synonym for "imply," actually means to deduce. "Do I infer that you think I'm a linguistic dolt?" The two words are used interchangeably by the uneducated, but they are *not* interchangeable. If you use such words incorrectly and the error gets into print, somewhere out there among your readers a number of linguistic purists will catch the error and will sneer at you. Cut the sneers to a minimum.

Don't Be a Careless Speller.   While you're looking in the dictionary, check for proper spellings. Some writers are good spellers, through years of practice and experience, but every writer has blind spots. Misspelled words are among the most visible of errors, and they always make you look bad. If you are a poor speller, wear out a dictionary per year if you have to. Check and double-check words you chronically misspell until you work your way past the mental block. And don't just look up difficult words, such as accommodate, boutonniere, connoisseur, eleemosynary and tonsillitis. Sometimes simple words will throw you. Gray/grey, for example. Even though you may see it spelled "grey" in print, it's wrong. "Gray" is the American spelling. "Grey" is British. Take the first dictionary preference if two are listed. Nor can you always depend on those handy spelling aids you learned as a child, such as "i before e, except after c." The memory guide may work most of the time, but there are notable exceptions. "Society," for one; "weird," "seize," "inveigle," "leisure," for others. If you aren't sure about a word, check the dictionary. In time, the correct forms will stay in your memory.

Avoid Jargon.   Stay away from phrases that crop up within various professions and make sense only to people who work in those professions. You've heard police officers on local television using terms such as "apprehend the perpetrator." That's fine for an officer filling out an arrest report. You're better off, though, saying "arrest the suspect." All fields of activity have their own jargon: Scholarly researchers use terms like "manipulated orientation" and "usual viewing mode" and "experimental protocols"; yacht lovers use "bowsprit" and "semi-circular deviation" and "gunk hole"; writers toss around terms like "graf" and "lead block" and "double-truck." Don't make your readers work overtime to understand. Of course, if you're writing for a specialized audience and a specialized market—about ski wax for a skiing magazine or debenture bonds for an investment magazine—you'll sound naive if you don't use the specialized jargon they expect. Just make sure you use it correctly.

Don't Use Sexist Language.   Mother Nature and Father Time are old hat. Many readers are offended by sexist terms like businessman, newsman, sportsmanship, mankind, founding fathers, maiden voyage and Lady Luck. They would prefer business executive, reporter, fair play, humankind, forebears, first voyage and just plain luck. Of course, you can go a little crazy and end up with clumsy writing when trying to desex every single word you put to paper, so use common sense. Don't change "manipulate" to "person-ipulate." Half the battle is being aware that words can offend. The best way to check a term for pejorative content is to ask yourself whether you would use the same term for the opposite sex and whether you would want it said about you.

Don't Mind-Read.   When writing about people and using the occasional paraphrase to season your direct quotes, there's a tendency to drift into word constructions such as, "The mayor feels that big business is wrecking the economy." Don't. It's better to say "The mayor *says* big business is wrecking the economy." The same advice holds for describing emotions. Don't say "The senator was angry." Tell us "The senator shook his fist at the audience and demanded silence." We'll get the idea. Mind reading is for clairvoyants and has no place in the professional job of reporting.

Avoid Partial Quotes.   Interview techniques take practice, and many beginning writers have difficulty "getting the entire quote," so they write happily along and "quote only as much" as they are certain is correct in their notes. But "partial quotes" are obtrusive and harder "on the reader" than full quotes, as you will naturally have noticed in these two sentences. If you have only a piece of a quote that seems important to you, ask your source to repeat it until you get it all. With practice and experience, you'll eventually learn to jot down quotes more quickly and fully.

Avoid Redundancies. Like clichés, some redundancies slip into the language and appear to grow roots. You see them so often that you begin to use them without thinking. You write "close proximity" and "assemble together" and "true facts" without considering the improper waste of words. You describe something as "plain and simple" or "right and proper" or "reasonable and fair," adding unnecessary verbiage. If you're a freelance writer getting paid by the word, this is *not* the way to increase your word count.

Don't Switch Tenses. Some apprentice writers have difficulty choosing tenses. Attributions hop back and forth from present tense to past tense:

> Jones says government waste must stop. He said, "It has become rampant."

Which is it to be? "Says"? "Said"? Pick one and stick with it. Check to see if you have placed your subject in space and time. If you have, past tense is better. "Jones, testifying at a special session last Tuesday, said . . ." But if your speaker is floating, pinned neither to a specific location nor to a specific time, present tense is often best. "Jones, a supporter of free trade, says . . ." Whichever you choose, use it throughout your story. Consistency is the hallmark of a good writer.

Don't Allow Inconsistencies in Style. A good writer also uses a consistent pattern in punctuation, spelling and other language basics. To help you maintain consistency, use a good style book. Many newspapers and magazines have their own style and consistency rules. If you work for a single publication, learn the proper style and use it. If you are a freelancer writing for several publications, you might decide to make it easier on yourself by using the Associated Press style book. Most editors are acquainted with the wire-service style book and will at least recognize that you've tried to regulate consistency in your writing. The main purpose of any set of style rules is to help you reach a level of uniformity. Editors will appreciate your copy more if you show consistency with spellings, punctuation, numerals, capitalizations, abbreviations and so on. They prefer their own style, of course. Just remember that style is basically only a matter of preference. It varies from publication to publication. The clever writer will pick up on style preference and give each publication the style it likes.

Avoid Common Grammatical Mistakes. Good grammar is a sign of an educated person. If you want to sound like a clod, save it for informal chatting with your friends and family. Don't inflict sloppy grammar on editors or on readers. There are, unfortunately, hundreds of rules and principles governing proper grammar and usage, far too many for easy memorization. Most people who commit grammatical gaffes do so without even realizing it. But ignorance is no excuse. Like someone sitting at a dinner table, eating peas with a spoon and mashed potatoes with a knife, you'll still look bad. Until you become more conversant with the mechanical details of good writing, the only salvation is to buy a good grammar handbook—something simple like Strunk and White's *The Elements of Style,* or something more complex, such as Perrin's *Reference Handbook of Grammar and Usage,* or any of the other detailed handbooks—and refer to it frequently. Even after you reach a good working relationship with the basic rules of grammar, it's a good idea to go back and review the rules every two or three years. Even good writers tend to forget the principles and need occasional tune-ups.

In the meantime, check your current awareness by looking at the following four examples, dealing with nominative versus objective pronouns, dangling participles, noun/verb/pronoun agreement and split infinitives. If you don't quickly recognize the all-too-prevalent error in each, you may be in trouble.

> The President refuses to answer Katie Couric or I.
>
> Hanging from the ceiling, Couric sees a long microphone.
>
> The Secret Service has guns under their armpits.
>
> To be a good grammarian, you have to successfully find all errors.

Don't Misuse Ellipses.   One of the quickest ways to irritate an editor or a copy desk is to use ellipses (those three dots . . . that separate copy) incorrectly. The ellipsis is a favorite device of the beginning writer, although no one has ever figured out why. Sometimes beginners use two dots, sometimes a half-dozen, but innovation in punctuation is frowned upon. If you want to appear professional, make sure you use ellipses only when necessary and only correctly. There are three proper uses for the ellipsis. One is formal: to indicate an omission from quoted or cited material. The other two purposes are dramatic. Use ellipses to denote pauses ("We could get the money, but it would be . . . wrong") or to suggest a sentence that trails off, without being completed ("Frankly, my dear, I don't give a . . .").

Avoid Exclamation Points.   Unless you're writing for a market that likes exclamation points (like James Lake's adventure magazines for men), you might as well put a piece of tape over that particular word processor key and never use it again. Frequent use of the exclamation point will mark you as the greenest of amateurs. You can't punch up a dull piece of copy by applying the ! to it. Once you learn to get along without the exclamation point, you can remove the tape and put it back into your writing repertoire for the infrequent occasion for which it will be handy.

Don't Mistreat Quotation Marks.   Another piece of standard punctuation that gives many writers fits is the simple quotation mark. It shouldn't be a problem. The rules are hard and fast. But the errors crop up anyway. Here's a rule worth remembering: For American publications, periods and commas that run adjacent to the quote mark go *inside* the quote. Always.

> "Those are the rules, Jack," he said.
>
> It has to be done with "finesse."

Question marks, colons and semicolons may be inside or outside, depending on the sense of the sentence and whether they are part of the quotation. If you're writing features and magazine articles, you'll be using lots of quotes, so you may as well turn to some handy guide and learn all the rules now.

Use Common Comma Sense. Some punctuation rules are definite—quotation marks, question marks, periods, ellipses, semicolons and colons. Other punctuation rules can be moderately soft, depending on the style rules used by your target publication. Hyphen rules fall in this category. So do some comma rules. The main thing about commas is to use them sensibly. Will you put a common before the "and" in a series or not? Formal English says yes. General English says it's optional, unless you're following a specific style guide, such as AP style, which says no. All comma rules aren't that soft. If you aren't sure, check your nearest style or grammar handbook.

Mastering all the available techniques will take time. Excellence in writing, like excellence at any pursuit, takes practice and application. But once you learn to gather your research materials, structure your writing, and use all the literary tools efficiently and properly, you are well on your way.

Every award-winning writer whose material appears in this book has gone through the learning process. Each has learned from his or her errors and gone on to write better features. Some writers don't. The key is one of commitment. If you are serious about writing, don't let mental and literary lapses get you down. By all means, avoid them whenever possible. But if a mistake slips through, don't ignore it. Learn from it.

WRITING SUBJECTIVELY

As your writing tool kit grows and your writing improves, you may find yourself tempted by one of the more alluring article categories—opinion writing.

Beginning writers love the idea. They view opinion pieces as the cushiest of writing jobs. And why not? On the surface, opinion pieces appear to be easy, lackadaisical off-the-cuff writing. Just string a few words together. No heavy-duty research. Tell it like you think it. That's dead wrong, of course. Opinion writing, from newspaper editorials to think-piece essays, requires a solid foundation of fact if you hope to persuade readers to a particular point of view. In addition, if you are a beginning writer, who cares what you think? Unless your name is fairly well known, or you have special expertise in some particular field, only your close friends will be interested in your opinions.

Okay, so pontificating on political détente and solving the world's woes may have to wait a while. What about reviews? Reviewing other people's professional work is also opinion writing, and a cool way to make a living. Just think of the many review jobs out there. You can sit around and read books, go to movies and chomp popcorn, watch TV with a beer in your hand or even play computer games all day long. And support yourself doing it.

If you're a good writer and willing to sacrifice a bit of time to get noticed, such jobs are available. Here's how one computer-game fancier did it. An academic and a busy magazine writer, he enjoyed playing computer games when he wasn't cranking out articles. But new computer games are expensive, selling for $30 to $50 each. So he decided to branch into reviewing for the most selfish of reasons, to get his hands on free review copies. Being a savvy writer, he knew none of the top gaming magazines would want to gamble on a neophyte in the field. So he volunteered to do free game reviews for a monthly newsletter at his local PC users' club. He reviewed anything he could get his hands on for about nine months, then he put all his newsletter reviews together, made copies, and sent them to a couple of magazine editors. The copies were accompanied by a cover letter, much like a regular query.

It worked. One of the two editors liked his sample reviews enough to make a tentative assignment. That first assignment clicked, and he was asked to do a couple more. As his portfolio of game reviews grew, he branched out and contacted other editors. Within a year, he was writing seven to ten reviews a month for four different magazines. Okay, game reviews aren't brain surgery. But his original plan, to get free games, was working fine. AND, he was getting paid for it.

If you're a serious writer, willing to demonstrate your abilities for free or for low pay, you could do the same thing. Maybe not for movies or TV criticism. Too many established staffers are lined up, salivating over those prospects. But book reviews, like game reviews, are easier. Try showing your writing credits to a local book editor and ask for an assignment. Pay is unpredictable (some publications pay well; others consider the free book as payment), but your chances of success are higher.

PUTTING IT ALL TOGETHER

Remember what you read at the beginning of this chapter about changing your voice to fit the market? That's true of all published material, even reviews. To demonstrate, you're going to read two brief computer-game reviews (each runs about 600 words), done for two different markets. The first ran in *PC Accelerator,* a snide magazine with attitude, aimed at a young macho male audience. The second was written for a popular family magazine called *MacAddict.*

How do their preferred voices differ? The *PC Accelerator* review thumps its manly chest and examines "Star Wars: Rogue Squadron" in such a blatantly sexist fashion that the husband-wife team of James Lake could as easily have written it for one of their men's adventure magazines. *MacAddict* prefers straight-laced writing, asking only that you sound totally committed to the Macintosh. The *MacAddict* review, therefore, deals more directly with a war game called "Medal of Honor: Allied Assault."

You'll also notice the use of gaming jargon. There's a whole new gaming vocabulary that an aspiring reviewer must learn, words like *shooter, quicksave, force feedback, AI* (or artificial intelligence), *multiplay* and so on. Your readers understand every word, so make sure you understand them, as well.

Here is the *PC Accelerator* review. See how many of this chapter's useful writing devices you can identify:

STAR WARS: ROGUE SQUADRON 3D
"MAY THE FORCE BEWITCH YOU"

One of the problems with beauty contests is that you sit for hours, watching gorgeous babes parade back and forth in gowns and swimsuits until your tongue is hanging out and you're ready to ask Miss West Virginia to marry you and bear your children (not necessarily in that order). Then she opens her mouth to answer serious questions about peace in the Middle East or saving the world from hunger and poverty, and you discover that you've fallen in love with Miss Air Head.

Rogue Squadron 3D is like a beauty contestant. It's stunning to look at, superbly built from top to bottom, and moves with fluid grace on the runway. You'll fall in love the moment you peel away the shrink wrap and insert the CD. It will be a wild, heated affair. But the time will come when you ask the game for something more serious, and it will let you down. This latest entry in the continuing Star Wars universe is no air head, but it does have a glaring weakness.

The good news first. It's a feast for the eyes and ears. The visuals will raise the hair on the back of your neck (3D accelerator required). Music is straight off the Star Wars sound track, accompanied by the sounds of explosions, screaming TIE fighters, intermittent chatter from your wingmen and shrieks from droids when you take a hit. You'll see smoke, engine glow, tracer streaks.

Don't worry about the plot. We're between movies. The Death Star is gone. Luke Skywalker hasn't yet become a Jedi. Fresh from the Battle of Yavin, he leads the legendary Rogue Squadron as they build a power base from which to take on the Empire. This is an action game, not a simulator. Controls are easy, whether you use a joystick, keyboard or gamepad, with lots of shooting and explosions. If you have force feedback, you'll even feel the jolt to your shields.

Game design is excellent. All missions are well executed, and they're ground-level, not just streaking through black space. You'll engage the enemy on Star Wars planets like Tatooine, Kessel, Sullust and Mon Calamari. You'll fly the X-wing, A-wing, Y-wing and the V-wing airspeeder over homesteads, sky cities, mountains, desert canyons, forests and oceans. You'll blow away giant walkers, droids, TIE fighters, storm troopers, and other Imperial scum. And, for the first time, you get a sneak flight on a secret ship which we're not supposed to name (hint—Han Solo did his smuggling runs in this surprisingly speedy clunker). The game is a hell of a lot of fun.

So what's the catch? The Force has gone solo (and we don't mean Han Solo). There's no multiplay. None. Just you and your machine and the special effects. Once you finish the 16 levels and probe the three secret levels, you'll spend the rest of your time going over the same ground, trying to improve your scores.

And that's the problem. Rogue Squadron is like the vacuous blonde with the eye-popping measurements. She may be the most gorgeous thing on the contest stage, and you might even want to whisk her off for a couple of weeks of outrageous pleasure. But once the bloom is off, how long can you sit over cocktails with someone who's still rehearsing her save-the-children-of-Ethiopia speech?

Oh well, maybe another month or two.

So? How many useful writing devices did you spot? Some are obvious, including specificity, active verbs, direct address, use of the question-asking device, descriptions, vivid figures of speech and humor. You also got a pretty good look at the analogy device, since the entire game is compared with an air-headed beauty contestant. There are missing devices, as well. Because it was a review, you didn't see much in the way of quotes or anecdotes.

And here is a less edgy approach, as seen in the *MacAddict* review.

MEDAL OF HONOR: ALLIED ASSAULT

Forget the usual array of zombies, goblins, aliens, and creepy monsters. Could anything be more satisfying than blowing away legions of steely-eyed Nazis? Jackbooted Germans are the villains de jour in *Medal of Honor: Allied Assault,* a stylish World War II first-person shooter with enough fiendish Nazis to keep you pinned down for days.

Powered by the Quake III engine, *Medal* is awash with Teuton-bashing action, so smoothly rendered that one forgets from time to time that it's only a game.

With only six major missions, the game may feel short, but that's probably because you're having such fun. Each mission is packed with sundry levels of mini-objectives, each cool enough and varied enough to avoid even a hint of tedium. As Lt. Mike Powell, U.S. Ranger and OSS agent, you'll go on search-and-rescue missions, infiltrate a Nazi submarine base, invade a secret Nazi lab, steal a 70-ton prototype tank, and even splash through the harrowing hail of gunfire on the beaches of Normandy as part of the vast D-Day invasion force.

After blasting parked Stuka dive bombers in North Africa, and sabotaging submarines in Norway, you'll join the great D-Day invasion in Normandy. The Omaha Beach landing is a tour de force. You and your comrades will bob shoreward in a Higgins landing craft, heading into the teeth of Nazi guns. Short of the beach, the ramp drops and you're up to your armpits in water. Bullets and artillery shells whiz around you. You'll see fellow soldiers struggle for footing, take hits, and cower behind steel anti-tank structures. You'll no doubt be hit several times yourself. (There's a medic near the beach who may restore your health . . . if you last that long.)

When you make it to shore, you'll be assigned sub-missions, including the use of banga-lores to clear out enemy bunkers and take out machine guns. But the Omaha landing isn't really about fulfilling those late mission goals. It's about getting to the beach. Simple survival. This slickly designed invasion sequence is worth the price of the game all by itself.

But beware. Not all of *Medal's* missions play fair. Just as you're getting the hang of things, you'll encounter a crumbling, bombed-out French village that looks innocently quiet, but is crammed with concealed German snipers. You'll need frequent use of the quicksave to get past them. They've taken cover behind walls, shattered windows, and all kinds of debris. And they never miss. They smack you down before you spot them, zeroing in from great distances. Your only respite may be a repetitious trial and error, saving after each kill, spotting the next bad guy as he guns you down, rebooting and taking him out, saving again, dying again, and so on until, gasp, you make it to safety.

Ah, *carpe diem.* In my book, that means carp at least once a day. In addition to the sniper sequence, I have another gripe with this excellent game. Graphics may be gorgeous, with rich textures and wild explosions, but such superb attention to detail makes for truly stiff system requirements. If you want to enjoy *Medal* to the fullest, you'll need a hefty Mac with the latest bells and whistles. Unfortunately, that's true of many new games these days. One begins to won-der if the gaming industry isn't involved in some wicked conspiracy to keep us adding new equipment every few months.

Even so, once you upgrade your older Macs and get past those pesky snipers, this shooter rocks. *Medal of Honor* is a surefire classic. You don't want to miss it.

Here's a final note about doing reviews or any other subjective criticism. Avoid becoming too negative. It's okay to mention, or even to stress, a work's weaknesses. But mention the good points, too, if there are any. Don't dump on everything that crosses your desk. Be selective about what you pan and what you praise. You don't want to build a reputation in the industry as a hatchet person, ready to trash every single movie, TV show or book that comes your way.

This all-encompassing nastiness occurs too often. It's what made Finnish composer Jean Sibelius once sneer, "No one has ever erected a statue to a critic." And perhaps that's the problem. The word *critic*. People who consider themselves serious critics sometimes think they must always criticize. Until you get your subjective bearings, it might be better if you think of yourself as a reviewer, not as a critic.

To have impact on the world, you have to be read. And to be read, you must write well. Writing may be a satisfying career aim, but it's also hard work. If you want to succeed, you must familiarize yourself with every tool at hand. If you reach for the right tools and use them properly, your next writing project might become the literary equivalent of a finely crafted automobile or piece of furniture, worth thousands of dollars on the open market. But if you ignore your tools and slap things together without care, you could end up with a lumpy ceramic ashtray that only your mother would love.

CHAPTER TEN

LEGAL AND ETHICAL CONSIDERATIONS FOR WRITERS

The press in this country is among the freest in the world. One very strong reason for this freedom lies in the wording of the First Amendment to the Constitution of the United States. It says:

> Congress shall make no law respecting an establishment of religion, or prohibiting the free exercise thereof; or abridging the freedom of speech, or of the press, or the right of the people peaceably to assemble, and to petition the Government for a redress of grievances.

The brilliance of our forebears was in linking press freedoms with the other guaranteed freedoms—religion, right of assembly and speech and redress of grievances. This intertwining of revered freedoms has made it doubly difficult to tinker with the free status of the press, no matter how volatile public opinion may become. (And, unfortunately, in times of national unrest, there are always a few "public-spirited" individuals who would like to see one or another of the First Amendment freedoms curtailed.)

Nevertheless, brilliance of linkage aside, the key words for you are these: "Congress shall make no law . . . abridging the freedom . . . of the press."

Sounds absolute, doesn't it?

It isn't. No government can afford to give blanket freedom to its press system. Even the most ardent First Amendment fanatic (and there are many) is forced to accept the absolute necessity for certain limitations. There are individual property rights to be considered, and the sanctity of reputation, protection from fraud, the privilege of privacy, right to a fair and impartial jury trial, statutes to protect and maintain community standards of decency and the inherent right of any government to protect itself against treasonable or seditious writing.

For example, how secure would you feel if there were no libel laws—if any newspaper or magazine or television commentator were free to say anything at all about you, no matter how true or false, no matter how damaging to your personal reputation or ability to make a living? How eager would you be to write articles if there were no copyright laws to protect your creative efforts—if any publication could pick up your back-breaking research and carefully crafted words and run them at will, without any recompense whatever to you as the writer?

So, as free as the press may be in this country, there are still certain restrictions and limitations that writers must keep firmly in mind. The most important of these, for your purposes, are the laws pertaining to libel, privacy and copyright. However, there are also some pertinent ethical restrictions not governed by law. Ethics are a personal, private matter to be decided by each writer according to the dictates of conscience, but publishing etiquette demands adherence to some basic ethical principles.

LIBEL

Libel is a false statement about a living person that does damage to that person's reputation in the community in which he or she lives. It may also cause embarrassment or humiliation, or affect a person's ability to make a living. The four most commonly cited, classic examples of libel (though some sound antiquated and naive), would be to charge someone falsely with the commission of a crime, or to suggest that a woman is unchaste, or to charge that someone has or has had a loathsome or contagious disease, or to bring discredit on someone in his or her profession, such as calling a doctor a quack or claiming that a lawyer is an ambulance chaser.

If you, through carelessness or malice, make a libelous statement about a person, you could easily end up in court. And that can cost you time, anxiety and money. There are three kinds of damages that a libel claimant can ask a court to award. The first is general damages, granted for injury to reputation. The second is special damages for specific pecuniary loss—which means a true monetary loss, such as an erosion of business or loss of one's job as a result of the libel. An outside source is usually required to prove the extent of special damages, unless the libel is per se, one of the four classic examples given above, in which case no proof of actual damages is necessary. The final form of damages is punitive, and is usually sought by the claimant as a punishment against an author or a publisher for making the mistake. Punitive damages can be awarded only if the writer or publisher has shown reckless disregard or malicious intent to harm, meaning he or she knew the statement was false or had reason to suspect it might be false.

Mistakes are easy to make. You might think that you have a solid piece of information, you might copy a name wrong from your research notes or you might quote a person incorrectly in a way that makes him or her look incompetent. So lesson number one in avoiding libel difficulties is: Be careful. Check and double-check your facts. If you've written something that appears to be libelous on the face of it, make sure you can trust your notes. Most good newspapers and magazines have legal advisers to worry and fret over possible actionable material, but even the best of lawyers miss a few. The job begins with the writer. If you are sure of your facts and can back them up, then much of the danger is behind you. If you're not so certain of your facts, think long and hard before you use them.

If a potentially libelous statement slips through and you end up in court, how do you protect yourself? For years, the most frequently used defenses were the common law defenses: truth, fair comment, fair report of a judicial or official proceeding. Then, in the landmark *The New York Times* v. *Sullivan* ruling in 1964, the Supreme Court opened a new door to libel defense. The plaintiff, Sullivan, was a public official, a police commissioner who charged that he had been libeled in a civil rights advertisement that ran in

The York Times. The Supreme Court, overturning an Alabama court decision that found in favor of Sullivan, said that a public official could not maintain a suit for damage to reputation unless the official could prove that the libelous statement was published with actual malice. You've heard the term before. It has nothing to do with the dictionary definition of "malice." Actual malice, as defined by the court, means that the writer or publisher either knew that the statement was false or went ahead and published it with a reckless disregard for whether or not is was false. This decision has since expanded to include public figures—people who are consistently in the public eye, such as very well known professional athletes and entertainers and other celebrities.

The New York Times v. *Sullivan* decision does not mean the courts have declared open season on public officials and public figures. There are nuances, and later decisions have seen that particular defensive door swing wider at times and narrower at other times, depending on the case, the climate and the individual judge. But at least the door is broader than it was before 1964.

To go back briefly to defenses that libel lawyers like to use or would prefer not to use, truth, oddly enough, is not one of the favorites. As Robert M. Callagy, a veteran libel lawyer, told an Author's League symposium in New York, "When you are dealing with either a public figure or a public official or even a private person, one of the things you do not want to do is to plead the truth as a defense, because then you are going to have to prove the truth. It's incredibly difficult to prove truth." So many libel lawyers prefer to fall back on a "reasonable research" defense, to state that a libel defendant used reasonable research and interview methods and did not know the statement to be false, and had no reason to suspect it was false.

Other possible defenses include "neutral reportage" and "opinion." It's important to remember, however, that both of these defenses have problems. "Neutral reportage" isn't accepted as a defense in all jurisdictions, and there's a great deal of disagreement over what does or does not constitute "opinion."

"Neutral reportage" usually occurs when a writer has written an accurate report about a public figure based on information received from a reliable source. Even if the reporter doubts the truth of the material, she is protected in some jurisdictions because she has made an accurate and "neutral" report.

The "opinion" defense is strong if the statement in question is obviously pure opinion. Movie and book critics, for example, often deal in opinion. A book critic can safely write, "Ann Jones is a terrible writer," even though many people, including Ann Jones, disagree. But the rules governing what is opinion and what is not are very complex, and they are far from consistent. Just tacking on the words "I think" or "I believe" doesn't make something an opinion. You can't write, "I firmly believe that Ann Jones plagiarizes all of her books," and expect to get away with it. But you could write, "I believe Ann Jones is a complete idiot," or even "Ann Jones is a complete idiot."

The problem is that libel law varies from state to state; interpretations can be inconsistent, and jurors can be fickle, and you never know what the outcome will be. So the very best libel defense is in preventive medicine. It's always a good idea to provide evidence on which an opinion is based. Be professional in your approach. Don't be careless or sloppy about gathering your facts. Be cautious in interview situations. Verify the credibility of your sources. Use common sense.

INVASION OF PRIVACY

If you think libel laws are confusing, wait until you get into the ticklish rights of privacy. From the standpoint of the writer, this is a scary and dangerous area. Like a mist-ridden moor in a Sherlock Holmes mystery, it can be serene and innocent to the eye, but if you get off on the wrong foot, you can sink up to your hipbones in nothing flat.

Traditionally, there are four separate divisions to the tort of invasion of privacy. You can fall afoul of the law if you cast someone in a false light; if you reveal intimate details of someone's life; if you misappropriate someone's name or likeness; or if you intrude physically into someone's private life.

The first area is vaguely similar to libel. You can cast someone in a false light in one of three ways. You can take a factual situation and embellish it (by adding dialogue or thought patterns, for example). You can take a factual situation and fictionalize it (the kind of thing we see in TV docudramas, complete with actions and reactions that may not have taken place). Or you can take a factual situation and distort it (by leaving things out or changing the meaning). Any of these situations can lead to a "false light" invasion-of-privacy suit.

But a key difference between libel and a false-light invasion of privacy is that the false-light tort does not require proof that the statement is defamatory. The classic example taught in most journalism law courses deals with one-time baseball player Warren Spahn, who brought suit against an unauthorized biography. The book was hardly critical. As a matter of fact, it said wonderful things about Spahn, holding him up as an excellent role model for children. Spahn said the material was fictionalized, that it had been written without his approval, and that it cast him in a false light. He won the case.

The second tort of privacy touches on the publication of intimate and embarrassing personal details of someone's life. It might be as simple as reporting that a professional football player sleeps on a bed of nails as a form of toughening up, or it might be a shocking revelation of the bizarre sexual preferences of a movie star. The real problem here is that even if you are telling the absolute truth, and have photographs and signed affidavits to prove it, the mere publication of hitherto unknown peculiar personal habits can get you in trouble.

The third form is easier to understand. It encompasses the misappropriation of someone's name or likeness for commercial purposes. Traditionally, that means you can't use someone's name or photograph in an advertisement endorsing a product without that person's express permission. Lately, however, this law has sprouted a few extra tentacles and has reached out to examine works of fiction in which real people are used as peripheral figures. In addition, it is well established that the estates of dead people can take issue with the use of a late celebrity's name or likeness for commercial purposes. These new applications are still fluid, but if they ever firm up, they could open new problem areas for writers and publishers.

The final area of invasion of privacy has only slight potential for involving newspaper feature and magazine article writers. It deals primarily with physical intrusion into a person's private life—unauthorized wiretaps, trespassing on private property to gather information, commiting fraud while gathering information, either by seeking interviews under false pretenses or through other dishonest acts, stealing photographs, unreasonable intrusion in a person's private affairs. In general, cases are decided by punishing the unreasonable intrusion, not the publication that develops from it. But if the publication falls in the second area—publication of intimate and embarrassing personal details—the method in which the information was gained might be considered a damning circumstance and go against you.

COPYRIGHT LAW

Copyright Protection

Copyright law is designed to protect the work of the individual writer, yet few writers seem to understand how it works and what it actually protects. For one thing, if you are the author of a copyrighted magazine article, you don't own the facts contained in that article. All you really own are the words you used to describe those facts. Facts and ideas can't be copyrighted.

There are several good reasons for a writer to do his or her best to understand copyright law, but the two main reasons are these: First, you have to learn as much as you can about copyright regulations in order to increase your own protection and rights as a writer; second, you'd better understand the rights of other writers before you start incorporating their facts and words into your own work.

A good starting place is a free circular called "Copyright Basics," which is available from the Copyright Office, Library of Congress, Washington, D.C. 20559 or from the Copyright Office's Internet site. The material provides an overview of the 1976 copyright law and important changes occuring later. You can keep up with the changes in copyright law by accessing the Copyright Office Web site at http://www.copyright.gov/.

In general, copyrighting an *unpublished* or *published* article is extremely simple. The law provides automatic copyright protection for all unpublished material from the moment it is written. Material written after March 1, 1989, which is later published, also receives automatic copyright protection. As a result, use of the familiar copyright notice (the word "Copyright" or the symbol ©, the year the work was created, and the name of the copyright holder) is voluntary—but recommended—for such material, as is registration with the Copyright Office. By the way, one copyright for a magazine is enough to protect all contributions in that issue of the magazine—including your particular article.

In summary, your unpublished or published work is automatically protected from the moment it is created until 70 years after your death or 95 years from the date it is published. There is a caution, however. You can't sue someone for infringing on your copyright until you create a public record of your copyright by registering your work with the Copyright Office. There also are other legal advantages to registering your work after publication; these are explained in the Copyright Office circular.

Let's back up a moment. We've said that anything you write falls immediately and automatically under copyright protection, as long as it is an original work of authorship. But that doesn't hold true for newspaper writers. Under the current law, if your writing efforts are "work made for hire," then the copyright falls to the employer. That means a newspaper reporter has no individual protection for stories written in the line of duty. A reporter may write a book or a magazine article on private time and get protection, but if he or she is writing as an agent of the newspaper, on company time, the stories belong to the parent organization. That's why columnists have to get permission before they can publish collections of their columns.

But assume you're a freelancer and that you own the rights to every original piece of work that you write. You are not actually selling your articles to magazines or newspapers when you submit them and collect your checks. Rather, you are licensing the publisher to reproduce your work and publish it. You are giving the publisher paid access to certain rights.

Rights vary, of course. Editors will usually tell you what rights they want to buy, and the terminology is usually self-explanatory. Here is a sampling of rights that magazines may request:

All Rights.   If a magazine requests your article under these terms and you agree, you give up the right to use the material in the same form at any later date. That means you can't sell it to anyone else for a reprint, use it later as part of a book, or option it to the movies.

First Serial Rights.   This means a magazine or newspaper (or any other periodical that publishes regularly in an ongoing, or "serial," fashion) has the right to run your article first. After that, the rights revert to you. First serial rights are usually designated as first North American serial rights, or first American serial rights. North American rights cover Canada as well, since many American magazines circulate there. American rights don't, which would allow you to sell rights for simultaneous publication by a Canadian periodical.

Second Serial Rights.   This usually refers to reprint rights after some other magazine has run your article, though it also covers first-time printing rights for a chapter or an essay from a book that you may have published.

Simultaneous Rights.   This won't happen often, but you may have occasion to use it. If you have a timely article that appeals to more than one market and the markets do not have overlapping or competing readerships, you may wish to specify to an editor that you are submitting the piece elsewhere at the same time and offer only simultaneous rights.

There are other terms, of course, such as world rights. Rights to the articles you have been reading in this book, for example, were assigned to the authors as nonexclusive world rights in all languages. That allows the authors of this book and the publisher, Allyn and Bacon, to market around the world, even in translation, without affecting any other rights of the original writers.

If you're a freelancer, then, what rights do you sell or pass along to a publication? Most writers are willing to give up first North American serial rights, if the price is right. But some publications insist on all rights. What do you do in that case? Turn them down flat? It often depends on your background of experience and your professional writing clout. If you're a beginner, you often have to go along with a publisher's demands in order to start building your reputation. But if you've already got a reputation, you may want to negotiate the rights down to something more acceptable, or simply pass and withdraw your submission. Articles often lead to books and even movies, and you don't want to have signed away your rights to something like that.

Copyright Infringement

Just as the copyright law protects you from piracy of your work, it also serves to protect other writers from misuse of their materials when you are researching a new article. The 1976 Copyright Act tries to give us a clear picture of what constitutes infringement. It states that anyone who violates the exclusive rights of the copyright owner has infringed on that copyright. Then it goes on to list those rights. They are:

1. reproduction of the copyrighted work
2. preparation of derivative works based on the copyrighted material
3. selling, renting or lending copies
4. performing the work in public
5. displaying the work in public

Basically, this means you can't pick up someone else's material and pass it off as your own. To lift another writer's words and incorporate them into your own work is plagiarism. And plagiarism is clearly an infringement of copyright. But infringement can take other forms, as well. Even if you paraphrase another writer's words, but use a major portion of his or her research, construction, and general thought—enough to diminish the value of that writer's work—you may be guilty of infringement.

It comes down to a ticklish question. How much can you copy or excerpt from another writer's work without stepping across the infringement boundary? There is a hazy doctrine called "fair use." Even without the author's permission, copyright law allows you to copy a portion of another writer's words, so long as you do so within reason. The problem is to determine how much is within reason.

There are no hard-and-fast rules, so you have to use common sense. But Section 107 of the Copyright Law provides some guidelines that may help you determine whether you may be exceeding the limits of fair use. For example, consider the purpose of your copying. If you are using someone else's words for critical or educational reasons, you may have more latitude than you would for commercial purposes. At the same time, consider the nature of the work you are copying. In theory, you can quote more safely from a textbook or scholarly work than you can from a popular commercial work. Also, you should give some thought to the ratio of words in relationship to the length of the copyrighted work as a whole. For example, 200 words from a full-length book might be perfectly acceptable, but 200 words from a 300-word article would be outrageous. With some copyrighted materials, even a fair and sane ratio won't help. Fair use is generally not applicable to poetry, musical lyrics, dialogue from a play, entries in a diary, private letters, charts and graphs, author's notes or case studies. Finally, be prepared to consider the effect of your copying on the potential market value of the work from which you are copying. If your borrowed words are apt to interfere with future sales or resales of the copied material, then you are probably guilty of infringement.

Can we be more exact about how many words may be used without permission? Not really. The doctrine of fair use is a doctrine of reason. The validity of the doctrine is determined in the courts, and the courts seldom agree with one another. There are no solid legal limits. But common sense tells us, for example, that a newspaper lead running perhaps

40 to 50 words can probably be used without permission as an example of good writing, while permission must be sought and secured to quote extensively from the article. That's why every full-length newspaper and magazine article in this book has been carefully acquired with a properly executed permission form.

What about crediting your source? Will that help you avoid the onus of copyright infringement? There are two answers. The first answer: Always credit your source if possible. It's simply good manners. The second answer: No, even if you do credit your source, it won't necessarily get you off the legal hook.

So let's go back to the first rule. If you plan to borrow portions of someone else's copy to make a point, use common sense.

ETHICAL GUIDELINES

When you attempt to fashion a system of personal ethical standards, you are embarking on a climb up the side of a self-constructed mountain, hoping for a morally acceptable view from the top. But the view is often murky. Ethics are a very personal thing. You set the standards for yourself. Laws, even when hammered into a confusing jumble of vague and seemingly conflicting social ideals, are meant for everyone. But an ethical stance can be determined by only one person, the one who intends to live within its parameters. You break the law, and you offend society. Go against your own ethical standards, and you offend mainly yourself.

Nevertheless, there are always attempts to create what one might call "group ethics." Journalists have them in the Canons of Journalism and the Code of Ethics of the Society of Professional Journalists. Broadcasters can turn to the Radio-Television News Directors Association or the National Association of Broadcasters for ethical guidelines. The American Society of Journalists and Authors has its Code of Ethics and Fair Practices. Almost every group in the field of communication offers some form of ethical direction to its members, including the Public Relations Society of America, the American Association of Advertising Agencies and even the Comics Magazine Association of America. But these group codes are usually quite general in nature, dealing primarily in nonspecific platitudes and idealism.

The reason for soft codes is probably obvious. Professional journalists are extremely jealous of their freedom. To allow some outside force to set to paper clear and usable rules and insist that they be followed would be a direct challenge to First Amendment guarantees. An individual newspaper or magazine or other publication might well create a solid set of guidelines and demand that anyone accepting work and payment from that publication must adhere to the parent organization's rules and regulations, but few publishers would cheerfully accept the enforcement of rigid guidelines from outside the organization, even if the outside source were an amenable society of like-minded individuals.

So you come back to personal ethics and the guidelines you will choose to enforce for yourself. Others may make suggestions. Editors may make suggestions. Your co-workers may make suggestions. But the only person who can force you to take the high road is you. Some of your choices may be made on moralistic grounds. Others may stem from your political or social upbringing. You may base some choices on the expectations of the markets for which you write. You may even make some ethical decisions for reasons of expedience, the knowledge that to do otherwise might wreck you forever with a particular editor or set of editors. Whatever your reasons, your decisions may make the difference between whether you are a good writer or an untrustworthy writer.

Let's take a look at some of the ethical situations you might have to face.

Truth and Accuracy.   Because you are a writer of nonfiction, this is one ethical condition that has no flexibility. Journalists are expected to report truthfully and accurately. The truth may not always be apparent, but it's your job to try to root it out. You'll make mistakes. Everyone does. But the quickest way to lose the respect of your editors, your peers and your audience is to falsify information deliberately.

Here's a classic example: In 1981, Janet Cooke, a 26-year-old *Washington Post* reporter, won a Pulitzer Prize for a feature called "Jimmy's World." It was a fascinating story about an 8-year-old heroin addict and the mean ghetto streets that produced him. She wrote emotionally, with solid quotes and raw description, painting a world that most of us will never see. Cooke's Prize-winning feature would probably be in this book, along with the other Pulitzer feature winners, except for one thing: It was a world that Janet Cooke had never seen. Jimmy didn't exist. Cooke made him up. Soon after the prize was awarded, questions began to surface. Two universities phoned the *Post* to say that Cooke had not received the degrees listed in her Pulitzer Prize biography. Editors called her in and grilled her for several hours. Finally, to their horror, Cooke admitted that the story was a fabrication. The Pulitzer award was returned to the Pulitzer Advisory Board and reassigned. Janet Cooke was forced to resign. A promising career lay in shreds.

Cooke may not have set out deliberately to falsify information or to mislead her editors and her reading audience. She was caught up in the pressures of a highly competitive business. Hired from the Toledo *Blade* with only two years of experience, she suddenly found herself surrounded by some of the best newspaper writers in the country. A compulsion to prove oneself can be overwhelming. But Cooke was caught tinkering with the one staple held most sacred by professional journalists—the truth. In the process, she embarrassed herself, her newspaper and journalists in general.

Fairness.   As a writer, you owe a debt to your sources and to the people you write about. You can't always write nice things about people. That isn't the way reporting works. But you can at least attempt to write fairly. If a person has good traits and bad traits and you intend to mention the bad traits, perhaps it would be more fair if you touched on the good traits as well. Even Attila the Hun had a dog and a mother who loved him.

A good way to check your material for fairness is to put yourself in the position of the person about whom you are writing. Examine your copy as though it had been written about you. Do you consider it accurate? Is it fair? If your answer to either question is no, maybe you should reconsider and take another look at your selection of facts.

Doctoring Quotes.   Does a writer have a moral right to tamper with someone else's words? It isn't always easy to formulate ethical guidelines, because sometimes—as with direct quotes—you'll find several distinct schools of thought, each with its own rational foundation. Many writers consider direct quotations to be inviolate. Such writers stick to verbatim quotes and refuse to change a single word. And they have a large following. Other writers are willing to dress up a quote, to change the structure entirely, as long as the essence remains the same. John Brooks, who writes for *New Yorker*, says, "I freely improve the subject's way of speaking. I don't put in any thoughts or any substantive words, key words that I haven't heard. But I write sentences. I knowingly quote people in sentences that are different from the way they said it, different and better."

Many writers aren't willing to go that far, but prefer a middle position. They might remove parenthetical expressions or repetitions from a subject's speech, but otherwise leave the quote as it stands. And many writers clean up a subject's accidental bad grammar, especially if it's the kind of innocent oral slip that we all make when talking. Martha Weinman Lear, formerly an editor with *The Times Magazine,* says, "I would clean up the grammar to the subject's advantage, but I would be loath to tamper with the quote in any other way. Putting words into the subject's mouth, I think, is really a primitive sin."

As you learned in the chapter on interviewing, when a subject uses consistent bad grammar or commits amusing linguistic muffs, some writers prefer to leave it in as revealing of character. But if it's just a slight goof, a temporary loss of syntax that has nothing to do with character or the meaning of the quote, most writers agree with Lear and feel duty-bound to correct it.

Lear's middle-ground approach to quotes was reinforced in the summer of 1991 when the U.S. Supreme Court unanimously ruled in *Masson* v. *New Yorker Magazine* that writers could be sued for inventing quotes or deliberately altering their meaning if the words used were significantly different from what was actually said. Jeffrey Masson, a psychoanalyst, had brought a $10 million libel suit against *New Yorker* writer Janet Malcolm over her series of 1983 articles examining his controversial views on Sigmund Freud. He alleged that she invented arrogant and boastful statements and placed them in his mouth. Masson's suit was disallowed by a lower court until the Supreme Court reinstated it. The key opinion, written by Justice Anthony Kennedy and endorsed by seven of the justices, stated that writers do *not* have "the freedom to place statements in their subjects' mouths without fear of liability." The opinion, however, went on to suggest that First Amendment protections required some flexibility for the writer beyond the simple cleaning up of a source's grammar or syntax. The opinion stated, "If an author alters a speaker's words but effects no material change in meaning, including any meaning conveyed by the manner or fact of expression, the speaker suffers no injury to reputation that is compensable as a defamation." Media specialists, who had feared that the Masson case would lead to a more restrictive ruling, expressed relief that the Supreme Court had taken such a moderate position.

On and Off the Record.   Most writers don't like off-the-record material. But if your source places something off-the-record and you listen to it without objection, then you are morally committed to keep it off-the-record. That could cause real problems if you later unearth the same information from another source. A frequently recommended procedure for those times when someone says, "This is off-the-record," is to interrupt immediately and tell the source, in that case, you'd rather not hear it. The source can then change his or her mind and put it on-the-record or pass on to something else. Nor should you allow her mind and put it on-the-record or pass on to something else. Nor should you allow anyone to make something off-the-record retroactively. When a subject tells you something and *then* says, "By the way, that was off-the-record," you shouldn't allow it to pass. If you have consistently stuck to your guns about not accepting off-the-record status, it will now be easier for you to say, "I'm sorry. I never listen to off-the record material. If you intended that to be off-the-record, you should have told me sooner so I could warn you not to say it." You may end up with some ill feelings between you and your source, but at least you won't feel morally inept.

Made-Up Names and Places.   As a general rule, you will not make up people or places. "Jimmy's World" isn't the only journalistic scandal involving fabricated names and locations. For example, a magazine writer was fired in the late 1990s by *New Republic* editors after they concluded he made up material in more than two dozen articles over a three-year period. Other writers as well have been caught with their imaginations showing, though not usually with such publicly disastrous results. One well-known magazine writer was recently criticized in print by his peers for having invented a bar in Spain where he supposedly heard a number of antigovernment political remarks. The writer maintained that the quotes were accurate, that his only error had been in making up the bar where he had heard them. But he presented the bar to his readers as truth, and when word leaked out that the bar didn't exist, it automatically cast doubt on his quotes—a high price to pay for a moment of fanciful invention.

There may be times when invented names or places or composite people will be acceptable, even mandatory, but the key is not to try to pass them off as real. If you want to show a hypothetical average man, or a representative average working mother, or a composite of several persons, make sure it's obvious that they're made up. The easiest way to do this is to use John or Mary Doe or some variation. Or put the name in quotes, to signal the reader that you're dealing with "hypothetical" cases. With or without quotes, hypothetical characters should have nice, simple names. It should be Sam and Mary who meet in a singles bar, or Bill and Betty who are trying to buy a new house, or Frank and Ellen who are facing the depression of divorce. Readers will often accept hypothetical illustrations if they deal with plain, average people, because readers realize it could happen to anyone. But if you jazz up your composite character, make him Hiram Grobnik, a one-legged farmer from Decatur, Illinois, who comes to Tampa Bay with his wife and 17 children to take a new job building elevated swimming pools, you run the risk of being charged with false reporting.

Confidential Sources.   If you promise anonymity and confidentiality to a source, you have a moral obligation to live up to your side of the bargain. Confidentiality has been with us a long, long time, and it has been extremely useful. Without it, Bob Woodward and Carl Bernstein would never have broken a number of their important Watergate stories. But there may have been an erosion of trust in confidential sources. Many editors now insist on knowing the identity of a confidential source before they will run the material that comes from it. Suppose you have made a promise of confidentiality to a source, and your editor puts you on the spot, demanding the name. What would you do?

Live up to your agreement? Take a chance on losing your job? Ethical crises can come in a number of forms.

Editorial Bias.   While discussing the subject of interference from editors and executives in the daily reportorial process, let's dismiss a public phantom. A number of people outside journalism seem to believe that editors and executives go around killing stories and hiding facts that disagree with their politics or their biases. It can happen, surely, but it's rare. Newspaper and magazine executives are usually better journalists than the reporters they oversee (that's often how they rose to executive positions in the first place), and they are as eager for the truth, as ready to break a story, as any writer. If you're worried about editorial influence in your future, don't be. Most editors and executives have as high a standard of ethics as yours will ever be, and they are not apt to influence your copy unduly. If you happen across one of the few exceptions, you must then make an ethical choice of your own. Will you accept improper influence to protect your job? Or will you move on to a better newspaper where such practices are not acceptable?

Pretense and Deception.   There will be times when you're after a story and it would be easier to get your information if you could only pretend to be someone else. What do you do? This is another of those hazy areas that depend largely on the circumstances and what role you wish to play. Can you pretend to be a police officer in order to question the victim of a crime? No. Can you pretend to be a customer in order to check alleged illegal practices at an auto inspection station? Probably. The main dividing line seems to be whether you actively engage in deception or merely go along with a pretense. If you tell someone you are an insurance salesman, you are involved in deception—you have lied about yourself to make your position more advantageous. On the other hand, if you attend a meeting of outraged citizens, knowing they intend to turn reporters away, and you sit among them without paper and pencil in evidence, and they assume that you are one of them and you allow them to continue with that assumption, have you really acted unethically? Many people would say not. The outraged citizens might disagree, of course, once they see your story in print. Some writers can never be comfortable in any role but the honest, obvious, straightforward presentation of themselves as writers. Others don't mind deception if it gets good results. You must make the final decision for yourself. And be sure your decision doesn't go against the policies of your publication.

Conflicts of Interest.   Newspaper and magazine writers, since they have to deal with the public day in and out, are usually friendly people. So they make friends. Being human, they may also make enemies. If you are assigned a story about a friend, a relative or even an enemy, you owe it to your editor and your conscience to make that personal relationship known before you go out to cover the story. The same holds true for any business-story assignment that involves a firm in which you hold some financial interest. You may be perfectly capable of covering such a story objectively and writing it objectively in spite of any personal connection, but the proper ethical position is to make sure the editor knows of your relationship in time to reassign the story, should that be the editor's preference. After all, others may know of your personal relationship as well, and appearances can sometimes be as damaging as actually mishandling the story.

Multiple Submissions. You've encountered this one earlier, but as a reminder for freelancers, a common ethical situation is whether or not to submit an idea or an article simultaneously to more than one potential market. The standard answer is no. Do not. Learn patience. Send your ideas and your finished articles to one publication at a time. But there is a different stance on this subject which is being taken by more and more professionals in the field. It holds that editors are not dumb, and they know that writers these days are often sending queries to several magazines at one time. So what do you do? No one can legislate your ethics for you. You'll have to decide how to handle this question on your own. But be aware that some editors may well be offended by the practice of multiple queries and may not be willing to consider future article ideas if they catch you at it. On the other hand, maybe such unyielding editors aren't the kind you care to work with anyway. The decision is yours. As for multiple submissions of a finished article, about the only time it is allowable is when you have a topic that is hot, timely and important. Even then, you should notify the editors that you are making multiple submissions.

Multiple Versions. Here's another ethical situation that confronts mainly freelancers. Once you've gone to a great deal of trouble to gather research and fresh information on a specific topic, there is always the temptation to use your material for more than one article, giving it a fresh slant, a different construction and a whole new set of words. Is this permissible? Generally, yes, as long as subsequent articles are submitted to markets that are not in direct competition with the market that purchased your first version. For example, if you worked hard to prepare a definitive article on database research and placed it with one of the leading computer magazines, you wouldn't then turn around and rewrite the same idea for a competitive computer magazine. Neither editor would be very happy to see the same general information appearing in the pages of a rival magazine. However, if you sell your original version to a computer magazine, then give your story angle a fresh twist and write a piece showing the value of database research to freelance writers and sell it to one of the writing magazines, there should be no cause for unhappiness on the part of either editor. You could then go on to rewrite the material for a business journal, or for a publication aimed at librarians or scholars or historians or any other specialized magazine directed toward a noncompetitive audience of people who might benefit from your information.

Making Ethical Decisions. Got the idea? There are many other ethical situations that can tease your conscience: freebies, paid junkets, personal gifts, when to use a concealed tape recorder, use of names of juvenile offenders, breaking a story when you know it may cause injury to someone, using "leaked" information. Consult your common sense. Anyone can tell when, for example, some minor gift from a source is only a pleasant gesture and when it is a would-be bribe. And above all, consult both your conscience and the policy of your newspaper or magazine.

You've now been briefly introduced to four very broad topics—libel, copyright, invasion of privacy and personal ethics. Volumes and series of volumes have been written about each of them. If you want to dig deeper, journey to your library and check out a few of the many books and articles available. As a matter of fact, you may well write something on one of these topics some day.

Because that's what this book is all about. Writing. In its pages, you've been exposed to feature and article ideas, research and interview techniques, marketing procedures, writing guidelines, specialized features, structure, leads, anecdotes, polishing and revision, law and ethics, and a variety of other helps, hints, and potential problems for the newspaper and magazine writer. If this book has performed its function properly, and you've absorbed the lessons and learned from the excellent examples, you should have the basics for a strong professional career.

The rest is up to you. So limber up your fingers and start writing. Good luck. Write hard. Write well.

CREDITS

INDEX